THE BOOKSTORE

THE BIBLE AND ARCHAEOLOGY

THE BIBLE AND ARCHAEOLOGY

Third Edition, Fully Revised

by J. A. THOMPSON

WILLIAM B. EERDMANS PUBLISHING COMPANY
GRAND RAPIDS, MICHIGAN

To Marion,
my Parents,
and my
past and present Students

Printing History:
Substantial portions of this book have appeared before under the following titles and copyrights:
Archaeology and the Old Testament, Copyright 1957, 1959 by Wm. B. Eerdmans Publishing Co.;
Archaeology and the Pre-Christian Centuries, © Wm. B. Eerdmans Publishing Co., 1958, 1959;
Archaeology and the New Testament, © Wm. B. Eerdmans Publishing Co., 1960.
Combined edition first published 1962; fourth printing 1969. Revised edition 1972. Third edition, fully revised 1982.

FOREWORD

The three shorter studies which have been brought together in this volume were first published in a series called Pathway Books. As I was one of the consulting editors of that series, I have a prior interest in introducing this work; but that is not my principal reason for doing so. My principal reason is that I believe this work, now revised, brought up to date, and so lavishly illustrated, to be a very useful handbook for Bible readers.

Dr. Thompson has for long made a special study of biblical archaeology. For a number of years he was Director of the Australian Institute of Archaeology in Melbourne. He has had practical experience in archaeological field-work with the American Schools of Oriental Research at the sites of Roman Jericho and Dibon. And as lecturer in Old Testament Studies in a theological school he knows how to relate the findings of archaeology to the wider interests of biblical study.

Archaeology certainly makes an important contribution to the study of the Bible. Large areas, especially of the Old Testament, have been so greatly illuminated by it that it is not easy to imagine what readers made of them before the days of biblical archaeology. Yet the scale of its contribution can be exaggerated, and it is one of the merits of Dr. Thompson's book that it does not make exaggerated claims for archaeology or try to make it fill a role for which it is unsuited. For all the light that archaeology throws upon the text, language, and narrative of the Bible, it is improper, and in any case unnecessary, to appeal to it to "prove" the Bible. Archaeology has indeed corroborated the substantial historicity of the biblical record from the patriarchal period to the apostolic age, but it is not by archaeology that the essential message of the Bible can be verified.

Sometimes, indeed, archaeology has made the interpretation of the biblical narrative more difficult rather than less so. It has happened at times that an earlier phase of research has appeared to solve one particular problem satisfactorily, whereas later study has thrown the whole question into the melting-pot again. This has happened, for example, with Professor Garstang's interpretation of the Joshua story in the light of his Jericho excavations, and with Sir William Ramsay's solution of the Quirinius problem in St. Luke's Gospel.

There is no finality in biblical archaeology. As more pieces of the jigsaw puzzle come to light, we see that we have sometimes put previously discovered pieces into the wrong place and produced a distorted pattern. Archaeological surveys for the Bible student must therefore be subjected to repeated revision in the light of new knowledge. Such a revision now lies before us, and it is to be hoped that Dr. Thompson's survey will have many readers, and will guide them to a better understanding of the Bible story.

University of Manchester   —F. F. BRUCE

PREFACE

The present volume contains the material which formerly appeared in the three smaller Pathway Books *Archaeology and the Old Testament* (1957, 2nd ed. 1959), *Archaeology and the Pre-Christian Centuries* (1958, 2nd ed. 1959), and *Archaeology and the New Testament* (1960). These smaller volumes have now been brought together into one volume with some rearrangement, and with the addition of more recent information, new maps, and numerous relevant and excellent photographs. Reference to more recent works is made in footnotes, and additional quotations from the ancient records of the Near East have been woven into the text.

The aim of the volume is to provide a concise resumé of the information that is now available for the study of the biblical records as a result of many years of excavation in Bible lands. In so short a compass there can be no pretense of being exhaustive. Indeed many important items have been mentioned only in passing, and significant books in French and German with their wealth of detail have been given very scant mention. Many have not even been cited. This results from the fact that this volume is intended in the first place for English-speaking readers who are not familiar with other languages. In a few cases the footnotes will point to some of these works. But the Bibliography at the end of this volume will provide a list of larger works in many of which the diligent reader will find comprehensive reading lists.

Regrettably, only passing reference can be made at present to the contributions of the Ebla archives. Despite the immense potential of the tablets for biblical studies, as yet they have been examined only cursorily, and much of the scholarly interpretation remains embroiled in controversy.

It is some gratification to the author to discover that the material of the three Pathway Books, which originally comprised lectures given in theological college, Bible college, and university classes in Australia in the past decade, should prove of value to similar classes in America.

Special acknowledgment should again be made of the help given by the author's wife in the preparation of this composite volume and of the encouragement of the Publishers.

The author's hope is that this larger volume will continue to prove useful to students who are learning their first lessons in Biblical Archaeology.

—J.A.T.

TABLE OF CONTENTS

PART THREE:

ARCHAEOLOGY AND THE NEW TESTAMENT

LIST OF MAPS

LIST OF CHARTS

LIST OF ABBREVIATIONS

AASOR: *Annual of the American Schools of Oriental Research*
AJA: *American Journal of Archaeology*
ANET: *Ancient Near Eastern Texts*
BA: *Biblical Archaeologist*
BAR: *Biblical Archaeology Review*
BASOR: *Bulletin of the American Schools of Oriental Research*
BJRL: *Bulletin of the John Rylands Library*
EAEHL: *Encyclopedia of Archaeological Excavations in the Holy Land*
ICC: *International Critical Commentary*
IDB: *Interpreter's Dictionary of the Bible*
IEJ: *Israel Exploration Journal*
JAOS: *Journal of the American Oriental Society*
JBL: *Journal of Biblical Literature*
JNES: *Journal of Near Eastern Studies*
JTS: *Journal of Theological Studies*
NBD: *New Bible Dictionary*
PEQ: *Palestine Exploration Quarterly*
QDAP: *Quarterly of the Department of Antiquities of Palestine*
RB: *Revue Biblique*
VT: *Vetus Testamentum*

LIST OF ILLUSTRATIONS

xvii

INTRODUCTION

1

BIBLICAL ARCHAEOLOGY TODAY

In the past forty years a new subject has entered the curriculum of Bible colleges and theological colleges. It is Biblical Archaeology. Its importance is beyond dispute. It is a vital branch of general biblical research, which has made tremendous progress in recent years. One outstanding worker in the field of biblical archaeology and general biblical research has recently written:

> There are few fields of human knowledge where the progress of discovery makes constant revision of handbooks and other aids to study more necessary than in biblical research.[1]

Biblical archaeology has all the fascination of the science of archaeology, which seeks to unravel the story of past ages by digging up their material remains. But it has the added interest that through this study we are better able to understand and interpret the textbook of our faith. Not the least fascinating part of these modern studies is that they go far toward authenticating the history of the written records which are the basis of our faith. Of course, it is impossible to authenticate archaeologically all that is in the Bible. Many of its statements lie beyond the sphere of archaeological investigation. No excavator can comment, in terms of his science, on the simple statement: "Abraham believed God, and it was counted unto him for righteousness." But in its own sphere this science does much for the student of the sacred record.

1. G. E. Wright and F. V. Filson, *Westminster Historical Atlas* (London, 1953), opening article by W. F. Albright, p. 9.

The late Professor Nelson Glueck, one of the foremost biblical archaeologists of the twentieth century, standing near Wadi Ein Irka in the Negeb. (Israel Office of Information)

THE VALUE OF BIBLICAL ARCHAEOLOGY

When we extract from the field of general archaeology all the material that is relevant to the Bible, and then organize our material into a formal study, we have the substance of a course in Biblical Archaeology. Such material has significance for the Bible student in at least four ways.

In the first place, it provides the general background of the history of the Bible. It is not sufficient merely to read the Bible if we wish to appreciate the significance of its narratives. The men of Bible history lived in an environment. Abraham, for example, moved in a world that had its own peculiar customs. It is necessary for us to learn from nonbiblical information what this world of his was like if we would understand more clearly the significance of the things he said and did. We realize that the picture we get of Abraham in the Bible has much about it that is reminiscent of the ancient Middle East in the period of about 1800–1500 B.C. The same kind of thing could be said of Joseph, Moses, Joshua, David, and the whole family of Bible personalities.

Secondly, the Bible is by no means a complete record. It would take a whole library to recount all the events necessary to give a complete account of the experiences of God's people. But there is now a vast amount of nonbiblical material available to supplement our Bible story. The authors of the Bible selected only certain aspects of the life of a man. They did not aim to give us a complete picture. They simply wrote about what was important for their purpose and passed over other things in silence. The archaeologist helps us to fill out the picture. We learn, for example, that King Omri, dismissed in six verses in the book of Kings, was known to the Assyrians and was the conqueror of Moab. We discover that King Ahab sent a large contingent of troops to a great battle against the Assyrians. Neither of these facts is mentioned in the Bible. These and many other items of information are made available to us by the archaeologist. In the following pages we shall discover many of them.

Then, thirdly, biblical archaeology helps us in the translation and explanation of many passages in the Bible that are hard to understand. Sometimes we find a word in a kindred language that gives an alternative meaning which will suit the Bible context better. Sometimes we learn that the Bible has preserved valuable geographical information which we have missed because we did not understand. At other times we gain a completely new impression of a passage in the light of fuller historical knowledge.

Finally, it is perfectly true to say that biblical archaeology has done a great deal to correct the impression that was abroad at the close of the last century and in the early part of this century, that biblical history was of doubtful trustworthiness in many places. If one impression stands out more clearly than any other today, it is that on all hands the overall historicity of the Old Testament tradition is admitted. In this connection the words of W. F. Albright may be quoted: "There can be no doubt that archaeology has confirmed the substantial historicity of Old Testament tradition."[2]

Even if some writers want to speak of divergences from the historical picture, they do so with caution and admit that there is no serious modification of that picture.

THE SOURCES OF INFORMATION

The archaeologist obtains his information from material objects left behind by the people of those far-off days. They are to be found in the ruined towns, graves, and inscriptions of the people. The objects now investigated by the excavator may be either quite exposed to human view even today, or covered up completely or partially by earth.

There are numerous structures that are still quite exposed. We need only refer to the pyramids and temples of Egypt, the Parthenon and other structures on the Acropolis in Athens, the great ziggurat at Ur of the Chaldees, various Roman temples, aqueducts, roads, and the like, scattered all over the East as well as in Europe, and the massive Crusader castles still to be seen in many lands. These buildings are more or less completely exposed and their inscriptions, art work, and general architectural features are readily available to the archaeologist.

Some buildings are partly covered and need to be cleaned up. Perhaps debris has gathered about their lower portions. This has to be cleared away before the complete structure is visible. Some of the buildings already referred to required a certain amount of clearing before they could be made to tell their story.

The completely covered remains, however, are the ones that require the skill of the trained excavator. How did they become covered? By a variety of means. Perhaps the buildings lay in the lower part of a town in early times. Once the town was deserted, the rains brought silt down from the hills around, which, in the course of centuries, covered the town. The marketplace at Athens and the forum at Rome were covered in this way.

Perhaps a town was overwhelmed by such means as volcanic ash. This was the fate of Pompeii and Herculaneum, near to modern Naples, in A.D. 79. Today the archaeologist can clear away the ash and view a Roman town of the first century A.D.

Some of the covered remains are in tombs and graves. These are very important because when people in the ancient world buried their dead, they placed in the grave objects that they believed would be needed by their departed friends in the afterlife. It is from graves that we obtain many of our fine museum

2. W. F. Albright, *Archaeology and the Religion of Israel* (Baltimore, 1955), p. 176.

Bethshan (Tell el-Husn), a town near Mount Gilboa in Israel, has been occupied almost continually since Chalcolithic times (ca. 5000-3200 B.C.). This view is from the Roman theatre. (W. S. LaSor)

pieces. There was no reason for them to be broken since they were protected by the walls of the tomb.

The most important type of covered ruin is that in which we find the remains of several towns one on top of the other. To us moderns this is strange. But in the ancient world, when a walled town was burned, or beaten down by battering rams, or destroyed by an earthquake, the newcomers who rebuilt the town did not remove the debris and the foundations of the old city. They selected the best material for re-use, leveled off the remains, and rebuilt on top of them. Some feet of debris from the previous town would thus be sealed off. The general pattern of houses and streets would remain, and a great many small items would be left in the rubbish.[3]

Most of the towns in Palestine known to us in the Bible are of this type— Bethel, Jericho, Samaria, Jerusalem, Megiddo, Bethshan, Bethshemesh, Debir, Gezer, and so on. Some of these towns had ten or twelve or even twenty strata of destroyed towns. Each recounts its own story. When the whole is excavated by cutting large trenches across the mound and comparing the finds, the story of the town slowly emerges. These sites are known to the archaeologist as "tells" or "mounds."

3. P. W. Lapp, *The Tale of the Tell* (Pittsburgh, 1975).

These, then, are the sources from which the excavator reconstructs his story. The items that speak are the ruined buildings with their walls and rooms and floors, the pottery, the metal implements and tools, the weapons, the ivory work, the glass, coins, and jewelry, the inscribed and written material, whether it be on stone, bone, or baked clay. Indeed, any item at all contributes to the final picture.

Among the most significant of the finds in an excavation are the written records, letters, receipts, census lists, contracts, and literary pieces, written on stone, broken pottery, leather, or papyrus. Material like this has been found in caves, wrapped around mummies, lying about in ruined buildings, or cast out on a rubbish heap. Such perishable material as leather and papyrus requires a dry climate, so that it is normally found only in Egypt above the level of the Nile floods, or in the dry parts of Palestine. Inscriptions in stone are likely to be found anywhere. Often inscriptions were filled with lead, but sometimes they were little more than scratches on the rock (*graffiti*). Occasionally written information was painted on the wall of a tomb, or marked in carbon on a coffin or a wall. Although this written material lacks popular appeal, it is possibly the most important of all the information that can be recovered from an ancient civilization, for it records the names of people and places and gives detailed information of events, laws, and customs.

Coins fall into a special class, for they are of value not only in dating remains, but also because they contain in themselves valuable historical material. They were important instruments of the propaganda machine in the ancient

Babylonian clay tablets (ca. 3100 B.C.) inscribed with linear characters that are directly derived from pictographs. The tablets contain accounts of fields, crops, and commodities. (British Museum)

world, and a study of them gives us a good deal of information about the appearance of kings and emperors, as well as about events. There are several references to coins in the New Testament, for example, the one where Jesus was questioned about the payment of taxes and He asked to see a coin. This was the occasion for an important lesson in loyalty: "Render therefore unto Caesar the things which are Caesar's; and unto God the things that are God's" (Matt. 22:21).

Finally, after several seasons of work, the story is told. The biblical archaeologist hastens to discover whether there are important items in the report of the excavator that bear on Bible history, and that will be of use in one of the ways we have suggested above.

BIBLICAL ARCHAEOLOGY AND THE NEW TESTAMENT

The average Bible reader sometimes gains the impression that the spectacular discoveries of the archaeologist apply only to the Old Testament. This is a serious misunderstanding. The New Testament, too, has benefited greatly from archaeological discovery.[4] To the credit of the modern excavator, there lies an impressive array of material that has not only thrown light on the history of the New Testament period but that has also had important repercussions in the field of New Testament study generally. It is not too much to claim that important modifications have been brought about in scholarly theories about the New Testament, almost entirely as a result of archaeological discovery. We shall notice some of these in this volume.

There is probably a good reason for the development of the idea that archaeology has little to say about the New Testament. The really significant discoveries that bear upon it are not nearly so striking as those that refer to the Old Testament. Many people who know very little about Bible history would nevertheless have heard of Sir Leonard Woolley and his excavations at Ur, the home of Abraham, or of Professor Garstang and his work at Jericho. Again, the excavations of Professor Koldewey at Babylon, the capital of the famous Nebuchadnezzar, seem to be commonplace in history books. The achievements of the great Assyrians have been known for over a century now since Sir Henry Layard, H. Rassam, and George Smith carried out their remarkable researches in the ruins of Nineveh and Nimrud. But all of these are of interest chiefly to the Old Testament scholar. Even the casual visitor to Egypt, Palestine, Syria, Lebanon, Iraq, and other countries in the East sees before his eyes massive structures like the pyramids of Egypt, the great ziggurat of Ur, the widespread ruins of Babylon, the Assyrian palaces of Nineveh, Khorsabad, and Nimrud, and the palaces of the Persians, all of which are of specific interest to the Old Testament

---

4. A. Parrot, *Discovering Buried Worlds* (London, 1955); E. M. Blaiklock, *Out of the Earth* (Grand Rapids, 1957); J. Finegan, *The Archaeology of the New Testament* (Princeton, 1969).

reader. Moreover, all of these are so old and carry with them so much of the mystery connected with those long-past days that, in comparison, Roman remains seem to come from yesterday and to lack the fascination of the more ancient past. Without this glamor, the antiquities of New Testament times have made less appeal to the public and so the impression has grown that there is little of value to be found in the excavation of remains of New Testament times.

Despite the absence of popular appeal, archaeological finds relating to the New Testament are by no means lacking. The most important of them are written records, inscriptions, and papyri. But there are some building remains and a considerable variety of other items which have their own special interest.

For many of the towns mentioned in the New Testament there are still considerable remains above the ground. For others there is a great deal that has become covered through the ages and needs to be excavated. The important town of Jerusalem, which we shall discuss in detail later, is rich in archaeological material.[5] However, when these towns are laid bare by the archaeologist there is much to be discovered, both about the life that was lived in these towns and about some of the buildings that are mentioned in the New Testament. We need only call to mind the great temple of Diana at Ephesus, or the marketplace at Athens. There are other towns unearthed by the archaeologist which, though not mentioned in the Bible, nevertheless tell us much about the life of the times. Such a town is Pompeii, which was overwhelmed by Mount Vesuvius in A.D. 79. Here we have a typical town of Paul's day, and a study of its remains will give us a clear idea of the sort of town in which Paul delivered his message.

5. For details see ch. 19.

PART ONE:

ARCHAEOLOGY AND THE OLD TESTAMENT STORY UP TO 587 B.C.

The remains of the ziggurat (temple tower) at Ur as seen from the southwest. It was built by Ur-Nammu and dates from the end of the third millennium B.C. The structure at Babel (Gen. 11) has been likened to such a tower. (University Museum, University of Pennsylvania)

2

ABRAHAM THE MIGRANT

IT would appear that the writer of the book of Genesis was concerned merely to lay down some general statements about mankind in his first ten chapters and to move as quickly as possible to the story of Abraham. Those general statements concern the creating hand of God behind all things material and living, the universality of human rebellion and of divine judgment, the fact of God's desire to save men, and the fact that men may be saved by faith in God and in obedience to Him.

The author of Genesis took from the information available to him certain data to illustrate his general principles. Unfortunately his sketches are so summary and so carefully selected that it is difficult to provide archaeological support for them. But some useful material is available for comparison along at least three lines.

(a) Creation. There are other ancient stories of creation, the best known being *Enuma Elish*, a Babylonian-Sumerian epic which tells of the origin of the gods from the primeval chaos in which two strange entities, Apsu and Tiamat, were commingled in a single body. From these came the gods. One of the younger gods, Marduk, finally overthrew Tiamat, cut her in two, and formed heaven and earth from her body. He then created man, as well as the rest of the universe. In comparison with this strange story recorded today on seven clay tablets, the majestic narrative of Genesis 1 and 2 stands out as a masterpiece. The one true God created all things in a series of divine utterances.[1]

---

1. J. B. Pritchard, *ANET* (Princeton, 1955), pp. 60ff., translation of E. A. Speiser; A. Heidel, *The Babylonian Genesis* (Chicago, 1942).

Two of the seven tablets in the Assyrian series containing the Creation epic. They are copies of the older Babylonian text and were made for the Assyrian royal library at Nineveh. The text may be traced to third-millennium Sumerian originals. (British Museum)

At one stage many Old Testament scholars suggested that the biblical story of creation owed much to *Enuma Elish* and made much of the supposed relationship between the Hebrew word *tehom*, "the deep," and the name *Ti'amat*, the goddess who personified the salt sea waters. In fact both *tehom* and *ti'amat* derive from a common Semitic root *thm* which in Ugaritic in the fourteen/thirteenth centuries B.C., and even in Ebla in the twenty-third century B.C., denoted very generally "the deep" or "the ocean abyss." The Babylonian *Enuma Elish* is itself not the original story but is derived from an earlier source. Today we have a number of Babylonian fragments which show a great deal of variation on details.[2]

(b) The Flood. The Babylonian tablets also have a flood story.[3] The hero Utnapishtim was saved in a ship with people and animals from a great flood. There are interesting parallels with the biblical story—the sending forth of birds to discover dry land, the building of an altar, and the offering of a sacrifice. But again, whereas the biblical story of the flood is monotheistic, the Babylonian

2. See A. Heidel, *The Babylonian Genesis* (2nd ed. 1951). Cf. J. V. Kinnier-Wilson in D. W. Thomas (ed.), *Documents from Old Testament Times* (New York, 1958), p. 14, who refers to "no connections of any kind"; W. G. Lambert, "A New Look at the Babylonian Background of Genesis," *JTS*, Vol. XVI, Part 2 (Oct., 1965), pp. 287–300, esp. pp. 289, 291, 293–299; A. R. Millard, "A New Babylonian 'Genesis' Story," *Tyndale Bulletin*, No. 18 (1967), pp. 3–4, 16–18.

3. J. B. Pritchard, *ANET*, pp. 42ff., translation of S. N. Kramer; A. Heidel, *The Gilgamesh Epic and Old Testament Parallels* (Chicago, 1946); A. Parrot, *The Flood and Noah's Ark* (London, 1955).

story is set in a strange polytheistic framework. There are, in fact, many differences between the two stories despite the resemblances, and it is more likely that both stories reach back to an original event than that the Hebrew story is a modification of the ancient myth.

Some features of the Babylonian Flood story have been illuminated by archaeology. The hero of the story, Utnapishtim, was, in fact, one of the early kings of the South Babylonian city of Uruk during the Early Dynastic II period.[4] According to the Babylonian story, this king went in search of immortality.

The story was widespread in the ancient Near East and excavations have yielded quite a number of texts or fragments which refer to the story of the Flood, although these differ in detail.[5] It is mentioned in the Sumerian King List, which gives a list of kings after the Flood and comes from about 2000 B.C.[6] From the seventeenth century B.C. at the latest comes the Epic of Atra-hasis. This originally included the fullest Babylonian account of the Flood.[7] There is a Sumerian Flood story from about 1600 B.C.[8] A Babylonian tablet about the Flood and referring to Atra-hasis was found in Ugarit and dated to 1400–1200 B.C.[9] Most of the Babylonian Epic itself is attested by copies from the early second millennium B.C., but the key Tablet XI is attested only in seventh-century B.C. copies. Ancient Mesopotamia has provided, up to the present, several Flood stories. Of special interest to Bible readers is a Gilgamesh fragment from the middle of the second millennium B.C., that is, from the Middle Bronze Age, found in Level VIII at Megiddo.[10]

Important Akkadian texts come from the library of the Assyrian king Ashurbanipal at Nineveh, although the Gilgamesh Epic is known from versions which antedate the first millennium B.C. A fragment of an Akkadian recension was found in the Hittite Archives at Boghazkoy, as were Hurrian and Hittite translations, both from the middle of the second millennium. Fragments of Tablets I–III and X come from ancient Babylonia and date to the first half of the second millenium.

That there were great floods in Mesopotamia which might have given rise to the Flood story is shown by considerable deposits of silt in several excavated sites such as Ur, Shuruppak, Erech, and Kish where strata of clay were laid down by large floods. The claim by Sir Leonard Woolley that he had found a deposit which marked the biblical Flood is no longer accepted.[11] The deposit there is a thick one but rather localized in one area of the city. The flood deposits in other

---

4. W. C. Hallo, *The Ancient Near East* (New Haven, 1971), p. 46.
5. J. B. Pritchard, *The Ancient Near East, Supplementary Texts and Pictures relating to the Old Testament* (Princeton, 1969), pp. 503–507.
6. W. G. Lambert and A. R. Millard, *Atra-hasis* (Oxford, 1969), pp. 16, 25.
7. *Ibid.*
8. *Ibid.*, pp. 138f.
9. *Ibid.*, pp. 131–133.
10. A. Goetze and S. Levy, "Fragment of the Gilgamesh Epic from Megiddo," *'Atiqot*, Vol. II (1959), pp. 121–128.
11. Sir Leonard Woolley, *Ur of the Chaldees* (London, 1938), pp. 21–23.

sites vary in thickness and in age. None can really be identified as a deposit laid down specifically by the biblical Flood. All we can say is that ancient Mesopotamian literature speaks consistently about a flood. The Flood deposits would seem to support the general truth of this picture. But the date and extent of the biblical Flood are at present beyond our knowledge.[12]

Attempts have been made to locate the remains of the Ark on modern Mount Ararat. Such attempts are virtually pointless since the Bible refers to the mountains (plural) of Ararat (Gen. 8:4) as the resting place of the Ark so that no specific mountain is identified. Further, the very name Ararat refers to the ancient land of Urartu, which covered a wide area. Pieces of timber found on modern Mount Ararat seemed to offer some hope of identification, but when these were dated by modern radiocarbon tests they were shown to be no older than the seventh–eighth centuries A.D.[13]

(c) King lists and their longevity in primaeval proto-history. One of the features of the Mesopotamian king lists is the very considerable age of the kings. The Sumerian King List commences with the words:

> When kingship was lowered from heaven kingship was (first) in Eridu. (In) Eridu A-lulim (became) king and ruled 28,800 years. Alalgar ruled 36,000 years. Two kings (thus) ruled it for 64,800 years.[14]

The line of kings continues down into historical times which are well known, and the length of the reigns becomes shorter. The significance of these lengthy periods is hardly to be understood literally and must have had some symbolic meaning. They were probably not intended to serve a narrowly chronological purpose in the modern sense. It is of some interest that the Bible also ascribes considerable length to the age of some of the descendants of Noah (Gen. 11:10–32). There is thus a certain parallelism between the biblical and the Sumerian material. But in the present state of our knowledge the significance of this is not clear. The biblical figures are much more modest than their Sumerian parallels.[15]

(d) The literary structure of early Genesis (1–9). Some interest attaches to the literary structure of the early chapters of Genesis, which follow the sequence of creation (chs. 1–2), man's alienation from God (chs. 3–4), a link by a ten-generation genealogy (ch. 5) to the Flood and the subsequent renewal (chs. 6–9), the development of mankind (chs. 10–11:9), and another nine-generation genealogical link from Shem to Terah the father of Abraham (chs. 11:10–25). This scheme is broadly parallel to that of the Sumerian King List, Atra-hasis, and the Sumerian Flood story.[16] It would seem clear that there was a

---

12. J. Finegan, *Archaeological History of the Ancient Middle East* (1979), pp. 23–26.
13. L. R. Bailey, "Wood from 'Mount Ararat': Noah's Ark," *BA*, Vol. 40, No. 4 (Dec., 1977), pp. 137–146; F. Navarra, *Noah's Ark, I Touched It* (translated from French, 1974).
14. J. B. Pritchard, *ANET*, pp. 265f.
15. See K. A. Kitchen, *Ancient Orient and Old Testament* (Downers Grove, 1966), pp. 35–41.
16. See K. A. Kitchen, *The Bible in its World* (Exeter, 1977), pp. 31f.

common literary tradition in the ancient Middle East differing in details from place to place but maintaining a certain similarity in literary outline. This tradition would seem to have arisen in Mesopotamia and was taken to the West to be given biblical expression at a later date.

The full implications of archaeological work in Mesopotamia have not yet been realized. As year follows year, excavations continue to provide exciting information about that ancient world against which the earliest stories of the Bible have to be set if they are to be understood properly.

After his introductory chapters, the author of Genesis moves into the story of Abraham, for which he provides a great deal more information.

THE ORIGINAL HOME OF ABRAHAM

The Bible places the home of Abraham at Ur of the Chaldees and suggests two stages of his migration to Palestine, first from Ur to Haran and then from Haran to Canaan. The identification of Ur has not been without some disagreement among scholars, some of whom see in the phrase "Ur of the Chaldees" a later editorial note since it seems inappropriate in the second millennium B.C. when the Chaldeans had not emerged into the light of recorded history. There may be some truth in this, but biblical tradition places Abraham's original home at Ur in Lower Mesopotamia (Gen. 11:31). Attempts to locate Ur in Upper Mesopotamia have not been at all successful.[17] Certainly many scholars feel that there are good reasons to give credence to the view that ancient Ur, the modern Tell el-Muqayyar, is the city referred to in Genesis.[18] Such a view is not necessarily tied to a proposal that Abraham was an Amorite and that his migration should be seen as part of the Amorite movements in the early part of the second millennium B.C. But if this identification of the biblical Ur is correct, then the forefather of Israel had contact with high civilization although he may not have actually been a city dweller. The excavations of Sir Leonard Woolley during the years 1922 to 1934 showed something of the splendor of the centuries before Abraham.[19] The royal tombs of Ur, dating to about 2500 B.C., produced a collection of magnificent golden vessels which are still the delight and wonderment of the students of the ancient world. Ur was a town with a complex system of government and a well-developed system of commerce, one with writing in common use for the issue of receipts, the making of contracts, and many other purposes. There were town drains, streets, two-story houses, a great temple tower (ziggurat), trade routes joining the town with other great towns to the north and the south, and various other evidences of a highly developed civilization.

17. See W. F. Saggs, "Ur of the Chaldees. A Problem of Identification," *Iraq*, Vol. XXII (1960), pp. 200–209.
18. D. J. Wiseman, "Ur of the Chaldees," *NBD* (1962), pp. 1304f.
19. L. Woolley, *op. cit.*

Statue (ca. 2500 B.C.) from the "Great Death Pit" at Ur of a he-goat with forelegs in a tree. Probably it was a holder for burning incense or for an offering bowl. The tree and the goat's legs and face are made of gold, the horns, eyes, and upper fleece are lapis lazuli, and the lower fleece is white shell pieces. The belly was made of silver, and the core of the statue was wood. (British Museum)

This area of southern Mesopotamia had formerly been occupied mainly by the Sumerians, who were the first settlers on the plains of Shinar. At an early date Semitic people began to infiltrate into these areas. These became known as the Akkadians. They lived peacefully among the Sumerians and took over their culture. Eventually they became the dominant group and replaced the Sumerians as the rulers of these lands. In later centuries yet other Semites came to dwell here, such as the Amorites and the Aramaeans. There is good evidence that the area was occupied by Semites at an early date. It is not at all unlikely, therefore, that a Semite like Abraham should come from southern Mesopotamia, although we may not be able to tell the precise Semitic group from which he came.

PEOPLES IN THE EAST
IN THE DAYS OF ABRAHAM

It is important to realize that the world in which Abraham lived was a very busy world indeed. We may say that the centuries following 2000 B.C. were centuries of great change all over the East. In addition to the older Sumerians and the Semitic Akkadians who were scattered throughout Mesopotamia, we find other important groups of people, such as the Amorites, the Hurrians, and the Hittities, coming into prominence in these lands.

We hear of the *Amorites* in the Bible among the inhabitants of Palestine and particularly of Transjordan. They were to be found, however, in many lands in the Near East at this time. Just before 2000 B.C. they began to move into Lower Mesopotamia, and by 1800 B.C. they were in possession of most of this region. At the same time they were active in the general area northeast of Galilee, as we learn from a valuable collection of execration (cursing) texts from Egypt. There were two groups of these texts that comprised curses written on small figurines or vessels and directed against potential rebel vassals of the Egyptians. The breaking of the objects on which the curses were written was believed to release curses. The first group of texts written on vases dates to the period between 1925 and 1875 B.C. and lists about thirty Palestinian and Syrian chiefs but hardly a town.[20] A second group of texts written on baked clay figurines and dating to the second half of the nineteenth century B.C., that is, a little later, refers to many more towns and fewer chieftains.[21] The two sets of texts give a picture of Amorites settling down in areas from Galilee northward and eastward. From this area they must have moved south into Transjordan and southwest into Palestine proper. At the time of the Exodus the Israelites overthrew Sihon and Og, kings of the Amorites in Transjordan (Num. 21:21–35), and fought with the Amorites in Palestine (Josh. 10).

An interesting document from Egypt tells the story of Sinuhe, an Egyptian official who fled to the same general area in the twentieth century B.C. He lived with an Amorite chieftain of the same kind as Abraham, Laban, or Jacob.[22]

It was the Amorites who gave to the world the great lawgiver Hammurabi, who ruled during the years 1792–1750 B.C. A study of his code of laws shows a number of interesting parallels with the law code of Moses.[23] This is not really surprising since the Israelite patriarchs came from these lands, and Abraham must have known and lived under similar laws before the days of Hammurabi.

---

20. First published in 1926 by K. Sethe in Berlin and known as the Berlin Texts.
21. G. Poesner, *Princes et Pays d'Asie et de Nubie* (Brussels, 1940).
22. J. B. Pritchard, *ANET*, pp. 18ff.
23. Compare Laws 250–252 with Exodus 21:28–36.

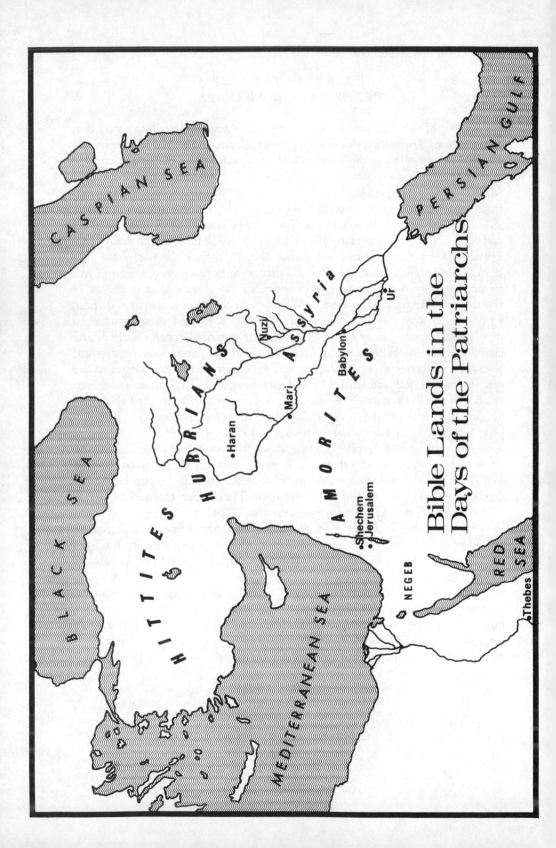

Bible Lands in the
Days of the Patriarchs

Two typical portraits of King Hammurabi of Babylon (1792–1750 B.C.) surrounded by the well-known Code of Laws. The portrait to the left is cut in limestone (British Museum). The eighty-inch diorite stele to the right depicts Hammurabi receiving the symbols of authority—the rod and the ring—from the god Shamash, seated. (Consulate General, Republic of Iraq)

An important question which has not yet been satisfactorily answered is whether the patriarchs were part of the Amorite movement. Both the forebears of later Israel and the Amorites, and for that matter the Aramaeans and other peoples in western Asia, were part of the general West Semitic stock. Biblical tradition links the patriarchs with the Aramaeans (Gen. 11:32ff.; 24; 29; 30; 31). But there is a good deal of uncertainty still about the ethnic origins of the patriarchs.[24] It is safe to assert, however, that the Amorites were a very significant element in the population of western Asia in the first half of the second

24. For well-documented but very critical assessment of the evidence see J. van Seters, *Abraham in History and Tradition* (New Haven, 1975), pp. 20–26, 33f., 43f., etc.; T. L. Thompson, *The Historicity of the Patriarchal Narratives* (New York, 1974), pp. 55–57, 67–88, 89–93, 118–143, 144–171. Both books have been the object of some very critical comment by other scholars.

millennium B.C. and were part of the scene in which the patriarchs lived and moved.

The second group of people that call for brief mention are the *Hurrians*. They began to enter the lands around the Tigris about 2000 B.C. Some clay tablets of this period introduce a new type of name, different from the other names of the area. These new names are now known to have belonged to the Hurrians, who during the next couple of centuries spread across central Mesopotamia and formed the main population in a number of very important kingdoms like the Mitanni kingdom which occupied the area between the Tigris and Euphrates rivers about 1500 B.C. In recent years the important town of Nuzi to the east of the Tigris has yielded an amazing collection of clay documents which have given insight into the customs of these lands.

Some of these customs bear some resemblance to some of the patriarchal customs portrayed in Genesis. The question will be taken up later in this chapter. But many of the customs which were current among the Hurrians had parallels in Middle Eastern society over many centuries. The Hurrians were only one section of a very complex society, and it is not inconceivable that some of Israel's forebears had contact with the Hurrians somewhere or other.

It may be asked whether Hurrians as such are known in the Bible. Some scholars feel that the Horites correspond to the Hurrians.[25]

The *Hittites* were a third group which became active about the time when the Israelite patriarchs were moving about in the East. This was a group of peoples which originated somewhere in Europe and formed part of the great Indo-European migration that reached as far as India. This group, which is of some interest to the Bible student, settled in Asia Minor. Here they found a more ancient people known as the Hatti people. The newcomers took over their name. References to Hittites in the Bible may not be to the Hittites of Asia Minor. According to the genealogical table of Genesis 10:15, a certain Heth was a son of Canaan. Interpreted in ethnic terms, there was a tribal element in Canaan which might be called the Hittites. Abraham purchased a field in which to bury Sarah from a certain Ephron the Hittite (Gen. 23:10), but he had to do business with the elders of Machpelah who are called "the sons of Heth" (Gen. 23:3, 5, 7, 10, 16, 18, 20). Nothing in this chapter requires that the term Hittite mean any more than a local Canaanite group. Indeed, the Hittites of Genesis are not to be connected with the ancient Hatti people nor to the Indo-European community that came into Asia Minor and gained control over the Anatolian plateau about 1900 B.C. Already in patriarchal times, however, they were active on the fringes of the patriarchal world. In the years *ca.* 1700–1190 B.C. they were to form an empire centered on Hattusa, and after their fall

25. There is wide discussion on the issue. See R. de Vaux, "Les Hurrites de l'histoire et les Horites de la Bible," *RB*, Vol. 74 (1967), pp. 481–503; *Histoire ancienne d'Israel* (Paris, 1971), pp. 69–71, 86–91; J. van Seters, *The Hyksos* (London, 1966), pp. 181–190; D. J. Wiseman (ed.) in *Peoples of Old Testament Times* (Oxford, 1973); H. A. Hoffner, "The Hittites and the Hurrians," pp. 221–226.

some Hittite centers lingered on in North Syria alongside the Aramaeans. There is no evidence of direct Hittite penetration into Palestine, although cultural influences no doubt were brought in by traders.[26]

Some reference should also be made to the Aramaeans who figure prominently in the patriarchal story (Gen. 25:20; 28:1-7; 31:20, 24; Deut. 26:5). This group of people is not greatly known on written documents in the early part of the second millennium B.C. although the name Aram, as a place name, is known in an inscription of Naram-Sin of Akkad as early as the twenty-third century B.C. Then there are references in documents from Drehem, a city of the Lower Tigris, to a region on the Upper Euphrates *ca.* 2000 B.C. There is also reference to a personal name in the Mari texts (seventeenth century B.C.) and at Alalakh (seventh century B.C.) and Ugarit (fourteenth century B.C.). From Egypt we have a reference to a place name in Syria from the days of Amenophis III (first half of the fourteenth century B.C.), as we do in the journal of an Egyptian frontier official in the days of Pharaoh Merneptah about 1220 B.C. From then on the name occurs frequently in Assyrian documents. It seems clear that a group, later to be known clearly as the Aramaeans from the land of Aram, were already known in the Upper Euphrates area from quite early in the second millennium. It is among these people that biblical tradition looks for the patriarchs and, however ill-defined they are at present, we must count them as one of the groups of people that were present in patriarchal areas in the first part of the second millennium B.C.[27]

To these peoples we must add numerous smaller groups, many of them subtribal in size and belonging to larger ethnic groupings. In Palestine itself from an early age there was already a very mixed population which had received, and was receiving all the time, infusions of migrants from various directions. The patriarchs, then, did not move in a vacuum but in a world that was peopled by a wide variety of ethnic and tribal elements, a picture that is reflected in the patriarchal narratives. Unfortunately we are unable to argue from the presence of these peoples in the biblical narratives anything about the date of the patriarchs since peoples mentioned there were known and were active in the Middle East for many centuries. On the basis merely of the peoples mentioned one could argue for a date for the patriarchs anywhere in the second millennium B.C. or even, with some modification in the meaning of the terms, into the first millennium B.C. Despite this, it is certainly a possibility that the patriarchs fit into the first half of the second millennium.

ABRAHAM'S JOURNEYINGS

The Bible describes the journeys of Abraham in some detail. Leaving Ur, he first traveled north to the town of Haran where he lived for a number of years before

26. H. A. Hoffner, *op. cit.*, pp. 197-221.
27. A. Malamat, "The Aramaeans," in D. J. Wiseman (ed.), *Peoples of Old Testament Times*, pp. 134-155.

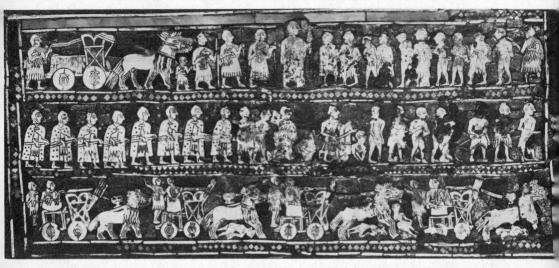

A masterpiece of early Sumerian art, this mosaic standard from Ur (ca. 2500 B.C.) is made of lapis lazuli, shell, and red limestone set in bitumen on wood. The top row depicts a chariot, soldiers, the prince (the large figure), and naked prisoners; the middle row, soldiers and naked prisoners; the bottom row, chariots being driven over a corpse-strewn battle field. (British Museum)

Thirty-seven Semites ("Asiatics") bring eye paint to Khnemhotep III (ca. 1900 B.C.) in a painting in his tomb at Beni Hasan, Egypt. This detail shows a boy with a spear, four women in multicolored garments (which contrast with the Egyptians' plain white robes), a donkey carrying bellows (perhaps for metal working?), and a man playing a lyre. (Oriental Institute, University of Chicago)

setting out again to journey to Palestine (Gen. 12). A later writer in the Bible described this first journey of Abraham as one in which "he went out, not knowing whither he went" (Heb. 11:8b). Recent research suggests quite strongly that this verse must not be applied in a physical sense. There were well-trodden trade routes throughout these lands, and we have no reason to think that Abraham left the usual roads when he made his journey. We should rather interpret this verse in a spiritual sense, namely, that having set out at the call of God, he did not quite know where this response was likely to lead him in the end.

Not only were there great roads from Ur to Haran, but other roads connected northern Mesopotamia with the Mediterranean coast and with Palestine. Still others connected Palestine with Egypt. There was a good deal of traffic between these latter two lands. This is shown by the numerous Egyptian items found in the tombs of Palestine dating to the years 2000–1500 B.C. This period covers the time of the great Twelfth Dynasty (ca. 1991–1786 B.C.), the second Intermediate Period, and the Hyksos Period (ca. 1720–1550 B.C.) during large parts of which Egypt exercised some sort of control over Palestine. Thus the Execration Texts, already referred to,[28] come from the Twelfth Dynasty, as does a valuable set of paintings from tombs found at Beni Hasan, 250 miles down the Nile, in which the artist has portrayed for us a group of semi-nomads who visited Egypt about 1900 B.C.[29] There were thirty-seven of these people, who were led by a man with a perfectly good Semitic name, Absha. The dress and the equipment of these people give us a good idea of the dress and equipment of the patriarchal family which moved into Egypt about the same time.

During the next two hundred years there was considerable movement to and fro between Egypt and Palestine. More generally there was movement for trade in many areas of the Middle East. One of the most notable examples is the movement of traders from Anatolia to ancient Assyria. From a center in Anatolia at Kanesh (Kultepe) caravans moved to Asshur and back again on a regular basis. Important documents found at Kanesh, the Cappadocian Documents[30] dating to ca. 1900 B.C., give valuable information about trade, caravans, legal procedures, and the like, and throw a flood of light on the customs of the period.

It is interesting to discover that the towns visited by Abraham according to the biblical records lie today in the zone where the rainfall is between ten and twenty inches annually. This is a zone where sheep can live. We have no serious reason to think that the general rainfall pattern has changed through the centuries.

28. See p. 19.
29. Photo in *Westminster Historical Atlas* (London, 1953), p. 23. See photo, p. 24.
30. O. R. Gurney, *The Hittites* (London, 1964), p. 18.

A drawing of what the ziggurat built by Ur-Nammu at Ur may have looked like. The temple buildings in the angles of the stairs are not shown. (University Museum, University of Pennsylvania)

PATRIARCHAL TOWNS, NAMES, AND BEASTS OF BURDEN

It may be asked whether we have any contemporary evidence about towns mentioned in the biblical records. There is, of course, good evidence for Ur. Some excavation has been undertaken at Haran in recent years, although only in the upper, later levels of the mound. It was known in the important Cappadocian texts of 1900 B.C. The name was still referred to in important texts from Mari on the middle Euphrates coming from about 1700 B.C. The site has never been lost. The name Nahor, as a town, is also attested in these northern areas in the Cappadocian texts, the Mari texts, and late Assyrian texts. It belonged to the district of Haran. Many other towns in this area are known from documents, and sometimes the same name is used for a person in the biblical record. The names Serug and Terah are cases in point.[31]

It is precisely in these northern Mesopotamian lands where the biblical

---

31. A discussion of place names, as well as of the whole range of modern knowledge now available, has been undertaken by R. de Vaux, "Les patriarches Hébreux et les découvertes modernes," *RB*, Vols. LIII (1946), LV (1948), LVI (1949). See also H. H. Rowley, "Recent Discoveries and the Patriarchal Age," *BJRL* (1949), pp. 3–38; R. de Vaux, *Histoire ancienne d'Israel* (Paris, 1971), pp. 189f.

records place the home of the patriarchs that we find these names. We may conjecture that a good deal of contact took place between Palestine and these lands to insure a continuity of culture. For this reason we look to northern Mesopotamia for the cultural background of the patriarchs.

We now have archaeological information about a number of the patriarchal towns in the Palestine area, such as Bethel (Gen. 12:8; 28:19; 35:1, 15, etc.), Shechem (Gen. 12:6; 33:18; 34:2, etc.), Jerusalem (Salem, Gen. 14:18), Mamre (Gen. 13:18; 14:13, 24; 18:1, etc.), Gerar (Gen. 20:1; 26:6, 17, 20), Beer-sheba (Gen. 21:14, 33; 22:19; 26:33, etc.), and Dothan (Gen. 37:17).[32] Continuous occupation began at Bethel in the Early Bronze IV Age (ca. 2200–2000 B.C.), but there was earlier settlement in the area. Bethel was still in existence in Byzantine times. There were settlements in the Beer-sheba area during the Chalcolithic period (ca. 3500 B.C.). The modern Tell Sheba dates only to the Iron II Age (ca. 1000–586 B.C.), so that no comment can be made about a site at Beer-sheba in the second millennium although the site of Ramat el-Khalil, two miles north of Hebron, was occupied early in the Middle Bronze II period, about 1800 B.C. This site may have been Mamre. The biblical story does not necessarily demand an actual town, however. The case is different with Shechem, which was a town of some sort early in the Middle Bronze Age (about 1850–1750 B.C.) and underwent numerous expansions in the centuries following. The Jerusalem area was inhabited in the Early Bronze I period (ca. 3150–2850 B.C.) and perhaps even earlier. But some kind of town existed here in the twentieth to nineteenth centuries B.C. and continued on until the present day. The site of Dothan goes back to the Early Bronze age when it was a large settlement surrounded by a wall. Occupation continued into Arab times. Nothing can be said of Gerar (Tell Abu Hureirah on the Wadi esh-Shari'ah to the south of Lachish) until the mound is excavated.

This brief discussion points to the possibility that events narrated in Genesis could have taken place early in the second millennium if all that was required in dating these events was that certain places referred to in the narrative existed in the early part of the second millennium. However, most of these towns also existed much later and some of them continuously for hundreds of years so that the narratives could be accepted as suiting geographical conditions over a long period of time.

As to personal names like Abraham, Isaac, Jacob, we are able to say today that these were current names in the areas referred to in the Bible. The details have been collected by a variety of writers in recent years. The Amorites in particular were fond of names of the type of Jacob and Isaac, names which are really verbal forms. However, a chronological problem attaches to names. The name Abraham (A-ba-am-ra-am in one form) appears under several variants in

32. Details about excavations at these sites are available in the *Encyclopedia of Archaeological Excavations in the Holy Land* (*EAEHL*), 4 vols. (1975, 1976, 1977, 1978).

Professor Nelson Glueck examines a piece of pottery from Abraham's time. (Israel Office of Information)

Akkadian and Amorite contexts over many centuries. It has several parallels in the same contexts, indicating that this type of name was widely current in nearly every period from which names of West Semitic peoples have been preserved. Certainly the name was common enough in the first half of the second millennium B.C.

The same observations may be made about names like Isaac, Jacob, and Israel. Unfortunately the name patterns alone do not enable us to date the patriarchal period with any sort of exactness.[33]

An analysis of the beasts of burden of Abraham and the other patriarchs shows that these were camels and asses. The asses seem to have been used more widely than the camels. It has been argued that camels were not used in the East at this time. This cannot be maintained any longer. It is probably true that camels had not come into very general use in Abraham's time. It was more like 1300 B.C. before this beast of burden became popular. However, there is clear evidence that the camel was used somewhat in earlier times. Small clay figures, some carvings, and some pieces of camel bone and camel hair are known from graves in both Egypt and Mesopotamia before 2000 B.C.[34] There is no need to regard these references in the patriarchal narratives, therefore, as anachronisms.

33. For a thorough discussion of this point see T. L. Thompson, *op. cit.*, pp. 17–51; J. van Seters, *Abraham in History and Tradition*, pp. 39–64.

34. J. P. Free, *JNES*, Vol. III (1944), pp. 187–193.

The whole question of the beginnings of the domestication of the camel is extremely complex. A South Arabian origin for the domestic camel is widely accepted today. Moreover, the manner of domestication varied widely in character since the camel may be and has been milked, ridden, loaded with baggage, eaten, harnessed to a plow or wagon, traded for goods or wives, turned into sandals and camel-hair coats, etc. The references in Middle Eastern literature to the camel from the later centuries of the second millennium B.C. give no clue to the process of domestication, which preceded such references. But the domestication of the camel must have been known in Northern Arabia and Syria much earlier. One recent study proposes that the process of camel domestication first got under way between 3000 and 2500 B.C.[35] Since it is impossible to fix a date for Abraham with any certainty, we need to exercise caution in regarding the reference to camels in passages like Genesis 12:16; 24:10, 19f., 22, 31f., 35, 46, 61, 64; 37:25 as a pure anachronism.[36]

THE CUSTOMS PORTRAYED IN THE PATRIARCHAL NARRATIVES

One of the most important contributions of modern archaeology to our understanding of the Bible is the information which is given about the laws and customs of the people. This material comes either from the formal law codes or from the many incidental references to the customs of the people to be found on the documents of everyday life such as receipts, letters, contracts, licenses, and the like.

We now have a great deal of this kind of material, in particular from patriarchal times. In the first place, we know of at least three Amorite law codes, one of which is complete, namely, the code of the great Hammurabi. But this code was but the later expression of the earlier codes of the town of Eshnunna and of the king Lipit Ishtar.[37] In the second place, we have a great variety of baked-clay tablets which give us remarkable glimpses into the customs of the ordinary people of the day.

One of the most interesting collections of written records is that of the ancient Hurrian town of Nuzi which lay to the east of the Tigris River. Its modern name is Yorghan Tepe. Here, in the years 1925 to 1931, Professor Chiera and his colleagues of the American Schools of Oriental Research found some 20,000 clay documents in the family archives of several of the villas of the town.[38] The date of these documents is given by the excavators as the fifteenth century B.C., which may be as much as three or four hundred years later than

---

35. R. W. Bulliet, *The Camel and the Wheel* (Cambridge, Mass., 1975), ch. 2, pp. 28–56, esp. p. 56.

36. E. A. Speiser, *Genesis* (New York, 1964), p. 90.

37. J. B. Pritchard, *ANET*, pp. 159–163.

38. R. H. Pfeiffer and E. A. Speiser, *One Hundred New Selected Nuzi Texts* (New Haven, 1936).

A beautiful example of Akkadian craftsmanship ca. 2300 B.C. This bronze head, presumably of Sargon I, was cast and then detailed further with a chisel. It is rather stylized
and nearly perfectly symmetrical, but note
the realism of the combed waves of the beard.
(Consulate General, Republic of Iraq)

the traditional date of the patriarch Abraham (eighteen century B.C. or even
earlier); but because customs persist, the tablets give important evidence about
the legal and social structure of society in these lands in previous centuries.

But insights into the life of the people of Mesopotamia in the centuries that
spanned the patriarchal period have come from other significant collections of
tablets as well, including those from Mari,[39] Alalakh,[40] and small collections
from numerous sites in Mesopotamia and Syria. What promises to be a remarkable collection of some 20,000 or more tablets has been found in ancient Ebla
(Tell Mardikh) in Syria. These tablets come from about 2300 B.C. and were
contemporary with the great Sargon I of Akkad who founded the first Semitic

39. Their publication in volumes of *Archives Royales de Mari* (ARM) will take many years to
complete.
40. D. J. Wiseman, *The Alalakh Tablets* (1953).

An example of the private cylinder seals with which Babylonians signed their documents. The seal was rolled across a clay tablet when the clay was still wet. (Consulate General, Republic of Iraq)

empire about 2350 B.C. He briefly subdued Ebla and other cities, but on his death two of his sons successively lost most of their father's empire. His grandson Naram-Sin (ca. 2250) restored the dominion of Akkad and destroyed Ebla. The archives of Ebla show that Ebla was in its day a strong rival of Akkad. We are now on the way to being able to study the life of people in northern Mesopotamia some 500 years before the traditional date of the patriarchs.

When the Nuzi documents were first published there was an enthusiastic response by biblical scholars to the information they contained, for they seemed to cast a great deal of light on a social milieu which appeared to be very similar to the society of the patriarchs.[41] More mature reflection on the material from Nuzi has led scholars to the conclusion that parallels occur between the patriarchal narratives and cuneiform texts from various parts of the ancient Near East at various times, so that the uniqueness of the relationship with Nuzi has been called into question. This later research has made it difficult to use these parallels in nonbiblical sources as a guide for dating, although their value in assisting our understanding of the society of the ancient Near East in the second millennium B.C. is undoubted and at present the large majority of relevant social parallels come from the second millennium B.C. The patriarchal customs were quite at home in the Mesopotamian culture of that period. We may infer that the biblical traditions in Genesis 12–50 which portray a thorough acquaintance with a Mesopotamian way of life came with the original migrants from Mesopotamia. And the general period must have been the earlier part of the second millennium since there was no long-term association with Mesopotamia

41. C. H. Gordon, "Biblical Customs and the Nuzi Tablets," *BA* (Feb., 1940); H. H. Rowley, "Recent Discovery and the Patriarchal Age," *BJRL* (Sept., 1949), etc.

in the first millennium B.C. to provide such an intimate acquaintance with these Mesopotamian customs.

Let us turn then to a discussion of some of the more important of these customs. It will be our method to refer to the Mesopotamian custom first and then to draw out some biblical parallels. For convenience we shall deal first with such major items as inheritance and marriage, and then refer briefly to one or two miscellaneous customs.

In Mesopotamia, inheritance was of major importance. Property was, theoretically at least, inalienable and could not pass from the family. In order to overcome this difficulty a fictitious system of adoption was used. By this device it was possible for a man to adopt any number of "sons" or "brothers," and then to pass over the property rights quite legally to the adopted party. Cases are known where there was a regular traffic in this kind of adoption.

A property owner who had no son would normally adopt an heir. The adopted "son" might be a freeborn man, a slave, or a relative. The tablet of adoption was written on clay after proclamation at the gate of the city. When party A adopted party B, he willed to B the major portion of his lands, buildings, and other items, in consideration of the fact that B promised to serve A during

Daggers and a sheath, ca. 2600 B.C., from Ur. The handles are made of lapis lazuli studded with gold; the smooth blades and filigreed sheath are also gold. Note the mark of the craftsman or owner on some of the blades. (Consulate General, Republic of Iraq)

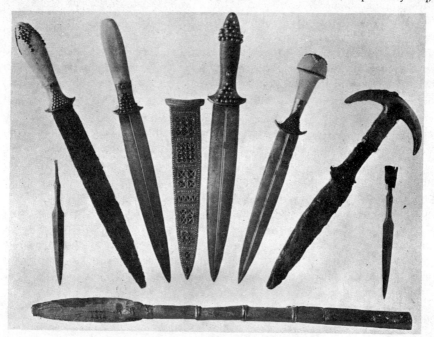

These copper miniatures (ca. 3000 B.C.) are fine examples of Sumerian art. The chariot, from Tell Agrab, is one of the earliest depictions of this vehicle; the driver straddles a centerboard and is drawn by four asses. The statuette of the wrestlers was found at Khafaje, east of Baghdad. The wrestlers wear only belts and may carry the large jars on a test of skill. (Consulate General, Republic of Iraq)

A's lifetime and then undertook to give him a decent burial on his death. There was generally a proviso that if A had no son, B would inherit the property outright. If, however, A had a son subsequent to the signing of the adoption document, then the natural son would become the heir and take the father's "gods," which were generally small clay figures used in family worship, but which seem to have become in time something like our modern title deeds. At any rate, the man who owned the property possessed the gods, and he passed these over when the property came into the possession of another.

There was another possibility that could arise in the case of a man who had no son. It was quite common for the man's wife to take a slave woman and present her to her husband in order to raise up a child for herself. In this case the son of the slave woman became the heir if there were no other sons. But here, too, should there be in due course a son born to the first wife, then the son of the slave woman took second place and had to surrender the inheritance to the true son. It was provided, however, that in that case the son of the slave woman should not be cast out but should have some share in the inheritance.

But there were in fact four possibilities available in the ancient Near East in cases where a childless couple lacked a son. They could adopt a son, the husband could marry a second wife, the husband might obtain a son through union with his concubine, or the wife might provide the husband with a slave girl. These solutions appear in texts from many periods and places, although all four were practiced at Nuzi. One of the most famous of the Nuzi texts is the Adoption Text HSS 5, 67.[42] This contract contains a clause that if the wife provided by the adopting man for his adopted son proved barren, she had to give a Lullu woman (i.e., a slave girl) to her husband although the first wife would exercise authority over any children born to the slave girl. In this respect this tablet provides a good parallel to the patriarchal narratives since the three elements of a barren wife, the wife's initiative in obtaining a slave girl, and the authority of the wife over the children occur in such passages as Genesis 16:2; 30:1-4, 9.

The Nuzi tablet in question reads as follows:

> The tablet of adoption belonging to Zike, the son of Akkuya: he gave his son Shennima in adoption to Shuriha-ilu, and Shuriha-ilu, with reference to Shennima, from all the lands . . . and his earnings of every sort gave to Shennima one portion of his property. If Shuriha-ilu should have a son of his own, as the principal son he shall take a double share; Shennima shall then be next in order and take his proper share. As long as Shuriha-ilu is alive, Shennima shall revere him. When Shuriha-ilu dies, Shennima shall become the heir. Furthermore, Kelim-ninu has been given in marriage to Shennima. If Kelim-ninu bears children, Shennima shall not take another wife; but if Kelim-ninu does not bear, Kelim-ninu shall acquire a woman of the land of Lullu as wife for Shennima, and Kelim-ninu may not send the offspring away. Any sons that may be born to Shennima from the womb of Kelim-ninu, to those sons shall be given all the lands and buildings of every sort. However, if she does not bear a son, then the daughter of Kelim-ninu from the lands and buildings shall take one portion of the property. Furthermore, Shuriha-ilu shall not adopt another son in addition to Shennima.[43]

This general custom according to which a barren wife gave her slave girl to her husband to raise children is known in a variety of texts apart from Nuzi. In some of these the practice was confined to priestesses in a restricted application of the same principle.[44] But Hammurabi Law 163 applied this provision to an ordinary wife and other old Babylonian texts refer to a girl who acted as a slave for the wife and a concubine for the husband.

42. See J. B. Pritchard, ANET, p. 220.
43. Ibid.
44. Hammurabi Law 144.

But there are other items of interest on this tablet. There is the provision that a handmaiden shall be given as a gift on the occasion of the marriage of Shennima to Kelim-ninu, and a proviso that if Shennima takes another wife besides Kelim-ninu after Kelim-ninu has borne children, then Kelim-ninu may take certain action against him.

The inclusion of a female slave in a dowry is mentioned in three old Babylonian marriage contracts (cf. Gen. 24:59, 61).

It must be noted, however, that the Nuzi tablet quoted is the only example of this exact custom, for five other Nuzi marriage contracts make provision for the husband to marry a second wife if the first was barren, and four imply that the husband could raise up offspring through his concubine in similar circumstances.

There was thus a good deal of flexibility in the arrangement, and the biblical narratives indicate only one of these.

With these illustrations of Mesopotamian law before us we may draw a number of comparisons between the customs of the patriarchs and those of the people of northern Mesopotamia as depicted here.

It would seem that in the first attempt of Abraham to secure an heir he resorted to the current practice of adopting a slave as his heir. It was "Eliezer of Damascus" who was chosen as heir and he was to Abraham "one born in my house" (Gen. 15:2, 3). At a later stage Abraham resorted to the method of taking a subsidiary wife. Actually the Bible makes the point quite clearly that it was Sarah the wife of Abraham who invited Abraham to take this woman. "It may be that I may obtain children by her" was Sarah's hope (Gen. 16:2).

When Ishmael was born, he presumably was regarded as the heir of Abraham. However, in due course Sarah herself gave birth to a son Isaac, who quite naturally took the place of Ishmael. Sarah wanted to cast out the bondwoman and her son, but this thing was very grievous in the eyes of Abraham (Gen. 21:10, 11). While Sarah does not seem to have had a great deal of compunction about this suggestion, it was, of course, quite out of keeping with the customs of the land, and Abraham revolted at the thought. Only a divine injunction led Abraham to allow the child and his mother to depart (Gen. 21:12).

Our discussion has already touched briefly on marriage. A study of some of the ways of the ancient Middle East is instructive here, too, because there are interesting parallels between these Mesopotamian customs and the biblical customs found in the stories of the patriarchs.

A number of other biblical parallels with ancient Middle Eastern practice may be illustrated from the following Nuzi document, which is the adoption tablet of a certain Nashwi who adopted a certain Wullu:

> The adoption tablet of Nashwi son of Arshenni. He adopted Wullu
> son of Puhishenni. As long as Nashwi lives, Wullu shall give him food
> and clothing. When Nashwi dies, Wullu shall be the heir. Should
> Nashwi beget a son, the latter shall divide equally with Wullu, but only

Nashwi's son shall take Nashwi's gods. But if there be no son of Nashwi, then Wullu shall take Nashwi's gods. And Nashwi had given his daughter Nuhuya as a wife to Wullu. And if Wullu takes another wife, he forfeits Nashwi's land and buildings. Whoever breaks the contract shall pay one mina of silver, and one mina of gold.[45]

In Genesis 29:24, 29 Laban gave both his daughters a maid as a marriage gift. The same custom is clear in the above document. It is also to be found in the document already quoted, which continues beyond the point given in our quotation with the words:

Furthermore, Yalampa is given as a handmaid to Kelim-ninu and Shatim-ninu has been made a co-parent. As long as she is alive she (i.e. Yalampa) shall revere her and Shatim-ninu shall not annul the (agreement). If Kelim-ninu bears (children) and Shennima takes another wife, she may take her dowry and leave.

The practice of providing a maid as a marriage gift was quite common in ancient Mesopotamia. In fact it continued until the Neo-Babylonian and Persian periods. It is not therefore of any special significance for dating purposes, although it is of value in portraying a general cultural milieu.

Again, the demand made by Laban on Jacob that he should not take another wife besides the two daughters and that he should not ill-treat the daughters (Gen. 31:51–54) occurs in a number of Nuzi texts and in Old Assyrian contracts.[46] The first text quoted above, the adoption tablet of Zike, contains this provision. This practice was also continued for many centuries and occurs in marriage contracts of the Neo-Babylonian and Persian periods.

When the Nuzi tablets were first published, writers like C. H. Gordon argued that the Jacob-Laban narratives could be understood in terms of an adoption arrangement between Jacob and Laban. This view has not commended itself to later scholars[47] and should probably not be pressed. The reference to Laban's *teraphim* (household gods), which were stolen by Rachel (Gen. 31:19, 33–35), is another feature in the Jacob-Laban story which earlier writers thought lent support to the idea of adoption. It was argued that Rachel stole the gods in order to guarantee Jacob's claim to the inheritance. However, since he was leaving the country, one wonders what value the possession of the household gods would have been. This much is clear. A number of Nuzi texts do refer to household gods (*teraphim*), and in nine of them the gods were given as part of an inheritance. Yet it was not merely the possession of the *teraphim* that guaranteed

---

45. J. B. Pritchard, *ANET*, pp. 219f., Tablet 2.
46. See J. B. Pritchard, *ANET*³, p. 543, document 4.
47. M. J. Selman, "The Social Environment of the Patriarchs," *Tyndale Bulletin*, No. 21 (1976), pp. 123–125; J. van Seters, *Abraham in History and Tradition*, pp. 78–85; T. L. Thompson, *op. cit.*, pp. 269–480.

Left: A bronze statuette, originally covered with gold or silver foil, of a Syrian god, possibly Baal. The kilt and headdress are Egyptian in style. It was found near Tyre and is dated ca. 1400 B.C. (British Museum) Right: Limestone votive statue, found in the Abu temple at Eshnunna (Tell Asmar). (Consulate General, Republic of Iraq)

the inheritance but also the father's act of bequeathing them.[48] In the Nuzi texts there were also heirs who participated in the division of the inheritance who did not receive the gods, which were normally given to the eldest son, though not automatically. But there is another interesting feature here: it was not unusual for Mesopotamians to carry *teraphim* with them when they went to another country.[49]

Despite a number of uncertainties in the drawing of parallelisms one cannot but be impressed with a number of features in the Bible and in ancient Near

48. See M. Greenberg, "Another Look at Rachel's Theft of Teraphim," *JBL*, Vol. 81 (1962), pp. 239–248.
49. Cf. M. Greenberg, *op. cit.*, pp. 246ff.; T. L. Thompson, *op. cit.*, pp. 277f.; M. J. Selman, *op. cit.*, p. 124.

Eastern documents which point to a community of ideas and practices. There are, of course, always variants of a particular practice as one moves from place to place.

The story of Abraham's purchase of the cave of Machpelah as a burial site for Sarah his wife (Gen. 22) is an instructive one since it gives information about a variety of customs relating to the procedures to be followed in the purchase of land. As a foreigner or landless resident alien (Hebrew ger wᵉtôšāḇ) Abraham was required to approach the local citizens or sons of Heth (cf. Gen. 10:15). Exaggerated politeness and protracted negotiations which are characteristic of oriental business dealings then took place, as was normal, at the city gate (Gen. 23:10). Abraham wanted only the cave, but he was obliged finally to take the whole field. The price was fixed at 400 pieces of silver—a mere bagatelle, they said (v. 15). The silver was weighed out on simple scale pans, presumably according to the standard weights used by the merchants (v. 16). The area in question was carefully defined (v. 17) and finally recognized as Abraham's property by the citizens, and Sarah was buried. It was the first piece of the promised land that Abraham could call his own.

The whole story has been interpreted in the light of Hittite laws.[50] Two of the Hittite laws which were used to explain the transaction are concerned with the feudal service which was associated with the property from which the owner was anxious to be free.[51] But once it is realized that the Hittites in the story are really a Canaanite group (Gen. 10:15), the Hittite association loses its significance. It was not a question of feudal dues at all, but simply a land sale in which the owner drove a hard bargain when he found someone in desperate need.

But despite this recognition that the story does not concern the Anatolian Hittites, it has many general characteristics in common with Near Eastern legal procedures from many periods. Thus the phrase "for the full price" (v. 9), which occurs also in the account of David's purchase of the threshing floor (I Chron. 21:23, 24), is the equivalent of an expression which occurs with slight variations in Akkadian sale contracts from several periods. Indeed, it runs back to Sumerian times. The expression occurs in the Mari texts and the Alalakh tablets, as well as in later texts, to denote that the complete price had been paid, with no balance remaining. What Abraham was saying was that he would give the full value of the field, that is, he would buy it. Allowing for minor variations in expressions, we are here dealing with a well-known legal formula.[52] As in most ancient Near Eastern deeds, the exact price of the sale is mentioned (v. 16) and the account of the transfer includes a description of the property (v. 17) in terms of the type of real estate (field), the name of the landlord, the general location (Machpelah), and the appurtenances of the land (cave and trees). However, the story in Genesis 23 does not mention guarantee clauses or provisions against

50. M. R. Lehmann, "Abraham's Purchase of Machpelah and Hittite Law," BASOR, No. 129 (Feb., 1953), pp. 15–18.

51. See Laws 46 and 47 of the Hittite Code, ANET³, p. 191.

52. G. M. Tucker, "The Legal Background of Genesis 23," JBL, Vol. 85 (1966), pp. 77–84.

suit, supported often by penalties. No list of witnesses is given, although this may be implied by the phrase "in the presence of the sons of Heth before all who went in at the gate of his city." But then, Genesis 23 is not a legal document but a narrative about title deeds. The procedures in evidence here carried on into the first millennium so that we are not able to link this story to a specific century or several centuries. But the style, structure, formulae, and contents of certain parts of the report are modeled on deeds of sale well known in the ancient Near East. The reader is thus enabled to see more clearly the meaning and context of the various elements of the story, thus enabling him to discern the significance of some of the details which are important for interpretation.

We have not exhausted the possibilities of such a study as this. The tells of the ancient Middle East still contain an untold wealth of tablet records which will throw light on the biblical period. At the moment, after a period of what seemed a growing clarity in our understanding of patriarchal times, we have become somewhat bewildered by the mass of data requiring careful reconsideration. And each year produces more and more tablets which will throw additional light on a puzzling age. But already we sense that the biblical narratives provide evidence of a society which, if it appears strange to modern readers, now seems to be realistic and authentic. We lack the sort of information which will enable us to pinpoint exactly the patriarchal era, but we have gained enormously from our understanding of social and legal practice in the ancient Middle East of the second millennium B.C. If we are not in a position to declare beyond question that the patriarchs fit into the first part of the second millennium B.C., we are certainly not in a position to deny such a proposition. Even if some of the customs were operative over many centuries, it is also true to say that they were operative in the period 2000–1500 B.C.

Some support for this view comes from an interesting line of research which has been initiated in recent years, namely, a consideration of the character of the major West Semitic tribal groups on the middle Euphrates in the nineteenth

Another cylinder seal and its impression (ca. 2000 B.C.). The two human figures, the tree, and the snake have been thought to depict a Babylonian version of the temptation of Eve, but no proof has been found in cuneiform texts. (British Museum)

and eighteenth centuries B.C. The important documents excavated at Mari dating to this general period have provided a wealth of data and have enabled a study of the relationships between the tribal groups and large urban centers like Mari. The two groups lived in a kind of equilibrium with one another, with a constant interchange between the pastoralists and the urban settlers who formed a dimorphic (two-shape) society.[53] Some workers in this field have seen close parallels between the Mari society and the society of the patriarchs[54] and have expressed a preference for the Middle Bronze Age (ca. 1800–1550) for patriarchal backgrounds. The picture that is painted in these more recent discussions is of a society living in simple villages on the nearer or further outskirts of large towns like Mari, tribally organized but having many contacts with urban society. They were sheep-breeders who moved their encampments periodically, normally annually, in search of water and pasturage. At points of contact between the two societies there were recognized modes of procedure. It has been further argued[55] that there is archaeological evidence in Palestine at the site of Givat Sharet for a "dimorphic society." Here a small unwalled satellite village comprising a mere dozen or so simple courtyard houses was built along a straggling path on a hillside about three-quarters of a mile southeast of the fortified Middle Bronze Age site of Bethshemesh in Palestine, and contemporary with it.[56] The houses show only one basic building type, and the pottery is homogeneous and contemporary with Middle Bronze Bethshemesh. Thereafter the village was abandoned. The date was about the eighteenth century B.C., that is, the Mari Age. To date, other examples have not been found, but this may be due to the lack of excavation, and it seems likely that others will be discovered. But that is a task yet to be undertaken.

It is evident that archaeological research has by no means completed its task in reference to the patriarchal period, and many fruitful avenues have yet to be explored more fully. We have by no means exhausted the study of the total cultural background of the ancient Near East. Only against that background can we come to a clear understanding of the background of the patriarchs. But progress is being made as scholars give attention to the further analysis of the social milieu of the patriarchs as reflected in Genesis; to the evidence of the ancient Near Eastern society as reflected in the numerous commercial and legal texts that are available; to the evidence of the Mari texts for the light they throw on the tribal societies of the Mari Age; and to the cultural history of Syria-Palestine as it is being reconstructed by modern archaeology.

53. J. T. Luke, *Pastoralism and Politics in the Mari Period* (1965), and V. H. Matthews, *Pastoral Nomadism in the Mari Kingdom* (ca. 1830–1760 B.C.) (1978), represent this line of research.
54. E.g., W. G. Dever, "Prolegomenon to a reconsideration of archaeology and patriarchal backgrounds," in J. H. Hayes and J. M. Miller, *Israelite and Judaean History*, pp. 102–120.
55. W. G. Dever, *op. cit.*, pp. 111f.
56. C. Epstein, "Bethshemesh," *IEJ*, Vol. XXII (1972), p. 157; D. Bahat, "Beth-shemesh," *IEJ*, Vol. XXIII (1973), pp. 246f.

3

IN THE LAND OF THE PHARAOHS

THERE must be few people who have never heard of the noble Joseph who was sold by his brothers into Egypt and rose to a place of prominence in that land. In due course he was able to have his whole family, numbering seventy people, brought to this new land. If we ask whether there is Egyptian evidence for the rise of this very Joseph to fame, the answer is that up to the present we have no formal evidence for the Bible stories about Joseph and his family. However, students of the history of Egypt have brought to light in recent years a considerable number of important facts which furnish a background into which the biblical narratives fit very naturally. This is the sort of thing we have seen in the case of the patriarchs. We shall see it again and again in this book.

THE COMING OF THE HYKSOS RULERS TO EGYPT

We must digress at this point to refer briefly to some facts of Egyptian history. Historians recognize some thirty more or less well-defined dynasties covering the period of Egyptian history from about 3000 B.C. to Roman times. In patriarchal times it was probably the Twelfth Dynasty that ruled Egypt. This line of rulers came to an end about 1786 B.C., to be succeeded by Dynasties Thirteen and Fourteen. The Thirteenth Dynasty (ca. 1786–1633 B.C.) ruled from Thebes but eventually lost their authority and became vassals of Asiatic newcomers who had been infiltrating the Delta region during the declining years of the Thirteenth Dynasty. These foreigners were groups of several western Asiatic peoples, chiefly Semites forced southward by widespread disturbances in lands to the north and east of Egypt. The tribal leaders or sheikhs of these people were called "Princes

41

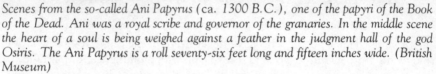

Scenes from the so-called Ani Papyrus (ca. 1300 B.C.), one of the papyri of the Book of the Dead. Ani was a royal scribe and governor of the granaries. In the middle scene the heart of a soul is being weighed against a feather in the judgment hall of the god Osiris. The Ani Papyrus is a roll seventy-six feet long and fifteen inches wide. (British Museum)

of the Desert Uplands" or "Rulers of Foreign Countries" (Hikau-khoswet, hence Hyksos). The last rulers of the Thirteenth Dynasty[1] became vassals of the Hyksos rulers. The Fourteenth Dynasty (*ca.* 1786–1603 B.C.) rulers, of which there were over seventy who reigned for the most part for very brief periods, operated from ancient Memphis (Ithet-Tawy) in the north until they were replaced by the Hyksos rulers who formed the Fifteenth and Sixteenth "Hyksos" Dynasties and ruled for roughly 140 years. They established a second capital in the eastern Delta at Avaris. These Semitic "pharaohs" took upon themselves the full rank and style of the local Egyptian kings and used the Egyptian state administration, employing regular Egyptian officials in the manner of the old regime. In the course of time naturalized Semitic officials took over many of these offices. Among these was a certain Hur, who was a kind of chancellor.

Eventually a line of princes from southern or Upper Egypt were able to rise and throw out the Hyksos rulers. A certain Kamose was able to re-occupy all Egypt for the Egyptians except Avaris in the northeast Delta. His successor Ahmose I founded the Eighteenth Dynasty and expelled the Hyksos rulers completely *ca.* 1570 B.C.

1. R. M. Engberg, *The Hyksos Reconsidered* (Chicago, 1939); A. Alt, *Die Herkunft der Hyksos in neuer Sicht* (Munich, 1954), pp. 26ff.; J. van Seters, *The Hyksos, a New Investigation* (New Haven, 1966); W. C. Hayes, *Cambridge Ancient History*, Vol. II, ch. II (1962).

We have a special interest in such a group because in the later chapters of Genesis we find the patriarchal family settling into their new home in Egypt, apparently with the goodwill of the rulers of the land. At a later day, when a "king arose who knew not Joseph," we find that the Israelite group was ill-treated. We conclude that at an earlier date the rulers were not Egyptians but people who were sympathetic to the patriarchal family itself and perhaps related to it in a broad ethnic sense. The Hyksos rulers would fit into this category very well.

WHAT THE HYKSOS RULERS GAVE TO EGYPT

Let us outline some facts about these people. Despite the fact that the Egyptians did all in their power to destroy all record of them once they had cast them out, they brought a great deal to Egypt that was to be for the benefit of the Egyptians themselves.[2] We now know that the rulers of the Eighteenth Dynasty went to great lengths to erase all traces of these Hyksos rulers. Their names were cut out of the monuments and every written record that could be found was destroyed. Only the keen eyes of the modern archaeologist have been able to discover clear evidence of the Hyksos invaders and to give us a picture of their achievements. These Hyksos rulers were, for the most part, of western Semitic stock, that is to say, they were largely Canaanite in origin. They evidently had a widespread empire in their time, for objects such as scarabs, which belong specifically to their culture, have been found in many lands in the East. Their most famous king was Khayan, whose name has been found on inscribed material in Egypt, Palestine, Mesopotamia, and even in Crete. This suggests that they had wide trade connections all over the East.

Many new features were introduced into Egypt at this time. We think today

2. J. A. Wilson, *The Burden of Egypt* (Chicago, 1951), ch. 7.

Tomb model of an Egyptian death ship carrying the mummified body to the underworld and "fields of peace." (British Museum)

Blue faience tile (sixteenth-fourteenth centuries B.C.) with a drawing in black of a typical Hyksos chariot, a driver, and two horses. The Hyksos introduced horses and chariots into Egypt. (Metropolitan Museum of Art, gift of J. Pierpont Morgan, 1917)

that the Hyksos people brought to Egypt such items as the horse and chariot, new types of daggers and swords, the strong compound Asiatic bow, and new types of fortification. Of special interest were the huge earth ramparts which enclosed fortified areas where chariots were housed. These have been found in several places in Palestine and Syria, as well as in Egypt. At places like Jericho and Shechem in Palestine great fortifications of this age were found during excavations there. It seems that Palestine itself was organized in a feudal manner at this time and consisted of numerous little states which owed allegiance to the Hyksos king.

PALESTINE IN THE SEVENTEENTH AND SIXTEENTH CENTURIES B.C.

In Palestine there was evidently great prosperity, if we are to judge from the wealth of the graves of the Canaanites of this period. These are among the richest of the tombs of all time in Palestine. During these years numerous new towns were built in the hill areas. Despite the picture of overall prosperity and of great urban development, there was evidently no public security, for there were many occasions when the towns were destroyed with violence. Excavation shows layers of burning in several towns dating back to this period. At no time in the history of Palestine were there so many walled towns in the land. We are quite naturally reminded of the spies of Moses who visited the land and reported, "The cities are walled, *and* very great" (Num. 13:28).

Joseph came from Palestine and was later able to arrange for the migration of his aged father Jacob and his brothers from his homeland to Egypt. There are many lines of evidence to suggest that it was during the Hyksos period that the events of Genesis 40–50 took place. We may suggest that Joseph came to prominence in Egypt about 1700 B.C.

THE HYKSOS CAPITAL AT AVARIS

The Hyksos rulers conquered northern Egypt and placed their capital in the Delta area, calling it Avaris. It seems that they allowed the Egyptians to continue to exercise some sort of governing power from a local capital at Thebes some four hundred miles up the Nile, although this authority was naturally supervised by the Hyksos rulers. Once the Hyksos conquerors were expelled, the town of Thebes again became the capital of Egypt.

The town of Avaris has been the subject of some discussion among the experts in recent years. Its location is now known with practical certainty. The land of Goshen, referred to as the area to which Jacob and his sons came, was in all probability the area around the Wadi Tumilat, which lay quite close to the capital of the Hyksos kings but a little to the southeast.

We have some reason to think that the new rulers, while they brought a good deal to Egypt, learned a great deal from Egypt. They soon adopted all sorts of ways and customs that were current in the land. For example, they copied Egyptian methods of writing and imitated the religious zeal of the Egyptians by building many new temples. An ancient god of Egypt, Seth by name, was honored in Avaris as Seth-Sutekh. This god bore a close resemblance to some of the Asiatic gods like Ba'al. His garments, headdress, and horns of divinity were Asiatic in type.

It is of some interest that when Horemhab, the last ruler of the Eighteenth Dynasty, was pharaoh (ca. 1340–1310), a vizier of Egypt named Seti came to the city of Tanis in the Delta region about the year 1330 B.C. to celebrate a four-hundredth anniversary. This took the form of the worship of the Egyptian god Seth, who is represented on the stele set up to celebrate his anniversary as an Asiatic deity in Asiatic dress. Some four hundred years earlier the Hyksos had begun their rule in Egypt in Avaris. The celebration thus commemorated the four-hundredth year of the rule of Seth as king and the four-hundredth year of the founding of Tanis. The Egyptians would not mention the hated Hyksos in such a commemoration, but the inference may be drawn. The vizier Seti later became the pharaoh Seti I, and the name Seti means "Seth's man."[3]

The Hyksos honored other gods besides Seth.[4]

In matters of court procedure we think that the Hyksos rulers took over a

---

3. J. B. Pritchard, *ANET*, pp. 252f.
4. J. van Seters, *op. cit.*, pp. 171–180.

great deal from the local rulers. In ordinary matters the newcomers soon took advantage of the experience of the Egyptians.

Because the Hyksos kings were Semites like the sons of Jacob, and in view of the biblical evidence that this family was made welcome in Egypt, we conclude that it was during the time of Hyksos rule that the small family, which was later to become Israel, came to Egypt. There is a further reason to associate the two groups. The Bible states that the time the children of Israel spent in Egypt was four hundred years. If we take the date of the Exodus as shortly after 1300 B.C.[5] and count back this period of time, we arrive at a date of about 1700 B.C., which is approximately the date of the Hyksos kings. These and other lines of evidence make the most likely time for Jacob's entry into Egypt as that during which Egypt was ruled by Semitic foreigners.

EGYPTIAN LOCAL COLOR IN THE JOSEPH STORY

A study of the local color of the Joseph story will soon lead the student to the conclusion that it is strongly Egyptian in character. This fact has been recognized for a long time and some scholars have made a special study of resemblances between the customs of Egypt and those of Genesis 40–50. The ordinary reader will profit greatly from the works of Professor Yahuda, even though some scholars think that he has seen too many resemblances.[6] The fact remains, however, that the Joseph narratives must have been written by someone who was well acquainted with the customs of Egypt.[7]

In the first place, it is clear that Joseph was by no means the only Asiatic Semite sold into Egypt about 1700 B.C. (Gen. 37:36; 39:1ff.), and also that Egyptian prisons were highly organized (Gen. 39, 40). An ancient papyrus in the Brooklyn Museum, once part of the register of criminals at Thebes, lists each offender by name, sex, crime, sentence, etc. This papyrus was re-used later on, and on the back was written a list of seventy-nine servants of a big Egyptian household, of which forty were Asiatics bearing good Semitic names.

Then, there are numerous titles that are well known in Egypt. Such titles as we find in Genesis 40:2, "the chief of the butlers" and "the chief of the bakers," are well known as the titles of certain palace officials in Egyptian writings. Joseph's designation as "overseer over his house" (Gen. 39:4) is also a title often used of officers in Egyptian noble houses. After Joseph's elevation to a place of real prominence in Pharaoh's court, the titles ascribed to him in the Bible are thoroughly Egyptian. Among these we may note "lord over my [Pharaoh's] house" (Gen. 41:40), "ruler throughout all the land of Egypt" (Gen. 45:8),

5. See next chapter, pp. 60–64.

6. A. S. Yahuda, The Language of the Pentateuch in Its Relation to Egyptian (London, 1933), or his more popular work, The Accuracy of the Bible (London, 1934).

7. J. Vergote, Joseph en Egypte, Génèse 37–50 à la lumière des études égyptologiques récentes (1959); K. A. Kitchen, "Joseph," NBD (1962), pp. 656–660. Note p. 658.

Wooden statue (ca. 1400 B.C.) of an Egyptian nobleman of high rank. He wears a tight-fitting, pleated, linen garment with a wide skirt. (British Museum)

"father to Pharaoh" (Gen. 45:8). The office of Joseph may have corresponded with that of a vizier of Egypt, though it could have been that a special high office, second only to the Pharaoh, was taken up by Joseph in the times of emergency. One other office not specifically mentioned in the Bible is that of "superintendent of the granaries." In a land like Egypt this was an important office, since so much depended on the storage and distribution of grain for the welfare of the country. Joseph probably had this title as well, for he certainly held the office.[8]

8. K. A. Kitchen, *Tyndale Bulletin*, No. 2 (Cambridge, 1957); W. C. Hayes, *A Papyrus of the Late Middle Kingdom in the Brooklyn Museum* (1955); K. A. Kitchen, "Joseph," *NBD* (1962), p. 658.

Various items of court procedure give us further evidence of an intimate knowledge of the Egyptian background. Joseph's elevation to an honored position in Egypt as we have it in the Bible follows the pattern of procedure in the Egyptian court. The Bible reference describes the manner in which the Pharaoh honored Joseph in these words:

> And Pharaoh took off his ring from his hand, and put it upon Joseph's hand, and arrayed him in vestures of fine linen, and put a gold chain about his neck; and he made him to ride in the second chariot which he had; and they cried before him, Bow the knee; and he made him ruler over all the land of Egypt. (Gen. 41:42, 43).

The investiture of an Egyptian vizier with a gold chain is depicted by the artists of Egypt. One famous picture from the days of Seti I (1308-1290 B.C.) shows this Pharaoh honoring a man in this way. It is acknowledged by most scholars that we have here in the Bible a description that is quite in keeping with Egyptian procedure. Incidentally, some writers have seen in this reference to "riding in a chariot" an important piece of local color for the time of the Hyksos rulers, for it was they who seem to have used the chariot for public occasions for the first time in Egypt. In any case, artistic productions and literary evidence point in the same direction. The Bible has faithfully represented the Egyptian way of honoring an important man in the land.

The dream of the Pharaoh at the time of the famine provides another group of interesting Egyptianisms. In the first place, dreams were regarded as of great significance in Egypt, as they were in many lands in Bible times (Gen. 41). There is meaning in the number of cows that feature in the dream. One of the chief deities of Egypt was a goddess, Hathor by name, who was regularly represented in the shape of a cow. Further, the male ox was used at times to symbolize the Nile. He was sacred to the god Osiris, the inventor of agriculture. In many of the pictures of ancient Egypt the Osiris bull was depicted accompanied by seven cows. There is a further possible symbolism here in that there were seven zones of the goddess Hathor in Egypt. It would seem to be entirely possible that a Pharaoh had been one day to one of the temples to worship and had seen a picture of the seven sacred cows. These had troubled him in his dream that same night.

We have a great deal of information about the famines of Egypt. Years of drought and bad harvests are well attested in Pharaoh's domain. There is even evidence of a seven-year famine. The famous King Zoser (about 2700 B.C.) once sent a message to the governor of one region down the Nile. Here are his words:

> I am very much concerned about the people in the palace. My heart is heavy over the calamitous failure of the Nile floods for the past seven years. There is little fruit; vegetables are in short supply; there is a shortage of food generally.[9]

9. Quoted in W. Keller, The Bible as History (New York, 1956), p. 105.

That great granaries were built and that steps were taken to appoint officers to control the storing and the issue of food for this great land is now well established. The message of the Pharaoh Zoser tells of the storehouses. However, in that case he sadly reported that

> ... the storehouses have been opened, but everything that was in them has been consumed.[10]

The instructions outlined in the Bible in Genesis 41:33–36 and 47–49 are therefore quite in keeping with what we now know of Egyptian practice.

Naturally, people outside Egypt sometimes visited the land in a time of famine to look for food. One papyrus (in a very fragmentary condition) is a report from a frontier official in the days of Seti II (about 1210 B.C.). Certain Bedu from the land of Edom had been allowed to pass the frontier, it seems, in a time of famine:

> We have permitted the transit of the Bedouin of Edom through the fortress of Merneptah ... in Theku to the pools of Pithom of Merneptah ... in order to sustain them and their herds in the domain of Pharaoh, the good sun of every land. ...[11]

We may suspect that this went on at other times, and that the events of Genesis 42–44, in the days of Joseph, were only typical of what happened many times through the centuries.

The practice of magic was widespread in Egypt. The Bible makes several references to magic and magicians in Egypt at the time of the Israelite sojourn there. The magicians of the land failed to interpret the dream of Pharaoh (Gen. 41:8). Later, Moses had dealings with these men (Exod. 8:7, 18; 9:11, etc.). It was the practice of magic that enabled the people of Egypt to hope for a continuance of the pleasures of this life in the next world. One needed only to represent the item hoped for in picture form on the walls of the tomb, and to add the necessary magic words, and all would be fulfilled in the next life. Even the picture was sufficient in some cases. By the use of magic one could even escape the terrors of the judgment day and achieve a safe passage through all the intricate pathways of the underworld. The Book of the Dead with its elaborate pictures gives us a good idea of the extent to which magic was practiced in Egypt.

The custom of embalming the dead referred to in Genesis 50:3 and 26 is quite typical of this land. The multiplicity of butlers and bakers, of which some were designated "chief" (Gen. 40:1, 2), the use of slaves of the state (Exod. 1:14), the festivities of the Pharaoh's birthday (Gen. 40:20), and the release of certain prisoners on this day are all well attested items in the general background of the life of Egypt.

These items will suffice for our purpose. There are many pieces of Egyptian coloring in the Joseph narratives that have been beautifully illustrated by Egyp-

10. *Ibid.*
11. "The Papyrus Anastasi VI," quoted by J. B. Pritchard in *ANET*, p. 259.

This wall painting from the tomb of Sebek-hetep (ca. 1420 B.C.) at Thebes shows Semites from Syria ("Retenu") bringing as tribute a little girl, an ointment horn, and gold, silver, and bronze vessels. They wear white garments wound below the waist and edged in red or blue. (British Museum)

tological discoveries of the type we have referred to in this section. W. F. Albright has written in this connection:

> The Egyptian sojourn of Israel is a vital part of early Israelite historical tradition, and cannot be eliminated without leaving an inexplicable gap. Moreover, we know from the Egyptian names of Moses and a number of the Aaronids that part of Israel must have lived in Egypt for a long time. Then there are a great many correct local and antiquarian details which would be inexplicable as later invention. Most striking is the obvious relation in which the Joseph story and the later history of Israel in Egypt stand to the Hyksos movement. The "king who knew not Joseph" and who oppressed the Israelites should be a pharaoh of the New Empire, after the expulsion of the hated Asiatics from Egypt.[12]

12. W. F. Albright, *From the Stone Age to Christianity* (Baltimore, 1946), p. 184.

The Egyptians believed strongly in a life after death and considered it their religious duty to preserve the body for the soul's use in the realm beyond. Not only were human beings embalmed but also certain animals and birds representative of deities. Above are a mummy of a falcon (sacred to Horus) and a mummified cat (sacred to Bastet). Note the artistic pattern of the linen bandages in which the cat is swathed. (British Museum)

The mummy of a woman, Katebet. Her face is covered with a mask, and jewelry is placed above the parts of the body that wore such items in life. Note the prominently displayed scarabaeus, the symbol of the sun-god Khepera and of resurrection. (British Museum)

SILENT YEARS IN THE LAND OF GOSHEN

According to the Bible it was to the land of Goshen that Jacob and the brothers of Joseph came when they finally settled in Egypt (Gen. 46:26ff.). This name is actually not known outside the Bible. Some scholars have tried to see in the word a sort of Semitism and have related it to a place in Palestine.[13] The name occurs elsewhere in the Bible, for example, in Joshua 15:51 where it is a town in southern Judah, or in Joshua 10:41 where it is a "country." In Joshua it is known as the country of "the Goshen" (literal Hebrew). M. Z. Mayani has recently suggested that the word was originally not a proper name but a common noun, referring to something that could be found in both Egypt and southern Palestine, the two strong areas of the Hyksos people. He notes the occurrence of the word in Genesis 47:4 where parallelism of thought suggests that the meaning is "pasturage."[14] Further, he finds interesting parallels to this word in the Indo-Iranian group of languages of which there are many living representatives in India today, most of them coming from the older Sanskrit. These words all have the sense of something to do with pastures and cattle. This discussion is of particular value to linguists, but for the ordinary Bible reader it is of some interest to know that there were groups of these same Indo-Iranian peoples in Palestine in the time of Joseph and Jacob. Indeed, they were a type of ruling class. They may well have left some elements of their language in the land, and the Hyksos conquerors may have taken this term with them to Egypt.

We may be fairly certain that this area was where the Wadi Tumilat is to be found today, in the eastern part of the Nile Delta. It is a narrow valley between thirty and forty miles long, connecting the Nile with Lake Timsah. It is a very rich area and is well described in the Bible as the "best of the land" (Gen. 47:1, 6, 11). We can think of the sons of Jacob carrying on their life here much the same as formerly, with an ever increasing tendency to live a settled life, but depending on their flocks for their main sustenance.

All Semites were to become objects of scorn and contempt to the Egyptians in later years, as they remembered the humiliating experiences of the Hyksos rule. In particular, however, those who were shepherds were "an abomination unto the Egyptians" (Gen. 43:32; 46:34). The reason for this may not be clear to us now, but it was a fact. It may have been because the flocks of the Egyptians were tended by men of a lower class. If these men were foreigners as well, the contempt would be still greater.

It is to be noted that there had been a continual stream of Semites into the Delta zone for centuries. The Israelite element was only one of the groups. We have a great deal of evidence to show that Semites from the general area of

13. *Ibid.*, p. 326.
14. *Revue d'histoire et de philosophie réligieuses* (1955), No. 1. Note by M. Z. Mayani, pp. 58–60.

Palestine were drifting into Egypt as early as 2000 B.C. or even earlier.[15] The pasture land of the Delta area was the place where these peoples settled. When the Hyksos irruption took place, the newcomers were of the same general stock as the people of Palestine. They were the Canaanites and Amorites of Palestine, and they spoke roughly the same language as did the family of Jacob. For example, one of the Hyksos princes had the name Jacob-hur, and one of the Hyksos viziers had the name Hur.

There was, then, a considerable collection of Semitic peoples in the Delta area of Egypt, especially at the time of the Hyksos rulers. When the native Egyptians rose in revolt, energetic leaders from Thebes expelled the foreigners about a century and a half after their arrival. The armies of the Hyksos rulers were chased out of the land and were pursued into Palestine. The large Semitic population of Egypt, however, remained in the Delta area. We can suppose that the little group of Israelites lived there quite unnoticed, among a mixed collection of Semites. The reaction of the Egyptians was now to place these peoples under some sort of supervision lest the same sad fate should befall Egypt again.

The book of Exodus opens with a picture of oppression for God's people. We must imagine that other people, too, shared in this general oppression. It was a "king who knew not Joseph" that now arose to oppress the people of God. This must have been a king of the new Eighteenth Dynasty which took over the government of Egypt after the expulsion of the Hyksos rulers.

It is impossible to say precisely how long a period is represented by the story we have in the first chapter of Exodus. It must occupy some four hundred years in all. If we have been right in making a strong link between the Hyksos conquerors of Egypt and the Israelites, we must think of the days of Joseph as being somewhere in the vicinity of 1700 B.C. It is evident that the court of the ruler at the time was not far from the land of Goshen, for the narrative in Genesis 46 and 47 suggests an easy passage from the Pharaoh and Joseph to the land of Goshen. This would mean that the capital was in the Delta area, a circumstance which would suit the times of the Hyksos rulers. Both before and after these times the capital was at Thebes, well down the Nile. The sojourn in Egypt lasted for some four hundred years. This lapse of time is referred to more than once in the Bible. Thus Exodus 12:40 states that

> the sojourning of the children of Israel, who dwelt in Egypt, was four hundred and thirty years.

It is interesting to notice that the story of these years is practically a closed one. The only details about them are given in Exodus 1. This chapter opens with a summary of the original migration to Egypt (vv. 1 to 6). Then there is a vivid description of the great increase in the numbers of these people, couched in the

15. See Beni Hasan Tableau, referred to in ch. 2, pp. 24f.

typical language of the Semite. The rise of "the king who knew not Joseph" is given in verse 8. We must think of this king as the first king of the Eighteenth Dynasty, who began to rule about 1546 B.C. From verses 9 to 14 the narrative is concerned only with the fact that these people had lost their freedom and had become servants of the Pharaoh. This period in Exodus 1 must represent about four hundred years in all. There is only one item of interest in all these years and it is probably to be placed toward the end of the time. It is the reference to the use of the Israelites in the building of the store cities of Pithom and Raamses. We shall return to these facts later, as they have an important bearing on the date of the Exodus. Finally, in this chapter we learn of the special means of oppression that were introduced just before the Exodus took place.

There is thus a considerable gap in the story of the Israelites from the days of Joseph till the days of the Exodus. We have considerable knowledge about the general history of Egypt during these years and can picture the sort of environment in which the people of Israel lived. But we lack any specific detail about their fortunes. Although the presence of Semitic peoples in Egypt is attested in a variety of ways, Egyptian records do not know of this little group as such. We have to be content to remain ignorant of the story of Israel for those years when they are struggling on toward independence and nationhood, not as a recognizable group in the annals of the Egyptians, but as a most significant group in the mind of God. We have to move on to the days of the Exodus before we find more tangible evidence.

We should raise a question concerning the exact composition of the group that was eventually to leave Egypt in the days of the Exodus. It has been pointed out already that a wide variety of Semites found their way to Egypt over many centuries. When eventually the descendants of Jacob came out of Egypt they were accompanied by a "mixed multitude" (Exod. 12:37). We can only speculate about the composition of that "mixed multitude" (or "a large number of other people," as the Good News Bible translates the phrase). A few general observations might help. The original patriarchal family that came to Palestine was only a small part of a much larger movement of peoples who left northern Mesopotamia and migrated to Palestine in the early part of the second millennium B.C. It is not unlikely that among these were many who had very broad kinship with Abraham's little group, and these, like Abraham, settled in the land. In the centuries that followed, some of these found their way to Egypt as captives of war, as traders, or as migrants. It would be impossible to estimate how many of the Semites who found their way to Egypt in the first half of the second millennium B.C. were related by some sort of kinship ties, however distant, to Abraham and to his descendant Jacob and his family. The "descent" of this wider group into Egypt took place over several centuries, and the particular "descent to Egypt" of Jacob and his sons (Gen. 46; Exod. 1:1-7) was only part of a much bigger movement from Palestine into Egypt, that is, the "descent into Egypt" in its wider sense may have been much more complex than the biblical account indicates. We may speculate that the "mixed multitude" spoken of in Exodus 12:37 comprised people who were drawn from this wider kinship group.

Such generalizations do not help us at all in providing an answer to the question of dating, which is quite as elusive as in the case of the patriarchs. But if archaeological and historical research has so far failed us in providing dates in these areas, we are still able to gain a good deal in cultural areas, as we have shown.

4

FROM EGYPT TO CANAAN

THE Bible speaks in several places of the wilderness wandering of the Israelites. It was a memory that was never forgotten. God's people had experienced a divine deliverance from Egypt and the strange period of wandering in the general area of southern Palestine and in Transjordan provided the liberated Israelites with opportunities to learn much about the ways of God and the ways of men. It was during these years, according to the biblical story, that the peoples so recently delivered from Egypt under the leadership of Moses received the law of God. Here, too, they revealed some of the inherent national weaknesses that were to be their sorrow in the centuries that followed.

The events surrounding the Exodus are still the subject of a great deal of discussion. In some areas of the discussion modern archaeological discoveries have provided valuable data. We have the same problems with chronology here that we found earlier. This arises partly from the fact that the compilers of the Hebrew records did not have the same outlook on exact dating that we of the twentieth century A.D. have. Thus, they are content to make such statements as "In the course of those many days the king of Egypt died" (Exod. 2:23), which, no doubt, is an exact enough date if one understands the precise time reference, but it is not exact enough for modern dating. Even so, we do have some clues from comparative historical and archaeological dating.

THE BACKGROUND TO THE EXODUS

When we speak of the Exodus, the reference is to the Exodus of the biblical story. But recently some writers have seen the total Exodus in a wider con-

An imposing aerial view of the pyramids at Gizeh, Egypt. At left is the Third Pyramid, of King Menkaure (Mycerinus); the smaller pyramids beside it are probably those of his queens. In the center is the Second Pyramid, of Khafre (Chephren), and to the right is the Great Pyramid of his father Khufu (Cheops). (Oriental Institute, University of Chicago)

text. Just as it may be argued that the total migration of people from northern
Mesopotamia at the time of the patriarch Abraham was far more numerous than
the tiny family of Abraham although it may well have included people who
were, broadly speaking, his kinsfolk, and just as it may be argued that the total
movement of Semitic peoples into Egypt was far more numerous than the family
of Jacob and probably contained many who were his kinsfolk in a broad sense
and who had moved into Egypt at various times, so we may argue that the total
Exodus was complex in character. It is known that Semitic peoples moved into
and out of Egypt a great deal during the second millennium B.C.—some for
trade, some returning "home" after a period in Egypt, and some forcibly removed when the Hyksos armies were driven out. This movement took place
over a period of time, perhaps over some centuries, so that when the Israelites
emerged as a recognizable group in Canaan in the thirteenth century there were
already many people in the land who were sympathetic toward them, being their
kinsmen in a general way.

All this is somewhat speculative and cannot be linked with any biblical
narrative, although there is considerable nonbiblical circumstantial evidence to
give support to such a picture. Our present concern, however, is with the
biblical story of the Exodus.

According to the Bible, the Exodus took place following a period of severe
oppression. We need to attempt to identify this period, and we probably have
useful help from both Egyptian history and archaeology.

In Imperial Egypt of the fourteenth and thirteenth centuries B.C. the
pharaohs engaged in enormous building programs throughout Egypt and Nubia.
For ordinary buildings like houses, storerooms, and offices, and even for palaces,
mud bricks were needed by the million. The temples needed stone, which had to
be cut, hauled from the quarries and shipped to the building sites, and then
placed in position. During the Eighteenth Dynasty (ca. 1570–1310 B.C.), after
the expulsion of the Hyksos rulers, the building program hardly reached the
Delta region. Only a limited number of royal buildings were erected in the east
Delta region. With the rise of the Nineteenth Dynasty (ca. 1310–1200 B.C.)
things changed in the east Delta region and in its principal town Avaris, a
formal capital of the Hyksos. Haremhab, the last ruler of the Eighteenth
Dynasty, refurbished the temple of the god Seth and began a new fashion.
Thereafter a considerable amount of building was undertaken in the Delta region. This required a great deal of labor. The land of Goshen where the Hebrews
lived was close to Avaris, now known to have been sited at Tel el-Dab'a and not
at Tanis as had been thought for many years. Avaris was well suited to be a focus
for communication between Canaan and Egypt on both economic and strategic
grounds, and after the death of Haremhab his official heir Pramessu became the
founder of the Nineteenth Dynasty (to be known henceforth as Ramesses I).
After a mere sixteen months the throne passed to his vigorous son Sethos (Seti)
I, who took strong steps to restore Egypt's control over Canaan and Syria. He
began massive building projects all over Egypt, for example, the great hall of

Seated statues of Ramesses II (1290–1224 B.C.) on the Pharaoh's temple at Abu Simbel. When the Aswan dam was built, the temple's facade was raised 60 meters to a cliff to escape flooding. (B. K. Condit)

sixty-six columns at the Karnak temple of Amun at Thebes. In the Delta region he built a summer palace which was the center of a new suburb of Avaris. His son Ramesses II, who reigned sixty-six years, undertook vast programs of building all over Egypt. One of his first acts was to proclaim the founding of a new capital city, Pi-Ramesse ("Domain of Ramesses"), around his father's summer palace to the north of Avaris. This was the Raamses of Exodus 1:11; 12:37 and Numbers 33:3, 5. It was laid out on a grand scale, with great stone temples of the gods at each of the four main points. Today the site is in complete ruins.[1]

1. M. Bietak, *Tell el-Dab'a II* (1975); K. A. Kitchen, *The Egyptian Nineteenth Dynasty* (1980).

THE OPPRESSION

In the carrying out of such projects great numbers of people were involved. We have valuable information today about the conditions of work in Egypt during the Nineteenth Dynasty, although such conditions are paralleled at other periods. The making of mud bricks was an important aspect of these large public works. Egyptian scenes depict Semites alongside Egyptians and others engaged in this task. Straw and chaff were used in the making of clay bricks in order to assist in the binding of the mud. The narrative in Exodus 5, which shows a concern to maintain the quota of bricks, is matched in the Anastasi papyri from Memphis dating to the thirteenth century where reference is made to men "making their quota of bricks daily" (cf. Exod. 5:8, 13–14, 18–19).[2] One official stationed in a border post complained that "there are no men to mould bricks and no straw in the district." The task of brick-making was given to officials who had a group of workmen under them. From the fifth year of Ramesses II there are brick accounts recorded on leather. One such record speaks of forty "stablemasters" each assigned a target-quota of 2000 bricks, that is, 80,000 in all. These would correspond to the "taskmasters" of Exodus 5:6, 10, 13–14.

The use of forced labor in these Egyptian projects is also known from Egyptian documents. Egyptian officers rounded up men from Nubia and the Libyan desert areas. It would be in line with such practices if the Hebrews of the east Delta area were rounded up in a similar way and set to strenuous forced labor from which there was no escape except by flight since the people subjected to such harsh and cruel treatment had no military power to resist.[3]

THE DATE OF THE EXODUS

It has been widely held that the Exodus took place about 1440 B.C. on the basis of the statement in I Kings 6:1:

> And it came to pass in the four hundred and eightieth year after the children of Israel were come out of the land of Egypt, in the fourth year of Solomon's reign over Israel . . . that he began to build the house of the Lord.

We have good reason to believe that Solomon began to reign about the middle of the tenth century B.C., that is, about 950 B.C. It would follow from this that the Exodus took place about 1430 B.C., in the time of the Eighteenth Dynasty which ruled Egypt from about 1570 to 1310 B.C.

Scholars have been very ready to point out that there are many features about such a date that appear to be impossible to reconcile with certain facts both of history and of archaeology.

2. See K. A. Kitchen, "From the Brickfields of Egypt," *Tyndale Bulletin*, No. 27 (1976), pp. 137–147.
3. *Ibid.*, where many fascinating details and a considerable bibliography are provided.

An Egyptian brick made of chopped straw and mud from the Nile ca. 1300 B.C. It is stamped with the name and title of Ramesses II and may well have been one of the bricks made by the oppressed Israelites. (British Museum)

In the first place, if we are to take the biblical narrative seriously (and there is every reason that we should), we are bound to notice that the picture in the Bible is easiest to interpret if we regard the residence of the Pharaoh as being in the region of the Delta at the time of the Exodus. The frequent going to and fro in the days of Moses, and the easy access to the ruler in the days of Joseph seem to require that the capital of Egypt was in the north of the land. There were two periods in Egyptian history when this was so—one under the Hyksos rulers, and the other under the Pharaohs of the Nineteenth Dynasty. All other evidence suggests that the period of the Hyksos was too early for the Exodus. The days of Joseph fit in there. It seems evident, therefore, that we must set these events at the time of the Nineteenth Dynasty (about 1310 B.C. to 1200 B.C.). The rulers of the Eighteenth Dynasty built only sparingly in the north and had their capital in the south, at Thebes. Modern excavation has demonstrated by contrast that there was intense building activity in the north in the years following 1310 B.C.[4]

As we have seen, the capital of Egypt during these years was called Pi-Ramesse, that is, "Domain of Ramesses," the Raamses of Exodus 1:11 and 12:37.

There has been some debate about the exact position of these two towns mentioned in the Bible. We are now able to give a reasonable identification of the two.[5] Pithom can now be identified with the site Tell el-Retabeh in the Wadi Tumilat.[6] Excavations here uncovered some massive structures including a fine temple from the days of Ramesses II but no traces of Eighteenth Dynasty

4. See K. A. Kitchen, *The Bible in its World* (Exeter, 1977), pp. 76f.
5. G. E. Wright and F. V. Filson, *Westminster Historical Atlas* (London, 1953), p. 37.
6. See J. Finegan, *Let My People Go* (New York, 1963), pp. 12f.

This huge sandstone head represents Amenhotep III (Amenophis), who ruled Egypt ca. 1413–1377 B.C. At one time he was thought to have been the pharaoh of the Exodus. (British Museum)

constructions. The prominence of the god Atum in the building work of Raamses suggests that the name Pithom may have been originally Per-Atum, that is, house of Atum. The town Raamses is the former Tanis-Avaris, the Hyksos capital in the Nile Delta. It was named "the house of Ramesses" (*Per Re'emasese*) and carried this name for two hundred years (*ca.* 1300–1100 B.C.). The excavations of the French archaeologist P. Montet have at last established this identification.[7]

We have a further pointer to a later date for the Exodus from Transjordan to which we shall refer in some detail later in the chapter. The argument is that if there is any historical value in narratives dealing with the contact of the Israelites in their journey through Transjordan with the rulers of Edom (Num. 20:14–21), Moab (Num. 22:1–25:9; Deut. 2:8–18), Ammon (Deut. 2:18–23), and the kingdoms of the Amorites and their rulers Sihon and Og (Deut. 2:26–36), then the narratives in question must refer to a time when these kingdoms in

7. P. Montet, *Le drame d'Avaris* (Paris, 1941).

Transjordan were in existence. Unfortunately, the archaeological story of Transjordan is not well known; however, something is known. Surface surveys conducted by the late Nelson Glueck pointed to a gap in the story of urban settlement in the area after about 1850 B.C. Transjordan was occupied by non-urban people living in insubstantial homes which have left little in the way of archaeological remains. Certainly for most of the Middle Bronze period from 1850 to 1550 B.C. there is little evidence of substantial towns, certainly not in sufficient numbers to give support to the biblical picture in the days of the Exodus.[8] There is a similar lack of evidence of urban settlement for most of the Late Bronze Age, although there is some. It would seem that toward the end of the Late Bronze Age (thirteenth century), and certainly in the Iron I Age (1200–1000 B.C.) and thereafter, there was abundant urban settlement in Transjordan.

This means that a date for the Exodus prior to the thirteenth century would not suit the biblical data referred to above.

To be sure, there is still a great deal of uncertainty about Transjordan due to lack of excavation.

A third line of argument has been proposed for a date in the thirteenth century for the Exodus, this time from Canaan where, according to the book of Joshua, the Israelites were able to capture a considerable number of towns (Josh. 1–12; note 12:7–24). This would suggest that we should find general evidence of destruction in Canaan, perhaps about the middle of the thirteenth century. A study of the list in Joshua 12 in the light of recent excavations suggests a list of sites about which the question of a destruction level in the thirteenth century should be asked. Among these are Jericho, Ai, Lachish, Gezer, Debir, Taanach, Megiddo, and Hazor. There may be others whose identification is not certain. There are difficulties in attributing a particular destruction level to the Israelites because there were other groups present who might attack and destroy a city. However, the possibility that at least some of this destruction was attributable to the Israelites cannot be ruled out. There is good evidence for destruction and an abrupt break in culture during the thirteenth century at Lachish and Hazor, at Eglon (Tell el-Ḥesi), as well as at Bethel, which is not in the list in Joshua 12.[9] While there are many problem areas, Jericho and Ai to name two, it can be said that the archaeological evidence confirms what can be deduced from written texts, namely, that the end of the Late Bronze Age and the beginning of the Iron I Age was a period of social and political turbulence and change in Palestine. If this can be linked with the Israelite invasion even in part, we have a further pointer to a later, rather than an earlier, date for the Exodus.

One important Egyptian monument prevents our speculation beyond a date

8. There were two sites in the Heshbon area at Jalul and Tell el-'Umeiri which point to sedentary occupation during the Middle Bronze Age. See R. Ibach, "An intensive surface survey at Jalul," *Andrews University Seminary Studies*, Vol. XVI, No. 1 (Spring, 1978), pp. 215–222.

9. J. Bright, *History of Israel* (2nd ed. 1972), pp. 127–130.

of 1220 B.C. for the final entry of Israel into the land. It is the stele of Merneptah who ruled Egypt from 1224 to 1216 B.C. In the fifth year of his reign he had
a long poem prepared that celebrates his victories over the Libyans. The conclusion of the poem describes the results of this victory. The peoples of Asia were
duly impressed and submitted to Egypt without trouble. In the list of Asiatic
lands and peoples we have for the first time the occurrence of the name Israel.
The relevant passage reads:

> The princes are prostrate, saying, "Mercy,"
> Not one raises his head among the Nine Bows.
> Desolation is for Tehenu; Hatti is pacified;
> Plundered is Canaan with every evil;
> Carried off is Askelon; seized upon is Gezer;
> Yanoam is made as that which does not exist;
> Israel is laid waste, his seed is not;
> Hurru is become a widow for Egypt:
> All lands together, they are pacified. [10]

This stele is dated about 1220 B.C. The reference to Israel shows that by this
date there was already a recognizable people of this name in Palestine.

It is clear on this evidence that we cannot come any further down in time
than 1220 B.C. for the time of the Conquest, although this stele does not really
tell us how much before this date the Exodus took place.

Most scholars today feel that the weight of evidence is for an Exodus from
Egypt about 1280 B.C. What, then, are we to say of the date implied by the
statement in I Kings 6:1? A comparison with the Greek Septuagint shows that
there was a difference of opinion in the minds of the translators about the time
when this text was prepared, say in the period between 300 and 100 B.C. The
Septuagint gives a period of four hundred and forty years as the time lapse
between the Exodus and Solomon. It has been suggested that there may be a sort
of symbolic usage of the numbers. Some scholars have pointed out that the list of
high priests in I Chronicles 6:3-8 includes eleven priests between Aaron and
Zadok, the priest of Solomon's time. If we think of a generation as forty years,
we can see how the four hundred and forty years of the Septuagint was deduced.
If, however, this is only a round number for a generation and if in fact the
generations were something less than forty years, we may arrive at a date for the
Exodus closer to the date suggested by the above evidence. The real answer to
these problems is not yet available.

THE JOURNEY FROM EGYPT TO THE WILDERNESS

If our suggestion that Israel left Egypt about 1280 B.C. is correct, then the
Pharaoh of those days must have been Ramesses II. He was a great man in many

10. J. B. Pritchard, *ANET*, pp. 376–378.

Granite statue of Ramesses II wearing the double crown of Upper and Lower Egypt and holding the symbols of his authority, the flail and scepter. He may have been the pharaoh of the Exodus. (British Museum)

ways, although he was also a great boaster. He sought desperately to recover the lost power of Egypt in Asia and had a good deal of trouble with the Hittites of Asia Minor, who naturally opposed him as he sought to extend his influence in Palestine and further north. It was really after he was compelled to recognize that the Hittites were a power to be reckoned with that he formed a non-aggression pact with them and returned with zeal to building.

The literary form of the treaty between Ramesses II and the Hittite king is of great significance for biblical scholars. Fortunately the treaty is preserved for us in both its Egyptian and Hittite forms.[11]

After a preamble there follow a historical outline referring to previous relations between the two countries, a list of treaty stipulations, divine witnesses to the treaty, and a list of curses and blessings, curses for any breach of the treaty and blessings which will follow if the treaty is kept. This pattern is very similar to the literary form in which the story of the making of the covenant between God and Israel at Sinai is told. It is, however, found in other parts of the Old

11. J. B. Pritchard, *ANET*, pp. 199–201, gives the Egyptian form.

Testament, especially where Israel's covenant with God is in question.[12] It is arguable that Moses saw God as Israel's divine King who had invited her to enter into a solemn covenant with him. There was a historical background to this, and there were covenant stipulations, curses and blessings. This concept of covenant[13] was quite fundamental to Israel's understanding of her relationship with Yahweh her God.

We have no opportunity here to comment on the plagues which preceded the final departure from the land apart from saying that they are neither improbable nor unusual. They are part of the local color of Egypt. No doubt they were more serious than usual, and without parallel. It has been pointed out by various writers that there is some hint in these plagues of an exposure of the weakness of the gods of Egypt, for most of them, if not all, were produced by creatures that were held to be gods in the land. While there is a good deal of information available in modern times bearing on these plagues, we shall concern ourselves rather with the journeyings of the Israelites, for which we now have valuable evidence.[14]

According to the Bible, the Israelites departed from Raamses (Exod. 12:37) and traveled to Succoth. Thence they journeyed to Etham (Exod. 13:20), and Pi-hahiroth (Exod. 14:2) "between Migdol and the sea, over against Baal-zephon." It was here that the Egyptians caught up with them. They were able to cross the sea by a wonderful intervention of God.

A brief comment may be made about the number of Israelites escaping from Egypt. The narrative in Exodus 12:37 refers to "six hundred thousand men on foot besides women and children." The meaning of this expression depends on the meaning of the word "thousand." The Hebrew term *elef* can carry a variety of meanings—clan, a subgroup of a tribe, a military group of some kind, an ox, etc. With different vowels and the same consonants the term can refer to a military officer of some kind. Hence the expression "six hundred *thousand* men" is of quite uncertain meaning. The calculation that allows one woman and several children to one man and arrives at a figure of three million or more would seem to be wide of the mark. A figure of a few tens of thousands would be more reasonable.

Thanks to modern research we have gone a long way toward discovering at least some of the path taken by the fleeing Israelites. Avoiding the "way of the land of the Philistines" (Exod. 13:17), which was traveled by the armies of Egypt, they turned to the south and moved from Raamses to Succoth, that is, in Egyptian terms, from Pi-Ramesse to Tj'eku some twenty-two miles away. In

12. See J. A. Thompson, *The Ancient Near Eastern Treaties and the Old Testament* (London, 1964), for a summary of ancient treaties and relevant Old Testament passages.

13. The Hebrew word *berith* translates both "treaty" and "covenant." See K. A. Kitchen, *Ancient Orient and Old Testament* (1969), pp. 157f.

14. See J. Finegan, *op. cit.*, pp. 47–57, for a valuable discussion of the plagues. See also K. A. Kitchen, *The Bible in its World*, pp. 79–85.

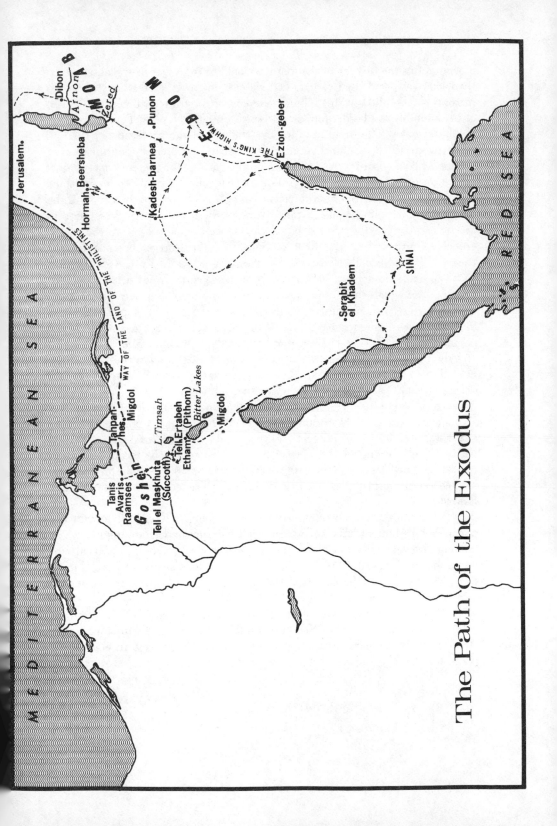

The Path of the Exodus

modern terms the first leg of the journey would be from Qantir traveling south, then southeast, and then east to Tell el-Maskhutah. It is of interest that two runaway slaves followed this route at the end of the thirteenth century.[15] Tell el-Maskhutah was a border fortress in the eastern area of Wadi Tumilat, west of the Bitter Lakes. The road then led by "the way of the wilderness of the Red Sea" (Exod. 13:18). Scholars continue to debate the precise identification of Etham, Migdol, Baal-zephon, and Pi-hahiroth, and at the present time no final identification can be given. It is possible that the name Pi-hahiroth is connected with the root *hrt* (= to dig) and refers to a location on one of the canals of the Nile.[16] Of one point we are certain. None of these towns was to be found in areas along the Red Sea proper but the evidence points to areas to the north, probably northward of the Gulf of Suez. Jack Finegan proposes a feasible theory.[17] From Succoth (Exod. 12:37) the path led to Etham (Exod. 13:20).

The name Etham can be derived from the Egyptian word *hetem,* meaning "fortress," of which there were many on Egypt's eastern frontier. The ruins of such a fortress with building remains dating to the days of Ramesses II were found at the eastern entrance to the Wadi Tumilat. It was at this point that the people turned back (Exod. 14:1f.) and camped at Pi-hahiroth between Migdol and the sea. Finegan conjectures that the sea in question was the large Bitter Lake. Etham lay between this and Lake Timsah to the north. Now to the west of the Bitter Lake is a height known as Jebel Abu Hasan overlooking shallow waters connecting the Bitter Lake to the Gulf of Suez. On this height are ruins of a square tower in which inscriptions of Seti I and Ramesses II were found. Such a tower was described by the Egyptian letters *m k t l,* which are to be compared with the Hebrew Migdol. The site of Baal-zephon cannot be located with certainty, but the place is known from various sources as a temple for mariners located on the arm of land that embraces the Gulf of Serbonitis (Sabkhat Bardwil).[18]

The term Red Sea can generally be translated Sea of Reeds. The translators of the Old Testament have been responsible for a misunderstanding here. The reference is evidently not to the Red Sea proper, but rather to some of its marshy extensions to the north in the region of Succoth. The name is too general for us to be able to identify the place today, but it was evidently well known, for the same name occurs in several Egyptian records.[19]

Attempts have been made to trace the path of the Exodus from the other side of the sea, across into the Sinai peninsula. These are not entirely successful, although the general path was almost certainly along the western edge of the peninsula. One of the best attempts to outline the journey is set out in the

15. J. B. Pritchard, *ANET*, p. 259, "The Pursuit of Runaway Slaves."
16. W. F. Albright, *BASOR*, No. 109 (1948), p. 16.
17. *Ibid.*, pp. 83–87.
18. W. F. Albright, *BASOR*, No. 109 (1948), pp. 15f.
19. H. Cazelles, *op. cit.*, p. 55.

Figures cut into the balustrade at Amarna, Egypt, of Pharaoh Akhenaton (1370–1353 B.C.), Queen Nefertiti, and presumably a daughter standing with offerings for the sun-god Aton. The sun-god is represented by the solar disk, whose rays stream in benediction upon the worshippers. Note that each ray ends in a hand, and that the hands just above the faces end in the ankh sign (the hieroglyph for "life"). (Metropolitan Museum of Art)

Westminster Historical Atlas. We shall not attempt to pursue our exposition any further, but proceed to some observations about the journey up to the point where the Israelites made their first contact with the kings of Transjordan.

After a stay of twelve months at Sinai and a further period of wandering in the areas to the south of Palestine, the Bible seems to indicate that they were ready to attempt an entry into the promised land from the south, moving in from the general area of Kadesh. At this point Moses sent twelve spies into the land to seek out information that would help the invaders. The instructions given to the spies and the report they brought back are set forth in Numbers 13. Three features of this report are of interest to us here. The spies reported walled cities, a mixed population, and fertile land. Each of these takes on a new meaning in the light of modern research. It is a fact that Palestine was studded with walled fortresses at the time. The feudal system under which the land was ruled made for small fortified centers. It was necessary for the local rulers to pay their annual dues to the Egyptian overlord or to his representative and to remain loyal to the Pharaoh. Apart from this they were allowed a good deal of independence, and they seem to have engaged in frequent petty wars among themselves. If ever the Pharaoh showed signs of weakness, there was immediate revolt. This happened in the days of the Pharaoh Akhenaton (about 1370–1353 B.C. or a little later), one of the pharaohs of the Eighteenth Dynasty. This ruler was more interested in religious reform than in the maintenance of his Asiatic empire. As a result of his neglect there were inroads into his domains on all sides. The local governors and princes who remained loyal to Egypt wrote letters to Akhenaton pleading for help from the Pharaoh, who had removed his capital to Amarna some distance up the Nile. Late in the nineteenth century a peasant woman, rummaging in the ruins of Amarna, discovered some of these letters written on baked clay. Others were found later. They are now known as the Amarna letters. They give a very good insight into the state of Palestine about a century before the Israelites came there. In particular they tell us of several of these walled towns and of how they were being taken over by the invaders. At one time it was thought that the picture given in these letters was a portrayal of the Israelite invasion, but further information now available has shown that the event was quite a different one. The Israelites did not attack the cities of Canaan till late in the thirteenth century. Nor is it possible to equate the Habiru with the Israelites even though the Israelites may have shown some characteristics of the Habiru.

A second aspect of the report of the spies is their reference to the mixed races of the land (Num. 13:29). Documents from the Palestine of that period have preserved many names which give a general idea of the elements in the population, in much the same way as names like Mackenzie, O'Reilly, Le Page, Schmidt, Kwei-Lian, and Ramamurthi in an American town give some indication of racial origins.

Finally, the description of the land as one that "flowed with milk and honey" had been given to the same land by Egyptian writers of an earlier day. There are

Two of the famous letters discovered at Amarna, Egypt, in 1887. The clay cuneiform tablets contain diplomatic correspondence from Babylonian, Canaanite, and other rulers to the pharaohs Amenhotep III and Akhenaton (fourteenth century B.C.). (British Museum)

extant today at last two accounts of the land in the general area of Palestine, and both give a glowing picture of at least some of its territory. We refer to the tale of Sinuhe the traveler,[20] dated to about 1900 B.C., and to the account of the campaigns of Pharaoh Pepi I,[21] about 2350 B.C.

The story of Israel's fear at the report of the spies and of her failure to proceed with the Conquest at that time is well known. The people turned back and remained in the wilderness for many years. When they finally decided to move, they proceeded at once to the east and, skirting Edom and Moab, were able to launch their attack from the east.

SOME ARCHAEOLOGICAL NOTES ON THE WILDERNESS PERIOD

Some references should be made to the contact of the Israelites with the Kenites. Moses had fled to their land in an earlier day and had married a Kenite woman, daughter of the priest of Midian (Exod. 2:16ff.). The name Kenite suggests the Hebrew word *qain*, which means "smith." That there may be significance in this

20. J. B. Pritchard, *ANET*, pp. 18–22.
21. *Ibid.*, p. 227.

name is shown by the fact that the area below the Dead Sea was, and still is, an area rich in minerals, an area "whose stones *are* iron, and out of whose hills thou mayest dig brass" (Deut. 8:9). The researches of archaeologists like Nelson Glueck have shown that copper was mined in this area at a very early date. The great Solomon seems to have undertaken mining and smelting activities in the region, as we shall see. It becomes a point of great interest to find that it was precisely in this region that Moses had the serpent of brass prepared (Num. 21:9). Moreover, one of the towns passed on the way to the land of Edom was Punon (Num. 33:42). This is the modern Feinan, an area rich in copper ores, where mining has been carried on at various times in the past.

Another point of interest on which modern discovery has shed light is the reference to Israel's success over some of the foes they met on the way. The Bible states that the people of Israel smote the enemy "with the edge of the sword" (Exod. 17:13; Deut. 13:15; 20:13; Num. 21:24). In Hebrew this phrase is literally "to the mouth of the sword." This now turns out to be a most precise description. Archaeological work has brought to light a great variety of swords, daggers, battle axes, and the like. Many of these have the representation of an animal mouth at the top of the blade, so that the blade appears to issue from the jaws of a wild beast.[22] The phrase "to devour by the mouth of the sword" is a very vivid one indeed.

It was during the wilderness period that the Israelites began to learn the significance of the laws that Moses had drawn up for them. It was the opinion of some scholars in the last century that not only were these laws largely the invention of a later day but that even the figure of Moses was largely legendary. Few would hold either of these positions today.[23] It has become increasingly evident that in the thirteen century B.C. legal and religious codes were well developed. The discovery of the ancient site of Ugarit (modern Ras Shamra) opposite modern Cyprus on the coast of Syria has given to the world great insight into the religious practices of the Canaanites. Baked clay documents found here have shown that even before the days of Moses the Canaanites had a most complex system of prayers and rituals, many of them bearing at least some resemblance to those of the Israelites. We may argue that if the people of Canaan had such development at the time, there is no serious reason why the people of Israel should not have had their own system also.

The same applies to the law codes of the ancient East. It was once thought that the earliest law code was that of the great Hammurabi, who was supposed to live about 2100 B.C. We know that he lived nearer to 1700 B.C. and that there were law codes before his time in Mesopotamia. In very recent years at least two codes have been discovered in excavations, namely, the codes of the town of Eshnunna and of King Lipit Ishtar.[24] Both of these precede the code of Ham-

---

22. T. J. Meek, "Archaeology and a Point of Hebrew Syntax," *BASOR* (Apr., 1951).
23. M. Noth, *The History of Israel* (Eng. trans., 2nd ed.), pp. 135f.
24. J. B. Pritchard, *ANET*, pp. 159-163.

The back of the throne chair of Tutankhamon (ca. 1360 B.C.), found in his tomb in the Valley of the Kings near Thebes. The panel is wood overlaid with gold, silver, blue faience, calcite, and glass. It shows the young king and his wife in ornate royal attire; she holds a small bowl, perhaps containing perfume, in her left hand and touches the king's broad collar with her right. The symbol of the sun-god evinces that the panel was made when the king still worshipped Aton. (Metropolitan Museum of Art)

murabi in time, and both show remarkable resemblances to it. Earlier still we have the Sumerian Laws of Ur-Nammu (*ca.* 2112–2095 B.C.), and earlier than that (*ca.* 2300 B.C.) we have the law code of Ebla, which has been reported but not yet published. There is no serious reason, therefore, why the Israelites should not have had a code of their own. There are, of course, a number of very remarkable resemblances between the code of Moses and that of Hammurabi. This is not to be wondered at since the patriarchal family came from Mesopotamia and would naturally bring with them something of the legal structure of the society which had been theirs until the time of their migration. Many of these laws would be necessary in any system, and we can understand that it would have divine approval.

Perhaps a few words about the Tabernacle in the wilderness would be in order here.[25] The idea of a traveling sacred ark was not peculiar to Israel. Tent shrines are depicted in the third century B.C. and the writer Diodorus tells of Phoenicians taking tent shrines into battle in the seventh century B.C. These are, of course, later than the Israelite period, but they provide a hint that this sort of thing was not unknown in the ancient world.

The shape and structure of the Tabernacle were both familiar to other peoples at the time, particularly to the Canaanites. The materials used were all such as could be obtained in the areas where the Israelites were wandering. Recent discussion has inclined scholars in general to take the biblical accounts of the Tabernacle in the wilderness more seriously than they have for the past century.

The rituals that were used in the Tabernacle would appear to have been quite elaborate according to the picture in Exodus and Leviticus. Even if we allow that these have been idealized somewhat, we should not dismiss the biblical material out of hand. Contemporary rituals in Egypt and at Ugarit are known to have been extremely elaborate. In Egypt they had fifty or sixty religious festivals at ancient Thebes and daily offerings of considerable proportions.[26] There was thus nothing unique about elaborate rituals, although the Israelite ritual was far less complex than the Egyptian one.

Comparisons with Ugaritic practices are instructive. At Ugarit they had "peace offerings" (or shared offerings), "sacrifices," "gift offerings," and "vows"—each of which in its Israelite form is known in the book of Leviticus.[27] The Ugarit picture comes from the centuries before Moses and demonstrates the complexity of its rituals.[28]

While questions of detail remain, the general point may be made that in the thirteenth century B.C. there were societies in western Asia which had complex religious practices long before the Israelites emerged on the pages of history. Much may be learned from a study of these neighboring cults which will help in our interpretation of biblical materials.

THE LAST STAGE OF THE
JOURNEY TO THE PROMISED LAND

Then came a day when Moses and the children of Israel decided to move on. But the decision was to go by an indirect way. There was a well-known trade road that wound its way through Transjordan, the King's Highway (Num. 20:17;

25. F. M. Cross, "The Tabernacle," BA, Vol. X (1947), pp. 45–68; W. F. Albright, BASOR, No. 91 (1943), pp. 39–44, and No. 93, pp. 23–25.
26. K. A. Kitchen, The Bible in its World, pp. 85f.
27. C. F. Pfeiffer, Ras Shamra and the Bible (Grand Rapids, 1962), pp. 36–39.
28. D. J. Wiseman, "Archaeology" in NBD (1962), pp. 70f.

21:22; Deut. 2:27, etc.). It is now established that this road existed from early times. It was used much earlier than the days of the Exodus. A string of Bronze Age fortresses, scattered here and there fairly close to the modern bitumen highway, shows that the road was in use even before 2000 B.C.[29] It was probably the conquest of this road that lay behind the invasion of the four kings of the East mentioned in Genesis 14. In later days the same road was again protected by small walled fortresses which stood at strategic points such as the descents into the wadis and at the edges of the plateau where the road came up again from deep valleys. It is still a matter of debate whether these fortresses were in existence in the days of the Israelite journeyings. Much more excavation of the small tells that are scattered along the King's Highway needs to be undertaken. It is interesting to learn that the Romans used the same path for their great road through Transjordan in the days of Trajan (A.D. 98–117).

Having made the decision to proceed to the Promised Land, the Israelites sent a message to the king of Edom asking permission to pass along the King's Highway. The promise was made that all food and water used would be paid for. The king of Edom refused passage to Israel (Num. 20:14–22). It may be asked why Israel did not attack the Edomites at once since, in any case, they did attack the Amorites a little later on. They had no intention of settling there because they were forbidden by an injunction from God to abhor Edom, who was their brother (Deut. 23:7). There were good reasons why Edom was not attacked. In the first place the plateau on which the kingdom of Edom lay stood high above the wadis[30] along which the Israelites moved, and the difficult climb up the sides of the wadis would put the newcomers at a disadvantage if any opposition was encountered. But further, there is some evidence that the plateau of Edom (as of Moab) was protected by a series of small fortresses strategically placed. Some of these lay along the north–south highway.[31] So Israel had to move north up the valley of the Arabah to the west of Edom, and proceed in an easterly direction, skirting Edom on its northern border along the Wadi Zered (Num. 21:4, 11–13; Judg. 11:17, 18). The king of Edom would not worry unduly about the passage of Israel to the east, away down in the valley. There was plenty of room for the people and their flocks and herds to pass through. Incidentally, it was about this time that the incidents of the brazen serpent and the death of Aaron took place (Num. 20:23–29; 21:5–9).

If Edom refused Israel the right to pass along the King's Highway, perhaps Moab would allow her to pass. Messengers sent to Moab were met by the same refusal. Israel did not attempt to force a passage for much the same reasons. The land of Moab had been given to the Moabites by God and was not for the

29. N. Glueck, AASOR, Vol. 15, p. 104; etc.
30. The altitude is of the order of 2500 feet, with some mountains rising to over 5000 feet.
31. N. Glueck, AASOR, Vols. 4, 15, 16–19, 25–28; The Other Side of Jordan (New Haven, 1940).

possession of Israel at this stage (Deut. 2:9). Moab, like Edom, was surrounded by fortresses and stood securely on her own plateau. So Israel moved along the Wadi Zered to the east.

> Then they went along through the wilderness, and compassed the land of Edom, and the land of Moab, and came by the east side of the land of Moab, and pitched on the other side of Arnon, but came not within the border of Moab: for Arnon was the border of Moab (Judg. 11:18).

Next a message was sent to the Amorite king Sihon. He, too, refused to allow Israel to pass along the King's Highway, but he made one foolish mistake. He left the shelter of his fortresses and came out to the plains in front of his kingdom. This gave Israel the chance she wanted. Sihon was defeated in battle and the way was open for the Israelites to move up to the highlands of the Transjordan plateau. Very soon the whole of Transjordan was in the hands of Israel. The two kingdoms of Sihon and Og were subdued and their lands given to the tribes of Reuben, Gad, and half the tribe of Manasseh (Num. 21:21-35; 32).

It should be noted that the archaeological picture of Transjordan is still very incomplete. There is good evidence of the emergence of urban settlement in the Iron I period and its continuance thereafter. But the precise date at which this development began escapes us. It cannot have been later than about 1200 B.C. and may have been somewhat earlier. In any case, the biblical account of the movement of the Israelites through Transjordan presupposes the existence of organized kingdoms. We must await the results of future research before our picture can be drawn clearly.[32]

THE CONQUEST OF THE LAND

The manner of Israel's settlement in Western Palestine raises many questions. Their appearance in the land of Canaan can be dated with reasonable assurance to the end of the thirteenth century. Already in 1220 B.C. the pharaoh Merneptah was speaking of some people named Israel.[33] No further detail is given. The Bible pictures military campaigns in the south (Josh. 1–10) and in the north (Josh. 11) of the land. The first chapter of Judges is thought by some scholars to indicate activity by groups which came from the south rather than from the east by way of Transjordan.[34]

In the biblical story in Joshua 1–10 we have a picture of towns being attacked and destroyed. Among these were Jericho, Ai, Lachish, Eglon, and

---

32. See Y. Aharoni, *The Land of the Bible* (London, 1966), pp. 184–192, for a good account of the biblical picture as well as for some useful archaeological notes.

33. The name may denote either a land or a people. To indicate which, the Egyptians prefixed the word by a special sign (a determinative). In this case the determinative denotes "people." See J. B. Pritchard, *ANET*, p. 378.

34. S. Hermann, *A History of Israel in Old Testament Times* (1975), p. 103; M. Noth, *The History of Israel* (1960), pp. 55–58.

At Jericho (Tell es-Sultan) Kathleen Kenyon excavated a tower, wall, and rock-cut ditch from Neolithic times (ca. 7000 B.C.). Joshua and the Israelites killed the inhabitants of Jericho, except Rahab and her family, and destroyed the city near the end of the thirteenth century B.C. (Jericho Excavation Fund, University of London)

Debir, in each of which archaeological work has been done in recent years. Insofar as there is a consistent picture anywhere, it would seem that there was considerable destruction in these towns about 1250 B.C. There are, of course, some problems yet to be solved. The town of Ai poses its own peculiar problem because it seems that the site that has been identified with Ai was destroyed about 2350 B.C. and lay in ruins at the time of the Israelite conquest.[35] Its very name means "ruin." Various suggestions have been offered to account for the fact that Ai is mentioned as being taken by Joshua. One is that it was merely an outpost of Bethel under the control of a military captain. He is styled "king," but this need occasion no difficulty as the Hebrew root simply means "ruler." If Ai was only a military outpost there may not have been any substantial buildings there and so nothing tangible would remain. However, this is one of the problems still remaining to be solved.

The town of Jericho raises questions also. Considerable excavations were undertaken here by the German excavators Sellin and Watzinger between 1907 and 1909, by Professor John Garstang between 1930 and 1936, and by Dame Kathleen Kenyon between 1952 and 1958. Earlier excavators had identified the upper stratum at Jericho as the ruins of Joshua's city. Nowadays it has been found that the material thus identified comes from the period before 1550 B.C., that is, from the end of the Middle Bronze Age. Any Late Bronze city has been largely weathered away and is marked by only a few remains and a few tombs.[36] As a result we have very little evidence of Joshua's city.

We are better placed in the case of Lachish, which was destroyed at the end of the Late Bronze Age, perhaps about 1250 B.C.[37] Other sites which were destroyed about the same time were Tell Beit Mirsim (which may be Debir), Bethel,[38] and Hazor, north of Galilee (Josh. 11:10, 11).[39] The rebuilding of these towns in the Iron I Age level took place soon after or after an interval in much poorer conditions and with cruder building techniques. There are other towns in Canaan which shared in the same widespread disturbances. It is tempting to link this phenomenon with the arrival of the Israelites and to see some correlation with the narratives in Joshua. The evidence is, however, only circumstantial and many critical historians agree that there is no proof that it was specifically the people of Israel who were responsible for these destructions since other peoples were in the area at the time.[40] Even so it would seem possible that at least some of the destruction was attributable to the Israelites, and the literary

35. W. F. Albright, *Archaeology of Palestine* (London, 1954), p. 76.
36. D. W. Thomas (ed.), *Archaeology and Old Testament Study* (Oxford, 1967), pp. 272f.
37. W. F. Albright, *BASOR*, No. 58, pp. 13f.; No. 68, pp. 23f.; No. 74, pp. 20–22.
38. W. F. Albright, *BASOR*, No. 58, pp. 13, 15.
39. Y. Yadin, *BA*, Vol. XIX (1956), pp. 2–11; Vol. XX (1957), pp. 34–37; Vol. XXI (1958), pp. 30–47; Vol. XXII (1959), pp. 2–20; Y. Yadin, et al., *HAZOR I—An Account of the First Season of Excavations 1955* (Jerusalem, 1958); *HAZOR II* (Jerusalem, 1960).
40. For a critical review of the material see J. M. Miller in J. H. Hayes and J. M. Miller (eds.), *Israelite and Judaean History* (London, 1977), pp. 252–262.

evidence in Joshua 1–11 cannot be dismissed. We need more evidence about yet other towns referred to in these chapters.

Another line of evidence which we shall pursue in the next chapter is the appearance of a great number of new settlements in the mountain areas of Palestine at the start of the Iron I period, that is, from about 1200 B.C. onward. That the land had new occupants from this time, and that there was a continuity in the occupation of some sites during the centuries to come, links those changes with the emergence of the Israelites.[41]

41. For a more detailed analysis of the many issues involved in the question see M. Weippert, *The Settlement of the Israelite Tribes in Palestine* (Studies in Biblical Theology, Second Series, 21; London, 1971).

5

SETTLING INTO THE LAND

THE emergence of the Israelites as a recognizable group dates from about 1210 B.C. If there is some difficulty about identifying exactly the people who brought about the destruction of so many sites in Canaan at the end of the Late Bronze period, archaeological evidence confirms what can be deduced from the written texts, namely, that the close of the Late Bronze Age and the beginning of the Iron I Age brought about considerable socio-political disturbance and change. On the material level some towns were destroyed and then rebuilt by people whose building skills were inferior to the old Canaanites, while other towns were built on bedrock. At places like Lachish and Hazor several Late Bronze temples were destroyed and not rebuilt, suggesting a change in occupants. This picture is not inconsistent with the emergence of a new group of people whose general culture differed in significant ways from that of the older Canaanite occupants of the land.

The archaeological evidence for the Iron I Age in Canaan presents three distinct pictures—an emerging group in the southwest corner of the land which comprised the Philistines, a new group on the central and northern highlands of the land representing the Israelites, and a continuing group which occupied the coastal and lowland areas representing the old Canaanite population. The literary picture in Judges 1:27–36 is a significant one. Important towns like Bethshean, Taanach, Megiddo, Gezer, Bethshemesh, and several others are listed as not having been occupied by the Israelites. These were, in fact, the old Canaanite towns, and some of these like Megiddo and Bethshean showed continuous occupation well into the Iron I period without any sign of severe destruction.

The story on the highlands is quite different. Here some towns like Bethel

The River Jordan. From its sources near Mount Hermon in the far north the river flows south to empty into the Dead Sea. (Israel Office of Information)

were destroyed and rebuilt almost at once. But what is of greater interest is that a considerable number of new towns emerged at the beginning of the Iron I Age. Only a few of these have been excavated, but careful surface surveys both in the central highlands and in the highlands of Galilee have brought to light scores of sites strewn with pottery typical of the Settlement period.[1] The story has yet to be told in detail, but already some significant excavations have been carried out. The little site of Izbet Ṣarṭah, three kilometers east of Aphek (Josh. 12:18; I Sam. 4:1; 29:1), lay on the road that led up from the coast to towns like Shiloh. Its archaeological story covered the period 1200–1000 B.C. There were three phases in its short history, the earliest covering the twelfth century. A fine example of an early "four-room" Israelite house was exposed in the center of the settlement. This house had walls about one meter thick. In the open space between this building and the surrounding houses were dozens of stone-lined silos dug down to bedrock. These silos were typical of the age. In one of them two sherds were discovered which fitted together and were found to contain writing, basically an early form of the alphabet with three lines copied above it, evidently by a learner. It would seem to represent a very early inscription from the period of the Judges, dating to about the twelfth century B.C.

A second site of considerable interest is Raddana, which lay on a hilltop surrounded on three sides by deep valleys on the eastern outskirts of Ramallah. It was a small Iron I Age settlement established toward the end of the thirteenth century B.C. Several typical houses were brought to light, as well as pottery which was characteristic of the age and an inscribed jar handle carrying three letters only but bearing testimony to the existence of writing in the days of the Judges (as does Izbet Ṣarṭah).[2]

A third site discovered on the southern outskirts of Jerusalem is Gilo. It was a small Iron I Age village which remained in existence for only a short period but was of the same general appearance as the other sites we have mentioned.

The complete story of the settlement in the Hill Country is now beginning to be unraveled. Two new technical advances furthered this settlement. First, there was the use of iron tools. Iron remained the monopoly of the Philistines for a time (I Sam. 13:19ff), during which they prevented the blacksmiths from working in Israel "lest the Hebrews make themselves swords or spears." Before long, iron tools found their way into Israelite areas (I Sam. 13:21). An iron plough point was found in Stratum II at Gibeah of Benjamin (Tell el-Ful) dating to the eleventh century.[3] Iron tools were stronger than bronze tools and soon made the task of clearing forests and preparing hilly areas for agriculture much easier.

---

1. M. Garsiel and I. Finkelstein, "The Westward Expansion of the House of Joseph in the Light of the Izbet Ṣartah Excavations," Tel Aviv, Vol. 5, Nos. 3, 4, pp. 193, 197.
2. J. A. Callaway and R. E. Cooley, "A Salvage Excavation at Raddana, in Bireh," BASOR, No. 201 (Feb., 1971), pp. 9–19.
3. W. F. Albright, AASOR, Vol. 4 (1924), p. 17.

This inscribed ostracon, found in two pieces at Izbet Ṣarṭah, Israel, is the oldest and most complete Hebrew abecedary yet discovered. The first four lines seem to be random letters, but the last is an alphabet written from left to right rather than in the right-to-left direction later established. (Institute of Archaeology, University of Tel Aviv)

The other technical advance was the invention of the plastered cistern in the Late Bronze Age.[4] This freed the population from dependence on wells and enabled any enterprising farmer who would sink a cistern into the limestone rock to have his own water supply. The device was not original to the Israelites, but they soon adopted it and it enabled them to found many small settlements independent of wells and wadis.

It would appear that the Israelites did not bring strong traditions of material culture with them to Canaan, but borrowed and adapted what they found in building constructions, weapons, art objects, and pottery.[5] Soon the Israelites developed their own characteristic methods. Y. Aharoni, who wrote an extensive discussion of the settlement of the Israelite tribes in Upper Galilee, was able to demonstrate this quite clearly.[6] Israelite activity in the days of the Judges transformed sparsely settled areas into densely populated areas. It was these highland regions which were to constitute the heart and strength of later Israel. When eventually Israel was able to dominate the plains, the conditions were already established for uniting the whole land into a political unity with considerable economic strength which resulted from the cultivation of extensive waste lands never before tilled.

But the emergent Israel was surrounded on all sides by hostile neighbors with whom there was a great deal of conflict. To these we now turn.

ISRAEL'S HOSTILE NEIGHBORS

Modern archaeology has done much to make clear to us the character of Israel's neighbors. On every side there were foes. To the northeast were the Aramaeans. To the northwest were the Canaanites, later to become known as the Phoenicians. In the coastal areas to the southwest the Philistines were a grave menace, while on the southeast were the Moabites and the Edomites, as well as various nomadic groups.

On the purely human level it is a marvel that Israel ever survived the attacks of these peoples. On many occasions she very nearly collapsed before the assaults of her enemies. Yet Israel emerged at last as an unified nation. It was in the purposes of God that she should survive.

From time to time these neighboring peoples made raids into the territory of the little nation of Israel which was fighting for a foothold in the mountain areas of the new land. On these occasions national leaders arose to defend the people. These leaders were the "Judges." Their resistance to Israel's enemies seems to have been confined to limited areas. Thus, in the southwest it was Samson who warded off the Philistines. Shamgar likewise opposed this enemy. In the north

---

4. W. F. Albright, *The Archaeology of Palestine and the Bible* (New York, 1931; 3rd ed. 1935).
5. Y. Aharoni, *The Land of the Bible* (London, 1966), pp. 219f.
6. *Ibid.*, p. 220.

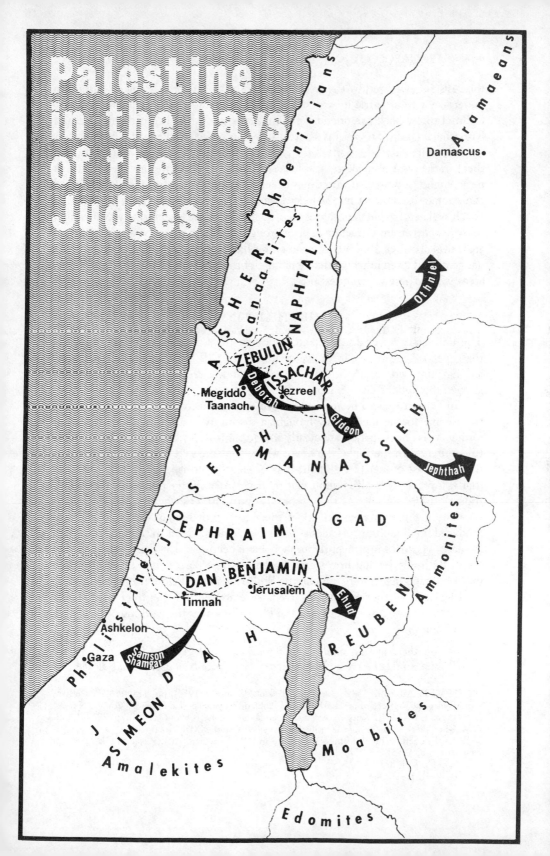

Palestine in the Days of the Judges

Aramaeans

Damascus•

Phoenicians

ASHER

Canaanites

NAPHTALI

ZEBULUN

Deborah

ISSACHAR

Jezreel

Megiddo•

Taanach•

Gideon

Othniel

MANASSEH

Jephthah

JOSEPH

EPHRAIM

GAD

DAN

BENJAMIN

Jerusalem•

Ehud

Ammonites

Philistines

Timnah•

REUBEN

Ashkelon•

Samson

Shamgar

•Gaza

JUDAH

SIMEON

Moabites

Amalekites

Edomites

the resistance was led by the woman Deborah, who urged the men of Israel to undertake a great battle in which a Canaanite coalition was overcome. Again, Othniel threw back the oncoming Aramaeans, who had been led by Chushan Rishathaim (Judg. 3). Gideon dealt with the nomadic peoples—the Amalekites, the Midianites, and the Sons of the East (or the Sons of Qedem, as we must call them in the light of modern knowledge). When the Moabites invaded the areas near Jericho, it was Ehud who threw them back. Jephthah the Gileadite defeated the Ammonites. Other minor Judges were active in other areas.

It will be of value to undertake a brief review of the fascinating way in which these peoples around Israel have been brought to life in recent years. We know a great deal about each of them today, and it has become very clear that the Bible has preserved a remarkably reliable picture of their customs and achievements in areas where these are in question.

THE PHILISTINES

The Philistines were part of the great movement of peoples which flowed out of the general Aegean area in the years around 1200 B.C. They are referred to by the Egyptian writers as the "Sea Peoples." It was these Sea Peoples who destroyed the famous city of Troy.

In Palestine these newcomers settled in the southwest and eventually gave their name to the land. They brought a distinctive culture with them. Their former areas of occupation are clearly recognizable today by the so-called "Philistine pottery." In the Bible, the towns where they are said to have lived are all in the southwest corner of the land. It is of great interest, therefore, to discover that it is precisely in this region that their very distinctive pottery is also found. Indeed, the occurrence of this pottery is quite rare elsewhere.[7]

The Philistines were skilled in the working of metals. Excavations have produced small melting furnaces at a number of sites. Gerar in the region of Gaza is a case in point. More recently furnaces have been found at Tell Qasile near Tel Aviv. Both copper and iron were worked in these places. It seems to be clear that iron implements were used on the Philistine plains before they were used on the highlands where the Israelites lived.[8] We are reminded of the biblical reference to the monopoly exercised by the Philistines over the working of metals for agricultural purposes:

> Now there was no smith found throughout all the land of Israel: for the Philistines said, Lest the Hebrews make them swords or spears: But all the

7. W. F. Albright, *The Archaeology of Palestine* (London, 1954), pp. 114, 116; T. Dothan, "Archaeological Reflections on the Philistine Problem," *Antiquity and Survival*, Vol. II, No. 2/3 (1957), pp. 151–164; K. Kenyon, *Archaeology in the Holy Land* (Oxford, 1965), pp. 221–239; G. E. Wright, "Fresh Evidence for the Philistine Story," *BA*, Vol. XXIX, No. 3 (Sept., 1966), pp. 70–86; K. A. Kitchen, "The Philistines," pp. 53–78 in D. J. Wiseman (ed.), *Peoples of Old Testament Times* (Oxford, 1973).

8. *AJA*, Vol. XLIII, No. 3, pp. 458ff.; Y. Aharoni, *op. cit.*, p. 219; W. F. Albright, *AASOR*, Vol. 4 (1924), p. 17.

Philistine-style dishes and bowl (Late Bronze Age, ca. 1600–1200 B.C.) found at Tell esh-Shari'ah (Gath?). (Israel Office of Information)

Israelites went down to the Philistines, to sharpen every man his share, and his coulter, and his ax, and his mattock (I Sam. 13:19, 20).

One object commonly found in excavated Philistine towns is the beer mug. This item was well known in the East at this time. Vessels large and small, equipped with side spouts and strainers, were commonly used for the barley beer which was the popular drink of the day. Professor Albright has observed that from the widespread occurrence of these vessels it is evident that the Philistines were "mighty carousers."[9] This picture is entirely in accord with the picture we have in Judges where we see Samson meeting his death at a Philistine feast where there was considerable drinking (Judg. 16:23–25).

According to the Bible, Samson met his death in a house where he was able, by his strength, to cause the two middle pillars to collapse and thus to bring about the destruction of the whole building. Excavations have shown that some of the large Philistine houses were built around a large central hall which was bisected by a row of pillars, used to support the upper story and the roof.[10]

The Philistines made considerable inroads into Palestine during the years 1200–1000 B.C. Finally they were able to overrun the whole land. At one stage they carried off the Ark of God from the little town of Shiloh. Excavation has shown that they did far more damage than merely to carry off the Ark. They burned the town to the ground at the same time. Shiloh was occupied again during the days of the kings but was later destroyed again. In the days of

9. *The Archaeology of Palestine*, p. 115.
10. *BA* (May, 1951), p. 44.

Jeremiah the ruins were still to be seen, and this prophet used them as a lesson to the people of Judah who were pinning their hopes of deliverance simply on the fact that the Temple of God stood in Jerusalem (Jer. 7:12–14).

Further evidence of the versatility of the Philistines is to be seen in their sea trade. It is clear from Egyptian records that some of the Philistine towns were engaging in a lively mercantile industry, exploiting the sea lanes between Egypt and Phoenicia. A fascinating story of the adventures of a certain Wen-Amon,[11] who was sent by the Pharaoh to buy timber from Phoenicia, gives us remarkable insight into the great activity in shipping along this coast at the time of the Judges. The Canaanites, too, were mixed up in this business. We have an important hint in the Bible that the Israelites, too, were engaged in some way in this traffic, although it seems certain that they were working with the Canaanites rather than with the Philistines:

> Gilead stayed beyond the Jordan; and Dan, why did he abide with the ships? Asher sat still at the coast of the sea, settling down by his landings (Judg. 5:17, RSV).

Groups of ships were under one control, suggestive of a mercantile organization.

In recent years the picture of the Philistines is slowly growing. Israeli archaeologists working in the old Philistine towns of southeast Palestine and in sites further north are beginning to fill out our knowledge of the Philistines in a remarkable way.

It is clear that there were substantial Philistine towns at Ashdod,[12] Askelon, Gaza, Bethshemesh, Tell Qasile,[13] Aphek, Tell Beit Mirsim, and Gezer. Surface surveys have been carried out over a wide area in such mounds, which carry Philistine-type pottery.[14] Attempts are still being made to identify the towns of Gath (Tell esh-Shari'ah?) and Ekron (Khirbet Muqenna). Traces of Philistine pottery have been found as far north as Bethshan and even in the northern Jordan River area east of Bethshan at Deir 'Alla (Succoth).[15] Thus, there was substantial Philistine occupation in the traditional Philistine towns. Elsewhere, along the Esdraelon Plain and into the northern Jordan plain there was at least some Philistine influence. There were also traces of the Philistine presence at places like Gezer and Tell Beit Mirsim in the lowland areas.

The general picture that emerges is that the Philistines were technically advanced and had obvious advantages over the Israelites. It is little wonder that they could press in and capture Shiloh (I Sam. 4), have a military post at

11. J. B. Pritchard, ANET, pp. 25–29.
12. A series of articles in IEJ in recent years has given preliminary reports. See also 'Atiqot, Vols. VII (1967—Ashdod I), IX–X (1971—Ashdod II and III).
13. Preliminary reports in IEJ, Vol. I (1950-1951), pp. 61–76, 125–140, 194–218.
14. G. E. Wright, op. cit., pp. 70–86.
15. H. J. Franken, VT, Vol. XIV (1964), pp. 377–379 and 417–422; PEQ, Vol. XCVI (1964), pp. 73–78.

The northern end of the Jordan River, in Upper Galilee. Mount Hermon is in the background. (Trans World Airlines)

Michmash (I Sam. 13–14), and finally defeat Saul in battle at Mt. Gilboa on the northern side of the plains of Esdraelon (I Sam. 29). It was to be the task of King David to throw them out of Israelite territory and confine them to the southwestern corner of Palestine.

THE CANAANITES

In the minds of many Bible readers the Canaanites constituted the main population of Palestine at the time of the Judges. They were indeed a very important element but by no means the only element in the population. The Bible refers to other groups, such as Amorites, Jebusites, and Hivites (Judg. 3:5). The Canaanites, however, were a highly cultured people and stood far in advance of Israel at the time.

When the incoming Israelites first met the Canaanites they destroyed many of their towns in a most ruthless fashion. An excellent lesson in comparative architecture is to be gained by setting the fine Canaanite town of Bethel, which the Israelites destroyed, alongside the towns which the Israelites subsequently built on the site. There were three such towns in the course of two centuries. W. F. Albright remarks that the change in culture is extraordinary. The new towns were quite rude in their construction in comparison with their Canaanite predecessors. Indeed, each phase of the new town deteriorated in construction. The third phase was by far the worst.[16]

This is not by any means an isolated case. There is an overall superiority of the Canaanite towns on the physical level. Such cities as Megiddo, Bethshan, and Salmonah in the north gave evidence of considerable wealth. Megiddo, for example, had a large and richly ornamented palace at the time. Although there was a degree of looting when it was finally destroyed, many fragments of what were once beautiful objects of gold, ivory, and alabaster remained strewn about the floors of the palace to gladden the hearts of the excavators.

There was, of course, a number of Canaanite towns that were not captured by the Israelites, as a study of Judges 1 will reveal. We have solid evidence to show that towns like Megiddo had no sign of the typical Israelite culture till well into the eleventh century.

The Canaanites, too, were engaged in trade by sea and, as we have seen, shared with the Philistines the export and import trade with Egypt. In the sphere of religion the Canaanites constituted a more serious menace to Israel. We know a great deal today about the religion of these people. The important documents which were found at Ras Shamra have given us a remarkable picture of the gods and goddesses, the temples and religious rituals, the hymns, prayers, and myths of the Canaanites. Many of their hymns were not unlike the later Psalms of Israel. The sacrifices offered in Canaanite temples resembled those which the Israelites offered to Yahweh, the God of Israel, in the names of the sacrifices and the beasts offered as well as in the ritual observed. But the religion was polytheistic and highly sensuous, with a strong emphasis on fertility rites. In the temples of the Canaanites there were male and female prostitutes ("sacred" men and women), and all sorts of sexual excesses were practiced. It was believed that in some way these rites caused the crops and the herds to prosper. Baal was the god who cared for the rain and the growth of the crops and the flocks. The goddess Asherah, the goddess of passion and the consort of Baal, was the inspiration of every form of passion whether in love or in war. Even during the days of the Judges the worship of these gods was finding favor in the eyes of many of the Israelites. The writer of the book of Judges makes the point that it was because Israel served the Baalim and forsook the Lord that they were delivered into the hands of oppressors (Judg. 2:11, 13, etc.).[17]

One of the outstanding contributions of the Canaanites in the realm of

16. BASOR, No. 56, pp. 11, 12.

17. A detailed account of the religion of Canaan is available in J. Gray, The Legacy of Canaan (1965, 2nd rev. ed.), VT Supp. V; H. Ringgren, Religions of the Ancient Near East (London, 1973), pp. 127–154.

Photograph and drawing of an ivory plaque (1350–1150 B.C.) from Megiddo showing a ruler receiving prisoners and tribute. The crowned woman before his throne hands him a lotus blossom; behind her are a woman playing the lyre, a soldier leading prisoners, a horse-drawn chariot and driver, and another soldier. (Oriental Institute, University of Chicago)

culture was that they were the real originators of the alphabet as a usable medium for writing. It was probably about 1700 B.C. when the first efforts were made to develop an alphabet. Flinders Petrie, the English archaeologist, found some of the earliest attempts at alphabetic writing at Serabit el Khadem in the Sinai peninsula.[18] Certainly by the time of the Judges this new form of writing was widely in use. The Canaanites, however, were versatile enough to be able to use several types of writing for their literature.[19] At Ras Shamra excavators found several scripts in use, including the cumbersome old Akkadian cuneiform (wedge-shaped) script which had been used in Lower Mesopotamia in the land of Akkad for the past two thousand years. An attempt to use a special type of cuneiform alphabet was one of the unusual experiments being tried here. A good deal of material was written in this type of script, even though it did not persist in later centuries.

18. W. F. Albright, *The Proto-Sinaitic Inscriptions and Their Decipherment*, Harvard Theological Studies, Vol. XXII (1966).
19. There is some question as to whether the people of Ras Shamra were really Canaanites. But, in any case, they showed the same cultural traditions, and an early text in the same cuneiform alphabet which was used at Ras Shamra has been found in Palestine at Bethshemesh.

The foundations of the Canaanite temple of the god Mekal (fourteenth century B.C.), the oldest of five temples discovered on the south flank of Bethshan (Tell el-Husn). The remains show the characteristics of both a temple and a high place. (University Museum, University of Pennsylvania)

The Canaanites, then, were a most dangerous group of enemies for Israel. Their clear superiority in art, in architecture, in trade, and in many other departments of life must have been most impressive to many of the Israelites. It is little wonder that some began to imagine that their superiority may have had a connection with their religion. This made it easier for some of the Israelites to accept the religion of Canaan.

From the point of view of military conquest Israel, as we have seen, did not succeed in taking all the Canaanite towns. The one major victory reported in the Bible came on the occasion when Deborah was able to urge the tribes of Israel to attack a Canaanite coalition in the north near the waters of Megiddo. Some scholars have seen in the information given in the Bible material for dating this event. The battle took place at "Taanach by the waters of Megiddo" (Judg. 5:19). It has been argued that the mention of Taanach in preference to Megiddo points to a period when Megiddo lay in ruins, but when Taanach was in existence. A date of about 1125 B.C. would fit the facts of archaeology and the facts of biblical history alike. After this battle the organized resistance of the Canaanites ceased, although many independent towns still remained to be captured by the Israelites.

One final feature of Canaanite life at the time of the Judges should be mentioned. Excavations have uncovered the important temple of Baal Berith,

Archaeological excavations at Tell esh-Shari'ah (Gath?) in the Lachish region. These foundations date from the Early Bronze Age (ca. 3200–2000 B.C.). (Israel Office of Information)

which stood at Shechem and which featured in the story of Abimelech, the son of Gideon (Judg. 9:4). The ruins of this temple produced evidence to show that it was used during the days of the Judges, although its original foundation goes back to an earlier date. It was a massive structure about twenty-five meters by twenty-one meters in size and was surrounded by a wall about five meters thick (nearly seventeen feet).[20] We can picture the sort of worship that went on there in view of the information to be found on the Ras Shamra texts.[21]

THE ARAMAEANS

The Aramaeans are rarely mentioned in the book of Judges. Yet they were to become a very significant group in later days. They are known in the English

---

20. W. F. Albright, *op. cit.*, p. 104; R. J. Bull, "A Re-examination of the Shechem Temple," BA (Dec., 1960), pp. 110–119; G. E. Wright, *Shechem, the Biography of a Biblical City* (London, 1965).
21. A good general review of the Canaanites is found in A. R. Millard, "The Canaanites," in D. J. Wiseman (ed.), *Peoples of Old Testament Times* (Oxford, 1973), pp. 29–52.

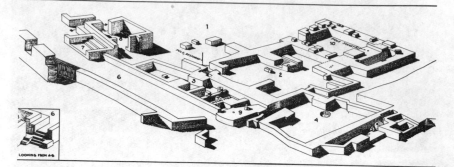

Perspective drawing of the temple of Mekal at Bethshan. It was dedicated by the Egyptian Pharaoh Thutmose III (1501–1447 B.C.) to that Canaanite god. (University Museum, University of Pennsylvania)

Bible as Syrians. From the days of King David onward they were a continual menace to the state of Israel.

Their origin has become clearer to us in recent times.[22] Already in about 1900 B.C. they were known in Lower Mesopotamia. In the centuries that followed they were moving toward the west and finding new homes for themselves in the general area we know today as Syria. The tablet records refer to them in the centuries before the period of the Judges. By 1300 B.C. they were well settled just to the northeast of the land of Canaan. It was one of their kings who invaded Palestine early in the days of the Judges. He is known in the Bible as Chushan Rishathaim (Judg. 3:8, 10).[23] This individual remains somewhat of a mystery. The date of this campaign was about 1200 B.C., but his incursion into Palestine was a foretaste of many later Aramaean (Syrian) incursions from the days of David onward. This group of people set up numerous small city states, many of which are known in the Bible, such as Zobah, Beth-Rehob, Tob, Maacah (II Sam. 8:3; 10:6–8), Damascus, and Hamath. Aramaean kings such as Hazael, Ben-Hadad, and Rezin are known in the books of Kings. The language of these people, Aramaic, became the *lingua franca* of the East in later days.[24]

22. A. Dupont-Sommer, *Les Araméens* (Paris, 1949); "Sur les debuts de l'histoire araméene," *VT Supp. I* (1953), pp. 40–49; A. Malamar, "The Aramaeans," in D. J. Wiseman, *Peoples of Old Testament Times*, pp. 134–155.

23. A. Malamat, "Chushan Rishathaim and the Decline of the Near East Around 1200 B.C.," *JNES* (Oct., 1954).

24. It is of some interest that in Genesis 31:47 the stone of witness between Jacob and Laban the Aramaean was called Galeed in Hebrew and Jegar-Sahadutha in Aramaic.

THE NOMADIC GROUPS

Not only were the Israelites troubled by more or less settled groups like the Canaanites, the Philistines, the Moabites, the Edomites, and the Ammonites, but nomadic groups made raiding excursions into the land in search of food (Judg. 6:5; 7:12, etc.). An interesting feature of these raids was the presence of camels among the nomads. Interesting material has come to light in recent years about the domestic use of the camel in the East from about 1200 B.C. onward. The camel, by no means unknown in previous centuries but used only spasmodically, now came to be widely used as a beast of burden.[25] There are increasing references to camels in the literature of the East after 1200 B.C. The picture of the desert nomads, Midianites, Amalekites, and the Children of the East using camels to conduct raids into Israelite lands in order to carry off crops and flocks seems to be entirely in accord with the picture we have from archaeology (Judg. 6:5; 7:12, etc.).

Much uncertainty surrounds the precise nature of these nomadic groups—Midianites, Amalekites, and Easterners (Sons of Qedem). It is widely agreed that the land of Midian was in northwest Arabia on the eastern shore of the Gulf of Aqabah. From this area they could penetrate into Sinai (Num. 10:29), Moab (Gen. 36:35), the eastern deserts in the area of Moab and Ammon (Judg. 7:25; 8:18-19), and even into the Jordan valley (Num. 25:6-7; 31:2-3) and Canaan (Judg. 6:1-6, 33; 7:1). They seem to be unknown archaeologically.[26]

The Amalekites seem to have ranged the desolate wastes from Sinai and the Negeb region into the Arabah south of the Dead Sea and east into Arabia. Archaeological excavations have thrown no light on them.[27]

We have a little information archaeologically about the Sons of the East, or Qedemites, from early texts which refer to the land of Qedem. An Egyptian fugitive from the king, named Sinuhe, found refuge for a time in the land of Qedem, which seems to have lain to the east of Palestine and then was taken up by a certain Ammi-enshi, a local ruler who placed him in charge of one of his districts. The fugitive referred to a certain Maki, ruler of Qedem, whom he gave as a referee concerning his conduct. The date of these events is during the reign of the pharaoh Sen-Usert I (ca. 1971-1929 B.C.). Evidently the Qedemites were known some seven hundred years before the Judges story.[28]

Incidentally, we may have some idea of the type of "pitcher" used by Gideon since the discovery in a tomb near Amman in Transjordan of a peculiar

---

25. W. F. Albright, *The Biblical Period* (Oxford, 1950), p. 21; J. P. Free, *JNES*, Vol. III (1944), pp. 187-193; R. W. Bulliet, *The Camel and the Wheel* (Cambridge, Mass., 1975), ch. 2, pp. 28-56, argues that camel domestication in some form got under way between 3000 and 2500 B.C.
26. See G. M. Landes, "Midian" in *IDB*, Vol. 3, pp. 375f.
27. G. M. Landes, "Amalek" in *IDB*, Vol. 1, pp. 101f.
28. J. B. Pritchard, *ANET*, pp. 18-22; Y. Aharoni, *op. cit.*, pp. 130f.

vessel with a handle, standing about ten inches high with an opening in the side about five inches by four inches. A small platform inside was used to support the typical open lamp of the day.[29]

THE TRANSJORDAN KINGDOMS

There were several newly emerged kingdoms in Transjordan in the days of the Judges, including Edom, Moab, Ammon, and the Amorite kingdoms of Sihon and Og. Israel had occupied the lands of the Amorites (Num. 21:21-35) but bypassed Edom, Moab, and Ammon (Judg. 11:13-28). However, in the days of the Judges areas of Israel were invaded by the Moabites (Judg. 3:12-30) and the Ammonites (Judg. 10:6-11:40). There is no mention of an invasion by the Edomites at that time, although this was to come in later years.

Archaeological investigation has provided important evidence about the emergence and development of these Transjordan kingdoms.

During the Middle Bronze and Late Bronze Ages settlement in Transjordan was largely non-urban. A renewal of sedentary occupation began at the end of the Late Bronze Age (thirteenth century) and continued therafter into the Iron Age. At the present time our evidence is very incomplete because of the comparative lack of excavation in these areas, so that the picture that we can give is far from complete. Nevertheless in the area of Ammon a Late Bronze–Iron I cemetery was discovered at Tell es-Sa'idiyeh,[30] a Late Bronze temple at Tell deir 'Alla, a Late Bronze building at Amman, and several Late Bronze–Iron I Age sites between the Yarmuk River and the Jabbok River. In the area of Moab several Late Bronze sites have been discovered between the Wadi Jabbok and the Wadi el-Hesa. In the area of Edom the existence of Late Bronze sites has yet to be demonstrated.

Archaeological evidence therefore points to the emergence of both Moab and Ammon in the Late Bronze Age during the thirteenth century. By the Iron I Age the emergence of these kingdoms had been established, and at the time of the Judges (ca. 1200-1050 B.C.) such people as Eglon the Moabite (Judg. 3:12-14) and the king of the Ammonites (Judg. 11:12) were ruling over well-established kingdoms in Transjordan.[31]

THE PLIGHT OF ISRAEL AND THE NEED FOR UNITY

Sufficient has now been said to make it clear that the picture in the book of Judges is greatly enlarged by our latest archaeological evidence. It becomes quite

29. *Quarterly Department of Antiquities, Palestine,* Vol. XI, Nos. 3, 4, Plate 17.
30. J. B. Pritchard, "Excavations at Tell es-Sa'idiyeh," *Annual of the Department of Antiquities of Jordan,* Vol. VIII (1964), pp. 95-98; *Archaeology,* Vol. XIX (1966), pp. 289f.; "The First Excavations at Tell es-Sa'idiyeh," *BA,* Vol. XXVIII (Feb., 1965), pp. 10-17.
31. See J. R. Bartlett, "The Moabites and the Edomites," in D. J. Wiseman (ed.), *Peoples of Old Testament Times,* pp. 229-258, for a useful general discussion.

clear that the general historical, geographical, cultural, and religious backgrounds of the book are consistent with the general Palestinian setting for the
period 1200–1000 B.C.

It might be well to recall, even if only in outline, that Israel's plight at the
time was serious indeed. She was, in the first place, torn by disunity. The
geographical problems were great. In these days of fast transport we do not
realize how difficult it was for the various tribal groups to maintain any sort of
cohesion. Imagine the difficulty of maintaining contact between the tribe of
Reuben in Transjordan, the tribe of Dan in the southwest, and the tribe of
Asher in the north when it involved traveling long distances on foot or by
slow-moving animals over unmade roads along the hilly terrain of Palestine.
Local disturbances could get quite out of hand before other tribal groups would
know of the trouble. Misunderstandings would easily arise, and did arise, as we
see in such incidents as the schismatic altar of Reuben and Gad (Josh. 22), or
the jealousy of Ephraim when she was not included in the force that Gideon
took to drive out the Midianites and their allies (Judg. 8). Further evidence of
intertribal misunderstandings and actual clashes is to be seen in the story of the
massacre of the men of Benjamin by men from the surrounding tribes after the
concubine of the Levite who stayed overnight at Gibeah had been cruelly killed
(Judg. 19).

There was another serious factor causing disunity during these years. This
was the tendency for many to follow the religion of the Canaanites. This declen-
sion of the Israelites may have been due in part to the subtle attraction of the
wealth of the Canaanites. They had fine homes, splendid art, a fine literature,
good trade connections around the East, and an apparent superiority in every
way over the people of Israel. The unthinking Israelite may have been inclined
to associate this wealth with some imagined favor of the gods of Canaan, and as
a result he may have forsaken the simpler nonsensuous faith of Israel. Once there
was religious apostasy in some areas, there was the possibility of serious disunity.
This undoubtedly took place.

The forces for disintegration were thus very strong indeed. There was, as
W. F. Albright points out, a strong centrifugal tendency, which was only increased
by the assaults of Israel's hostile foes on every hand.[32] For not only did those
enemies attack the tribes in isolated areas, but they compelled some of them to
leave their homes in order to find new safe areas in which to live. The tribe of
Dan is a case in point (Judg. 18:1ff.).

Throughout the land, both east and west of Jordan, there were aggressive
moves from surrounding peoples. It was indeed a day when "every man did *that
which was* right in his own eyes" (Judg. 17:6). This descriptive phrase, applied to
the Israelites themselves, characterized the whole political condition of the land
at this time.

---

32. W. F. Albright, *The Biblical Period*, p. 19.

As against these disruptive forces, however, there were some unifying forces. The people of Israel possessed, after all, a common language, common customs, a common religion and loyalty to Yahweh, and a common Mosaic tradition of law. Moreover, despite apostasy, there was a central sanctuary at Shiloh which must have exercised some sort of cohesive force. What Israel needed was a great leader who would command the respect of all the tribes, and who would unite Israel's resources of manpower in order to throw off her aggressors. It was left to the last judge, Samuel, to gather together the national hopes for a king and to focus these on Saul, who emerged as Israel's first monarch.

6

ONE NATION—ONE KING

Before Israel finally reached the stage where she was able to choose a king who would be acceptable to all the tribes at once, there were a number of experiments in kingship. Perhaps the best known of these was the attempt of the tribes to make Gideon king after his success in beating off the marauding nomadic groups. On his return home the men of Israel said, "Rule thou over us, both thou, and thy son, and thy son's son also." Gideon was unwilling to undertake such a responsibility and said, "I will not rule over you, neither shall my son rule over you: the Lord shall rule over you" (Judg. 8:22, 23).

A second abortive attempt at kingship was that of Gideon's son Abimelech, who conspired with the Canaanites of Shechem (Judg. 9:6ff.). He had all his brothers put to death, except the one who escaped, and after a short-lived rule he was killed when a woman dropped a millstone on his head while he was attacking the besieged city of Thebez.

ARCHAEOLOGY AND THE DAYS OF KING SAUL

It was in the days of the Judge Samuel that general agreement among the tribes was obtained. The need for a king had become quite clear in the minds of the people and they began to cry out for a king "like all the nations" (I Sam. 8:5). At first Samuel seemed to be unwilling to agree to their request, realizing, no doubt, that the people had a wrong motive. They wanted a king at all costs. What they needed was a ruler who would recognize that God was their Sovereign and that any other ruler should be but the vice-regent of God. Israel was essentially a theocracy whose kings needed to be men after God's own heart. After a time,

Samuel was able to choose Saul the son of Kish, a man Israel needed. Saul was indeed God's choice. In due course Saul was anointed and was able to demonstrate both his physical prowess and his spiritual qualities. In his defeat of the Ammonite king at Jabesh Gilead (I Sam. 11), he showed that he could lead men in battle. In his sharing the experience of the prophets (I Sam. 10) he showed a heart willing to yield to the influences of God's Spirit. He was accordingly acclaimed king and widely accepted by the people.

Saul's life was one long struggle against the hostile neighbors that surrounded Israel. As we read the story of his life in the first book of Samuel we trace the steps of a life which began with promise and ended in tragedy. There were several serious acts of rebellion against God. Many of his actions earned the contempt and keen opposition of the best men in Israel. Finally he met his death by falling on his sword after the battle of Mount Gilboa in which the Philistines defeated the army of Israel (I Sam. 31).

Archaeological research has given us some useful light on certain aspects of the story recounted in the book of Samuel. His chief opponents, the Philistines, are now more clearly delineated for us after the many excavations in the Philistine plains. There is no need to repeat the detail given in the previous chapter. We can, however, add a note to the Philistine story as it touches on the last part of the story of Saul. When Saul died after that tragic battle at Mount Gilboa, the Philistines desecrated his body, which they found lying where it fell. His head was cut off and placed in "the temple of Dagon," his armor was taken to "the house of Ashtaroth" in Bethshan, and his body was fastened to the wall of the same city.[1] We can be fairly certain that one of the two temples excavated at Bethshan during the years 1921 to 1933 by C. S. Fisher, Alan Rowe, and G. M. Fitzgerald was this actual temple. Here were typical temples of the day where the cult of the gods of Canaan was carried out. Numerous items of religious significance were found in these temples. Which of the two temples was the one referred to in the story is, of course, impossible to say. It is now quite clear, however, that there was a temple in Bethshan at the time.

The most important single item of archaeological interest is the fortress of Gibeah, which was excavated by W. F. Albright.[2] It was the second occupation at Gibeah and replaced the little town that had been destroyed by fire in the days of the Judges (Judg. 19, 20). After the destruction of the first town the site remained unoccupied for about a century. It was succeeded by this little fortress, which probably served as Saul's headquarters during the Philistine wars. It was larger than the subsequent fortress which eventually rose on its ruins.[3] It was not a luxurious place, although it was marked by a "certain measure of rustic lux-

1. I Samuel 31:9, 10; I Chronicles 10:9, 10.
2. W. F. Albright, *Archaeology of Palestine* (London, 1954), pp. 120–122; P. W. Lapp, "Tell el-Fûl," *BA*, Vol. XXVIII, No. 1 (Feb., 1965), pp. 2–10.
3. See above, p. 82, n. 3.

*Northwest corner of the fortress
dating from the time of Saul at
Gibeah (Tell el-Fûl), a site ca.
five and a half kilometers north
of Jerusalem. (Paul W. Lapp)*

ury."[4] It was a two-story building and contained a variety of pottery vessels, including a number of large cooking pots, and an iron plough point which suggested that some sort of agriculture was carried on in the area. W. F. Albright proposed a very neat square fortress with towers at each corner for Saul's fortress, which stood from about 1025 B.C. to 950 B.C. More recent work at Gibeah, the modern Tel el-Fûl, has confirmed only one tower at the southwest corner. In fact the whole area has not been excavated.[5]

But there are some other items of interest on which archaeology has shed light. It would appear from a study of biblical texts in Samuel and Chronicles that the extent of Saul's domains took in the central highlands from about a line reaching west from the bottom end of the Dead Sea, along the foothills skirting the Philistine areas, the hill country of Galilee, and the area of Gilead in Transjordan southward to the River Arnon.[6] Surface surveys in much of this region have revealed sites of the Iron I Age which included Saul's lifetime (the last decades of the eleventh century). Towns mentioned in Judges 1 remained in

4. *AASOR*, Vol. IV, pp. 51f.
5. P. W. Lapp, *op. cit.*, pp. 2–10.
6. See Y. Aharoni, *The Land of the Bible* (London, 1966), Map 20, p. 256.

Canaanite hands. Excavations at Tirzah (Tell el-Far'ah), Bethel, Ai, Gibeon, Beer-sheba, and other towns have revealed that these towns were occupied at the time. If we take the year 1000 B.C. as marking the end of Saul's reign, it is now possible to say that after the initial settlement the Israelites were already living in many urban situations by that time. There was already some industry at Gibeon,[7] as well as private houses. At Tirzah, immediately above the ruins of the Late Bronze Age, houses appeared which stood in an orderly fashion along well-marked streets.[8] There was a town at Bethel to which Samuel went on circuit (I Sam. 7:16). This town survived and grew in later centuries. We have referred already to Gibeah where a small village was founded in the twelfth century and where Saul had a small fortress. Jerusalem was occupied by a Canaanite enclave known as the Jebusites. The village Izbet Sartah on the road from Aphek to Shiloh was founded in the twelfth century B.C. Here three occupational strata covered the period 1200 to 1000 B.C. It was destroyed about Saul's time, perhaps by the Philistines. As we have seen, excavations here produced the remains of houses and an ostracon on which the alphabet was written. The site of Ai to which we referred earlier is also of some interest. There was some sort of occupation there in the period 1050–1000 B.C. Evidently the settlers used the ruins of the old Bronze Age city to reconstruct simple houses. No attempt was made to restore the former fortress, however. Pottery of the Iron I period lay among the ruins of this occupation period.[9] Shiloh (I Sam. 1–4), too, was occupied in Saul's time. A fine house some four meters by three meters was discovered, as well as several stone jars with a collar rim, typical of the age. The house was destroyed along with other parts of the city in the second half of the eleventh century.[10]

The town of Beer-sheba, represented today by Tell Sheba on the outskirts of Beer-sheba, was settled in the days of the Judges about 1200 B.C. as an unwalled settlement, to judge from pottery discovered in one area. Its fortification did not begin till David's time when it was surrounded by a solid wall.[11]

Some eight miles east of Beer-sheba lies Tell Masos where there was an early Israelite settlement from the thirteenth to the eleventh centuries B.C. Several four-room houses with vertical pillars to support the roof were brought to light. The settlement was quite large for the times and covered the days of the Judges down to Saul's time. Nearby lay the ruins of a fortress of the days of the Kings. These sites provide only a glimpse into the state of affairs in Saul's day. With the coming of David there was something of an upsurge in building activity in Israel.

7. J. B. Pritchard, "Industry and Trade at Biblical Gibeon," BA (Feb., 1960), pp. 23–29.

8. R. de Vaux, "Tirzah," in D. W. Thomas (ed.), Archaeology and Old Testament Study (Oxford, 1969), p. 376.

9. J. A. Callaway, "The 1964 Ai (et Tell) Excavations," BASOR, No. 178 (1965), pp. 38–40.

10. A. Kempinski, EAEHL, Vol. IV (1978), pp. 1098–1100.

11. Y. Aharoni (ed.), Beersheba I (1973).

DAVID, ISRAEL'S GREATEST KING

Bible history relates how David had to flee from Saul and find a home among the Philistines (I Sam. 27). It seems that David became a sort of vassal of these enemies of Israel. When Saul was killed in battle, David was allowed to become king in Hebron (II Sam. 2:1–4), while Saul's son fled across the Jordan and became king in Mahanaim (II Sam. 2:8). From the Philistine point of view it was probably a desirable thing to have two kings ruling over Israel. "Divide and conquer" is an old principle. The arrangement was, however, short-lived. After seven years the two parts of the kingdom were re-united and David became king over all Israel (II Sam. 5). Although he was forced back by the Philistines to his fortress (II Sam. 5:17), he was able eventually to fight his way out and deliver his whole nation as well.

David's life was filled with a number of magnificent achievements. On every side he was able to push back Israel's enemies. Philistines, Moabites, Edomites, Aramaeans, Ammonites—all suffered at his hands (I Sam. 5, 8, 10, etc.). At his death, David left a kingdom at peace from her foes. In addition to these military achievements there were remarkable advances in the spheres of government, commerce and trade, religion, and international affairs. The whole organization of government was undertaken in a workmanlike fashion. Officers were appointed over the several departments of state (I Chron. 27:25–34). Trade connections were made with the Phoenicians and perhaps with others. In matters of religion the Temple services were organized and the music of the Temple was arranged. It was one of David's greatest hopes to build the Temple, but he was denied this privilege (I Sam. 7). It was left to his son Solomon to complete the task according to the pattern of his father David. One of David's greatest achievements, however, was the setting up of Jerusalem as the national capital. But it had to be captured from the Jebusites (I Sam. 5). There was shrewd design in choosing this site, for it lay outside the borders of Judah, and therefore a member of the tribe of Judah could not be accused of partisanship in the choice of a site for his capital. The place was, moreover, strategically placed in the central hill country, and rather inaccessible to an invading foe. It was in all probability a place which had honored associations with Abraham.

Excavations at sites in the general southeastern areas of Palestine have revealed several towns with a well-known type of fortification, the so-called casemate walls, which are really two comparatively thin walls braced across by transverse walls and giving the appearance of great solidity. These date to about the start of the tenth century B.C. and can be attributed either to Saul or to David.[12] The biblical picture would seem to suggest David rather than Saul, since Saul was far too busy with his enemies to be able to devote his energies to building. The sites are strategically placed in regard to the Philistines. There is

12. W. F. Albright, *op. cit.*, p. 122.

nothing at all surprising in the fact that David should feel it necessary to undertake some sort of fortification against the Philistines in this area. Such a system would provide some check on their inroads.

One of the clearest pictures we have of David in the biblical record is that of musician and organizer of the Temple music (I Chron. 25). It is now clear that Palestine was well known around the East for many centuries as a land where music was widely enjoyed. As early as 1900 B.C. Egyptian artists painted Palestinian nomads who visited their land with asses and goods for trade.[13] Among the people pictured were some who carried stringed instruments like harps. Egyptian monuments of the New Empire from about 1550 onward refer to a variety of types of music from the land of Canaan.[14] The Ras Shamra texts from Ugarit, the famous Canaanite town on the mainland opposite Cyprus, have produced an abundance of religious poetry and a number of references to a class of temple personnel known as *sarim*.[15] These appear to have been more or less similar to the Hebrew "singers" of the days of David and after. Later records of the Assyrians also refer to considerable musical activity in this land.

Further evidence is probably to be obtained from a study of the names of some of the men employed by David in this service. At least some of these have Canaanite names,[16] and others are said to have been "aboriginals"[17] of the land. It is legitimate to think that David compelled some of the local inhabitants to serve him in the capacity of musicians in much the same way that he forced other conquered people to do other work.

The tantalizing reference to the capture of Jerusalem in II Samuel 5:6–8 speaks of David's men reaching the gutter (water shaft). David said on that day, "Whosoever getteth up to the gutter, and smiteth the Jebusites . . . *shall be chief and captain*" (II Sam. 5:8). The translation of the Hebrew word here is open to various interpretations. If the reference is to some kind of water tunnel we may find an explanation in the wonderful water systems of the Canaanites. At a variety of places in Palestine underground tunnels, which enabled the people to take water into the city, have been brought to light. The best of these was that at Megiddo. We may imagine that the Jebusites of Jerusalem exploited a similar kind of arrangement. What was necessary for David's men was to find the entrance to this water tunnel, enter it, slay its defenders, and then wait there till other people from the town came for their water. By eliminating them one by one the final surrender of the town through thirst was assured.

There is, however, one other possibility. W. F. Albright translates the word gutter as "hook" by comparison with a similar word used by the Assyrians.[18] He

13. On the Beni Hasan wall paintings, see p. 24. See also W. F. Albright, *op. cit.*, p. 209.
14. W. F. Albright, *Archaeology and the Religion of Israel*, p. 125.
15. C. H. Gordon, *Ugaritic Manual*, Vol. III (Rome, 1955), p. 327.
16. W. F. Albright, *Archaeology and the Religion of Israel*, p. 127.
17. Hebrew *ezrah*: aboriginal (I Kings 4:31; I Chron. 2:6).
18. W. F. Albright, "The Old Testament and Archaeology," in H. C. Alleman and E. E. Flack (eds.), *Old Testament Commentary* (Philadelphia, 1954), p. 149.

Spring Gihon in the Kidron Valley of Jerusalem may have derived its name from the Hebrew word for "gush," because it gushes for forty minutes every six to eight hours. It still supplies water for part of the region. David used the Gihon passage to capture Jerusalem from the Jebusites, and Hezekiah diverted the spring to protect the city's water from the Assyrians. Beyond Gihon in this picture is the eastern entrance of Hezekiah's tunnel. (Garo Nalbandian)

imagines the use of some kind of climbing apparatus whereby hooks were used to grasp the wall. He translates the sentence: "Whoever getteth up with the hook and smiteth the Jebusites." In that case the capture of Jerusalem was by quite a different method. Whatever the method, the stronghold of the Jebusites was at last taken. The method by which it was captured is probably one of those secrets which must be left to the archaeologist to explain as his knowledge of ancient methods of warfare is enlarged.

If we date David's reign about 1000–960 B.C. we have already moved into the early decades of the archaeological period Iron II A (1050–900 B.C.).

Interesting evidence comes from Gibeon, now known as El-jib. It was excavated in the years 1956 to 1962 by J. B. Pritchard. It is clear that Gibeon

Gibeon, a city ca. *ten kilometers north of Jerusalem, produced and exported much wine in the eighth and seventh centuries B.C. Excavations there have revealed wine cellars, wine presses, fermentation tanks, and jars of various sizes. This handle, inscribed gb'n ("Gibeon") gdr, is from a jar for exported wine. (University Museum, University of Pennsylvania)*

was a thriving town during the Iron I and Iron II periods. In the course of the excavation, one of those things happened that every archaeologist hopes for. Inscribed materials in the form of Hebrew writing on the handles of large jars gave the exact name of the place as *gb'n,* that is, Gibeon.[19] These jar handles were found among the debris in a very large pool excavated into the native rock inside the north wall of the city. The pool was 11.3 meters in diameter and 10.8 meters deep and was in use from shortly after 1200 B.C., it would seem. It was therefore there in David's time. The excavator has suggested that this is the pool referred to in II Samuel 2:12–17 where the servants of David and the servants of Ish-bosheth, Saul's son, met and did battle.

The site of Tell Qasile overlooking the River Yarkon on the northern outskirts of modern Tel Aviv, which was once in the hands of the Philistines, probably fell into the hands of the Israelites in David's time. The Israelites built on the ruins of the Philistine city at the start of the tenth century. The site remained continuously in Israelite hands during the days of the Kings, as a variety of Hebrew inscriptions testifies.[20]

During David's time the town of Beer-sheba, a mere unwalled settlement in

19. J. B. Pritchard, *BA* (Dec., 1956), pp. 66–75; *Illustrated London News* (Oct., 1956), pp. 695–697; (March, 1958), pp. 505–507; *VT Supp. VII* (1960), pp. 1–12.
20. A. Mazar, "Qasile, Tell," *EAEHL,* Vol. VI (1978), pp. 963–975.

the days of the Judges, became a walled city and was surrounded by a solid wall some four meters thick with offsets during the tenth century B.C. A fine gateway flanked on either side by two guardrooms and a tower lay on the south side of the city. In an open square near the gate a platform (or *bamah*) was found, with a carefully constructed incense altar next to it (cf. II Kings 23:8f.). A similar cultic platform was found at the fortified town of Dan in the far north of the land, giving rise to the suggestion that Dan and Beer-sheba marked administrative limits of the land at the time. Hence the biblical phrase "from Dan to Beer-sheba."[21]

Some of the larger Canaanite towns which resisted the Israelites in the days of the Judges and Saul (Judg. 1:27-33) seem to have fallen to the Israelites in the days of David. Bethshan was still in the hands of the Canaanites during the eleventh century, although it may have been Solomon's time before the Israelites took over. When that happened, substantial buildings were replaced by the poor constructions of Level IV.

The town of Tirza (Tell el-Far'ah) seems to have been occupied by the Israelites in the tenth century B.C. Gezer was certainly an Israelite town in Solomon's day (I Kings 9:15-17), and does not seem to have been taken by David.[22] Hazor was an unfortified town in David's day. Lachish, for which there are no biblical references between the days of Joshua and those of Rehoboam, accords with the apparent lack of building activity on the mound between the twelfth and tenth centuries B.C. Megiddo remained in Canaanite hands till about the end of the eleventh century. Finally, in David's time, the city was occupied by the Israelites. The relatively haphazard construction of the houses and the absence of fortifications suggest that it was settled by the Israelites before they began the careful planning of the important royal cities which were a feature of the days of the Kings. Beginning with David and continuing on into Solomon's day Megiddo was rebuilt in a grand way.

THE ACHIEVEMENTS OF SOLOMON

Archaeological discoveries relating to Solomon's time are quite remarkable. Professor Albright has observed in his useful volume on the archaeology of Palestine that "the age of Solomon was certainly one of the most flourishing periods in the history of Palestine. Archaeology, after a long silence, has finally corroborated Biblical tradition in no uncertain way."[23]

Solomon entered on the marvelous inheritance left to him by his father David. It lay in his hands to make a great nation out of the now united tribes. At first he succeeded in a measure. By the end of his life he had ruined his work and

21. Y. Aharoni, "Beersheba, Tel," *EAEHL*, Vol. I (1975), pp. 162-164.
22. W. G. Dever, "Gezer," *EAEHL*, Vol. II, pp. 428-443.
23. W. F. Albright, *The Archaeology of Palestine*, p. 123.

allowed the growth of such serious discontent that shortly after his death the whole structure which had been built up so carefully by David came tumbling down.

At the time when Solomon ruled over Israel, Phoenicia was one of the greatest powers in the East. Its people, who represented the northern section of the Canaanites, had by now given up military ambitions and were concentrating on trade. The Phoenicians were excellent technicians and were evidently in great demand all around the East, to judge by the widespread occurrence of clearly Phoenician influences in art and architecture in all the surrounding countries. The Bible makes it clear that Solomon availed himself of the skills that these Phoenician tradesmen were ready to offer to anyone who was able and willing to pay. Hence, in building, in metal working, in shipbuilding, in the manning of ships, and indeed in many other ways the influence of these people became important during the days of Solomon.

A study of the description of the Temple and of the art work used in it in I Kings 6 and 7 will reveal many remarkable resemblances between the work of the Phoenicians and the artistry in the Temple. Chapter 6 makes a special reference to the woodwork which lined the Temple. It was largely cedar which had been imported from the king of Tyre (I Kings 5:10). Solomon used a great deal of this cedar to build the house of the Lord (I Kings 6:9, 10, etc.). Woodworkers carved cherubim, palm trees, open flowers, and the like (I Kings 6:29, etc.) into cedar boards. A similar picture is given in the case of the metalwork as described for us in chapter 7. The details here are a good

A view of Mount Zion in Jerusalem (left), the religious and national center of the kingdom of David and Solomon. The alleged tomb of King David is close to the prominent belfry of the Benedictine Church of the Dormition. (Israel Office of Information)

deal more complete. The copper used in the various items was fashioned into the same kinds of patterns. Reference is made to cherubim, lions, oxen, palm trees, pomegranates, network, flowers of lilies, and so on (I Kings 7:18, 26, 29, 36, etc.). Now a study of the motifs used in the Phoenician ivory inlay work, which has been discovered in many ancient sites excavated in recent decades, will make it quite clear even to the non-technical reader that the motifs used in both the woodwork and the metalwork of Solomon's Temple were strongly influenced by Phoenician patterns. This is to be expected since there is specific reference in the Bible to the employment of Phoenician tradesmen in each case.

In the matter of the architecture of Solomon's buildings we have some interesting material from modern excavations. Perhaps the most striking fact that has emerged is that the whole pattern of the Temple of Solomon is very close to that of other temples in the East at this time. The idea of two main parts in the Temple, a holy place and a most holy place, although it follows the arrangement of the ancient Tabernacle in the wilderness, can be paralleled in a number of places.[24] Even the two big, free-standing pillars in Solomon's Temple referred to as Jachin and Boaz have their parallels in the temples of the East. It seems clear that Solomon relied in part on the Phoenician architects in the actual design of the Temple. Even if Solomon's Temple followed in a general way the ancient Tabernacle model, the working out of these details in an actual Temple seems to have followed patterns that were fairly usual all around the East at the time.

According to I Kings 7:12, the court around one of the houses Solomon built "had three courses of hewn stones, and a course of cedar beams; like as the inner court of the house of Jehovah, and the porch of the house." In the great excavation at Megiddo, carried out during the years 1925 to 1939, precisely this arrangement was found in the town that was there in Solomon's day. It was commented on at the time by R. S. Lamon and G. M. Shipton, the excavators. In describing a certain building they wrote:

> One feature of the building . . . is that the piers of its podium consist of three rows of hewed stones. Wherever the third course was preserved, the upper surface was burned black, and therefore some combustible material, presumably wood, must have overlain the stones. On the floor of the courtyard, near the northwest corner of the building, there was found a large piece of wood charcoal in a deposit of ash which lay along the west wall of the building and which, when analysed, proved to be that of cedar. In addition to indications of timber above stonework there were still to be seen lying on top of the podium walls sufficient remains of mud brick to show that this material too entered into the composition of the superstructure. This evidence accords well with the type of construction in Solomon's temple in Jerusalem as described in I Kings 7:12.[25]

24. G. E. Wright and F. V. Filson, *The Westminster Historical Atlas* (London, 1953), p. 48.
25. R. S. Lamon and G. M. Shipton, *Megiddo I* (Chicago, 1939), p. 59.

The occurrence of the so-called proto-Ionic capitals in the buildings of Solomon's time, and for that matter in later buildings as well, is a further indication of the strong influence of the Phoenicians at the time.[26] The use of wood in the interior of the Temple of Solomon can be compared with the contemporary usage of wood in several structures in the area of Syria.

During his lifetime Solomon strengthened Israel's army. In particular he built up a considerable force of chariots. These were concentrated at strategic points where chariot cities were built and where horsemen were trained (I Kings 4:26; 10:26–29, etc.).

It was proposed by P. L. O. Guy, one of the excavators of Megiddo, that the nature of Solomon's chariot cities had become much clearer since the excavation of that city.[27] He discovered many units in a complex group of buildings each of which consisted of a central passage about three meters wide, flanked by two rows of stone pillars which seem to have served both as tie-posts and as supports for the roof. Behind each row of posts was an area of some three meters wide for the horses. Each unit accommodated about thirty horses. Similar groups of "stable" units are known at Taanach, Hazor, Tel el-Ḥesi (Eglon?), and Gezer. More recent research[28] has shown beyond any doubt that the ruins discovered by P. L. O. Guy overlay Solomonic material so that the "stables" at Megiddo must be attributed to Ahab. However, the "stables" of Solomon's day were no doubt very similar in appearance and may even have stood in the same area.

More recently there have arisen some doubts as to whether these structures were stables at all. Rooms with pillars down the center have been found at other places: among them Hazor, Tell Sheba, Bethshemesh, Tell Beit Mirsim, and Tell en Nasbeh. It would be difficult in some of these cases to think in terms of stables. The view that these structures were storehouses rather than stables is now generally accepted. Professor Yadin in his excavations at Hazor has concluded that the large "pillared building" of Solomon's period was "nothing less than a royal storehouse."[29] More recently, excavations at Tell Sheba,[30] a Solomonic town on the outskirts of Beer-sheba, have uncovered a similar pillared room with a beaten earth floor in the center and paved stone floors on either side, as at Megiddo and Hazor. On the floors of the side rooms there was a variety of large pottery vessels, suggesting that the structure was a storeroom and not a stable. It is being argued that the central beaten earth passage was where the pack animals stood while the stores were being unloaded into the storerooms. The so-called hitching posts and feed boxes at Megiddo were for the

26. W. F. Albright, *The Archaeology of Palestine*, pp. 126f.

27. *Ibid.*, pp. 123f. Cf. Y. Yadin, "Hazor Ruins," *IEJ*, Vol. 8 (1958), pp. 80–86.

28. Y. Yadin, "New Light on Solomon's Megiddo," *BA* (May, 1960), pp. 62–68.

29. Y. Yadin and others, *Hazor I, An Account of the First Season of Excavation, 1955* (Jerusalem, 1968), pp. 11–14; *Hazor II, An Account of the Second Season of Excavation, 1956* (Jerusalem, 1960), p. 9.

30. Y. Aharoni, "Beersheba, Tel," *EAEHL*, Vol. I, pp. 160–168; *Beersheba I: 1969–1971 Seasons* (1973).

These remains at Megiddo, Israel, were once thought to be the floors and hitching posts of Solomon's stables but are now dated from Ahab's time. Archaeologists now question whether the remains are stables at all, since structures like them unearthed at other sites have proved to be storehouses. See above discussion of "stables" and "storehouses." (Oriental Institute, University of Chicago)

animals who were tied up while they fed and were being unloaded. At Megiddo the large "water tank" served to water the animals. It has been pointed out that there is no specific reference in the Bible to the fact that Megiddo was a chariot city, nor indeed is any specific chariot city mentioned. Megiddo, Hazor, and Gezer are listed in I Kings 9:15 as towns that Solomon built, and I Kings 4:26 and 10:26 refer to Solomon's chariot forces. But I Kings 9:15 refers very generally to Solomon's "store cities," "the cities for his chariots," and "the cities for his horsemen," along with the towns he built—Jerusalem, Hazor, Megiddo, Gezer, Beth-horon, Baalath, and Tamar. It is possible that sometimes a store city was also a chariot city, but there is no specific statement about which store cities were also chariot cities. Until some literary or archaeological data are available to prove the point, the question must be left open.

This discussion provides an excellent illustration of the way in which the interpretation of archaeological finds needs to be kept flexible. Sometimes the first tentative explanations need to be modified in the light of later evidence and subsequent consideration of the data. The aim must always be to arrive at the true interpretation of the facts, or at least the most likely interpretation, in the light of all the evidence. In the present case the evidence seems to point strongly to the fact that these famous structures were after all not stables, but storehouses.

Solomon had to import horses from other lands. According to I Kings, 10:28, 29, Solomon obtained his horses from Egypt. This passage in the Authorized Version of the Bible has an odd ring about it: "And Solomon had horses brought out of Egypt and linen yarn" (I Kings 10:26). The word for "linen yarn" might well mean "from QWH," where QWH refers to a country. At the time of the translation of the Authorized Version of the English Bible such a land was unknown, but today we translate this passage rather differently in the light of our discovery of the ancient land of Que (QWH), which lay in the area of Asia Minor at the time of Solomon. The Hebrew of the passage can now be translated as follows: "And Solomon had horses brought out of Egypt and out of Que."

We have referred to the cities Jerusalem, Hazor, Megiddo, and Gezer, which were typical of cities Solomon rebuilt in a grand style. The city of Jerusalem remains something of a mystery to us since, although lots of excavation has gone on in and around it, the city of Solomon's day is still virtually unknown. The Temple has disappeared because of the great amount of destruction that has taken place there. Whether some ruins lie somewhere beneath the surface of the large area enclosed within Herod's walls is not known because excavation here is forbidden. But we now have a good picture of the cities of Megiddo and Hazor and of some parts of Gezer. Each of these cities had an impressive fortification surrounding it. The walls were generally of the casemate variety, that is, they were double walls braced across at intervals by short cross walls. The gateway into the city was normally of a standard pattern. There were three guardrooms on each side of the main roadway into the city, with a large tower flanking each side of the entrance. The casemate wall extended on both sides of the gateway.[31] Precisely this type of gateway was found at Hazor,[32] Gezer,[33] and Megiddo.[34] The gate at Beer-sheba was slightly different, with only two guardrooms on either side of the entrance.[35] In Solomon's day the wall was evidently solid, although in the next century the casemate wall appears.[36] This type of gateway is now referred to as the Solomonic Gateway. It is of some interest that the gateway leading into Ezekiel's ideal temple had the same shape (Ezek. 40:5-16).

Inside the fortification of these cities lay a wide variety of structures.

31. Y. Yadin, "Megiddo," *EAEHL,* Vol. III, p. 851.
32. Y. Yadin, "Hazor," *EAEHL,* Vol. II, pp. 486f.
33. W. G. Dever, *op. cit.,* pp. 436f.
34. G. Loud, *Megiddo II: Seasons of 1935-1939* (1948).
35. Y. Aharoni, *Beer-sheba I,* Plate 84.
36. *Ibid.,* pp. 9-10.

Solomonic gate at Megiddo showing the typical triple piers. The guardrooms were later sealed off by rubble filling the spaces between the pillars, which stood at the ends of the piers. (Oriental Institute, University of Chicago)

At right are the Solomonic (ninth century B.C.) gate and casement wall of Hazor, Area A. In the background are the remains of a pillared building. (Israel Exploration Society)

Perhaps the most common of these was the typical Israelite four-room house. It consisted of a rectangle, one end of which was cut off to provide a room or rooms and the remaining larger portion of which was divided into three segments, the central one being the courtyard and the portions on either side for rooms, or one or both of them an extension of the courtyard. They were generally roofed over.

It is clear from the Bible that Solomon must have had considerable sources of copper. Many tons of copper would have been required for all the brass (Hebrew "copper") items used in the Temple. The Bible has a specific reference to the casting of metals in the plains of Jordan (I Kings 7:46). There can be no doubt about the existence of mines and metal-working furnaces in the area of the Jordan in these times. Nelson Glueck has made this clear in a variety of ways. In his delightful book *The River Jordan* he remarks:

> I found fragments of slag on some of the tells north of Admah and especially upon the site of ancient Succoth. In Solomon's time this entire district in the Jordan Valley hummed with industrial activity devoted to the turning out of finished metal articles for the adornment of the new Temple.[37]

It seems possible that copper was worked in areas to the south of the Dead Sea where there is a good deal of copper ore to be found. Indeed, when Nelson Glueck excavated the site of Tell Kheleifeh, a low mound with Iron Age and Persian Age remains located some 500 meters from the present north shoreline of the Gulf of Aqabah about midway between the eastern and western sides of the Gulf, he thought that he had discovered a smelting and copper refining plant from Solomon's day.[38] More mature consideration of the proposal following criticism of his suggestion[39] led Glueck to change his interpretation so that what he once thought to be Solomon's smelting works he now described as a fortified storehouse and granary.[40] The large building he excavated was 13.2 meters square, with the outside walls 1.2 meters thick and the partition walls one meter thick. This building originally had six rooms, three small square rooms at the north end and three rectangular rooms to the south, each 7.4 meters in length. The structure was built of mud bricks 40 by 20 by 10 centimeters. The outer walls had two horizontal rows of apertures piercing the width of the walls. The lower row was a meter above the base of the walls, and the second row 70 centimeters higher. Glueck originally thought these were holes for admitting a draught of air to a furnace, but it seems clear now that these apertures held wooden cross-beams inserted into the walls for bonding or anchoring the structure. This type of building is known at Samaria as well as at sites outside Palestine (cf. I Kings 6:36). A sloping ramp of mud bricks supported the outer

37. N. Glueck, *The River Jordan* (Philadelphia, 1946), p. 146.
38. N. Glueck, *The Other Side of the Jordan*, pp. 50–113; BASOR, No. 188 (1967), pp. 8–38.
39. B. Rothenberg, *PEQ* (1962), pp. 5–71.
40. N. Glueck, "Ezion Geber," *BA*, Vol. XXVIII, No. 3 (Sept., 1965), pp. 70–87.

sides of this building. Surrounding the whole was an enclosure with casemate walls each side of which was 45 meters in length, built of larger mud bricks (43.5 × 23.5 × 13 cms.). These casemate walls are characteristic of Solomon's time and have been found at Hazor, Megiddo, and Gezer, as we have seen. A gateway with its opening to the sea was built in the south side.[41] It is thought that the site may mark the ancient town of Ezion Geber. It is known to archaeologists as Ezion Geber I. The town was to have a long history reaching down to the fourth century B.C. It was destroyed several times in its long history.[42] The above discussion gives another example of the ongoing work of reinterpretation of archaeological results. It is still possible, of course, that there were smelting works somewhere in the region, but their ruins have not yet been found. The presence of copper ores to the north of the Gulf of Aqabah would suggest some such activity.

A linguistic item points in an interesting way to the activities at this port. The Bible tells us that Solomon had a "navy of Tarshish" here (I Kings 10:22). The very word "Tarshish" may betray the purpose for which the port was used. Professor Albright has suggested that this word has linguistic links with a Semitic root which is used of the flow of liquids or, perhaps by a metaphorical use, of the flow of molten metals.[43] In that case a Tarshish fleet may well be a refinery fleet. The activity of the Phoenicians here can be compared with their activity in the island of Sardinia where activity in the production of copper at this time is now established.[44]

Incidentally, this work seems to add point to the story in the Bible that the Queen of Sheba paid a visit to Solomon (I Kings 10). There is clear evidence that there were trade connections between Palestine and southern Arabia at the time. The ancient kingdom of Saba (Hebrew "Sheba") was situated in the southwest corner of Arabia. Quite recently this area has been visited by a party of archaeologists. A great deal of evidence was obtained, but unfortunately the local Arabs made continuance of the work impossible.[45] Sufficient has been discovered, however, to show that this area was a flourishing place in the days of Solomon. If we are to have further evidence of the Queen of Sheba it will probably come from this area.

One valuable piece of written evidence from this age is the now famous Gezer calendar written in the old Phoenician script on a piece of limestone. The writing gives us valuable insight into the agricultural activities of the land at the time. A recent translation by W. F. Albright reads as follows:

41. This building was destroyed in the last quarter of the tenth century, probably by Pharaoh Shishak. The site was later rebuilt and a new series of fortifications erected, probably in Ahab's time.

42. See N. Glueck, "Kheleifeh, Tell el-," *EAEHL*, Vol. III, pp. 713–717.

43. W. F. Albright, "New Light on the Early History of the Phoenician Colonization," *BASOR*, No. 83, pp. 21ff.

44. *Ibid.*, pp. 14ff.

45. W. Phillips, *Qataban and Sheba* (London, 1955).

His two months are [olive] harvest,
His two months are planting [grain],
His two months are late planting;
His month is hoeing up of flax,
His month is harvest of barley,
His month is harvest and feasting;
His two months are vine-tending;
His month is summer fruit.[46]

Some very important information has recently come to light from the ancient site of Arad. On rising ground to the north of the ancient city the Israelites had an open, unwalled settlement in the twelfth and eleventh centuries B.C., that is, during the Iron I Age. Then in the second half of the tenth century B.C. a walled citadel was erected. It was some 50 by 55 meters in area and was surrounded by a casemate wall with protruding towers. This was in Solomon's time. One feature of this citadel which was to be continued on into later citadels was a sacred area where some kind of temple stood. It consisted of a large rectangular structure some 65 feet long and 49 feet wide, with an entrance on the eastern side. At the western end a portion was cut off to form a sort of holy of holies. This part had a small projecting room in the center of the western side approached by three steps. On the steps stood two small stone altars on which the excavators found charred material, suggesting that incense or some other material had been burned here. Inside this western room was a small paved "high place" (bamah) and beside it a fallen stone pillar (maṣṣebah), well finished and rounded on its upper end. Two plastered flint slabs, more crudely fashioned, were leaning against the wall. The larger room had plastered benches around the walls, probably for offerings and cult vessels. An altar for burnt offerings lay in the center of this room. It was a square structure built of earth and small field stones (cf. Exod. 20:25) and was covered by a large flint slab surrounded by two plastered grooves evidently for collecting blood.[47] This temple was a forerunner of several others at Arad which were in use during the days of the kings of Judah.

The structure continued in use till the end of the seventh century B.C. (Stratum VII) when it was rebuilt without the altar and high places, probably in the days of Hezekiah (II Kings 18:1-4). Finally in Stratum VI the place of worship disappeared completely, probably in the latter part of the seventh century, that is, in the days of Josiah (II Kings 23:6-20). We have here a reminder of the shrines and high places which were scattered throughout the land and earned the condemnation of the prophets (e.g., Hos. 10:8; Amos 7:9; Jer. 7:31; 17:3; 19:5, etc.).

Our immediate interest, however, lies in the fact that in Solomon's day, in

46. J. B. Pritchard, ANET, p. 320.
47. Y. Aharoni, "Arad: Its Inscriptions and Temple," BA, Vol. XXXI (Feb., 1968), pp. 18-20; "Arad," EAEHL, Vol. I, pp. 85f.

the territory of Judah, there was a temple, apparently used by the Israelites, which was not merely a rival to the temple in Jerusalem, but also seems to have contained some "unorthodox" features.

THE CLOSE OF SOLOMON'S LIFE

Solomon's reign, which began with such promise, was to end tragically. We have seen how very remarkably the biblical account of his reign has been illuminated by modern archaeological discovery. The Bible gives us a sad picture of the collapse of the kingdom at Solomon's death. Yet it is not to be wondered at that the revolution came. In a variety of ways Solomon sowed the seeds of revolt by his own foolish methods of government. It was not altogether wise to divide the land into new zones in the way he did (I Kings 4). Some of the new boundaries cut across the old tribal boundaries and this led to certain tribal disagreements. Moreover, the king resorted to heavy taxation and to a sort of forced labor in order to carry out his work of erecting great buildings, like his own palace and the Temple. Israelite men were sent in courses to Lebanon to cut the cedar trees—a month in Lebanon and two months at home. There was something of extravagance in the royal building program. In addition to this, the king offended the religious scruples of many of the people by allowing his foreign wives to erect their shrines in the very shadow of the Temple of God (I Kings 11). Many foreign favorites were apparently encouraged in the court, the most notable among them being the Phoenicians.

All of these grievances were the basis for considerable dissatisfaction among the people. On Solomon's death the people quite naturally hoped for some relief from his son Rehoboam. Had this son been wise he might have made concessions so as to overcome the many legitimate grievances of the people. But he unwisely followed the advice of his friends and as a result the whole kingdom collapsed. Thereafter there were to be two kingdoms in the land (I Kings 12).

7

THE KINGS OF ISRAEL

AFTER the death of Solomon the northern kingdom of Israel founded by Jeroboam set out on its disturbed course which was to come to a sad end after only two hundred years of independent existence. In that time there were to be no less than nineteen kings. These belonged to nine different families in all. There was great insecurity in government. If we use the term "dynasty" for a ruling house, then we can say that only the Fourth and the Fifth Dynasties achieved any stability at all.

Three features about these days are important to remember. In the first place, Israel had periods of conflict and periods of friendship with her neighbor and brother Judah. Secondly, the great nation Assyria lay in the background of the history of these days like an ogre and was to cause a great deal of trouble to Israel and Judah alike. Thirdly, these were the days of the great preaching prophets—Elijah, Elisha, Hosea, Amos, Micah, and Isaiah.

Before we discuss the kings of Israel it will be necessary to give some account of the Assyrians so that we may appreciate their significance for the history of Israel. We owe a great deal to Assyrian records in interpreting the story of Israel since information was recorded in the Assyrian palaces about at least seven of Israel's kings—Omri, Ahab, Jehu, Joash, Menahem, Pekah, and Hoshea. Furthermore, several of the Assyrian kings are known to us in the Bible. It was not for nothing that Israel referred to the Assyrians as a rod (Isa. 10:5), a razor (Isa. 7:20), and a flood (Isa. 8:7, 8). We turn, then, to give a brief review of the history and culture of the great Assyrian nation.

THE ASSYRIANS: THEIR HISTORY, CULTURE, AND SIGNIFICANCE FOR BIBLE HISTORY[1]

The heart of the Assyrian nation lay in the very fertile region surrounding the middle Tigris River in the general area of modern Mosul. In the days of the Israelite patriarchs the Assyrians were already a recognizable group. They were trading with the old Hatti people in Asia Minor. One of their remarkable king lists[2] tells of their earliest kings who "lived in tents." The second group comprised kings "whose fathers were known." The third group, of only six, had three foreigners. From king number 33 on to the last king, number 107, we have considerable information. One of the great kings of early times was Shamshi-Adad, a contemporary of Hammurabi. He reigned from about 1748 to 1716 B.C. This was about the time of the Hyksos kings in Egypt. The great Egyptian Dynasty Eighteen, which was so powerful in Palestine and in western Asia generally, was prevented from expanding too far to the east by the Assyrians. In the days when the religious reformer Akhenaton neglected his empire in Asia, the Assyrians were able to push to the west and occupy the land between the Tigris and the Euphrates rivers. This was in the time of the strong Assur-Uballit (1354–1318 B.C.).

During the days when Israel was moving into the Promised Land, and all through the unsettled period of the Judges, the Assyrians were consolidating their position at home. At the time of the Exodus there was a very strong king, Adad-Nirari (1304–1273 B.C.), who subdued the king of Babylon. With the collapse of the powerful nations like Egypt and the Hittites at the time of the invasion of the Sea Peoples about 1200 B.C., Assyria was ready to exploit the new situation. Just at the start of the eleventh century the first Tiglath Pileser (1118–1078 B.C.) was pushing into the areas occupied by the Aramaeans (Syrians). From that time onward it became quite a regular feature of Assyrian practice to invade lands to the west for plunder and economic gain.

The great figure in Assyrian expansion was King Ashurnasirpal (883–859 B.C.). He moved the capital from Ashur to Calah (Nimrud), and set about to organize the Assyrian army into a tremendous machine. Nimrud was the base where the army was recruited and trained. Bowmen, spearmen, and slingers made up the infantry. The more mobile units were the cavalry, armed in much the same way. Then there were the charioteers, one of the most dreaded units of the Assyrian army, whose thunder from afar struck terror into many a nation. These are vividly described by the prophet Nahum (Nah. 2:3, 4; 3:2, 3). Other units were trained in siege warfare, which the Assyrians worked out to a fine art.

---

1. W. L. Hallo, "From Qarqar to Carchemish, Assyria and Israel in the Light of New Discoveries," BA (May, 1960), pp. 34–61; H. W. F. Saggs, "The Assyrians" in D. J. Wiseman (ed.), *Peoples of Old Testament Times* (London, 1973), pp. 156–178.
2. JNES (July, 1942; Oct., 1942; Jan., 1943).

Siege apparatus included battering rams, large wooden or cane shields to protect the attackers before the walls, scaling ladders, and great slings. There were special techniques for building earth ramparts on which the battering rams could be run up. Still other units of the army were trained to cross rivers, to climb mountains, to undertake anything that was necessary for the transport of the Assyrian army. All this Ashurnasirpal established on firm foundations, building on the past no doubt, but providing that final drive that made the whole war machine the wonder and the terror of the East. He campaigned in a great half-circle around his land. Although he did not reach the little kingdoms in Palestine, he did mention many states in the vicinity, like Tyre and Sidon, from whom he took tribute; and although he did not refer to the contemporary King

The ruthlessly ambitious King Ashurnasirpal (883–859 B.C.) and his successors built not only the Assyrian empire but also cities that are magnificent even in ruins. This picture shows the remains of the citadel and towered city wall that fortified Ashurnasirpal's new capital, Nimrud (biblical Calah), on the east bank of the Tigris twenty miles south of modern Mosul. (Consulate General, Republic of Iraq)

Detail of the monument that Ashurnasirpal set up in the courtyard of his palace at Nimrud (Calah). Around his image in the center are the astral symbols of Assyrian gods. The 154 lines of text relate that his prisoners of war built the city and that when it was completed he gave a banquet for its 64,000 inhabitants and for 5,000 distinguished guests from the farther parts of the empire. (Consulate General, Republic of Iraq)

Omri of Israel, it is of some significance that the Assyrians later referred to Israel by the term "Bit-Humria," that is, "House of Omri."

The successor of Ashurnasirpal was Shalmaneser III (859–824 B.C.). He is not known in the Bible but his records tell us that King Ahab was involved in a war with him. He left us a picture of King Jehu on a large black obelisk to be seen today in the British Museum. It is the only picture of a Bible king that we have.[3] In his day the great prophet Elijah was preaching in Israel.

After the death of Shalmaneser III the Assyrians lost very much of their vigor for the best part of a century. During these years they had troubles nearer home and were unable to indulge in some local wars. We can say that from 823 to 745 B.C., except for a few years around 800 B.C., the Assyrians were of no great danger in western Asia. In 745 B.C., however, one of the Assyrian generals usurped the throne and took the name of one of the great kings of the past, calling himself Tiglath Pileser III. He reigned from 745 to 727 B.C. At home he was able to restore control, subdue some of the enemies who had kept Assyria from expansion all those years, and then turn once again to the west. He established a vital connection with Israel and is referred to in the Bible (II Kings

3. J. B. Pritchard, *ANET*, pp. 280f.

Tiglath Pileser III (745–727 B.C.) stands in his war chariot, accompanied by his driver and a man holding an umbrella. Detail of a relief from Nimrud (Calah) of the Assyrian capture of Astartu, perhaps the biblical Ashtaroth. Tiglath Pileser is called Pul in Babylonian texts and in the Bible. (British Museum)

15:19, 29; 16:7, 10). At a time of dispute between Israel and Judah, the king of Judah foolishly called on the king of Assyria for help. This led to the overthrow of the king of Syria,[4] who at the time was an ally of Israel. Then Tiglath Pileser invaded Israel and took many captives (II Kings 15:29, 30). At the same time Judah herself had to pay tribute and, in effect, lost her liberty. The king of Israel at the time was Pekah. When he died in 732 B.C., Israel had only ten more years of independence remaining. They were sad years in which Pekah was murdered and his successor was taken captive to Assyria by Shalmaneser V (727–722 B.C.), who went on to capture Samaria, the capital, in 722 B.C. Although the next ruler, Sargon II, took the credit, it was properly the achievement of his father, Shalmaneser V.

Judah continued alone as great Assyrian kings continued to rule in the East—Sargon II (721–705), Sennacherib (704–681), Esarhaddon (680–669), Ashurbanipal (668–626). Finally Assyria herself fell before the combined attacks of the Medes and the Chaldeans during the years 612 to 609 B.C. The kingdom of Judah outlasted the great Assyria by over twenty years.

Artists were encouraged in Assyria. We still delight in some of the wonderful ivory work that was produced by the artisans of those days. But excellent work was also done in metals, precious stones, and other artistic media. Perhaps the most spectacular art work from Assyria was that done by the stone masons. Huge winged lions and bulls with human heads, weighing several tons, adorned

4. The "Syria" of the Bible is strictly "Aram." Generally it refers to Damascus.

Ashurbanipal (668–626 B.C.) hunting lions. Carved on flat slabs of alabaster, this and other reliefs of many aspects of Assyrian life lined the walls of the king's palace at Nineveh. The representations have a certain conventionalism but also a stark realism, which is shown here by the postures of the dead and dying lionesses. (British Museum)

the entrances to palaces and temples. Splendid flat slabs of alabaster were used to line the walls of the palaces. These were carved with detailed pictures taken from the whole range of Assyrian life. Here we can see the nation at war, at work, and in the daily round of life. From such bas-reliefs we gain a great deal of information about the equipment of the army and the methods of battle and siege warfare. We see the hundreds of slaves engaged in hauling great carved bulls into the palaces, and we observe the tools of the workmen. We see the king engaged in hunting lions (Nah. 2:11, 12). We learn something of the gods of Assyria and the procedures in the temples. All this and much more is still to be seen by the visitor to the great museums of the world where these excavated bas-reliefs are on display. In addition to the pictures there were literally miles of written records which preserved valuable historical information.

Some of the Assyrian kings were men of literature who went to great pains to collect the stories of the ancient world into their palaces. Thanks to this, the world is able to read the ancient Flood story and the Babylonian story of creation, carefully recorded on baked clay tablets. There is a great number of local historical records on which we can draw today for our history of this great nation.

Assyrian architecture was a great achievement in itself. The first stage in the erection of a palace was the construction of a huge raised terrace covering

Ashurbanipal, holding the weapons of the hunt in his left hand, pours a libation over the four dead lions at his feet. In front of him are an offering table and two musicians playing lyres; behind him two pages whisk away flies. Limestone relief from Kuyunjik. The Assyrian empire fell to the Medes and Chaldeans within twenty years after Ashurbanipal's reign. (British Museum)

several acres. This was made of large unbaked bricks and for added stability was built with sloping sides and sometimes faced with stone slabs. On this terrace the king constructed his palace of massive baked mud bricks. Some of the palaces contained over one hundred rooms. The inside walls were lined at the bottom with slabs of alabaster carved in the way we have indicated. The upper parts of the walls were decorated with bright paint and glazes. Huge carved-stone figures stood at the entrances. An impression of splendor and power must have been created in the mind of the visitor from a foreign land. Incidentally, the pictures on the walls would have a good propaganda effect on the foreigner. Perhaps these things might happen in his land some day!

The religion of the Assyrians was polytheistic. There was a great deal of religion of a formal kind, with prayers for every occasion. Some of the Assyrian gods are known in the Bible—Tammuz, Ishtar, Nebo, and Nisroch. It was quite a common practice for the Assyrian kings to set up in a captured town an Assyrian altar and other religious symbols as a sign of conquest. It was probably such an altar that Ahaz of Judah saw in Damascus. He had a copy of it made in Judah (II Kings 16:10–11).

In contrast with all this culture, there was unspeakable cruelty in the nation. As a regular practice, after a battle hundreds of the conquered people were taken off to a strange land. Many were selected for torture. Heads were removed,

This human-headed bull, more than three meters high, was one of a pair guarding the gateway to Ashurnasirpal's palace at Nimrud (Calah). It has the wings of an eagle, the curly hair of a lion on its chest, flanks, and hind parts, bovine ears with dangling earrings, and extra legs so that observers from the side will always see at least four. (British Museum)

hands cut off, ears taken off, tongues pulled out, eyes gouged out, skins taken off in one piece and often tacked to the walls of the town as a warning. Indeed, it seems that there was no piece of brutality known to man that the Assyrians did not use. Not only did they do these things, but they portrayed them on the bas-reliefs and described them in some detail in their official records. The cruel Ashurnasirpal described his dealings with the cry of a certain Khulai in these words:

Six hundred of their warriors I put to the sword; three thousand captives I burned with fire; I left not a single one among them alive to serve as a hostage. Khulai their governor I captured alive. Their corpses I piled into heaps; their young men and maidens I burned in the fire; Khulai, their governor, I flayed and his skin I spread upon the wall of the city of Damdamusa; the city I destroyed, I ravaged, I burned with fire.[5]

Assyria remains in the memory of men today as possibly the supreme example of a nation with the highest culture, with a highly formal religion and skill in all the arts of mankind, but lacking in its inner soul that love of righteousness and that fear of God of which the prophets of Israel spoke so fervently. Of what use is culture if a man or a nation lacks righteousness?

THE FIRST THREE DYNASTIES OF ISRAEL

The first house began with Jeroboam I (922–901 B.C.).[6] His son Nadab ruled after him for only two years and was then slain by a certain Baasha (I Kings 15:25ff.). This was the first of many conspiracies that removed kings from the throne in Israel.

We have some interesting archaeological light from the days of Jeroboam. Reference is made in the Bible to the invasion of Palestine by Pharaoh Shishak of Egypt, five years after the death of Solomon (I Kings 14:25–28; II Chron. 12:2–12). The story in Kings refers only to the attack on Jerusalem. More detail is given in Chronicles where the walled cities of Judah are mentioned (v. 4). In actual fact the invasion touched Judah rather severely.[7] We know from the records of Shishak in Egypt that his campaign seriously affected Israel also. A list of the towns he attacked is given on the walls of his partly ruined temple in Karnak, close to modern Luxor in Egypt. This list includes many towns in Israel. In particular the town of Megiddo is mentioned. When Megiddo was excavated some years ago, one of the striking finds was part of a broken stele (inscribed stone slab) bearing some of the names of Shishak, and showing that he had probably set up here in Israel a commemorative inscription.

We have nothing else at present to enlarge our biblical picture of the house of Jeroboam, but we may have some light on the golden calves set up by him in Bethel and Dan (I Kings 12:29). It has often been suggested that these were objects of worship. We think today that this may not be the correct picture,

---

5. E. A. Budge and L. W. King, *The Annals of the Kings of Assyria* (London, 1902), pp. 291f.

6. We follow the dates of W. F. Albright in *Biblical Period* (Pittsburgh, 1950), p. 66. The alternative chronology in R. Thiele, *The Mysterious Numbers of the Hebrew Kings* (Grand Rapids, 1958), pp. 74ff., differs in some respects. Yet another system is that offered in *EAEHL*, Vols. I–IV, which gives a date of 928–907 B.C. for Jeroboam I, some six years earlier than Albright's date. But at present there is no generally accepted dating. The difference between the systems is minimal.

7. B. Mazar, "The Campaign of Pharaoh Shishak to Palestine," *VT Supp. Vol. IV* (1957), pp. 57–66.

"Jeroboam the son of Nebat . . . made Israel to sin" is an ominously recurring phrase in the Old Testament history of the kings. Jeroboam made two golden calves and placed them in Dan and Bethel. Earlier the Israelites had worshipped a golden calf at Sinai. The golden calves may have resembled this bronze calf statuette of Apis, the fertility-god of Memphis, Egypt. (British Museum)

although no doubt many of the unthinking Israelites would worship these images, and to that extent Jeroboam "made Israel to sin." It has become clear, however, that people like the Hittites and the Canaanites symbolized the presence of their gods by animals. There are in existence a number of pictures and statues where gods are standing on the backs of animals.[8] Perhaps Jeroboam agreed that the God of Israel could not be represented in any form, but he wanted to symbolize God's presence in some way. So he chose the method of the pagans. This was a most dangerous procedure, for it led many to attach significance to an image and, in fact, broke the second commandment.

The Second Dynasty of Israel was introduced by Baasha when he slew Nadab, the son of Jeroboam. He and his son Elah ruled from 900 to 876 B.C. Of the twenty-five years, Elah ruled only two before he was murdered by the usurper Zimri.

8. W. F. Albright, *From the Stone Age to Christianity* (Baltimore, 1940), p. 228; O. R. Gurney, *The Hittites* (London, 1964), Fig. 8, pp. 142, 143.

Baasha was soon involved in a war with Judah (I Kings 15:16–22). Two features about this story in the Bible can be illuminated from archaeology. Asa of Judah found that Baasha was building a fortress on his frontier. In fear, he sent to the neighboring king of Damascus for help. This king, Ben-hadad son of Tabrimon (v. 18), is now known from an inscription found in Syria.[9] It is an Aramaic text telling of a vow made by "Bir-hadad, son of Tab-ramman, king of Aram."

The second item concerns the fortress of Geba (v. 22). When the Syrian armies arrived at the invitation of Asa, Baasha left off building the fortress and retired to fight. Asa immediately crossed the border, pulled down the fortress of Baasha, carried the materials to his own side of the frontier, and erected two fortresses there! One of these was Geba or Gibeah. It was the third occupation of the site. There had been a building here in the days of the Judges. When the surrounding tribes attacked the tribe of Benjamin on the occasion of the physical humiliation of the Levite's concubine, the town of Gibeah was burned (Judg. 19, 20). King Saul built the second fortress here, as we have seen.[10] It was Asa who built the third. Excavation has revealed a remarkable correlation between the biblical information and the extant remains at this site.[11]

Recent excavations reveal an occupation of the site during the Iron II period. Asa lived at the beginning of the period. But during the last decades of the Iron II period Gibeah was strongly fortified, and its population increased as the sixth century wore on. The city was probably destroyed in Nebuchadnezzar's campaign of 597 B.C.[12]

The end of Israel's Second Dynasty came when Elah was slain. His murderer, Zimri, did not rule more than a week (I Kings 16:11–20). We must, however, count him as a third ruling house in Israel. Archaeological discovery adds nothing to the biblical narrative. The army captain who slew Zimri was Omri, the father of Ahab, and a great man in his own right. It looked as if there was to be some stability at last in Israel, for this house was to rule for over thirty years.

THE DYNASTY OF OMRI

This Dynasty comprised four kings in all: Omri (876–869 B.C.), Ahab (869–850 B.C.), Ahaziah (850–849 B.C.), and Joram (849–842 B.C.). It is described in the Bible in derogatory terms. Very little is given about Omri, and only the worst features of Ahab are mentioned. Ahaziah and Joram were probably of little account in any case. Modern discovery has a different picture to give, and adds

---

9. W. F. Albright, "A Votive Stela Erected by Ben Hadad I of Damascus," BASOR (Oct., 1942), pp. 23ff.
10. See above, p. 82.
11. AASOR, Vol. IV, pp. xxxivf.
12. P. W. Lapp, "Tell el-Fûl," BA, Vol. XXVIII, No. 1 (Feb., 1965), pp. 2–10.

considerably to the Bible picture. It is a principle of biblical interpretation that the Bible deals with people from the religious angle. Very often it says little about other aspects of their life, such as their political and economic significance. Kings like Omri and Ahab merit only denunciation in the religious sphere, but archaeology shows that the case is quite different in the political and economic spheres.

The story of Omri is given in but six verses in the Bible apart from the account of his murder of Zimri (I Kings 16:23-28). Two things are mentioned about him. He bought a field from Shemer and founded the capital of Israel there. He was a wicked man and "did worse than all that were before him." There is only a hint of "the might that he shewed."

Thanks to archaeological work we can now greatly enlarge this picture. The town of Samaria has been excavated.[13] The foundations of the city were laid by Omri, although the bulk of the first city was probably built by his son Ahab. But it is in the realm of international politics that Omri is best known. Both the Assyrians and the Moabites knew him, and his name was recorded in their annals.

We have no details in Assyrian records about Omri himself but we think that he was not merely known, but also respected, forever after, for after his time Palestine became known in Assyrian records as Bit-Humria, that is, House of Omri. The Assyrian king at the time was the great and cruel Ashurnasirpal (883-859 B.C.). Just why Omri was esteemed thus becomes clear from the wonderful record left in Moab by her famous King Mesha (II Kings 3:4). Moab had been conquered by David and held by Solomon. After Solomon's death it was lost again. The Bible tells us that King Mesha of Moab paid tribute to Israel (II Kings 3:4). It was never known who had subdued Moab again till an English missionary in 1868 visited ancient Dibon in Moab and found a large black basalt stone with thirty-four lines of writing on it. Every effort was made to get this stone to Jerusalem, but the local Arabs proved difficult and finally destroyed it in 1873. Fortunately a copy of the stone was made before it was destroyed, and this told the story of how King Mesha of the Bible had at last been able to throw off the yoke of Israel. Of special interest to us here is that the stone tells us that it was Omri, king of Israel, who had subdued Moab and humbled it for many years, and that this state of affairs had continued under his son. But then Chemosh the god of Moab had again occupied the land. We infer that Mesha had been able to free Moab from Israel. This revolt began in the days of Ahab. Probably Mesha at first refused to pay tribute at a time when Ahab was busy with his Syrian wars. Mesha declared that this was the time when Moab gained her freedom. The Bible states that it was after the death of Ahab that Moab rebelled. The two

13. For a good simple outline of the story of Samaria see A. Parrot, *Samaria* (London, 1958). See also N. Avigad, "Samaria," *EAEHL*, Vol. IV, pp. 1032-1050, who provides further bibliography.

Omri the king of Israel had forced Moab to pay tribute, but during Ahab's reign Mesha the king of Moab withheld payments and soon after became entirely free from Israel's control. On the so-called Moabite Stone (ca. 840–820 B.C.), Mesha tells of his revolt and lists the villages that he "with the help of Chemosh [the Moabite god]" took from Israel. (Oriental Institute, University of Chicago)

accounts are not contradictory. They look at the events from two different angles. From the viewpoint of Moab the revolt dated from the refusal to pay tribute to Ahab. But from Israel's point of view Moab did not gain her freedom until after the failure of the punitive expedition recorded in II Kings 3.

This valuable nonbiblical record from Moab reads as follows:

> I [am] Mesha, son of Chemosh-(. . .), king of Moab, the Dibonite—my father [had] reigned over Moab thirty years, and I reigned after my father,—[who] made this high place for Chemosh in Qarhoh (. . .) because he saved me from all the kings and caused me to triumph over all my adversaries. As for Omri, king of Israel, he humbled Moab many years [lit., "days"], for Chemosh was angry at his land. And his son followed him and he also said, "I will humble Moab." In my time he spoke [thus], but I have triumphed over him and over his house, while Israel hath perished for ever! [Now] Omri had occupied the land of Medeba, and [Israel] had dwelt there in his time and half the time of his son [Ahab], forty years; but Chemosh dwelt there in my time.

And I built Baal-meon, making a reservoir in it, and I built Qaryaten. Now the men of Gad had always dwelt in the land of Ataroth, and the king of Israel had built Ataroth for them, but I fought against the town and took it and slew all the people of the town as satiation [intoxication] for Chemosh and Moab. And I brought back from there Arel [or Oriel], its chieftain, dragging him before Chemosh in Kerioth, and I settled there men of Sharon and men of Maharith. And Chemosh said to me, "Go, take Nebo from Israel!" So I went by night and fought against it from the break of dawn until noon, taking it and slaying all, seven thousand men, boys, women, girls and maid-servants, for I had devoted them to destruction for [the god] Ashtar-Chemosh. And I took from there the (. . .) of Yahweh, dragging them before Chemosh. And the king of Israel had built Jahaz, and he dwelt there while he was fighting against me, but Chemosh drove him out before me. And I took from Moab two hundred men, all first class [warriors], and set them against Jahaz and took it in order to attach it to [the district of] Dibon.

It was I [who] built Qarhoh, the wall of *the forests* and the wall of the citadel; I also built its gates and I built its towers and I built the king's house, and I made both of its reservoirs for water inside the town. And there was no cistern inside the town at Qarhoh, so I said to all the people, "Let each of you make a cistern for himself in his house!" And I cut *beams* for Qarhoh with Israelite captives. I built Aroer, and I made the highway in the Arnon [valley]; I built Beth-bamoth, for it had been destroyed; I built Bezer—for it lay in ruins—with fifty men of Dibon, for all Dibon is [my] loyal dependency.

And I reigned [*in peace*] *over* the hundred towns which I had added to the land. And I built (. . .) Medeba and Beth-diblathen and Beth-baal-meon, and I set there the (. . .) of the land. And as for Hauronen, there dwelt in it (. . .) [And] Chemosh said to me, "Go down, fight against Hauronen." And I went down [and I fought against the town and I took it], and Chemosh dwelt there in my time. . . .[14]

So Omri was a man of importance after all. We are able to put together a more adequate picture of the achievements of this king today with the help of the archaeologist.

The story of Ahab is told in some detail in the Bible, the best part of six chapters being devoted to it. The emphasis, however, is on the aspects of Ahab's life that are important from the religious point of view. His clash with Elijah, his theft of the vineyard of Naboth, his evil wife Jezebel, his encouragement of the false prophets, his conflict with the prophet Micaiah, and his final defeat in battle are the main points of interest for the Bible writer. There are hints of other achievements in the account of two successful wars against Syria, and in the reference to "the ivory house which he made and all the cities that he built"

14. J. B. Pritchard, *ANET*, p. 320.

(I Kings 22:39). These matters are recorded in "the book of the chronicles of the kings of Israel," but since this work is now lost we have no record of them. If we are to learn more about Ahab, then, we are dependent on the discoveries of the archaeologist. In this we are not disappointed. A variety of additional pieces of information is available for us from this source.

The story of the conflict of Ahab with Elijah gains much from modern discovery. It was at a time of severe drought. This drought is attested in the writings of Josephus,[15] who quoted from the Greek writer Menander, who in turn had drawn on some Phoenician sources. Of greater interest, however, is the fact that the god Baal, who features so much in this story, is now depicted for us in very great detail as a result of the tablet discoveries from Ras Shamra, the former Ugarit, a great Canaanite town and the site of several temples. Baal was peculiarly the god of fertility. He controlled the seasons and was responsible for the storm and the rain. If a drought was upon the land, it was due to Baal's working. The devotee would appeal to him for relief of these conditions.[16] With scorn, Elijah, on Mount Carmel, exposed the emptiness of this belief (I Kings 18). If Baal failed, the God of Israel would not. At the word of Elijah, and in answer to his prayer, the rain came.

There is another feature of this story. In the Hebrew text there are in fact two gods referred to in I Kings 18:19. These are Baal and Asherah[17] (translated in the Authorized Version as "the groves"). The documents excavated at Ugarit show us that Asherah was a female goddess, the consort of Baal, a sensuous, lustful creature. She, like Baal, had her prophets in Israel, four hundred of them (I Kings 18:19). The Authorized Version of the Bible needs to be revised here to read: "the prophets of Baal four hundred and fifty, and the prophets of Asherah four hundred."

The story of Naboth receives some explanation, too, in the light of Canaanite mythology. One of the myths of Canaan told of a goddess who found a young hunter one day with a beautiful bow, the gift of another god. She tried all she could to persuade him to give her the bow. He would not part with such a precious possession. Then she gained permission from El, the chief of the gods, to take measures to obtain the bow. She selected a man of brutal character, turned him into an eagle, placed him in a flight of eagles, and had him swoop down one day to peck the young hunter to death. She then took the bow with impunity.[18] Might was right in Canaanite mythology, and if gods and goddesses behaved in this selfish fashion, could it be expected that their worshippers would be any better? Naturally, Jezebel, a Canaanite woman, believed that her hus-

---

15. Josephus, *Antiquities* VIII.xiii.

16. See J. Gray, *The Legacy of Canaan* (1965), pp. 163–169; H. Ringgren, *Religions of the Ancient Near East* (London, 1973), pp. 131–135.

17. See J. Gray, *op. cit.*, pp. 169–178; H. Ringgren, *op. cit.*, pp. 140–143.

18. *Aqhat* III.i.5–43 in G. R. Driver, *Canaanite Myths and Legends* (Edinburgh, 1956), pp. 57f.; J. Gray, *op. cit.*, pp. 111–116.

band had the right to possess a man's vineyard regardless of his claim that it was a family possession, and so she said to him: "Dost thou now govern Israel? arise and eat bread and let thine heart be merry. I will give thee the vineyard of Naboth" (I Kings 21:7).

Ahab is known on the Assyrian monuments as one of a coalition of twelve kings who opposed the great Shalmaneser III at the battle of Karkar in 853 B.C. The Assyrian claimed to have won the battle. It is significant, however, that he did not make war for a few years afterward. It is probable that both sides were badly mauled. In the Assyrian account of the battle we are given a list of the forces of the coalition. The following extract from the annals of Shalmaneser gives interesting details of the participants in the coalition.

> ... I approached Karkara. I destroyed, tore down, and burned Karkara, his royal residence. He brought along to help him 1200 chariots, 1200 cavalrymen, 20,000 foot soldiers of Adad'idri (Hadadezer) of Damascus; 700 chariots, 700 cavalrymen, 10,000 foot soldiers of Irhuleni from Hamath; 2000 chariots, 10,000 foot soldiers of Ahab the Israelite; 500 soldiers from Que, 1000 soldiers from Musri....[19]

Other places are listed, including Arabia and Ammon. It is clear that Ahab provided the greatest contingent of chariots and the second largest number of soldiers. If the stables discovered at Megiddo belonged to Ahab and not to Solomon, we understand where some of his horses and chariots were kept.[20] This significant battle is not even referred to in the Bible. The forces of Israel since the days of Solomon must have been considerable. It was probably as a result of this battle that Ahab's army was so weakened as to give encouragement to Moab to rebel and to refuse to pay tribute. No doubt Ahab intended to subdue Moab again, but he died before he was able to accomplish this.

Excavations have given us much insight into the building programs of Ahab. The first palaces at Samaria were very fine indeed. Some of the finest masonry of all time was laid down by the builders of Ahab.[21] Another feature of the palace ruins here was the clear Phoenician influence, revealed particularly in the type of carved capital at the top of the columns used to support the roof. In the same palace area a considerable amount of carved ivory was found. It was the fashion of the day to decorate the interior walls with ivory friezes and to ornament the palace furniture in the same way. Palaces of this type have been found at Nimrud in ancient Assyria and in Phoenicia. The magnificent ivories found at Nimrud in ancient Assyria include numerous pieces from the time of Ahab, that is, in the ninth century B.C. Ahab's ivory house (I Kings 22:39) in particular now finds a good parallel and an explanation in a room in one of the palaces of

---

19. J. B. Pritchard, *ANET*, p. 278, col. 2, and p. 279, col. 1.
20. See above, pp. 110–112.
21. Examples of the wide variety of structures which have been brought to light in excavations will be given in ch. 9, pp. 161–183.

Nimrud where the mud-brick wall was once overlaid with a great ivory screen.[22]

Incidentally, Ahab's arch-enemy Ben-hadad was eventually slain by a certain Hazael (II Kings 8:15). This fact is attested in the records of Shalmaneser III, who referred to Hazael as the "son of a nobody," the usual description of a usurper. The annals of Shalmaneser read thus:

> I defeated Hadadezer of Damascus together with twelve princes, his allies. . . . Hadadezer himself perished. Hazael, the son of a nobody [a commoner], seized the throne. . . .[23]

We have nothing of real importance to add to our picture for the two successors of Ahab. Joram tried to subdue Moab again with the help of Judah and Edom, but failed. It was probably in these years that Hazael became king of Damascus and began his raids on Israel. It was at the time of one of the Syrian raids, perhaps before the reign of Hazael, that the Syrians were besieging Samaria and fled at the sound of what they thought were the armies of the Hittites and the Egyptians. More recently we have discovered that there was a land to the north of Palestine known as Musur. This land features often on the tablets. It is thought that what the Syrians feared was a coalition of Hittites and Musurites rather than a coalition of Hittites and Egyptians. In the days of the first translations of the Bible into English, the word MSR was mistaken for Egypt, since the two words have the same consonants. There are other places in the Bible where we are able to make changes like this in the light of more recent knowledge. Indeed, the Bible has an intimate knowledge of ancient geography and we are only now coming to understand its value as a source of ancient geography.

Here we must leave the dynasty of Omri. It is clear that modern archaeology has done much to increase our knowledge of the times, and to give us a fuller picture of the kings of Israel in this period.

THE DYNASTY OF JEHU

Various groups in Israel grew tired of the weak successors of Ahab, and a change was imminent. There was a revolution, supported by the prophet Elisha and the prophetic party as well as by other faithful adherents of the faith of Israel. Finally an opportunity came and an army captain named Jehu decided to act after the armies of Israel had been mauled in a battle in which the king was wounded. Jehu slew the king as he lay at Jezreel recovering from his wounds. The same day

---

22. M. E. L. Mallowan, *Iraq*, Vol. 13, pp. 1–20; Vol. 14, p. 8; and succeeding volumes. Note Vol. 20, p. 104. Illustrations of the ivories occur in *Illustrated London News*, No. 221, p. 256; No. 223, pp. 199ff.; No. 228, pp. 130ff.; and No. 231, pp. 869–873, 934–937, 968ff. J. W. and G. M. Crowfoot, *Early Ivories from Samaria* (London, 1938).

23. J. B. Pritchard, *ANET*, p. 280, col. 2.

he caused the death of the king of Judah, who happened to be visiting the king of Israel. The wicked Jezebel was sought out and cast to the dogs (II Kings 9 and 10). Jehu thus commenced a new dynasty which was to have five kings who ruled from 842 to 745 B.C., nearly a century in all.

Jehu is best known to us as the one king in either Israel or Judah whose picture we have today. The great Shalmaneser III was still reigning at the time of Jehu's accession. He evidently had some dealings with Jehu in the year 842 B.C., for the large black obelisk found by the early excavator Sir Henry Layard at Nimrud in 1840 has a picture of Jehu bowing before Shalmaneser and offering: "Silver, gold, a gold beaker, golden goblets, pitchers of gold, lead, staves for the hand of the king, javelins."[24] This incident happened when Shalmaneser, who had been busy for some years and had allowed the king Hazael of Damascus to get a little out of hand, decided to pay a visit to the west. Hazael was subdued, as were others. The rulers of Tyre, Sidon, and Israel thought it better to pay tribute. This fact passes unnoticed in the Bible. We have nothing else to report about Jehu from archaeological discovery, but in a general way the Assyrian story brought to light by the excavators helps to explain much in the next century.

Events in the eastern parts of the Assyrian domains kept their kings busy from about 837 B.C. till 802 B.C. The Syrians were able to molest Israel a great deal when they had no fear of the Assyrians. Thus, despite early promise, Jehu suffered at the hands of Hazael and lost Israel's lands in Transjordan (II Kings 10:32, 33). His son Joahaz was practically a subject of Hazael and his successor Ben-Hadad (II Kings 13:1-7). Then in the year 802 B.C. Damascus herself was prostrate before the Assyrians. Joash, the third king of the Jehu dynasty (801–786 B.C.), seized the opportunity to regain the lost lands of Israel (II Kings 13:25). The name of King Joash was discovered on an important inscribed stele of Adad-Nirari III (811–783 B.C.) during excavations at Tell al Rimah in northern Iraq in 1967. This Assyrian king records that in the first year of his reign:

> He received the tribute of Ia'asu (Joash) the Samaritan, of the Tyrian (ruler) and of the Sidonian (ruler).[25]

The days were auspicious from another point of view. Events in the general area of Damascus of which we have been ignorant till recent years provided Israel with further welcome relief. An important monument found near Aleppo tells

---

24. *Ibid.*, p. 281. Several scholars have raised doubts over the years as to whether the figure on the second row of Shalmaneser's monument is really Jehu. Recent discussion, however, supports the identification. See S. Herrmann, *A History of Israel in Old Testament Times* (London, 1975), p. 232; Alberto R. Green, "Sua and Jehu: The Boundaries of Shalmaneser's Conquest," *PEQ* (Jan.–June, 1979), pp. 35–39.

25. S. Page, "A Stela of Adad-Nirari III and Nergal-Eresh from Tell al-Rimah," *Iraq*, Vol. XXX, Part 2 (Autumn, 1968), p. 143.

The inscribed, four-sided Black Obelisk of Shalmaneser III (858–824 B.C.) from Nimrud (Calah) shows the kings of the Gilzanites, Israel, Musri, and Suhi and the tribute that they brought to this Assyrian king. The tribute on the panels pictured here includes gold and silver, copper vessels, staffs, camels, monkeys, stags, lions, ivory, and linen garments. (British Museum)

This panel of the Black Obelisk shows "Jehu son of Omri" (or his emissary) bowing before Shalamaneser III. At either side of the panel are Assyrian attendants. This is the only contemporary portrait of an Israelite king. (British Museum)

of struggles between Zakir, the Aramaean king of Hamath, and a strong coalition headed by Ben-Hadad of Damascus.[26]

This monument, in the form of a stele, tells of a siege of Hazrek, the biblical Hadrach (II Chron. 9:1). It commences with these words:

> The stela which Zakir king of Hamath and Lu'ash set up in honor of 'Ilu-wer.... I am Zakir, king of Hamath and Lu'ash. I am a humble man, but Baal-Shamain (Lord of Heaven) called me and has held to me, and Baal-Shamain has caused me to reign over Hazrek. And Benhadad, son of Hazael, king of Aram, united against me twelve [?] kings—Benhadad and his army, Bar Gush and his army, the king of Que and his army, the king of 'Umq and his army, the king of Gurgum and his army, the king of Sam'al and his army, and the king of Meliz and his army... and all these kings besieged Hazrek and raised up a rampart higher than the rampart of Hazrek, and digged a ditch deeper than its ditch. Then I raised my hands to Baal-Shamain and Baal-Shamain heard me and Baal-Shamain spoke to me by seers and... Baal-Shamain said to me, "Fear not! It is I who caused you to reign and it is I who will be with you. It is I who will deliver you from all these kings which have set up siege against you...."

Zakir was delivered. But the preoccupation of so many of these Aramaean kings in the general period 800–775 B.C. meant that Israel and Judah were not troubled by them. Indeed, it was because of these troubles in Syria that Joash of Israel (about 801–786 B.C.) was able to re-establish Israel's prestige. On his death, his competent son Jeroboam II set out on a period of remarkable prosperity for Israel.

During these years also the great Assyrian nation was more or less immobilized. Adad-Nirari III (811–783), the one referred to in II Kings 13:5 as "a deliverer (saviour) for Israel who rescued them from the power of Aram," was occupied with the powerful Urartu people from the Caspian region for the first quarter of the eighth century, and his son Shalmaneser IV (783–773) was still fighting defensive actions against this people. Even Assyrian governors close to home were virtually independent. Among these, Shamshi-ilu of Bit-adini ruled in royal style. He is probably the one Amos had in mind as "him that holdeth the sceptre" in Bit-adini ("house of Eden") (Amos 1:5). Ashur Dan III (773–755) and Assur-nirari V (755–745), the two rulers who followed, could do no better. Owing to the discovery of written records in the excavations of Assyrian cities, we now have this picture.[27]

Thus while the Assyrians, the Aramaeans, and the Urartu people fought one another to a standstill, Israel and Judah with the long-lived rulers Jeroboam

---

26. *Ibid.*, p. 501. Cf. A. Dupont-Sommer, *Les Araméens*, pp. 45ff.; M. F. Unger, *Israel and the Arameans of Damascus* (1957), pp. 85–89. Cf. also M. Black, in D. W. Thomas (ed.), *Documents from Old Testament Times* (New York, 1958), p. 246.

27. W. W. Hallo, *op. cit.*, pp. 41–46, summarizes the material.

II and Uzziah were able to regain something of the economic strength and the territorial extent they had known in the days of Solomon.

The biblical record in Kings dismisses Jeroboam II in very few verses (II Kings 14:23–29). His reign was a sad one from the religious point of view, for apostasy and insincerity abounded, and the king allowed the worship of false gods to continue unchecked. Yet these were days of great economic prosperity. Evidence of this is given in the words of the great eighth-century prophets (Isa. 3:18–26; 5:8–13; Amos 5:11; 8:4–6; Mic. 2:2). The more sober records in Kings do not give this impression. Something of the splendor of the days and of their prosperity can be gained from excavations.

The buildings in Samaria and in Megiddo dating from this time give evidence of careful planning. The excavators refer to the remarkable layout of the town of Megiddo in these days. It is, however, the town of Tirzah that gives what is perhaps the best picture of the times. Here the great gate into the city led at once into a massive structure which was evidently the palace of the local governor. Nearby were two large buildings with fine stone foundations. Behind these three buildings lay the rest of the town, which was of a very ragged style and spoke of poverty. No better picture of the considerable class distinction in Israel could be hoped for. The excavator, Père de Vaux, made special reference to this fact.[28]

One sign of the prosperity of the times was a great grain-storage pit at Megiddo. Here was a pit some twenty-three feet deep, some thirty-seven feet across at the top, and some twenty-three feet across at the bottom. Its capacity was about 12,800 bushels. It had two sets of winding stairs inside. Chaff was found between the chinks in the uncoursed stones that made up the sides.

Further evidence of prosperity comes from Samaria. Just inside the gate about seventy receipts written on pieces of broken pottery (ostraca) were found by the excavators. The date of these records, known as the Samaria Ostraca,[29] has been the subject of a great deal of scholarly discussion. The first proposal was to date them to the days of Ahab.[30] Then the days of Jeroboam II (786–746 B.C.) were proposed.[31] A later suggestion was to date them to the days of Menahem (745–738 B.C.).[32] Yet another proposal was to date some to the days of Joash (801–786 B.C.) and some to the days of Jeroboam II.[33] A date somewhere about the time of Jeroboam II seems at last to be acceptable. The dating

28. R. de Vaux, "La quatrème campagne de fouilles à Tell el-Far'ah, près de Naplouse," RB, Vol. LIX (Oct., 1952), pp. 551–583, but note p. 566 and Plate XI.

29. D. W. Thomas, Documents from Old Testament Times, pp. 204–208.

30. J. W. Jack, Samaria in Ahab's Time (Edinburgh, 1929); G. A. Reisner, C. S. Fisher, and D. G. Lyon, Harvard Excavations at Samaria (Cambridge, Mass., 1924), pp. 227–246.

31. J. B. Pritchard, ANET, p. 321.

32. S. Yadin, "Ancient Judaean Weights and the Date of the 'Samaria Ostraca,'" Scripta Hierosolymitana (Jerusalem, 1960), Vol. III, pp. 1–17.

33. Y. Aharoni, "The Use of Hieratic Numerals in Hebrew Ostraca and Shekel Weights," BASOR, No. 184 (Dec., 1966), pp. 13–19, esp. p. 18 n. 30; The Land of the Bible, A Historical Geography (London, 1966), pp. 315–327.

depends on the interpretation of some important signs on the ostraca that stand for numbers. These discussions illustrate the kind of problem that sometimes arises in the interpretation of archaeological data. Apart from the date, the documents speak of oil, barley, wine, etc. being received in Samaria. They refer to many place names and provide evidence of local geography.

One important feature of these receipts is the considerable variety of names on them. Many of these were composed with the element Jah or Iah, showing some link with the name of Israel's God. Such names as Elijah, Jedaiah, and so on, are typical. Alongside these were many names with the element Baal, like Elibaal, Abibaal, Jeribbaal. In fact, for every eleven Jah names there were seven Baal names. This points to a certain popularity for names involving Baal and suggests a widespread devotion to this pagan god. While it is true that many people do not pay much attention to the meaning of a name, yet it is evident that these names were common in Israel and were used without much compunction by the people. All of this fits in with the picture of apostasy given in the prophets.

We have the feeling that there is much yet to be discovered about these days in Israel. What we have is of great importance in explaining and in corroborating the biblical narratives referring to this age.[34]

At the close of Jeroboam's life a new terror appeared in the East. The Assyrians had a new king, Tiglath Pileser III, who ruled from 745 to 727 B.C. It was the end of liberty for the small kingdoms to the west. Before a quarter of a century was over, the kingdom of Israel had fallen. When Jeroboam II of Israel died, he was replaced by his son Zechariah. But this king ruled for only six months and was killed in a revolt. It was the end of the Jehu dynasty.

THE LAST KINGS OF ISRAEL

After the death of Zechariah in 745 B.C. Israel was to have only about a quarter of a century of independence remaining. In that time there were five kings, of whom three were murdered, one was taken captive, and only one died naturally. Our information for these days, apart from the Bible, comes from the Assyrian records. Three of the last kings were referred to in these records.

The usurper who slew Zechariah was Shallum. He reigned only a month and was himself liquidated by Menahem. It was in the days of Menahem that the Assyrian inroads became serious. Tiglath Pileser made a move toward Israel but Menahem was able to buy him off. The figure of fifty shekels referred to in II Kings 15:20 is now known to be the average price for a slave. Menahem was asked to assess his men at the price of slaves and to buy his freedom thus. It was probably in the year 743 that Tiglath Pileser referred to Menahem as paying

34. Further discussion of the cities of the days of the Kings will be taken up in ch. 9, pp. 161–183.

tribute to him. It seems that Menahem was captured and then released. The account of Tiglath Pileser refers to his attack on Gaza, and then he adds:

> As for Menahem I overwhelmed him like a snowstorm and he fled like a bird alone, and bowed to my feet. I returned him to his place and imposed tribute upon him. . . .[35]

There follows a list of the tribute collected.

Menahem died in his bed and was succeeded by his son Pekahiah (II Kings 15:22). We know no more about this man, and in any case, after two years he was slain by an army captain named Pekah.

Pekah is a notorious character in Bible history, for he made an alliance with Rezin, king of Damascus, and sought to invade Judah. Rezin had paid tribute to Tiglath Pileser as early as 743 and his name is mentioned in the list which quotes Menahem in these words:

> I received tribute from Kustashpi of Commagene, Rezon of Damascus, Menahem of Samaria, Hiram of Tyre, Sibitti-bi'li of Byblos, Urikki of Que, Pisiris of Carshemish, I'nil of Hamath . . . [etc.].[36]

But Rezin, emboldened by Tiglath Pileser's preoccupation elsewhere, headed a new anti-Assyrian coalition in which Pekah of Israel joined. They sought to bring Judah in and planned to set up a certain Ben Tabeel (Isa. 7:6) in place of King Ahaz. The place name *Tab-el* has now been discovered on a tablet from Nimrud, so that the Ben Tab'al of Isaiah 7:6 may well have been the son of Ahaz and a princess from Tab-el.[37]

When Pekah and Rezin moved on Jerusalem (II Kings 16:5; II Chron. 28:5–8), King Ahaz of Judah in a panic called on Tiglath Pileser for help. The Assyrians marched west, imposing tribute on Judah, Ammon, Edom, and Moab, and taking large numbers of people from the Galilee and Gilead areas of Israel into captivity (II Kings 15:29). At that time the fortress of Hazor was destroyed and the proud kingdom of Israel was reduced to a tiny vassal state only part of its original size.[38] It is strange that both Hosea and Isaiah refer to Ephraim, which would have been fairly correct geographically. These events took place in the years 734–732.[39]

In 732 Tiglath Pileser turned to Damascus. The Bible tells us of the attack of the Assyrians on this ancient foe of theirs (II Kings 16:9). The city which had held out so long finally fell. In the same year a pro-Assyrian revolt in Samaria cost Pekah his life and brought Hoshea to the throne as a loyal Assyrian vassal,

35. J. B. Pritchard, *ANET*, pp. 283f.
36. *Ibid.*, p. 283, col. 2.
37. H. W. F. Saggs, *Iraq*, Vol. 17 (1955), pp. 131–133; W. F. Albright, *BASOR*, No. 140 (1955), pp. 34ff.
38. Y. Yadin, *BA*, Vol. 20 (1957), pp. 34–37.
39. The record of Tiglath Pileser is damaged but the general sense is clear. See J. B. Pritchard, *ANET*, p. 283, col. 2.

at least for a short time. If Tiglath Pileser did not actually put Hoshea on the throne, he seems to have approved. His record reads:

> They overthrew their king Pekah (Paqaha) and I placed Hosea (Ausi') over them as king.

The strain of the Assyrian annual tribute was too much for Hoshea and he began to intrigue with Egypt. Retribution was swift. The new king of Assyria, Shalmaneser V (726–722), took action in 725 B.C., and the Assyrian armies came to Israel. Shechem was captured and Samaria was besieged. Hoshea the king was captured outside the city and deported before the fall of Samaria (II Kings 17:4). The siege went on for nearly three years, but in August or September of 722 the city fell. Shalmaneser died in December, 722, that is, after the fall of Samaria. Sargon his son and successor claimed the final capture of the city on his monuments, and no doubt he was present, and possibly even in command of the armies, so that he had a share in the fall. The Babylonian Chronicle notes the destruction of Samaria (Sa-ma-ra-'i-in) as the outstanding event of the reign of Shalmaneser. It is of interest to note that in Ezra 4:10 Samaria, normally spelled in Hebrew as *Shomron*, is spelled *Shamrayin*, as in the Babylonian Chronicle.

An Israelite wall at Samaria, one of many built by Ahab. These strong fortifications withstood one attack, and the city fell to the Assyrians in 722 B.C. only after a three-year siege. (Bastiaan VanElderen)

Shalmaneser V took exiles off to Assyrian lands like Guzana (Gozan) and Haran (I Chron. 5:26). In due course these exiles evidently reached the capital cities of Nimrud (Kalah) and Nineveh, where Israelite names have been found on written records. Ostraca from Nimrud and Nineveh carry twenty-two Israelite names, such as Menahem and Hoshea.[40]

In Sargon's account of the fall of Samaria he takes the credit for himself although, as we have seen, it was his father Shalmaneser V who took the city. Sargon's annals read as follows:

> I besieged and conquered Samaria, led away as booty 27,290 inhabitants of it. . . . The town I rebuilt better than it was before and settled therein people from countries which I myself had conquered. I placed an officer of mine as governor over them and imposed upon them tribute as is customary for Assyrian citizens.[41]

There are parallels between this narration and the story in the Bible in II Kings 17.

So ended the kingdom of Israel. The importance of archaeology for the enlargement of our knowledge of these kings and for the corroboration of many of the statements in the Bible is evident. Perhaps the most important feature of this additional material is that it enables us to place the kings of Israel in a true perspective. In that light they appear politically to be of far more significance than we would think them to be were we dependent on Bible history alone. As to their worth in the eyes of God, the Bible writers had a true perspective. It remains a fact that mere physical achievement has no justifying worth before God.

40. J. B. Segal, "An Aramaic Ostracon from Nimrud," *Iraq*, Vol. 19 (1957), pp. 139–145; W. F. Albright, *BASOR*, No. 149 (1958), pp. 33–36.
41. J. B. Pritchard, *ANET*, pp. 284f.

8

THE KINGS OF JUDAH

WHEREAS Israel ceased as an independent nation in 722 B.C., Judah continued until 586 B.C. Factors similar to those which influenced Israel are found in the case of Judah: the continual menace of Assyria, the possibility of conflict with her own sister state, and the ministry of the prophets. To these we may add conflict with Edom, which acted as a natural rival to Judah in much the same way Syria did for Israel. Modern archaeology has added to our knowledge of Judah in ways similar to those we have seen for Israel. Judah had but one line of kings during all this period. There was a short interregnum when the woman Athaliah ruled, but the royal prince was in hiding and came to the throne after six years. It will be convenient to treat the story of Judah in three sections, the period contemporary with Israel's first four dynasties, the period contemporary with the rest of Israel's history, and the period when Judah stood alone.

THE FIRST EIGHTY YEARS: 922 B.C. TO 842 B.C.

Rehoboam (922–915 B.C.) was involved in the campaign of Shishak of Egypt. The Bible refers only to the invasion of Judah and, indeed, Judah appears from I Kings 14:25 to have been the principal target of Shishak, although, as we have seen, the campaign was far more extensive. Shishak mentioned several towns of Israel[1] on his temple at Karnak. It is clear, however, that a number of places, regions, settlements, forts, and families in the area of the Negeb as well as along

---

1. B. Mazar, "The Campaign of Pharaoh Shishak to Palestine," *VT Supp.* IV (1957), pp. 57–66.

the Philistine coast were reached by Shishak's troops at the time. It would seem that the defensive positions in the southern part of the kingdom of Judah erected by David and Solomon were probably destroyed—a fact that explains why Rehoboam was compelled to erect a new line of fortifications that encircled the Shephelah and the mountains of Judah.[2] At this time the important town of Ezion Geber on the Red Sea, the port of Solomon, was destroyed by fire. This was a loss to Judah, but later, in the days of Jehoshaphat, when the Egyptian menace was past, the people of Judah were able to rebuild the port.

From the time of Asa (913–873 B.C.), we have evidence of the building of the fortress of Gibeah.[3] This has been referred to in our account of the kings of Israel. Thanks to the discoveries of Ras Shamra we are able to understand the reforms of Asa more clearly: "He took away the sodomites out of the land ... and Maachah his mother... he removed from *being* queen, because she made an idol in a grove" (I Kings 15:12, 13). We now know that these sodomites (*qedeshim* in Canaanite) were sacred male prostitutes. The Canaanites had these in their temples along with sacred women. These men and women performed rites in the temples designed to encourage fertility in flock and field. The very name *qedeshim* is the same in Hebrew and Canaanite and means "holy men," although the practices of these men were far from holy. The reference in this text to "an idol in a grove" is really a reference to "an idol of Asherah." The RSV translates "She had made an abominable image for Asherah," that is, for the Canaanite goddess we have already discussed.[4] Here, too, the Authorized Version of the Bible needs to be revised.

Jehoshaphat (873–840 B.C.) came to the throne about the same time as King Omri of Israel. There began a period of friendship between Judah and Israel which lasted for thirty years. There was close cooperation between Ahab and Jehoshaphat during their reigns. They were present together at the battle in which Ahab was slain.

The main archaeological interest in these years lies with Israel. The one feature we have for Judah concerns the rebuilding of the port of Ezion Geber. The Bible indicates that Jehoshaphat "made ships of Tarshish to go to Ophir" (I Kings 22:48). Though the ships were wrecked, the biblical statement suggests that the port was rebuilt. This seems to be supported by Nelson Glueck's excavation there. The second city of Ezion Geber is datable from pottery to the early part of the ninth century.

FROM THE REVOLUTION OF JEHU TO THE FALL OF SAMARIA

The revolt of Jehu in Israel brought about the death of Judah's king also (II Kings 9:27). This enabled the queen mother, Athaliah, the sister of Ahab of Israel

2. *Ibid.*, p. 66.
3. See above, pp. 82, 101, 128.
4. See above, p. 90.

Panorama of Bethlehem in Judah, where both David and the "Son of David" were born. (Trans World Airlines)

(II Kings 8:26), to seize the throne for herself and to destroy the seed royal. Fortunately, the king's sister rescued his baby son Joash and brought him up. During the six years that Athaliah ruled, Canaanite worship was encouraged. In particular, Baal was worshipped and Mattan, a priest of Baal, was installed. The name of Mattan is Canaanitish, typical of many names ending in "an" to be found on the baked clay tablets unearthed in recent years.[5] Perhaps Mattan was actually a Canaanite who was brought to Israel by Athaliah to lead the sensuous Canaanite worship which has been revealed to us by such documents as those found in the Ras Shamra (Ugarit) library.

There is little of archaeological interest during those years. Assyrian evidence for Judah is lacking, although the king of Syria, Hazael, who invaded the area around Gath and thought of turning to Jerusalem, is known to the Assyrians. He was the "son of a nobody," that is, a usurper.[6]

With the ascent of Uzziah to the throne, Judah embarked on a period of great prosperity. It was the eighth century. External foes were occupied elsewhere and both Judah and Israel were free to exploit the days of freedom. The narrative in Kings, as we have seen, dismisses Jeroboam very quickly. Its treatment of Uzziah is almost as brief (II Kings 15:1-7). However, the account in II Chronicles 26:1-23 is quite detailed. The days were prosperous, as we learn from this chapter. In particular there was expansion in the southern parts of Judah toward the Negeb. Recent discovery and excavation in this area have shown how true the picture in Chronicles is. A good deal of surface survey has been carried out in the Negeb in recent years, and it is now clear that during the eighth century settlement extended over almost the whole area. This was an important transit area between the coast and the Arabian lands behind.[7] Uzziah had good contacts with the Arabs at the time. It would appear that the later settlement at Qumran which produced the Dead Sea Scrolls used a fortress built by Uzziah. Certainly these people reoccupied an eighth-century fortress and made it the core of their own very much enlarged structure. It is the view of the excavators that we have here one of Uzziah's "towers in the wilderness" (II Chron. 26:10).[8]

One other point of interest is that the Bible speaks of the restoration of Eloth or Ezion Geber in the days of Uzziah. This was the third city on the site. For the first time in its history the place assumed the semblance of a real village and not merely a large fortified granary. Pottery dates the town to the days of Uzziah. In its debris was a royal seal bearing the name Jotham, which was probably the seal of the crown prince.

There is still some dispute about the name "Azriyau of Ya'udi" referred to in

5. W. F. Albright, *Archaeology and the Religion of Israel* (Baltimore, 1953), p. 127.
6. See J. B. Pritchard, *ANET*, p. 280, col. 2, para. 3.
7. N. Glueck, *Rivers in the Desert*, gives details.
8. R. de Vaux, "Fouilles de Khirbet Qumran," *RB*, Vol. LXIII (Oct., 1956), pp. 535-537.

records of the Assyrian king Tiglath Pileser III. This name has been interpreted as Azariah of Judah. Azariah was an alternative name of Uzziah (II Kings 15:1–17). Writers like W. F. Albright are inclined to identify the two.[9] Other scholars associate this name with a ruler of the little state of Sam'al to the north of Israel on the Syrian coast which was also known as Ya'udi. Indeed, it seems that the kingdom of Israel represented the extreme edge of the Assyrian sphere of power at this time and that the kingdom of Judah lay outside the area of Assyrian influence. The king Azriyahu of Ya'udi who paid tribute to the Assyrians in 738 B.C. was almost certainly from this small state in Syria. The state is known from several inscriptions as being one of the first to pay tribute to the Assyrians in northern Syria.[10] But even if there is no extrabiblical reference to Azariah (Uzziah), there is some additional evidence from excavations to supplement the narratives of the Bible for the days of Uzziah.

After Uzziah's death in 742 B.C. the Assyrian menace became severe. The great Tiglath Pileser was soon to begin his attacks on Israel, and Judah was caught up in the struggle very quickly.

It was in the days of Ahaz (735–715 B.C.) that Judah became seriously involved with Assyria. The threat of Pekah of Israel and of Rezin of Damascus caused Ahaz to call on the Assyrians for help despite the advice of Isaiah to the contrary (Isa. 7:1–9). Ahaz was summoned to Damascus to pay homage and to witness the symbols of Assyrian lordship set up there. We have suggested[11] that a pagan altar was among these, and that Ahaz had a copy of this made in Jerusalem (II Kings 16:7–11). Ahaz, under his alternative name Jehoahaz, is mentioned in a list of tributaries of Tiglath Pileser, a list which, incidentally, includes rulers of such countries as Edom, Moab, Gaza, Askelon, and Ammon.[12] All of these were in the vicinity of Judah and suggest the seriousness of the Assyrian inroads at this time.

Tiglath Pileser's list reads as follows:

> . . . in all the countries . . . I received tribute of Kushtashpi of Commagene, Urik of Que, Sibitti-be'el of Byblos, Enil of Hamath, Panammu of Sam'al . . . Sanipu of Bit-Ammon, Salamanu of Moab, . . . Mitinti of Ashkelon, Jehoahaz [Ia-u-ha-zi] of Judah [Ia-u-da-a-a], Kaush-malaku of Edom . . . Hanno of Gaza. . . .

There is strong evidence in the Bible that Ahaz was inclined to receive religious influences from the East. The reference to the passing of his son through the fire (II Kings 16:3) links up with the discovery that the god Muluk or Malik was widely worshipped in the lands to the east of Palestine.[13] One of

9. W. F. Albright, *The Biblical Period* (Pittsburgh, 1950), p. 40.
10. S. Herrmann, *A History of Israel in Old Testament Times* (London, 1975), p. 246.
11. See above, p. 124.
12. J. B. Pritchard, *ANET*, p. 282.
13. W. F. Albright, *Archaeology and the Religion of Israel*, p. 163.

The State of Israel has conducted extensive archaeological research in historical sites. To determine the significance of a site and to identify it, on-the-spot photography is essential; these photographers are at work in the central Negeb. (Israel Office of Information)

the rites associated with this god was that of offering children in sacrifice. The deity Adrammelech, referred to in II Kings 17:31 as being the god of those people whom the Assyrians settled in Samaria after the exile of the Israelite population, is now attested in Syria as Adad-milki. There are references to the sacrificial cremation of sons to the god Adad in documents from northern Mesopotamia extending from the tenth down to the seventh centuries.[14] If we are to understand the significance of the religious practices of Ahaz we will need to call on the discoveries of the archaeologist.

It was during the days of Ahaz that Israel finally fell, leaving Judah alone in the land as a more or less independent Hebrew state, although there was a degree of subservience to Assyria.

FROM HEZEKIAH TO THE DOWNFALL OF JUDAH

From the days of Hezekiah (715–687 B.C.) we have some valuable material. The Assyrian records are a great help here. Quite early in the reign of Hezekiah, King Sargon of Assyria came to the areas to the southwest of Judah where the king of Ashdod was causing trouble of some kind. Ashdod had even tried to

14. *Ibid.*, p. 221.

Archaeological activity at Wadi Kurnub in the Negeb. The presence of armed men indicates the political unrest in this area of the Near East. (Israel Office of Information)

obtain the aid of Judah, but without success. In 712 B.C. Sargon sent troops to attack Ashdod. The event is referred to in the Bible in Isaiah 20. This reference is of special interest because it was the sole reference to Sargon preserved in the records of the ancient world until the excavations in old Assyria showed what a great king he was. In his records he made reference to the revolt of Ashdod of 712 B.C. Sargon's annals speak thus:

> Azuri king of Ashdod had schemed not to deliver tribute [any more] and sent messengers [full] of hostilities against Assyria to the kings in his neighbourhood. On account of the misdeed which he [thus] committed, I abolished his rule over the inhabitants of his country and made Ahimiti, his younger brother, king over them. But these Hittites always planned treachery, hated his reign, and elevated Iamani [or Iadna] over them, who, without claim to the throne, knew, just as themselves, no respect for authority. [In a sudden rage] I marched quickly—in my state chariot and with my cavalry which never, even in friendly territory, leaves my side—against Ashdod, his royal residence, and I besieged and conquered the cities Ashdod, Gath, and Asdudimmu. ... I reorganized these cities and placed an officer of mine as governor over them and declared them Assyrian citizens and they bore my yoke.[15]

15. J. B. Pritchard, *ANET*, p. 286, col. 1.

An interesting letter from Nimrud, mentioning tribute from Egypt, Gaza, Judah, Moab, Ammon, Edom, and Ekron, may well date from this campaign.[16]

In 701 B.C. the next Assyrian king, Sennacherib, invaded Palestine and crushed a rebellion. In the southwest, Egyptian forces were defeated and the town of Lachish was besieged. This siege is vividly depicted in the bas-reliefs found in the palace of this king at Nineveh. He followed up his success at Lachish by attacking the walled cities of Judah, forty-six in all, according to the Assyrian record. The Bible tells of the promise of Hezekiah to Sennacherib to pay heavy tribute. The Assyrian king was not content and proceeded to besiege the capital, Jerusalem. The prophet Isaiah urged Hezekiah to hold out. This he did and the Assyrians retired. The biblical account in II Kings 18:1 to 19:7 has many parallels with the account of Sennacherib. Here are a few extracts from the annals of Sennacherib:

> As to Hezekiah the Jew, he did not submit to my yoke. I laid siege to forty-six of his strong cities, walled forts and to countless small villages in the vicinity and conquered them by means of well-stamped earth-ramps and battering rams brought thus near to the walls. . . . Himself I made a prisoner in Jerusalem, his royal residence, like a bird in a cage. I surrounded him with earthwork in order to molest those who were leaving his city's gate. . . . I reduced his country but I still increased the tribute and the presents due to me as his overlord which I imposed upon him beyond his former tribute to be delivered annually. . . . Hezekiah did send me later to Nineveh . . . thirty talents of gold, eight hundred talents of silver. . . .[17]

The correlations between the two records are quite remarkable and have often been noticed. Among the more important we could draw attention to the mention of Hezekiah the Jew in both records, the attack on his walled cities (the exact number being given by Sennacherib), the siege of Jerusalem, in which Hezekiah was living, the tribute imposed, especially the thirty talents of gold, which is mentioned in both records, and Sennacherib's return to Nineveh (II Kings 19:36). Each record gives additional facts as well, so that the complete picture is obtained from a combination of the two.

There has been some discussion about whether Sennacherib paid one or two visits to Palestine. Some writers feel[18] that the Bible record requires this, and the external facts allow it. The second visit is said to be recorded in II Kings 19:8–37. This remains a subject for debate, however. The Assyrian records are silent on the matter. But since they are silent for Sennacherib after 689 B.C., we await future discovery to clear up the point. Probably the weight of opinion is that there was only one visit.

16. H. W. F. Saggs, *Iraq*, Vol. 17 (1955), pp. 134ff.
17. J. B. Pritchard, *ANET*, p. 288.
18. J. Bright, *A History of Israel* (London, 1960), pp. 282–287.

In II Kings 15:13–16 we read: "In the
fourteenth year of King Hezekiah Sennacherib King of Assyria came up against
all the fortified cities of Judah and took
them. . . . And Hezekiah gave him all the
silver that was found in the house of the
Lord, and . . . stripped the gold from the
doors of the temple of the Lord . . . and
gave . . . [them] to the king of Assyria."
The cuneiform inscription on this hex-
agonal clay prism (686 B.C.) from
Nineveh confirms that Sennacherib received such tribute from Hezekiah.
(British Museum)

The death of Sennacherib at the hand of assassins, referred to in the Bible
(II Kings 19:37), is known in Assyrian records.

> I tore out the tongues of those whose slanderous mouths had uttered
> blasphemies against my god Ashur and had plotted against me, his
> god-fearing prince; I defeated them. The others I smashed alive with
> the very same statues of protective deities with which they had smashed
> my own grandfather Sennacherib—now as a belated sacrifice for his
> soul. I fed their corpses, cut into small pieces, to dogs, pigs, zibu-birds,
> vultures, the birds of the sky and to the fish of the ocean.[19]

19. Ibid., pp. 288f.

Israelite city wall, late eighth or seventh century B.C., in the present-day Jewish quarter of Jerusalem. This view is from the south. (Israel Exploration Society)

Stone lintel from the tomb of (Shebna)-yahu at Silwan, southeast of Jerusalem. It is inscribed with three lines of archaic Hebrew and is dated ca. 700 B.C. Possibly this Shebna is the same man that Isaiah rebuked for having prepared an elaborate sepulcher (Isa. 22:15ff.). (British Museum)

One final detail from the days of Hezekiah is concerned with the way in which "he made a pool and a conduit and brought water into the city" (II Kings 20:20). German students in 1880 found a long tunnel connecting the pool of Siloam and the Virgin's Fountain. On exploring it they found an inscription on the wall inside, in a script that was in use in the days of Hezekiah.[20] The writing is only the scratching of one of the workmen as he described how the last few blows were struck before the waters flowed. There is, however, no reason for doubting that the workman's remarks are true and that this tunnel is indeed the conduit of King Hezekiah. The so-called Siloam inscription, now housed in the Museum at Istanbul in Turkey, still provides some excitement for the reader as he senses the thrill of those who finally broke through the wall of rock:

> (. . .).[when the tunnel] was driven through. And this was the way in which it was cut through:—While (. . .) [were] still (. . .) axe[s], each man toward his fellow, and while there were still three cubits to be cut through, (there was heard) the voice of a man calling to his fellow, for there was *an overlap* in the rock on the right (and on the left). And when the tunnel was driven through, the quarrymen hewed [the rock], each man toward his fellow, axe against axe; and the water flowed from the spring toward the reservoir for 1,200 cubits, and the height of the rock above the head[s] of the quarrymen was one hundred cubits.[21]

Hezekiah's successor, Manasseh, who had one of the longest reigns in Judah, ruled from 687 to 642 B.C. He is referred to briefly in the annals of

20. J. B. Pritchard, *ANET*, p. 321.
21. *Idem.*

Esarhaddon (681–668 B.C.) where he is listed with others who paid tribute to help in the building of a royal palace.

> I called the kings of the country of Hatti and of the region on the other side of the river: Ba'lu king of Tyre, Manasseh [Me-na-si-i] king of Judah [Ia-u-di], Qaushgabri king of Edom, Musuri king of Moab, Sil-Bel king of Gaza, Metinti king of Ashkelon, Ikausu king of Ekron, Milkiashapa king of Byblos, Matanbaal king of Beth-Ammon, Ahimilki king of Ashdod—twelve kings of the seacoast.[22]

The religious practices of Manasseh can be better understood from a knowledge of Eastern religion in those centuries. Archaeology has much to say about these. We have no other information about Manasseh apart from the account in the Bible and the one reference in the annals of Esarhaddon. Evidently Judah was still under some sort of allegiance to the Assyrians. It is of some interest to note that the prophet Jeremiah was probably born in the days of Manasseh and as a boy grew up in the midst of a strange syncretism in religion. He was later to attack such non-Yahwistic practices (Jer. 7:30–8:3, etc.).

A significant collection of documents from this same Assyrian king, Esarhaddon, has been found in recent years in the form of some three hundred fragments of baked-clay cuneiform writing which, when assembled, proved to comprise eight large tablets, practically identical in content, which constituted the written document of a treaty Esarhaddon had made with his vassals to the east of Assyria in which they swore to support the accession of Ashurbanipal's sons after his death.[23] No doubt such treaties were drawn up for all of Esarhaddon's vassals. Certainly after his death there was a period of seventeen years of peace which was broken only when the sons Ashurbanipal in Nineveh and Shamash-shum-ukin in Babylon fought each other in a bloody war, and though Ashurbanipal won, it was at the price of Assyria's strength. She was in decline from 648 to her fall in 609 B.C.

These documents, apart from their historical interest in showing something of the procedures of government, give a very clear picture of the formal structure of a covenant between a suzerain and his vassal, and provide important parallels between the biblical covenants and the secular covenants of the day. It would seem that these nonbiblical covenants may have provided a useful illustration of the way in which Yahweh, Israel's King, was related to Israel, who was His vassal.[24]

But to return to the internal strife between the two sons of Esarhaddon, it is to be noted that there were repercussions all over the Assyrian world and many peoples took the opportunity to revolt. Already in 641 Elam was in revolt. In 640 in Judah, Amon, a pro-Assyrian king, was murdered (II Kings 21:20ff.;

---

22. Ibid., p. 291.
23. D. J. Wiseman, The Vassal Treaties of Esarhaddon (London, 1958).
24. See above, pp. 65f.

II Chron. 33:21ff.). Ashurbanipal marched west to deal with Judah and other rebels in the area. He may have had to punish Samaria again, for Ezra 4:9ff. speaks of foreigners being settled in that town by Asnapper.[25] In Judah the "people of the land" punished the rebels and made Josiah king, thus avoiding Assyrian retribution (II Kings 21:24; II Chron. 33:25).

But Josiah began to pursue an anti-Assyrian line both in politics and religion, one that had already been followed by Hezekiah when he sent an invitation to the Israelites in the Assyrian province of Samaria to join in the Passover (II Chron. 30:1–31:1). The death of Ashurbanipal in 627 assured Josiah of success and he extended his reforms to all Israel. The last kings of Assyria were powerless to resist. Indeed, it was in Josiah's reign that the end came for Assyria. The great coalition of Media and Babylon on the east and the hostile groups like Judah on the west encircled Assyria. In 612 Nineveh, Nimrud, Assur, and Dur-Sharrukin had fallen. Only Egypt remained loyal to Assyria in her dying throes and Pharaoh Necho set out to assist her at Harran whence her last king Assur-uballit II had fled after the fall of Nineveh.[26] Josiah's little army opposed him as he passed through Palestine, but Josiah lost his life (II Kings 23:29, 30). By 609 the collapse of Assyria was complete. The words of the prophets of Judah concerning Assyria's doom were fulfilled (Isa. 10:12–15; Zeph. 2:13–15; Nahum). This reconstruction of the activities of Pharaoh Necho is clear from the Babylonian Chronicle for the year 610 B.C. which reads as follows:

> In the sixteenth year, in the month of Iyyar, the king of Akkad called out his army and marched to Assyria. From the month of Sivan to the month of Marcheswan they marched about victoriously in Assyria. In the month of Marcheswan the Umman-manda who had come to help the king of Addad and united their armies and to the city of Harran after Assur-uballit who had sat upon the throne of Assyria they marched. As for Assur-uballit and the army of Egypt which had come to his help, fear of the enemy fell upon them; they abandoned the city and... crossed the river Euphrates.... The king of Akkad reached Harran... the city was captured and they carried off much spoil from the city and temple.[27]

The Babylonian Chronicle for the year 609 B.C. adds:

> In the month of Tammuz Assur-uballit, king of Assyria, a great Egyptian army... crossed the river, marched against the city of Harran to conquer it....[28]

---

25. A. Malamat, "The Historical Background of the Assassination of Amon, King of Judah," *IEJ*, No. 3 (1953), pp. 26–29.

26. A. Parrot, *Nineveh and the Old Testament* (London, 1955).

27. D. J. Wiseman, *Chronicles of the Chaldaean Kings (626–556 B.C.)* (London, 1956), pp. 60–63.

28. *Ibid.*

Thanks to such historical information gained from baked clay documents discovered in excavations, we can now translate the small Hebrew preposition 'al in II Kings 23:29 more accurately. The word has several meanings—"above," "upon," "beside," "against." The translators of the Authorized Version, assuming that Egypt was going to fight against Assyria on this occasion, translated accordingly. We now translate, the king of Egypt went up "*alongside* the king of Assyria," rather than "*against* the king of Assyria."

Necho had deposed the son of Josiah, who naturally became king after his father's death, and chose another son, Eliakim, whom he renamed Jehoiakim. This man was probably pro-Egyptian in his sympathies (II Kings 23:34). By 605 B.C. the Egyptian armies were defeated at Carchemish in Syria and the Babylonian general was marching into Palestine. Jehoiakim was allowed to rule, but as a tributary of Nebuchadnezzar who by now was king in Babylon. This state of affairs continued till the death of Jehoiakim in 598 B.C. Within three short months his son Jehoiakin had to face an invasion from Nebuchadnezzar. It is not clear whether this eighteen-year-old king was being punished for the intrigues of his father or whether he was involved in some personal intrigue. In any case, the Babylonian armies marched into Judah, besieged Jerusalem, and took the king into captivity. At the same time, by a shrewd move all the men of ability, the leaders and technicians, were taken away. In this way Nebuchadnezzar hoped to weaken the rebels (II Kings 24:12–16).

Two valuable inscriptions bear on these times. The Babylonian Chronicle[29] gives the first nonbiblical reference to the first attack of Nebuchadnezzar on Jerusalem. The record reads:

> In the seventh year, the month of Kislev, the king of Akkad mustered his troops, marched to the Hatti-land and encamped against the city of Judah and on the second day of the month of Adar he seized the city and captured the king. He appointed there a king of his own choice, received its heavy tribute and sent them to Babylon.

The second record comes from the archives unearthed by the German excavator Koldewey in Babylon. Here were hundreds of receipts for oil issued to various captives in the city. The name Yaukin (Jehoiakin), king of Judah, appears on three of these.[30] One of them refers to his five sons as well.

> 1½ sila [oil] for 3 carpenters from Arvad, ½ sila each; 11½ sila for 8 carpenters from Byblos, 1 sila each. . . . 3½ sila for 7 carpenters, Greeks, ½ sila each; ½ sila to Nabu-etir the carpenter; 10 [sila] to Ia-ku-u-ki-nu [Iaukin] the son of the king of Ia-ku-du [Judah], 2½ sila for the 5 sons of the king of Ia-ku-du [Judah].

29. *Ibid.*, pp. 71–73.
30. J. B. Pritchard, *ANET*, p. 308.

These receipts date about the year 592 B.C. and testify to the presence of Jehoiakin and his family in Babylon some years after his captivity.[31]

The king appointed by Nebuchadnezzar to replace Jehoiakin was the latter's uncle Zedekiah. For several years he gave his allegiance to the Babylonian king. Then he, too, began to intrigue with Egypt. As a result Nebuchadnezzar came to Palestine, bent on destruction. We have a very full account in the Bible of the last days of Judah (II Kings 25). Some very valuable materials bearing on the last eighteen months of Judah's history have been brought to light from excavations.

Both excavations and surface surveys conducted in southern Judah have confirmed the fact that there was considerable destruction carried out here at the start of the sixth century B.C. Numerous excavated mounds revealed that they were occupied till just after 600 B.C. but that there was a drastic break in their occupation after that, so that they were not occupied again till post-exilic times. Some of them were never again occupied.[32]

In Lachish we have the best picture of the destruction. Indeed, there were two destructions close together. The final destruction was violent, and so fierce was the fire which destroyed the city that the limestone of the buildings turned to lime. The most important item in the town of Lachish was the collection of inscribed potsherds or ostraca, known as the Lachish ostraca. These turned out to be military letters quickly written out in the days of feverish haste as the Babylonian armies were closing in. As we read these short notes we gain the impression that southern Judah was in a state of stress. There were urgent orders passing to and fro, special arrangements being made for fire signals, the sending of a military mission to Egypt (Jer. 26:20-23), the inspection of guards, and general increase of military activity. The whole correspondence suggests an atmosphere of nervous tension in the early stages of the war before Jerusalem fell. Here is the letter that speaks of messengers going to Egypt.

> Thy servant Hoshaiah hath sent to inform my lord Yaosh: May Yahweh cause my lord to hear tidings of peace! And now thou hast sent a letter, but my lord did not enlighten thy servant concerning the letter which thou didst send to thy servant yesterday evening, though the heart of thy servant hath been sick since thou didst write to thy servant. And as for what my lord said, "Dost thou not understand? call a scribe!" as Yahweh liveth no one hath ever undertaken to call a scribe for me; and as for any scribe who might have come to me, truly I did not call him nor would I give anything at all for him!
>
> And it hath been reported to thy servant, saying, "The commander of the host, Coniah son of Elnathan, hath come down in order to go into Egypt; and unto Hodaviah son of Ahijah and his men hath he sent to obtain (. . .) from him."

31. W. F. Albright, The Biblical Period, p. 47.
32. W. F. Albright, Archaeology of Palestine (London, 1954), pp. 140f.

Excavators at Lachish (Tell ed-Duweir), a site ca. thirty meters southeast of Jerusalem, found twenty-one ostraca in classical Hebrew that have great philological and historical value. Most are letters from the beginning of the Chaldean siege of Lachish (ca. 590 B.C.). The senders are apparently Yaosh, commander of the Lachish garrison, and his subordinate, Hashaiah, at an outlying post. In Ostracon IV, pictured here, Hashaiah mentions Yahweh and tells his commander that he has followed all orders and is watching for the arranged signals from Lachish. (Israel Department of Antiquities and Museums)

> And as for the letter of Tobiah, servant of the king, which came to Shallum son of Jaddua through the prophet, saying, "Beware!", thy servant hath sent it to my lord.[33]

Another letter tells that the soldiers in an unnamed post were looking for the fire signals of Lachish, because those of Azekah were already not visible. It would seem that the state of affairs was already more advanced than that described in Jeremiah 34:7, where all the cities of Judah had fallen except Lachish and Azekah. The letter reads as follows:

> May Yahweh cause my lord to hear this very day tidings of good! And now according to everything that my lord hath written, so hath thy servant done; I have written on the door according to all that my lord hath written to me. And with respect to what my lord hath written about the matter of Beth-haraphid, there is no one there.
> And as for Semachiah, Shemaiah hath taken him and hath brought

---

33. J. B. Pritchard, *ANET*, p. 322.

him up to the city. And as for thy servant, I am not sending *anyone*
thither [today (?), but I will send] tomorrow morning.

And let [my lord] know that we are watching for the signals of
Lachish, according to all the indications which my lord hath given, for
we cannot see Azekah.[34]

Another group of valuable ostraca has now come to light from southern
Judah. During several seasons of excavation at the site of Arad in southern
Judah[35] upward of two hundred ostraca were found. About half of these were in
Aramaic (from about 400 B.C.). But the rest were in Hebrew from the days of
the Monarchy. In particular a group came from the last Israelite fortress
(Stratum VI) that seems to belong to the period preceding Nebuchadnezzar's
first campaign of 600-598 B.C. Seventeen of these belonged to a certain
Eliashib, son of Eshyahu, who seems to have organized relations and provisions
in the area.[36] Of special interest is a letter that refers to the sending of men from
Arad to another town Ramath-Negeb to prepare for an Edomite attack. The
excavator suggests that the attack in question should be linked with events
described in I Kings 24:2 and Jeremiah 35:11 (reading Edom for Aram). In any
case the Edomites took advantage of Judah's defeat after the fall of Jerusalem and
invaded the southern areas of Judah.[37]

We shall devote some space in the next chapter to a discussion of some of
the unauthorized shrines and places of worship which existed in Judah and Israel
during the days of the Kings.[38] Josiah undertook considerable reforms in the area
of religion and destroyed these shrines (II Kings 23:4-20; II Chron. 34:3-7).
One of the towns where this program was carried out very effectively was Arad.
Here Josiah had alterations made to the walls of the citadel. The new walls cut
right across the old temple.[39] We probably have evidence of the same activity at
Beer-sheba.[40]

Until recently it has not been possible to obtain direct evidence about
events in Jerusalem apart from what we have in the Bible. But recent excavations carried out by Dr. Kathleen Kenyon on the little spur that runs south from
the south wall of the Temple area have produced some remarkable evidence.[41]
Dr. Kenyon cut a trench east-west across this spur in search of ancient walls. She
was rewarded with some significant data about Jerusalem early in the sixth
century B.C. All along the hillside, which falls away quite steeply to the east,

34. *Ibid.*
35. See above, pp. 166, 177f.
36. Y. Aharoni, *IEJ*, Vol. XVI (1966), pp. 1-7; *BASOR*, No. 184 (1966), pp. 13ff.; J. B.
Pritchard, *ANET, Supplementary Texts and Pictures* (1968), pp. 568f.
37. See the prophet Obadiah.
38. See pp. 177-180.
39. See pp. 177f.
40. See pp. 178f.
41. K. Kenyon, *Jerusalem: Excavating 3000 Years of History* (London, 1967), pp. 78-104.

there had been built a series of terraces that supported houses. Finally, some distance down the slope the wall of the period was discovered. Evidently Nebuchadnezzar's battering rams had breached the wall and had been able to loosen the terraces and send the houses tumbling down the hillside. There was an enormous task awaiting the excavator. Many tons of fallen stones had to be removed before the foundations and lower walls of the houses were revealed. But then a remarkable picture of the shape and contents of the houses came to light. When Nehemiah came to rebuild the wall about a century and a half later he built at the top of the slope beyond the fallen debris.[42]

Thus Judah came to an end and the land passed under the control of the Babylonians. Not all the Jews by any means were taken to captivity, although only the poorer people remained in the land to care for it (II Kings 25:12). Some of the Jews, including Jeremiah the prophet, went to Egypt (Jer. 43). It was perhaps fifteen hundred years since Abraham had left Ur of the Chaldees to come to Palestine. It was surely a strange thing that after all those years some of his descendants should be returning there, not as free men, but as captives. Yet they learned many lessons from this captivity, and after their return they were to undergo further experiences that were to take them on to the "fulness of times" when the Messiah would come.

42. Note Nehemiah 2:13-14.

9

CITIES OF JUDAH AND ISRAEL IN THE DAYS OF THE KINGS

WE have made some general remarks in passing about some of the features of some of the towns in Palestine in the days of the Kings. But the Israelite town in the days of the Kings is important enough to devote more space to it.

The period of the Kings lasted for about 400 years from just before 1000 B.C. to just after 600 B.C. Archaeologically the period covers Iron Age IA (1200–1150 B.C.), Iron Age IB (1150–1000 B.C.), Iron Age IIA (1000–900 B.C.), Iron Age IIB (900–800 B.C.), and Iron Age IIC (800–586 B.C.). During these centuries both Israel and Judah were invaded more than once by Egyptians, Syrians, Assyrians, and Babylonians. Several of the towns were destroyed more than once and rebuilt subsequently. Evidence of the destruction of towns comes from ash layers in the cities. It is an interesting exercise to attempt to link destruction levels with historical events. Admittedly the interpretation of archaeological evidence is not always possible, but it sometimes is.

The excavated site gives information about many facets of town life—town planning, water supply, houses and domestic utensils, public buildings and architecture, industry, shrines and temples, artistic work, and the like. The Bible has many references to such things. Clearly our understanding of biblical references is greatly enhanced by archaeological discovery. Even a cursory study of one archaeological report will reveal a new world to the non-specialist.

TOWN PLANNING IN AN ISRAELITE CITY

A number of Israelite towns have now been excavated so that certain features of the city plan in the days of the Kings have become clear.[1]

The walled city was entered through the city gate (or gates). Cities of the Solomonic period normally had the typical Solomonic gate,[2] which was set in a casemate wall. But there were other possibilities. The town of Beer-sheba, as we have seen,[3] had a gate with only two guardrooms on each side. At first it had a solid wall, but in the post-Solomon period a casemate wall was built over the solid wall. The town represented by Tell en Nasbeh some 12 kilometers north of Jerusalem and generally identified with biblical Mizpah (Judg. 20:1f.; I Sam. 7:16f.; I Kings 15:17–22; II Kings 25:22–25; Neh. 3:7; Jer. 40–41) had been deserted for about two thousand years and was reoccupied at the beginning of the Iron Age, in the eleventh century B.C., probably by the Israelites.[4] The city has been extensively excavated. It was surrounded by a great wall whose total length was 660 meters. Constructed of salients and recesses, it incorporated nine or ten towers each of which was strengthened by a glacis (sloping earth ramp). A ditch (*fosse*) seems to have surrounded the whole city. The wall was not of uniform construction, indicating that it was probably built by forced labor and perhaps in a hurry (I Kings 15:22). The gate is the best yet discovered. At the entrance there was an open square (8 by 9 meters), with benches all around. Other benches were found in the guardroom. Inside the gate was another open square. The city walls of the gate were not continuous but separated by about eight meters so that the east wall overlapped the continuation of the same wall so as to allow the gateway to be built. Towers protected each side. A second gate was placed some 60 meters to the south of the main gate. The main gate area was drained by a covered channel, a phenomenon found at Beer-sheba.[5]

The open areas and the benches at Tell en Nasbeh probably provide evidence of the arrangements in ancient Israel for conducting public business and trials at the city gate (Isa. 29:21; Amos 5:10, 15, etc.). Another example of benches at the city gate was the northern city of Dan.[6]

Immediately inside the city gate it was quite common to place important public buildings, storehouses, the local governor's residence, and so on. We shall speak in more detail below about the storehouses near the city gate. The cities of Megiddo and Beer-sheba provide good examples. These cities also contained substantial structures close to the gate which seem to have been the

---

1. Y. Shiloh, "Elements in the Development of Town Planning in the Israelite City," *IEJ*, Vol. 28, Nos. 1–2 (1978), pp. 36–51.
2. See above, pp. 112f.
3. See p. 112.
4. M. Broshi, *Naṣbeh Tell en-EAEHL III*, pp. 912–918; C. C. McCown, J. C. Wampler, and others, *Tell en Nasbeh 1–2* (1947), p. 61.
5. Y. Aharoni, *Beersheba I*, p. 14.
6. A. Biran, "Dan, Tel," *EAEHL*, Vol. I, pp. 318–320.

governor's residence.[7] Thus at Beer-sheba there was a building some 15 by 18 meters, much larger than a normal house and containing more rooms. There was an open space in front of this dwelling. At Megiddo, too, there were remains of what must have been a substantial building in Solomon's day.[8] There had been a palace here in earlier times in Stratum VII (ca. 1350–1150 B.C.), and in the post-Solomon period there was a very substantial structure on the right side of the gateway with very thick walls throughout.[9] This had been built over the Solomonic structure and largely destroyed it. But enough of the Solomonic building has been preserved to show something of its character. Hazor, too, had an impressive structure quite close to the gate, although this was probably a storehouse. An adjoining structure may have been an administrative building.

In a number of excavated towns there was an elevated area, perhaps a sort of raised central "acropolis" (fortified area or citadel). Examples of such an area occur at Beer-sheba[10] and Lachish.[11]

Apart from these large public buildings were numerous houses with their associated domestic items. We shall describe these below.

As to the layout of a city, plans varied a great deal. The city of Beer-sheba, which was something of a model city, was laid out with a circular ring road around it. Between the road and the walls lay houses of various kinds and perhaps some public buildings. Other roads crossed the town, with houses on both sides of the street. It seems that open spaces were left here and there at intervals, although the complete picture is not clear because the mound has not been excavated completely.[12] It is quite normal to build houses against the city wall in ancient Israel. At Tell Beit Mirsim (identified by some geographers with Debir, although this identification is questioned by others), houses of the Iron II period in the areas excavated were built against the wall. There is no clear pattern of a simple ring road for this town, although it was possible to go around the city by a zigzag road which followed the wall.[13] Other examples of rows of houses built against the city wall are Bethshemesh,[14] Tell en Nasbeh,[15] and Megiddo.[16] However, the detailed and easily recognizable overall city plan, dominated by the continuous circular street, is so far unique to Beer-sheba.[17]

7. Y. Aharoni, op. cit., p. 14.
8. G. Loud, Megiddo II: Seasons of 1935–1939 (1948), Level IV, Fig. 389.
9. R. S. Lamon and G. M. Shipton, Megiddo I: Seasons of 1925–34 (1939), Fig. 89, Stratum III.
10. Y. Aharoni, op. cit., p. 17.
11. Y. Aharoni, Lachish III, pp. 78ff.
12. Y. Aharoni, Beersheba I, Plate 84; "Excavation at Tell Beersheba, Preliminary Report of the Fifth and Sixth Seasons, 1973–1974," Tel Aviv, Vol. 2, No. 4 (1975), pp. 146–168. Note the map of the city on p. 148.
13. Y. Aharoni, Tell Beit Mirsim III, Plates 1–6.
14. Y. Aharoni, Ain Shems II: Map of Iron Age II–III; Vol. V, pp. 68f.
15. Y. Aharoni, Tell en Nasbeh I: Survey Map.
16. Y. Aharoni, Megiddo II, Fig. 23, p. 23.
17. Y. Shiloh, "The Four-Room House—Its Situation and Function in the Israelite City," IEJ, Vol. 20, pp. 180–190.

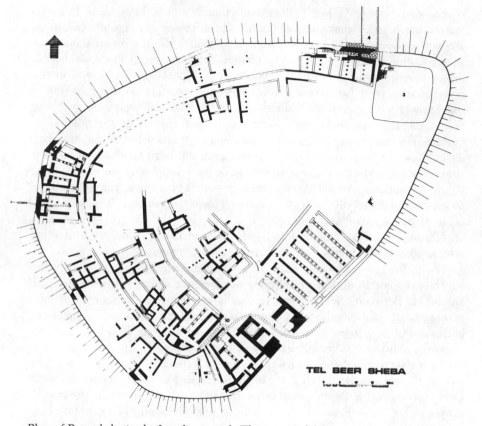

Plan of Beer-sheba in the Israelite period. The ring road forms a concentric circle with the city wall.

Two more cities call for special discussion because of some unique features which have become clear in excavation, namely, Jerusalem and Tell el-Far'ah (Tirzah).

Jerusalem in the days of the Kings was built partly along the spur which runs south from the Temple area. The terrain to the east runs quite steeply into the Kidron valley. The significant excavations of the late Dame Kathleen Kenyon in the period 1961–1967 added much new light on the character of the city of Jerusalem along this slope. By means of a large trench cut across the side of the ridge she was able to bring to light a remarkable story. A series of walls discovered down the hillside marked the limits of the city at various times. In this area Jerusalem from the days of David onward consisted largely of domestic dwellings built on a series of terraces which had been constructed up the hillside. A substantial wall was set into the hillside and filled with earth and stones behind.

Other terraces were built in a similar fashion. On these terraces small houses were built.[18] The rooms were small and the walls built of rough stones slightly dressed and coated with mud, although one large room was built on the pattern of the four-room house, the usual plan in the Iron II Age. It has been conjectured that this method of filling behind terrace walls for construction explains the references in II Samuel 5:9 and I Kings 9:24 to David and Solomon building the Millo (literally, filling). Such a mode of building was precarious since heavy rains or earth tremors would tend to dislodge parts of the retaining wall. Nebuchadnezzar discovered this when he battered down the city in 586 B.C. Dame Kathleen Kenyon discovered an enormous accumulation of stones in the area where she dug. It was apparent that in a general collapse in the area, retaining walls and house walls went tumbling down the hillside.[19] Little is known about what the city of Jerusalem was like in other areas, and we must await further excavation. However, we have some significant information about the western side of the wall of Jerusalem in the seventh century B.C. During excavations in the area formerly known as the Jewish Quarter, a fine stretch of wall was discovered belonging to the late eighth or seventh century B.C. The wall lay some 275 meters to the west of the Temple area and was curved, suggesting a bend at this point. Its general direction was from northeast to southwest. At its southern end it turns sharply west. The wall was seven meters thick, and so far some 40 meters have been uncovered. It is built entirely of large stones both dressed and undressed and laid with no binding. Two to seven courses have been preserved to a height of 3.30 meters in one place. It would appear that the area uncovered was only the foundation, for it lay on bedrock. On either side of the wall the earth contained pottery from the Iron Age II period (*ca.* 1000–586 B.C.).[20] It is of some interest that when Nehemiah went on his night excursion to explore the walls of the city, "there was no place for the beast that was under me to pass" (Neh. 2:14).

The town of Tirzah (Tell el-Far'ah) in the days of the Kings reveals an interesting story. The city of the Israelite period (Stratum III) was built on the ruins of the Late Bronze Age town. It seems to have been well planned, with parallel streets and blind alleys. Typical Iron Age houses lined the streets. Apart from one quite large structure close to the gate which may have been the residence of the local governor, the houses were fairly uniform in size and structure, reflecting a society in which there was little social stratification.[21] This town was destroyed about the middle of the ninth century, possibly at the time of Omri's conquest of Tirzah (I Kings 16:17–18), and was then deserted for

18. See K. Kenyon, *Jerusalem: Excavating 3000 Years of History* (London, 1967), Plates 46–50 following p. 116.

19. See the remarkable photo in *ibid.*, Plate 9.

20. Y. Yadin (ed.), *Jerusalem Revealed* (Jerusalem, 1975), pp. 5, 42–44. Note the photo on p. 42.

21. See R. de Vaux, "La quatrième campagne de fouilles à Tell el-Far'ah, près de Naplouse," *RB*, Vol. LIX (Oct., 1952), Plate 10 facing p. 576.

a time. The next city (Stratum II) was much more impressive.[22] A number of well-built houses were constructed according to a plan similar to that of Stratum III but somewhat larger and of superior construction. The walls were better built, with dressed facings on both sides and well-joined corners. In place of the one larger dwelling in Stratum III there were now several. These were the homes of the wealthy. They were separated from the quarter of the poor citizens by a long, straight wall. The poor quarter contained small houses, closely packed together with thin, rough walls. In contrast to the uniformity of the tenth-century residences this great difference between the dwellings of the poor and of the wealthy in Stratum II demonstrated the serious social differentiation which emerged in Israel in the ninth and eighth centuries. In fact Stratum II belonged mainly to the eighth century and is a tangible commentary on the protests of the prophets Isaiah and Amos against this class distinction in Israel (Isa. 5:8–10; Amos 3:15; 8:4–6, etc.).[23]

With an ongoing program of excavation in Israel the character of Israelite cities will become much clearer as the years go by.

WATER SUPPLY

Walled cities of any size would require considerable quantities of water. Palestine lacks rivers on the highlands, although some small rivers run into the Mediterranean Sea. In the Jordan Valley area there is abundance of water from the River Jordan and from the Wadi Far'ah, which is watered by a fine spring. Galilee is a fresh-water lake, and in areas to the north of Galilee the headquarters of the Jordan provide good water. But in the mountain areas people depended on two main sources of water, springs and cisterns. Some towns like Jerusalem and Megiddo had fine springs just outside the city walls. Other like Hazor and Beer-sheba had access to underground water. Even where there were springs or when water supplies from a spring were inadequate, the people had to dig cisterns into the limestone rock and plaster these with lime plaster.

There were no problems in obtaining water in times of peace. People could move out beyond the city walls to the spring and carry water back to their homes in the city. In times of war, however, this was not possible. In order to gain access to the spring without risk of enemy harassment the people of Israel devised a remarkable system in which they dug a vertical shaft deep into the ground inside the city and then dug a horizontal shaft to the spring outside the city walls.

At Megiddo a great vertical shaft, 35 meters deep, was sunk from the surface of the ground. The upper part of the shaft was dug partly through the accumulated occupation debris of past centuries and partly through solid rock. The

22. *Ibid.*, Plate 11.
23. R. de Vaux, "El-Far'a, Tell," *EAEHL*, Vol. II, pp. 400–404; *RB*, Vol. LIX (Oct., 1952), p. 566.

upper part was lined with masonry. At the base of the vertical portion, the shaft took an angular direction and finally turned horizontal for 63 meters to the spring. As a finishing touch to this remarkable engineering feat a stone wall was built to block the mouth of the cave so that the water supply was accessible only from within the city. As to the date of this remarkable achievement, it probably goes back to the time of Solomon or perhaps shortly after.[24]

Jerusalem, too, had an internal water shaft dug through the solid rock inside the city walls—first at an angle, then roughly horizontal, then vertical, and then horizontal to the fine Gihon Spring which was situated on the western side of the Kidron valley and delivered its waters into the valley. This system was already in use by the Canaanites before David captured the city (II Sam. 5:7, 8).[25] Modern investigation has shown that a maze of tunnels was constructed with the Jerusalem spring over the ages. The most famous of these is the Siloam Tunnel dating from about 700 B.C., which is to be associated with the conduit built by Hezekiah (II Kings 20:20; II Chron. 32:5, 30). This tunnel followed a complicated course. First it ran back into the hillside, then it turned south and followed the ridge with some slight deviations, next it turned west, and finally it ran into the Pool of Siloam inside the city walls. The shaft was dug from two directions at the same time. As a result there had to be an adjustment in levels. It remains a puzzle to modern engineers as to how the two sides met. Finally, at the point of meeting there was a slight overlap. The triumph of the meeting is recorded in the Siloam Inscription found in 1880, which reads:

> This is the story of the boring through: whilst (the tunnellers lifted) the pick each toward his fellow and whilst three cubits (yet remained) to be bored (through, there was heard) the voice of a man calling to his fellow, for there was a split in the rock on the right hand and on (the left hand). And on the day of the boring through, the tunnellers struck, each in the direction of his fellows, pick against pick. And the water started to flow from the source to the pool, twelve hundred cubits. A hundred cubits was the height of the rock above the head of the tunnellers.[26]

This tunnel enabled the people of Jerusalem to survive the siege of the Assyrian army of Sennacherib during Hezekiah's reign (II Kings 18:13–19:37).

It may be conjectured that other cities were able to develop similar internal water systems in order to reach the spring on which the city depended for water.

The alternate source of water to be reached by a shaft was the water table which lay in the valley outside the city walls. Three well-known examples of this device are those at Hazor, Gibeon, and Beer-sheba.

24. R. Lamon, *The Megiddo Water System* (Chicago, 1935); Y. Yadin, "Megiddo," *EAEHL*, Vol. III, pp. 854f.

25. K. M. Kenyon, *op. cit.*, pp. 19–22.

26. This translation follows that in *ibid.*, p. 70.

Siloam Tunnel inscription (ca. 400 B.C.). It relates the completion of this Jerusalem tunnel, which was dug by two teams that started at opposite ends and finally met. (Israel Department of Antiquities and Museums)

At Hazor a shaft 30 meters deep connected with a sloping tunnel some 25 meters in length, taking the total depth to 40 meters. This shaft was constructed in Stratum VIII in the ninth century B.C., that is, in the days of the Omri dynasty. The upper part of the shaft was cut through the strata of earlier occupation levels and the lower portion was quarried out of the rock. The entrance to the shaft was quite extensive, being some 19 meters by 15 meters. It was supported by huge supporting walls. Eventually the tunnel ended in a sort of pool situated at the natural water level.[27]

At Gibeon two water systems were in use—one leading to ground-water and the other to a spring in the village nearby. The first was a cylindrical shaft cut into the rock beneath the city some 11.3 meters in diameter and 10.8 meters deep. A spiral staircase was cut along the north and east sides of the pool. At the bottom, the stairway continued downward into a tunnel which led to a water chamber 13.6 meters below. By means of this spiral staircase of seventy-nine steps the citizens of Gibeon could gain access to fresh water lying 24.4 meters below the level of the city. It has been conjectured that this construction is the "pool of Gibeon" referred to in II Samuel 2:13. It has been calculated that about three thousand tons of limestone would have been removed in this enterprise.

The second device for obtaining water at Gibeon in a time of siege was a stepped tunnel which led from inside the city to a spring in the village below. This passage of ninety-three steps cut through the rock was dug later in the Iron

---

27. Y. Yadin, "Hazor," *EAEHL*, Vol. II, pp. 490f., 494; "The fifth season of excavations at Hazor, 1968–1969," *BA*, Vol. 32, pp. 63ff.

This Iron Age (ca. 1200–300 B.C.) pool at Gibeon may be the one mentioned in II Sam. 2:13. The spiral staircase leads down to a tunnel and thence to a water supply, which is well below the level of the city and thus protected in time of siege. (University Museum, University of Pennsylvania)

Age II period, perhaps at a time when the flow of water into the water chamber of the pool of Gibeon was inadequate.[28]

A third system of which something is known was that at Beer-sheba. It was located at the northeastern corner of the city. Steps about 3.30 meters wide led into a deep shaft which was about 17 meters square at the entrance. The circular flight of stairs resembled those at Megiddo, Gibeon, and Hazor. Unfortunately the excavators at Beer-sheba did not carry their work to the source of water, but it is clear that the Beer-sheba project was a gigantic one, comparable to that at Hazor.[29]

The water cistern provided another source of water. Normally this consisted of a neck of about two or three feet in diameter which was sunk into the rock for

28. J. B. Pritchard, "Gibeon," *EAEHL*, Vol. II, pp. 447, 449; *The Water System at Gibeon* (Philadelphia, 1961).
29. Y. Aharoni (ed.), *Beersheba I*, p. 16.

three or four feet. This neck opened into a much larger, bulbous-shaped reservoir whose capacity varied considerably. The interior of the cistern was then plastered over with lime plaster to prevent leakage. Whenever it rained, water from rooms or the ground surface was directed into the cistern. The cistern was commonly the adjunct of the Israelite house (II Kings 18:31; Prov. 5:15; Jer. 2:13, etc.). At times the cistern was used as a place of imprisonment (Gen. 37:24 where pit=cistern; Jer. 38:6). Jeremiah likened the men of Israel who forsook Yahweh and followed strange gods to the farmer who had a flowing spring on his property but ignored it and hewed out a cistern which was cracked and would not hold water (Jer. 2:13). He was imprisoned in such a cistern for a time. With a wry sense of humor the narrator sets us at ease by telling us that "there was no water in the cistern, but only mire, and Jeremiah sank in the mire" (Jer. 38:6). In order to get him up from the cistern, old clothes had to be sent down and placed under his arms to protect his armpits from the ropes by which he was drawn out (Jer. 38:12, 13).[30]

We shall draw attention to household cisterns when we discuss Israelite houses. One interesting archaeological by-product of cisterns is that over the centuries the women who came there for water sometimes dropped their water-carrying vessels into the cistern where they broke and fell among the silt and mud (Eccl. 12:6). If this went on over a long period of time, there were stratified pottery deposits on the bottom of the cistern. It has become regular procedure for the modern archaeologist to excavate cisterns. In this way he is able to recover significant objects and to obtain a good picture of the development of pottery styles over the years. Sometimes imported vessels whose date is known in the land of their origin become a useful date indicator for local wares.[31]

HOUSES

Several decades of excavation in Palestine have provided important evidence about ancient Palestinian dwellings of all ages.[32] The first Israelites built on the same plan as their Late Bronze predecessors, but their dwellings were much poorer. They re-used such items as silos and oil presses in some cases. The simplest and poorest houses consisted of a courtyard with a single room on one side. Good examples were found at Tell Qasile.[33] Another crudely built house was found at Bethshemesh. It had a courtyard 34 by 20 feet, with three equal-

30. In 1951, during the first season of excavation at Dibon in Transjordan, the writer was set the task of identifying cisterns on and off the mound. He recorded 66 in all. See F. V. Winnett and W. L. Reed, "The Excavations at Dibon (Dhiban) in Moab," AASOR, Vols. 36–37 (1961), p. 6 n. 8.

31. P. Lapp, "The Pottery of Palestine in the Persian Period," in E. D. A. Kuschke and E. Katsch (eds.), Archäologie und Altes Testament (1970), pp. 179–197. Note p. 180.

32. H. K. Beebe, "Ancient Palestinian Dwellings," BA, Vol. XXXI, No. 2 (May, 1968), pp. 38–58.

33. B. Maisler, BA, Vol. XIV (1951), p. 48.

sized rooms on one side each eleven feet by ten and a half feet. There was stone paving in the court and in two of the rooms. Sometimes one half of the court-yard was covered over to provide more shelter. A house of this type dating to about 900 B.C., just after Solomon's day, was found at Hazor.[34]

Some houses were more ambitious than the simple dwelling and had a courtyard with rooms on two adjoining sides or on three sides. One fine house at Megiddo dating from about 1050 B.C. had two entrances onto the street, each of which led into a corridor off which was a group of rooms.[35] The end of each corridor led into the large courtyard. A stairway at the back of the house led to a second story. The overall dimensions of this house were 104 by 97 feet, so that it must have belonged to a person of wealth or importance. The floors were paved with fine lime plaster.

The most common type of house in the days of the Kings consisted of a courtyard with rooms on three sides. This was, in fact, a style of house which was used in Palestine from 1700 B.C. onward. Some archaeologists have called this type of house the "four-room house."[36] It consisted of a room built across the whole length of the short axis of the courtyard plus the courtyard itself, which was divided into three parts by two rows of pillars set along the long axis of the court. These pillars supported a part of the courtyard area, although the actual courtyard was left open. Generally the back room was subdivided into two or three smaller rooms while the side wings of the courtyard could be walled up between the pillars to provide more rooms. There was a wide variety of pos-sibilities. Usually the house was one story and had an entrance to the street. In the courtyard were found ovens and silos, various stone grinders and saddle querns, stone bowls and kitchen pottery. Sometimes houses of this type were built back to back with a common back wall but facing parallel streets. When the walls of the house were substantial enough, a second story was added. Stairs were provided either outside or inside the house to reach the second story.

An interesting "four-room" house was found at Shechem.[37] An original house was later expanded by its owner by the addition of two rooms along the long axis and two rooms along the short axis of the original courtyard. The courtyard contained a storage bin, a large open hearth, a saddle quern, and stone grinders. Cobblestones covered the floors of the first room on each side of the entrance. Querns and a small silo in one room at the back suggest a kitchen which had access to a large silo in an adjoining room. The ceiling was made of beams of half logs laid in pairs, and a mixture of clay and straw mortar about two inches thick covered the beams.

34. Y. Yadin, Hazor I, p. 14, House No. 48.
35. G. Loud, Megiddo II, Fig. 83, p. 37.
36. W. F. Albright, AASOR, Vol. XXI–XXII (1943), p. 55; R. de Vaux, PEQ, Vol. LXXXVIII (1956), p. 133; J. B. Pritchard, BA, Vol. XXVIII (1965), pp. 10–17; G. E. Wright, Shechem, the Biography of a Biblical City (London, 1965), pp. 159–162; B. Maisler, BA, Vol. XIV (1951), pp. 47f., etc.
37. G. E. Wright, op. cit., pp. 158–162, Plate 976.

Large houses of the four-room type have been found at Hazor dating to the eighth century B.C.[38] In one such house, rooms on the two sides of the courtyard were entered from the courtyard. The row of stone pillars was off center in this case. They supported a roof over the narrower part of the courtyard, which was paved. The main courtyard was open and had an oven and storage jars. The overall size was 44 by 42 feet, suggesting it was the residence of a government official or a man of wealth.

The presence of water cisterns was not uncommon. At Tell en Nasbeh the standard four-room house was common. During excavations fifty-three cisterns were discovered and cleared, all of them private ones and somewhat smaller than those found in other sites.[39]

The domestic pottery found in these houses is generally badly smashed, but it may be related to the pottery found intact in the tombs because of distinctive rims, handles, bases, decorations, and the like, so that it is possible to give a reliable picture of the pottery belonging to each age.[40]

PUBLIC BUILDINGS AND ARCHITECTURE

While architectural features are associated with all buildings they are more pronounced in the larger public buildings. A number of the more impressive of these will now be reviewed.

Masonry is often a distinctive feature of a period. Solomon's age was given to the use of large ashlar blocks (large hewn stones). These were found in such cities as Megiddo and Hazor. The recognition of this type of masonry in the foundation of the so-called "stables" at Megiddo enabled Professor Y. Yadin to link it with the Solomonic gate and to demonstrate that the overlying "stables" were post-Solomonic. We may presume that in Solomon's day the use of these large ashlar blocks was widespread in much the same way as the characteristic masonry of the later Herod was used all over his domain.

One feature described in I Kings 6:36, namely, a courtyard built of three courses of hewn stone and a row of cedar beams, has been discovered in Megiddo.[41]

The town of Samaria has preserved some beautiful masonry of the ninth century B.C. dating to the days of Ahab and Omri. The outer city wall consisted of blocks of stone with a marginal draft arranged in a neat order of one "header" (the stone laid lengthwise) and two "stretchers" (the stone laid end on). Each stone was carefully smoothed and laid without mortar. The inner city wall was

38. Y. Yadin, *Hazor II*, Plate CCIV.
39. C. C. McCown, *Tell en Nasbeh I*, ch. 12, "Some Cisterns and Silos," pp. 129–147.
40. R. Amiran, *Ancient Pottery of the Holy Land* (Jerusalem, 1969).
41. R. G. Lamon and G. M. Shipton, *Megiddo I, the Seasons of 1925–1934, Strata I–V*, p. 59, Building 538.

made of smoothed masonry similarly laid without mortar.[42] The discovery of large quantities of ivory within the palace precincts probably sheds light on a feature of the internal architecture, namely, the decoration of the walls inside the palace with friezes of ivory in the style of the Assyrian palaces. We have here an explanation of Ahab's "ivory house" (I Kings 22:39).[43]

An interesting feature of the Solomonic period and the periods following at Megiddo is the use of the Proto-Aeolic capital, probably in public buildings. The same feature was discovered at Hazor from the ninth century B.C. where there was a monumental entrance to an open area.[44] Megiddo, too, produced several of these capitals. They were evidently widely used in the tenth and ninth centuries B.C.

Domestic architecture was generally much simpler. The poorest houses were built of one thickness of rough stones whose interstices were packed with smaller stones and covered with mud plaster. Bigger houses were built of double thicknesses of stones, often smoothed off, at least on the inside, and covered with lime plaster. Frequently the ends of walls and doorjambs were built of squared stones. Amos seems to have been referring to the large houses of the wealthy in his reference to the winter houses and the summer houses, houses of ivory and great houses (Amos 3:15; cf. Jer. 36:22). His reference in 5:19 to the man who fled into his house on the Day of the Lord, leaned with his hand on the wall, and was bitten by a serpent would seem to be to a poorer house where a snake might lurk among the stones. Incidentally, Amos gives us a glimpse of building methods in 6:7 where he refers to a wall built with the aid of a plumb line. Probably the ancient Palestinian built his own house with such materials as were readily accessible, for example, roofing timbers, stones, and mud bricks. Such complex structures as vaults, long known in Egypt and Mesopotamia, seem not to have been used, at least to any extent, in Palestine till the Persian period.[45] Large public buildings could draw on specialist builders local and foreign (I Kings 5:18). This would account for Phoenician, Egyptian, and Greek influences in architecture.

Clearly the study of architecture in any land is a vast one. All we have attempted to do is to provide a few glimpses into what is known at present. We know a lot more about building materials and building methods, about houses, rooms, roofs, doors, courtyards, architectural features, dimensions of houses and courtyards, and the like than before recent archaeology had done its work. It

---

42. J. W. Crowfoot, K. M. Kenyon, and E. L. Sukenik, *The Buildings at Samaria* (1942).

43. J. W. and G. M. Crowfoot, *Early Ivories from Samaria* (London, 1938); N. Avigad, "Samaria," *EAEHL*, Vol. IV, pp. 1038, 1044, 1046.

44. R. S. Lamon and G. M. Shipton, *Megiddo I*, pp. 14–15; Y. Yadin *et al.*, *Hazor III–IV*, Plates CCCLXII–CCCLXIII.

45. See O. Tufnell, *Lachish III*, Plate 120; R. W. Hamilton, *IDB*, Vol. I, p. 120. More recently there has been a hint of such structures in Deir Alla. See H. J. Franken, *VT*, Vol. XI (1951), p. 367.

would appear that houses and other buildings were intended to be used over long periods, and extensive repairs, additions, and internal adjustments were carried out over many years except in the cases of war, earthquake, or fire. Each new piece of knowledge we gain enables us to understand the written records of the Bible and sometimes to correct former interpretations.

INDUSTRY

There are references in the Bible to potters, dyers, metal workers, stone masons, weavers, wine makers who tramp out the grapes, men who press oil from the olive, farmers, merchants, and others. Modern archaeological investigation has shed some light on all these.

It would seem that some industry was carried on in the home, which may also have been used as a shop. In Tell Beit Mirsim there were cylindrical stone vessels varying between 70 and 90 centimeters in height and diameter in which there was hollowed out a relatively small and roughly spherical basin between 30 and 45 centimeters in diameter with a mouth one-half to two-thirds as wide. Around the rim ran a circular groove with a small hole at one point to allow liquid to run back into the basin. These vessels have been described as dye vats. They normally occurred in pairs, and they were found in several areas of the city. The presence of many loom weights in the city lends support to the view that at this town there was a dyeing and weaving industry. It is even possible that the stone pillars which are such a common feature of Israelite houses may have had a double function—as roof supports and as bearers of looms.[46]

Gibeon was a center for the production and export of wine in the eighth and seventh centuries B.C. Excavations here brought to light sixty-three rock-cut cellars for the storage of wine at a constant temperature of 18° C. The cellars were bottle-shaped and averaged 2.2 meters in depth, 2 meters in diameter at the bottom, and .67 meters in diameter at the opening. In the same area wine presses carved from the rock and with channels for conducting the grape juice to the fermentation tanks and settling basins were discovered. The jars in which the wine was stored had a capacity of nearly ten gallons. It is estimated that the sixty-three cellars would have provided storage space for jars containing 25,000 gallons of wine. There also were smaller jars with inscribed handles on which the name Gibeon (gb'n) often appeared with a proper name, probably that of the maker. Stoppers to close the jars and a funnel for filling the jars also were found.[47]

Numerous pottery bowls in small rooms facing a street suggest that food was sold in some houses. A house at eighth-century Hazor provides a good example. Houses which contained more than the usual number of saddle querns for a

46. W. F. Albright, AASOR, Vol. XXI–XXII (1943), pp. 50–53. Note p. 50.
47. J. B. Pritchard, Winery, Defenses and Soundings at Gibeon (Philadelphia, 1964).

family may point to a corn-grinding business. Narrow rooms attached to the exterior housewalls and lined with rows of jars full of carbonized grain point to shops for the sale of grain.

One of the best-known structures in the general area of production and distribution is the storehouse, which is well represented now in cities like Beer-sheba, Megiddo, Tell el Hesi, Tell Abu Hawam, Tell Qasile, Hazor, and Tell Malhata.[48] As we have seen,[49] these structures were first identified at Megiddo as Solomon's Stables from the references in I Kings 4:26 and 9:19, although some unease about this identification was expressed by J. B. Pritchard.[50] The discovery of similar structures at Beer-sheba containing a wide variety of vessels—bowls, cooking pots, storage jars, jugs, decanters, flasks, etc.—seemed to confirm the view that this type of structure was a storehouse. Certainly at Beer-sheba and Megiddo structures of this kind lay near the gateway. We can picture transport animals laden with their goods, passing through the city gate and moving only a short distance to the storehouse. It is of interest to notice some details of these structures at Beer-sheba and Megiddo.

At Beer-sheba one entered the city through the gateway, which had two guardrooms on each side, and turned right where three storehouses lay. Each was similar in structure and consisted of three long rooms approximately 10 by 18 meters. Two center rows of pillars divided the area into three long, narrow rooms. The width of the central room was about 2.0 meters and that of the side rooms about 2.5 meters. The side rooms were paved with stones of various sizes. The central room rose about 40 to 50 centimeters (about the level of the two side rooms) and had a floor of beaten earth level with the street outside, so that the side rooms seem to be sunken in relation to the street. The outer walls of the building and the wall separating the three sections were made of sun-dried bricks built on a stone foundation and then plastered with lime plaster about 2 to 3 centimeters thick. Each section had 9 to 11 pillars of squared stone about 50 by 50 centimeters. The space between the pillars remained open so that easy access was possible to the storage area. The main entrance to each section opened to the street. The total area of the storehouse complex was 600 square meters. The variety of vessels found suggests that a variety of products was stored here. We may conjecture that such things as grain, wine, and oil were the normal commodities to be found here. Several ostraca which seem to be receipts resemble in their general contents those found at Samaria,[51] which named a certain product from two localities of the district. It would seem that at Samaria and Beer-sheba, and no doubt at many other towns, there were centers of district administration,

48. See Z. Herzog, "The Storehouses," in Y. Aharoni (ed.), *Beersheba I*, pp. 23–30, for a general description of these.

49. Above, pp. 110f.

50. J. B. Pritchard, "The Megiddo Stables: A Reassessment," in J. A. Sanders (ed.), *Essays in Honour of Nelson Glueck, Near Eastern Archaeology in the Twentieth Century* (1970), pp. 268–276.

51. See above, pp. 138f. See also Y. Aharoni, *Beersheba I*, pp. 71–77.

and that royal stores were maintained in these places according to regions and localities.

The structures at Megiddo were similar but more numerous, and were set in two areas of the city. On the southern side of the city, near to the water system, lay five such structures side by side. In front of these was a large courtyard, perhaps to rest the animals or to provide an area for conducting business, or both. On the northern side of the city and to the right of the main gateway lay three blocks of storehouse units, one with five sections, one with two sections, and another with five sections, that is, seventeen in all, arranged around three sides of a rectangle. A feature of the Megiddo storehouses was the presence of several hollowed-out stone blocks placed beside the pillars, which seem to have

Grain storage silo at Megiddo from the time of Jeroboam. It is stone lined and can hold 12,800 bushels of grain. (Allen Myers)

served as water troughs or feed boxes for the animals.[52] The date of the Megiddo storehouses is post-Solomon, possibly in the days of Omri or Ahab in the middle of the ninth century B.C., so that they belong to Stratum IV A and are thus contemporary with the water system.

So the picture that now emerges about these interesting structures at Beersheba, Megiddo, Tell el Hesi, Tell Abu Hawam, Tell Qasileh, Hazor, Tell Malhata, and perhaps also at Taanach and Gibeon is that they represent storehouses where the local administration collected commodities brought in to key cities, possibly as taxes. Perhaps these storehouses should be identified with the *mishkenot* (Hebrew) mentioned in the Bible in the days of Solomon and Hezekiah. A significant description that defines the role of these structures is found in II Chronicles 32:27-29, which refers to storehouses for the increase of corn and wine and oil. They should be linked with the system of collection and distribution for which evidence is found in the ostraca of Samaria, Arad, and Beer-sheba.

Some indication of the quantities of grain that might be gathered at one place is shown in the large storage silo at Megiddo. This huge, stone-lined storage pit capable of holding 12,800 bushels of grain was discovered by excavators. The bin was at least 7 meters deep. Its rim may originally have been somewhat higher than the highest preserved point. It was 11 meters in diameter at the top and 7 meters at the bottom. The entire structure was of uncoursed rubble which was probably not plastered originally since chaff and grain were found in the chinks between the stones.[53] Similar olive-oil presses were found at Gezer[54] and at Bethshemesh.[55]

HIGH PLACES, SHRINES, AND TEMPLES

The stress on the legitimacy of the central sanctuary in Deuteronomy 12 and the constant complaint of the prophets about illegitimate high places scattered around the land raise questions about the extent to which high places, shrines, and rival temples existed in Judah and Israel. Modern excavation has produced some vivid illustrations of the practice. There is a growing body of archaeological evidence that other places of worship besides Jerusalem did exist in the days of the Kings.

The best preserved of these is probably that at Arad, which was discovered in the northwest corner of the citadel. It was found originally in the tenth century (Stratum XI) in Solomon's time and continued in use through Strata X to VII, that is, from the ninth to the seventh century B.C. It was modified a

---

52. Y. Yadin, "Megiddo," *EAEHL*, Vol. III, p. 848; R. S. Lamon and G. M. Shipton, *Megiddo I: Seasons of 1925-1934*, pp. 32-47, Fig. 44 (p. 37), Fig. 53 (p. 41).

53. W. F. Albright, "The Excavation of Tell Beit Mirsim, The Iron Age," *AASOR*, Vols. XXI-XXII for 1941-1943, pp. 62f., Plate 49.

54. R. A. Macalister, *Gezer II* (1912), pp. 61-65.

55. E. Grant, *Ain Shems I* (1931), pp. 25ff.; *Ain Shems V* (1932), pp. 75f.

good deal in the late eighth century (Hezekiah's day) and finally destroyed at the end of the seventh century in Josiah's day when a casemate wall was built across the middle of it. At the time of King Uzziah (ca. 769–733 B.C.) the sanctuary consisted of a broad courtyard with an entrance from the east end and an altar for burnt offerings approximately in the center of the room. From this room one passed into a second, narrower room, at the back of which was the Holy of Holies and which was approached up a flight of three steps. On one of these steps were found two stone incense altars 40 centimeters and 51 centimeters high respectively. The tops of these altars were concave and covered with a layer of burned organic matter, perhaps the remains of animal fat. Inside the Holy of Holies was a paved platform (bamah or high place) and a stone pillar (masṣebah) about one meter high, smoother and painted red. Two earlier pillars were built into the wall and covered by plaster. The altar for burnt offerings which stood in the center of the courtyard was built of mud brick and small stones in accordance with biblical law (Exod. 20:25, etc.). It was about 2.5 meters square and is reminiscent of the altar of the Tabernacle (Exod. 27:1) and perhaps like the original altar in Jerusalem (2 Chron. 6:13). The altar was covered by a large flint slab surrounded by two plastered grooves, evidently for collecting sacrificial blood. During the ninth century some changes in structure were made, but the essential elements remained. About the end of the eighth century both the altar of burnt offering and the high place were covered over, probably as a result of the reforms of Hezekiah (II Kings 18:1–50). It seems that the place of the sanctuary was reduced to a large open room. In the next century even this was wiped out, probably when Josiah finally destroyed all unauthorized places of worship (II Kings 23:4–20; II Chron. 34:3–7). We have some other glimpses into this sanctuary recorded on some of the ostraca found in the city. Two of these, found in the sanctuary, contain references to the priestly families of Pashhur and Meremoth, and one refers to "The House of Yahweh," which may be a reference to the local sanctuary regarded by the people of Arad as a legitimate place of worship. It was operated, it seems, by members of priestly families.[56]

The second city where religious activity of some kind was carried on was Beer-sheba. In the second season of the excavations (1970) two altars characteristic of the period were found in a room of an eighth-century B.C. house. One was a flat, square object on four short legs with a hollowed out cavity on top. It was 3.5 by 6.5 by 6.5 centimeters. Such small limestone altars from later in the Iron Age have been discovered at Tell Malhata, perhaps at the end of the seventh or beginning of the sixth century B.C.[57] But of much more significance was a remarkable large horned altar built of numerous pieces of a distinctive white stone. The altar had been dismantled at some stage and its parts used in a wall as filling under a roadway. But the altar was reassembled when the distinctive stone pieces were collected from two different areas, which were, however, not far apart. It would appear that the altar stood about 157 centimeters (65 inches) high or three large (royal) cubits, similar to the height of the altar at Arad and in the Tabernacle (Exod. 27:1) and perhaps to the one in Solomon's Temple (II Chron. 6:13). The width of the altar was uncertain since there may have been additional stones between the horns which have not been found. But it is possible that it was a square of five cubits like the altars at Arad and the biblical altars.[58] The placement of the altar in the city is not certain either, and there has been a good deal of scholarly discussion about this.[59]

We have some evidence of the existence of a place of worship at the town of Lachish. Lachish was an ancient religious center. In the Late Bronze Age there was a shrine on the tell and another in the fosse below the tell which had been destroyed twice and rebuilt during the Late Bronze Age. Excavators brought to light remnants of a high place from the Israelite period (Strata V–III). These lay beneath a later Hellenistic temple and included a large stone pillar (*maṣṣebah*), the remains of the trunk of an olive tree (Asherah?), several pits containing broken stone pillars, and votive objects. Nearby was a small room 3 by 4 meters with plastered benches along the walls and a raised platform in one corner. On the benches and near the platform was a large collection of cult vessels including a stone incense altar with horns, four pottery incense burners, chalices, bowls, lamps, and other pottery vessels. This small cult room attributed to Stratum V was destroyed in the latter part of the tenth century B.C. (Solomon's day), but the finds add weight to the view that the ruins of the nearby high place in Levels V–III were based on a tradition of an earlier cult in the area. It has been conjectured that we have here a Jewish temple similar to the Yahwistic temple at Arad.[60]

At the northern extremes of Israel the town of Dan had an unusual structure. At the northern side of the mound the excavators discovered an unusual, almost square platform 18.7 by 18.2 meters built of fine masonry laid in headers and stretchers. Such a structure was characteristic of the Israelite period.[61] The evidence suggests that the platform was probably built in the days of Jeroboam I and enlarged in the days of Ahab and Jeroboam II. The space enclosed by the four outer walls was then filled with basalt stones laid closely one on top of the other. A flight of steps 8 meters wide was built against the southern wall of the platform. It has been proposed that we have here an open air high place

58. Y. Aharoni, "The Horned Altar of Beer-sheba," BA, Vol. 37, No. 1 (1974), pp. 1–6.

59. H. Shanks, "Yigael Yadin finds a Bama at Beer-sheba," BAR, Vol. III, No. 1 (1977), pp. 3–12; A. F. Rainey, "Beer-sheba Excavator Blasts Yadin—No Bama at Beer-Sheba," BAR, Vol. III, No. 3 (1977), pp. 18–21, 56.

60. D. Ussishkin, "Lachish," EAEHL, Vol. III, pp. 747–749.

61. See above, p. 172.

(*bamah*). Pottery sherds collected from the stone steps suggest a date of about 850 B.C., but this represents one of the stages of building. The general area seems to have a tradition of sacredness since in Hellenistic and Roman times there were shrines in the area. It is of some interest that the extent of the territories of ancient Israel was "from Dan to Beer-sheba" (I Sam. 3:20; II Sam. 3:10; 17:11; 24:2, 15; I Kings 4:25, etc.). King Rehoboam I set up a golden calf at Dan and another in Bethel, the two towns marking the northern and southern limits of Jeroboam's domains, which were known as Israel (I Kings 12:29). It seems, therefore, that the presence of some sacred area at Dan is to be expected.

A further structure, very much smaller, stood at the entrance to the city of Dan. The outer gateway gave entrance to a stone-paved courtyard built of large basalt stones, some 19.5 by 9.4 meters. Here people would gather for private or official purposes. The excavator has proposed that we may have here an illustration of the "street" (*rehob*) referred to often in the Bible (e.g., Judg. 19:15; II Chron. 32:6).

It was in this court just before the inner gate that an unusual structure and a bench were found. The structure, built of limestone, was a small platform with a single broad step in front and four decorated bases surrounding it, probably the bases of columns which supported a canopy. The use to which this structure was put remains a puzzle. It may have provided support for the king's throne or a cult statue. The bench, which was 5 meters long, may have been used by elders of the community.[62]

Kathleen Kenyon found evidence that even in Jerusalem under the shadow of the Temple there was a small shrine. This is not surprising in the light of some of Jeremiah's words (Jer. 7:30f.; 19:4-6; 25:6; 44:8, etc.). In her excavations she discovered a small room in which were two standing pillars. These do not seem to have been roof-supports since the room was too small to require them. She proposed that they were *maṣṣeboth* (sacred pillars). Some support for the idea that this was a sacred area came from the discovery that at the back of this room, set on bare rock, was another small stone structure set apart by itself which Kenyon interpreted as the base of the altar. There are some puzzling features about the whole complex, but at least it is suggestive of a cult center of some kind.[63]

Evidence is growing that the prophets were not speaking against imaginary cult centers in various parts of the land but against actual shrines and temples which existed alongside the Temple in Jerusalem. In these places there was a real danger that the people might become involved with kinds of worship which were foreign to the pure worship of Yahweh. It was this danger that Josiah sought to eradicate in his great reform (II Kings 23:4-20). We may expect that further excavation in the years ahead will elucidate the question still more.

62. A. Biran, "Dan, Tel," *EAEHL*, Vol. I, pp. 318-320; *IEJ*, Vol. 20 (1970), pp. 92ff.
63. K. Kenyon, *op. cit.*, pp. 65-66, Plates 33-35.

ARTISTIC WORK

According to the Decalogue Israel was forbidden to make representations in the form of graven images or likenesses of anything that is in heaven above, in the earth beneath, or in the water under the earth. The law forbade the worship of all such things. As a result artists in Israel were restricted in the subjects they could represent. The whole range of geometrical patterns and of plants could be depicted by the artists. But representations of human or animal forms were forbidden.

Yet despite such limitations the artisans of Israel were able to achieve some artistic creations in architectural features, in pottery and faience, in jewelry, and the like.

We have already alluded briefly to some of the features of Israelite architecture.[64] There is beautiful artistry in some of the masonry of Samaria, Megiddo, and Hazor, in the arrangement of squared stones in walls, in the use of the Proto-Aeolic capitals, in the design of gateways, storehouses, administrative buildings, and so on.

Some of the pottery of the Iron Age also has a beautiful symmetry about it, and although it was almost completely devoid of painting of any kind it achieved some attractive results by its widespread use of burnishing on reddish pottery. The water decanter, Jeremiah's earthen flask (baqbuq, Jer. 19:1), was among the most attractive and graceful of all Iron Age pottery vessels. But the bowls with their heavy profiled rims and ring bases, decorated inside and often outside as well by burnished rings, had a charm of their own. It has often been claimed that when set alongside the beautifully painted vessels of the Late Bronze Age many of which were imported, and even of some of the painted vessels of the Iron I period, the pottery of the days of the Kings (Iron II period) was peculiarly drab and uninspiring. This view is a serious over-statement of the contrast, as anyone who has worked with Iron II pottery will readily agree.[65]

A study of both the private and official seals which were in use for the sealing of documents during the days of the Kings reveals some skill in artistic activity, although questions must have been raised in some quarters when representations of animals appeared on some of these. One of the most attractive of these is the roaring lion that appears on the seal of Shema, steward of Jeroboam, from eighth-century Megiddo.[66] But there are others, such as the winged griffin with a falcon's head and a lion's body from eighth-century Samaria,[67] and the fighting cock from Tell en Nasbeh at the end of the seventh century B.C.[68]

64. See pp. 172-174.
65. R. Amiran, op. cit., pp. 191-293, Plates 60-100.
66. A. Reifenberg, Ancient Hebrew Seals (London, 1948), p. 27.
67. Ibid., p. 31, No. 9.
68. Ibid., p. 36.

Bronze cast of a seal that depicts a roaring lion—a common symbol for Judah—and is "[Belonging] to Shema, servant of Jeroboam." The two biblical occurrences of the title "servant of the king" make evident that Shema's was a high position. The original jasper seal, dated to the eighth century B.C., was excavated in 1904 at Megiddo but subsequently lost in Istanbul. (Israel Department of Antiquities and Museums)

Ivories from the days of the Kings provide a good insight into an important aspect of Israel's artistic skills. The most spectacular are the Samaria ivories.[69] Many of these carried geometric designs and flowers. But some carried human and animal representations. The influence of Phoenician craftsmen is clearly seen at Samaria where the Queen Jezebel was a Phoenician. She brought with her an army of supporters in religious and artistic areas. Egyptian and Syrian influences are also evident. Samaria is not the only town which has produced ivories, but it represents the finest collection available today.

Other media as well as ivory were used for artistic expression. Thus Arad of the seventh century B.C. produced a beautifully executed decorated shell.[70] Bone and stone were also used for artistic work. Stone was the normal medium for the hundreds of seals that are now available for study.

Among the metals gold, silver, and bronze were commonly used. The use of gold and bronze in Solomon's Temple is well illustrated in I Kings 6 and 7 and in the lists of booty carried away by those who invaded Israel from time to time (I Kings 15:25-27; II Kings 18:16; 24:13-14; 25:13-17). Because of the high value

69. J. W. and G. M. Crowfoot, *op. cit.*; N. Avigad, "Samaria," *EAEHL*, Vol. IV, p. 1039.
70. Y. Aharoni, "Arad," *EAEHL*, Vol. I, p. 88.

Ivory plaque (1350–1150 B.C.), possibly an inlay of a cask, showing a griffin. This plaque and many other ivory objects were found at Megiddo. (Oriental Institute, University of Chicago)

attached to metals in the ancient world, many of Israel's artistic works in metal must have been carried off. Nevertheless we have some representative pieces which give us a glimpose into the quality of the workmanship. In order to discover what has remained behind from those centuries one needs to consult the standard excavation reports of great cities like Samaria, Megiddo, Hazor, and Lachish where items are listed generally in their various categories and with photographs of sketches of the particular items.[71]

Our review of the cities of Judah and Israel in the days of the Kings is far from exhaustive. It will have become clear, however, that information about the several areas we have discussed is very important for our understanding of the life of the people of Israel and Judah in those centuries and quite basic for the exegesis of numerous biblical passages.[72]

71. As an example, the objects found at Megiddo are given in P. L. O. Guy, *Megiddo Tombs* (1938), pp. 162–191, Plates 164–170. The objects are from different ages, but the general range of items is clear. Similar information is to be found in other excavation reports.

72. General reviews may be found in such books as S. M. Paul and W. G. Dever, *Biblical Archaeology* (New York, 1973); G. E. Wright, *Biblical Archaeology* (London, 1957), ch. XI, Plates 183–201.

PART TWO:

ARCHAEOLOGY AND THE PRE-CHRISTIAN CENTURIES

The Ishtar Gate and Procession Way at Babylon, ca. 605–562 B.C., in a painting by M. Bardin based on the reconstruction by archaeologist E. Unger. Note on the right side the famous "hanging gardens" and beyond them the ziggurat. (Oriental Institute, University of Chicago)

10

DAYS OF EXILE

WHEN the people of Jerusalem went into exile in the days of Nebuchadnezzar, a period of history closed for Israel. The tribal units that had entered Palestine in the time of Joshua had been united under King Saul about 1050 B.C. Following the death of Solomon and the division of the land into two kingdoms, each had gone its own way and had fallen in turn before a great conqueror—Israel in 722 B.C. before the Assyrians, and Judah in 586 B.C. before Nebuchadnezzar and the Babylonians (or Chaldeans).

After each disaster thousands of captives were taken to lands far away from the homeland. We know little of the fate of the exiles from Israel, but we do have some knowledge of the exiles from Judah.

THE FATE OF THE EXILES FROM ISRAEL

According to II Kings 17:6 Israelites were carried away to Assyria and placed in Halah, on the Habor, the river of Gozan, and in the cities of the Medes. According to the record of the Assyrian King Sargon, there were 27,290 captives. This information in II Kings 17:6 complements Sargon's record by giving the destination of the exiles. The River Habor is well known as the great tributary of the Euphrates on which Abraham's city Haran lay. It was in the ancient region of Aram-naharaim. Gozan is the Akkadian Guzana, which may be Tell Halaf in the same general area. It is clear from this entry that a lot of the people of Israel were taken to a region represented today by the northeastern corner of Syria. The other area to which the captives were taken was much further to the east in the land of Media in the region of modern Iran.

We have little direct information about these two groups, but centuries later there were large Jewish colonies in the northern Tigris-Euphrates region[1] and in Persia. The hero of the apocryphal book of Tobit was one of those deported at this time. He lived in Nineveh but had compatriots in Media (1:1f., 10, 14). We now have a contemporary picture of such a deportation by the Assyrians in a document from Kirkuk.[2]

In addition, an ostracon from Calah (Nimrud) of about 720/700 B.C.[3] contains a list of twenty-one names of men, and in most cases of their fathers, thought to be workmen or slaves. Of these ten are in biblical Hebrew: Elisha, Haggai, Haziel, Hanan, Hananeel, Michael, Menahem, Uzza, Achbor, and Shubael. Other names are probably Aramaean. But it is now thought that we have here some tangible evidence of the presence of North Israelites in Assyria toward the end of the eighth century B.C. Similar names have been identified on other documents.[4]

These are only glimpses into the dispersion of these northern Israelites. What happened to them we do not know. They may have been partly assimilated into the Assyrian-Aramaean amalgam of peoples in northern Mesopotamia, but Jeremiah certainly hoped for their return a century later (Jer. 3:12-18; 31:2-22).

THE HOME OF THE EXILES IN BABYLONIA

Bible history makes it clear that the people of Judah were invaded more than once by the armies of Nebuchadnezzar, and each time captives were taken. In 597 B.C. King Jehoiachin and many of his notables, among whom was the prophet Ezekiel (Ezek. 1:2), were taken away to Babylonia. When Jerusalem fell to Nebuchadnezzar in 586 B.C., another group of people from Judah joined the party that had been exiled some eleven years before. It is of great interest to us to read the letter that the prophet Jeremiah wrote to these first exiles. Jeremiah stayed behind in Jerusalem and was still there when the city finally fell to the Chaldeans. But he wrote to the first group of exiles words of encouragement, urging them to build houses, plant gardens, take wives, raise children, and pray for the peace of the city to which they had gone (Jer. 29:1-7). All of this argues for a degree of freedom for the exiles in that foreign land.

The first group was already settled in the region of the River Chebar. Thanks to archaeological discovery, the general area where these people lived can now be identified with some certainty. Much of our information comes from the ancient site of Nippur in southern Mesopotamia, which will be referred to

---

1. J. Neusner, A History of the Jews in Babylonia, Vol. II (Leiden, 1966), p. 91 (map).
2. E. Chiera and E. A. Speiser, JAOS, Vol. 47 (1927), pp. 56ff.
3. M. H. Segal, "An Aramaic Ostracon from Nimrud," Iraq, Vol. XIX, Part 2 (1957), pp. 139-145.
4. W. F. Albright, "An Ostracon from Calah and the North-Israelite Diaspora," BASOR, No. 149 (1958), pp. 33-36.

again in this book. This town has been excavated in part, and excavations are still proceeding there. Among the cuneiform tablets discovered in the ruins were two, dating respectively to 443 B.C. and 424 B.C., which refer to a waterway named *naru kabari* or *nehar kebar*, the "River Chebar."[5] This waterway was evidently an artificial canal which started from the Euphrates River just north of Babylon, and which can be traced further south until it joins the Euphrates again south of Ur of the Chaldees. Nippur itself is some sixty miles southeast of Babylon, and the canal flowed through Nippur. There was therefore a connection by water beween the general area where the exiles lived and the capital of the great Nebuchadnezzar.

It is interesting to note that the place name Tel Abib (Ezek. 3:15) is a Hebrew adaptation of a Babylonian name Til Abubi.[6] The Babylonian words mean "the mound of the flood." The actual site is not known but it was no doubt one of the many old mounds or tells formed from the debris of ruined cities. These had been long unoccupied and some of them were thought to go back to the days before the great Flood. Apparently some of these mounds were resettled. Similar sites, for example Tel Melah and Tel Harsha (Ezra 2:59; Neh. 7:61), are referred to in the Bible as having been occupied by the exiled Jews. G. A. Cooke says that the name Tell Abubi was a common name in Babylonia at all periods. It was known in Hammurabi's code and on one of the inscriptions of the Assyrian king Tiglath Pileser.[7]

Actually, in the vicinity of Nippur there are several old mounds and, as we shall see later, there is clear evidence that there were Jews living in this area between 500 and 400 B.C.[8] We may conjecture that these later Jews were descendants of the earlier exiles deported from Judah just after 600 B.C.

We can picture the Jewish exiles, then, settled in a foreign country among the heathen, and engaged in some sort of forced labor under Nebuchadnezzar. Here they were to dwell for many years until finally many of them returned home just after 540 B.C. as a result of the decree of the conqueror Cyrus. Their lot may not always have been hard, for preachers like Ezekiel were evidently free to preach to the people, who seem to have had some sort of limited local government with "elders." Their true condition remains largely a matter of conjecture. F. F. Bruce has made the fascinating suggestion that the exiles were drafted into a forced-labor gang working on the Babylonian irrigation system.[9]

BABYLON THE GREAT

The great capital was about sixty miles away from the exiles. Very likely few of them ever saw the great city. Yet it is of some importance for us as Bible students

5. G. A. Cooke, *The Book of Ezekiel*, ICC (Edinburgh, 1936), p. 4.
6. *Ibid.*, p. 42.
7. *Ibid.*
8. See below, pp. 237f.
9. F. F. Bruce, *Bible Study Notes* (Jan.–Feb., 1951), p. 34.

to know something about this city which is described in such glowing terms in several passages in the Bible. Thus the book of Isaiah refers to it as "Babylon, the glory of kingdoms, the beauty of the Chaldees' excellency" (Isa. 13:19).

Babylon was an ancient city with a long history of occupation. Nebuchadnezzar determined to restore and to extend it so as to make it one of the most wonderful of all the cities in the East. In this he succeeded. Today, thanks to the work of Robert Koldewey and his team of German archaeologists, we have a good idea of the splendor of the city of those days.[10] During the years between 1899 and World War I the ruins of the inner city of Babylon were thoroughly excavated. A vast system of fortifications, streets, canals, palaces, and temples was brought to light. Well might Nebuchadnezzar have described this city in the words of Daniel 4:30, "Is not this great Babylon, which I have built for the house of the kingdom [royal dwelling place] by the might of my power, and for the honour of my majesty?"

The inner city where the king had his palaces is seen today as a remarkable complex of ruins. Entrance was gained through the great Ishtar Gate, a double gate leading through double fortification walls. It was adorned with magnificent enameled bricks into which patterns of flowers, geometrical figures, life-size animals, bulls, lions, and dragons were worked. The Ishtar Gate must have been startling in its beauty. Once inside this magnificent gate, the visitor would pass along the stone-paved procession way in the heart of the city proper. This way was walled up with enameled bricks decorated with life-size lions. To the right of the procession way lay the palace area, likewise adorned with beautiful enameled bricks. One fine room decorated with bricks of gold and blue must have been the throne room. Some writers have made the suggestion that this was the place where the finger wrote on the wall, although the Bible does not actually assert this. In the same general area is a strange structure, thought by some to be the remains of the famous "hanging gardens." Whether or not this particular set of ruins can be identified with this well-known world wonder, it remains true that one of the features of the mighty Babylon was a remarkable set of gardens supported on terraces and thrust up into the air. They were built, according to tradition, for the wife of the king, a woman from the cool mountain regions to the north, to give her both beauty and coolness.

Further down the procession way on the right lay the temple area where the priests' quarters as well as the temple of Marduk, known as Esagila ("house whose top is lofty"), were to be found. The most spectacular of all the buildings in the sacred area was the great ziggurat or temple tower, which rose up into the sky in eight stages, according to the Greek historian Herodotus.[11] There were other notable buildings in the heart of this splendid city. Outside the main city area were various fortification walls at intervals of miles apart, all designed to

---

10. R. Koldewey, *The Excavations at Babylon* (London, 1914).
11. Herodotus, *The Histories* (London, 1954), p. 86.

The imposing ruins of the Ishtar Gate, built by Nebuchadnezzar (ca. 605–562 B.C.), show why the Babylonians boasted of their building accomplishments and why their city was called "Babylon the Great." (Consulate General, Republic of Iraq)

make Babylon impregnable. Truly this was an outstanding city and one to be proud of.

And Nebuchadnezzar was proud indeed, as the inscriptions show. Among the ruins of the city Koldewey found a sizeable number of inscribed materials, partly on bricks and stones and partly on baked clay tablets. Many of the written records indicate the pride and confidence of Nebuchadnezzar, as a selection of these inscriptions will show:

> A great wall which like a mountain cannot be moved I made of mortar and brick.... Its foundation upon the bosom of the abyss I placed down deeply... its top I raised mountain high. I triplicated the city wall in order to strengthen it, I caused a great protecting wall to run at the foot of the wall of burnt brick....[12]
>
> When Marduk the great lord named me the legitimate son and to direct the affairs of the land... Babylon his mighty city..., its great walls I completed. Upon the thresholds of their great gates strong bulls of bronze, and terrible serpents ready to strike, I placed. That which no

12. W. H. Lane, *Babylonian Problems* (London, 1923), p. 179.

Babylon's ziggurat, called the "House of the Foundation of Earth and Heaven,"
and the principal temple of Marduk in a painting by M. Bardin. The river is the
Euphrates. A comparison of Bardin's reconstructions of Babylon with the actual
ruins drives home forcefully the veracity of God's predictive word concerning the
city. (Oriental Institute, University of Chicago)

king had done my father did in that he enclosed the city with two
moat-walls of mortar and brick. As for me, a third great moat-wall, one
against the second, I built with mortar and brick, and with the moat-
wall of my father joined and closely united it. Its foundation upon the
bosom of the abyss I laid down deeply, its top I raised mountain
high. . . .[13]

13. *Ibid.*, p. 178.

The produce of the lands, the products of the mountains, the bountiful wealth of the sea, within her I gathered ... great quantities of grain beyond measure I stored up in her. At that time the palace, my royal abode ... I rebuilt in Babylon ... great cedars I brought from Lebanon, the beautiful forest to roof it. ... [14]

Concerning one of the temples, Nebuchadnezzar spoke in the following terms:

Huge cedars from Lebanon, their forest with my clean hands I cut down. With radiant gold I overlaid them, with jewels I adorned them ... the side chapels of the shrine of Nebo, the cedar beams of their roofs I adorned with lustrous silver. Giant bulls I made of bronze work and clothed them with white marble. I adorned them with jewels and placed them upon the threshold of the gate of the shrine. ... [15]

In contrast to all these grandiose words we listen to the words of the prophets of Israel with something of awe:

And Babylon, the glory of kingdoms, the beauty of the Chaldees' excellency, shall be as when God overthrew Sodom and Gomorrah. It shall never be inhabited, neither shall it be dwelt in from generation to generation (Isa. 13:19, 20).
Babylon shall become heaps, a dwelling place for dragons, an astonishment, and an hissing, without an inhabitant.
Though Babylon should mount up to heaven, and though she should fortify the height of her strength, yet from me shall spoilers come unto her, saith the Lord.
Thus saith the Lord of hosts; The broad walls of Babylon shall be utterly broken, and her high gates shall be burned with fire (Jer. 51:37, 53, 58).

Babylon was not beaten down by an enemy. It was taken by the Persians in 539 B.C. and became a sort of second capital. In the days of Alexander the Great it was still occupied, although Alexander undertook the clearing up of certain deserted areas. In Roman times there was a town here. The town, however, was slowly abandoned and today the state of ruin of the once magnificent city is a telling commentary on the proud words of the man who made it in his day the wonder of all the East.

ARCHAEOLOGY AND THE PROPHET EZEKIEL

It was during the days of exile that the prophet Ezekiel sought to show the exiles that they were suffering the just consequences of their sins. It has been the traditional view of the Christian Church that the book of Ezekiel should be taken at its face value so that we regard the prophet as having done his preaching

14. *Ibid.*, p. 181.
15. *Ibid.*, p. 187.

during the period 597 to 573 B.C. in the land of Babylonia. More recently there have been those who have sought to show that this prophet lived in Palestine for at least part of his ministry. Others have tried to show that the prophecy came from a date much later than the exile. In these discussions archaeology has done a good deal to support the traditional view.

Already we have made reference to some of the place names, which are not inconsistent with a Babylonian residence for Ezekiel. Indeed, they require it, if the geographical data are to have meaning. But there are other pointers. In Ezekiel 4:1 the prophet is commanded to take a brick and draw on it a map of Jerusalem. The Hebrew word here refers to a sun-dried brick, and while it was quite usual to draw sketches on such mud bricks in Babylonia, we are not aware that this sort of thing was ever done in Judah.[16] Again, the fact that Ezekiel was commanded to "dig through" the walls of the house as he acted a parable of the removal of people from the doomed city of Jerusalem points to Babylonia (Ezek. 12). Excavations show that the usual medium used for house construction in these lands was mud or adobe. In Palestine, on the other hand, the walls were made of stone, and the act of digging through a wall would invite the collapse of the wall (Ezek. 12:5–7).[17] It has been maintained that walls of mud were non-existent in Palestine in the sixth century B.C. but were in fact the only walls in use in Mesopotamia.[18] Other passages in Ezekiel's prophecy refer to the same type of house. Thus Ezekiel 13:10–15 refers to a house where the rainstorms will wash away the plaster. The same picture of adobe walls in the houses is found in Ezekiel 22:28.

Evidence that Ezekiel wrote at the time of the Exile comes from a most unusual source, namely, the description of the east gate in the ideal temple described in Ezekiel 40:5–16.[19] There is enough data here for the careful reader to be able to reconstruct the ground plan of the gateway. It turns out to be a gate with provision for three doors, one behind the other, in a space of twenty-five cubits. Archaeologists point out that this type of gate was of a very old pattern. It was quite common in the days of King Solomon, for example, and is known in excavations at Megiddo, Gezer, and Hazor, in towns that go back to the days of Solomon. Another interesting fact is that this type of gate disappeared from the ancient Near Eastern scene in the ninth century B.C. and was replaced by a new style of gate altogether. A certain number of the older type of gate must have remained in use for years after their construction, but sooner or later they would all disappear, so that by Ezekiel's day it would be almost impossible to find one. How then would Ezekiel in a vision see a gate, the like of which was known in Solomon's day, but which had long since gone out of use in the East? The answer

16. E. Chiera, The Wrote on Clay (Chicago, 1938), pp. 160–164.
17. Mud houses are to be seen, however, in some places in Palestine today.
18. C. C. Howie, The Date and Composition of Ezekiel (1950), p. 18.
19. Ibid., pp. 43ff.

is that he must have seen the Solomonic gate in the Temple in Jerusalem prior to its destruction by Nebuchadnezzar in 587 B.C.[20] The destruction of the Temple would have removed what was probably the last gate of this kind to be seen in the East. In any case, here is a reasonable explanation of why Ezekiel would see such a gate in his vision, and incidentally a reason for thinking that he lived at the time of the Exile.

There is another possible link with Babylonia which, although not accepted by all commentators, seems to the present writer to have some value. It is that the strange imagery in Ezekiel 1 owes something to the Babylonian environment. In his vision Ezekiel saw strange creatures with human heads and wings, and in the imagery we see the face of a man, a lion, an ox, and an eagle (Ezek. 1:5-11). The partly human, partly animal forms are reminiscent of the guardian figures of the Babylonian temples, which may have been known to Ezekiel. It is quite within the range of the facts of biblical history and of our own experience today that God takes up the events and experiences of life as a starting point for speaking His mind to us. It was the storm that gathered on that day that was the prelude to God's revelation to Ezekiel. The storm was merely an attendant on God's throne. So, too, God called on the visual impressions so familiar to Ezekiel to grant to him a vision of the divine splendor.

SOME LATER MILITARY EXPLOITS OF NEBUCHADNEZZAR

Bible readers are familiar with those military events that concern the fall of Jerusalem. We referred in an earlier chapter[21] to the publication of an important document which refers to the campaign of Nebuchadnezzar in 598 B.C., which led to the captivity of Jehoiachin (II Kings 24:10-16). Reference has also been made to the valuable receipts from Babylon which refer to the presence of Jehoiachin here in 592. Unfortunately, written evidence of the campaigns of Nebuchadnezzar is sparse at present. That he had other campaigns is certain, and some of these are referred to in the Bible. Thus he had dealings with both Tyre and Egypt. Ezekiel 29:18 speaks of his siege of Tyre, but we still await archaeological evidence of this event. Concerning Egypt, however, we have one inscription which, though far from complete, does tell of a campaign in that land.[22] The prophet Ezekiel spoke in several places of the judgment God intended for Egypt at the hands of the Babylonian king (Ezek. 29:19; 30:10; 32:11). A fragmentary historical text dating from the thirty-seventh year of Nebuchadnezzar, which is the year 567 B.C., speaks of fighting between

20. The size of the gate described in Ezekiel 40 is not significant because it is in any case visionary. It is the pattern that concerns us. There is little point to argue, as some have done, that the size of Ezekiel's doorway would have been too big for the temple known in Solomon's time and still standing in Ezekiel's earlier years.

21. See above, p. 156.

22. J. B. Pritchard, ANET, p. 308.

The Babylonian Chronicle mentions Nebuchadnezzar's capture of Jerusalem in 597 B.C., the appointment of Zedekiah as king, and the removal of Israelite prisoners, including Jehoiachin, to Babylonia. (British Museum)

Pharaoh Amasis and the king of Babylon. Unfortunately the tablet is so badly damaged that we can draw little reliable information from it. It may have been confined to the area of the Delta only, and again we await further archaeological light.[23] By this date Nebuchadnezzar was already old and his days of fighting were over.

A further tantalizing inscription from these days refers to an expedition to the general area of Syria and Lebanon.[24] This, too, is incomplete and lacks definite evidence as to the date and the occasion. What interests us is that the prophet Ezekiel infers that for many years after the fall of Jerusalem the Babylonians were active militarily. It is Babylon that is to be the agent of divine judgment on Tyre and Egypt. The inscriptions, though meager in number and content, do at least point to a continuation of the campaigns of the great king for a number of years. We live in hope that yet further excavation will bring to light additional significant evidence about these times which are so vital in Bible history.

THE CLOSING YEARS OF CHALDEAN POWER

When Nebuchadnezzar died in 562 B.C., after a reign of forty-two years, he was followed in quick succession by three weak kings, first by his son Amel Marduk

---

23. There are useful discussions in H. L. Ellison, *Ezekiel* (Grand Rapids, 1958), p. 102, and H. R. Hall, *The Ancient History of the Near East* (London, 1950), p. 549.

24. J. B. Pritchard, *ANET*, p. 307.

(562–560 B.C.), whom Jeremiah calls Evil Merodach (Jer. 52:31; II Kings 25:27), then by Nergal-shar-usur (Neriglissar), one of the nobles and a son-in-law of Nebuchadnezzar, who replaced the inefficient Amel Marduk in a revolution and reigned from 560 to 556, and finally by the weak son of this last king, Labashi Marduk, who was expelled after a second revolution a few months after he came to the throne. One of the conspirators, Nabonidus (Nabunaid), then ruled as the last king of Babylon (556–539 B.C.).

The names of these three kings are known in written records. Thus Neriglissar's name appears on contract tablets as early as 596 B.C. Apart from Evil Merodach, who according to the Bible released King Jehoiachin (II Kings 25:27), we have no special interest in these rulers. The last king of Babylon is, however, of very real interest to us, for it was in his time that the collapse of Babylon became imminent.

Nabonidus ascended the throne amid bloodshed. Already the people of the land had shown considerable discontent with the Chaldean rulers and in two revolutions had managed to replace them. The new ruler was a man of culture with such a keen interest in antiquity that he has been described as the world's first archaeologist. He restored the temple of the moon in Haran where his mother was probably a priestess. Perhaps he was in fact a Syrian and from the outset stood little chance of gaining popular approval. But he took steps at once to make an impression on the people. An important basalt stele, now preserved in Istanbul, tells of his rise to power. He declared:

> I am the real executor of the wills of Nebuchadnezzar and Neriglissar, my royal predecessors. Their armies are entrusted to me and I shall not treat carelessly their orders. . . . [25]

Referring to the previous king he declared that

> Labashi Marduk, a minor who had not yet learned how to behave, sat on the royal throne against the intention of the gods. [26]

The inscription goes on to tell how one night in a dream Nebuchadnezzar and his attendant appeared to Nabonidus on Marduk's command, to interpret strange signs in the heavens as a portent of a long reign. Other gods, too, sent favorable signs. It is evident from the inscription that the new king wished to indicate to the people that he had the personal approval of both Marduk the god and the former Nebuchadnezzar.

Important new inscriptions from Haran were found in 1956 during an examination of the mosque which now stands on the old site. [27] Three basalt stelae about two meters high by about a meter wide had been found and reused in the mosque, but they were ancient and carried cuneiform inscriptions relating to the

---

25. *Ibid.*, p. 309.
26. *Ibid.*
27. These documents have been published by C. J. Gadd in *Anatolian Studies*, Vol. VIII; J. B. Pritchard, *ANET Supplementary Texts* (Princeton, 1969), pp. 560–563.

days of Nabonidus. Two of these tell of the reign of this ruler and of his restoration of the temple of the moon goddess Sin at Haran. Nabonidus said that it was Sin "who called him to kingship." It would seem, however, that he earned the hostility of the people for his support of Sin, and it may have been partly for this reason that he retired to Teima for several years. The third stele is an account of the life of Nabonidus' mother, who was a votaress of the moon goddess.

In an attempt to win the esteem of the priests, Nabonidus undertook various works of restoration in the temples of Babylon. He richly endowed many of these, restored the temple of Marduk in Babylon, and journeyed through the land bestowing gifts on the gods of each sacred shrine: Sin at Ur, Shamash at Larsa, Ishtar at Uruk. Before long, however, he offended the priests greatly and paved the way for his own downfall. The year after his accession he was called to the west to quell a revolt. Moving on to Hamath and turning south toward Edom, he discovered the oasis at Teima and he settled down there, to remain till perhaps his sixteenth year as king. This was a fatal mistake, for it was necessary for the king to be present each New Year in Babylon for the special annual procession of the gods. In his absence the procession could not be held. It was an occasion when pilgrims flocked to the great city and when the coffers of the temples profited greatly. As the king stayed away year after year, the anger of the priests grew.

Back home in the capital the king appointed his son Belshazzar to be the actual ruler. One cuneiform inscription reads as follows:

> He entrusted a camp to his eldest, first-born son; the troops of the land he sent with him. He freed his hand; he entrusted the kingship to him. Then he himself undertook a distant campaign, the power of the land of Akkad advanced with him; toward Teima in the midst of the westland he set his face.... He slew the prince of Teima... then he himself established his dwelling in Teima....[28]

The important Nabonidus Chronicle, issued later, in all probability at the inspiration of Cyrus, makes the point that in the seventh, ninth, tenth, and eleventh years "the king was in the city of Teima. The son of the king, the princes, and his troops were in Akkad...."[29] More important is the repeated statement that "the king did not come to Babylon for the ceremony of the month of Nisan."

It is interesting to comment here that since it was Belshazzar who exercised the co-regency in Babylon, and probably did so to the end, the book of Daniel is correct in representing him as the last king of Babylon (Dan. 5:30). A man like Daniel who was honored would thus be "third" in the kingdom.[30] Incidentally,

---

28. Quoted in J. Finegan, *Light from the Ancient Past* (Princeton, 1946), pp. 189f.
29. J. B. Pritchard, *ANET*, p. 305.
30. The Aramaic word means literally "third," but it came to mean, more generally, a prominent officer of state.

the reference in Daniel 5:18 to Nebuchadnezzar as "father" of the king may simply follow Semitic usage which allows language like this in the case of family relationships, or it may follow on the claims of Nabonidus that he was the legitimate heir of Nebuchadnezzar.

The days of Babylon were drawing to a close. Further to the east a petty king, Cyrus the Persian, had in a remarkable way become ruler of both Media and Persia and had embarked on a program of expansion. In 546 B.C. he had conquered Lydia. In the following years he was able to bring most of the East under his control, leaving only Babylonia as a last pocket of resistance. These ominous events led to some action on the part of Nabonidus. The Nabonidus Chronicle tells us that the king was still at Teima in the eleventh year, that is, 546 B.C. He may have stayed there longer, for the chronicle has a gap at this point and does not resume till the seventeenth year, which was the last year of his reign. There must have been something of a panic, for the record tells us that "Bel went in procession," that is, the New Year festival was held. Moreover, the gods from neighboring cities were entering Babylon. We think that in a vain hope to gain some protection from them Nabonidus gathered gods into Babylon. Some cities resisted this summary carrying off of their gods to Babylon, if we are to judge from the chronicle: "The gods from Borsippa, Kutha . . . and Sippar did not enter."[31]

In October of 539 Babylon fell to the Persians. There were battles in the outskirts of Babylon some days before. On the fourteenth day Sippar was seized and "on the sixteenth day Gobryas ['Ugbaru] the governor of Gutium and the army of Cyrus entered Babylon without battle. Afterwards Nabonidus was arrested in Babylon when he returned there."[32]

The end of the two co-rulers Nabonidus and Belshazzar was death at the hands of the Persians. A new age had dawned for the people of the East and in particular for the Jews in exile. It was to usher in days of return and restoration.

ARCHAEOLOGY AND THE PROPHET DANIEL

We do not intend here to enter the lists and fight a battle with the literary critics about the date of this important book in the Old Testament. That decision rests on a number of considerations. There are, however, a number of comments that may be made from the archaeological angle, for undoubtedly the author of this book was reliably informed on a number of issues. In particular the fifth chapter has a number of items which suggest a well-informed writer. This, in itself, does not provide any exact evidence about the date when Daniel was written since a later writer who was well informed about the period of the Exile could still record information that was accurate. But it does suggest that the source materials used by the writer were reliable at this point.

31. J. B. Pritchard, ANET, p. 306.
32. Ibid.

The references in various places in the book of Daniel to soothsayers, magicians, astrologers, and the like (Dan. 1:20; 2:10; 4:7; 5:11, etc.), are all authentic items in the background of the times. Excavations have produced a considerable amount of material about the religion of Babylon, and it is clear that magic and divination played a large part.

Another feature of the book of Daniel which has an authentic ring is the great importance attached to dreams. We have already noticed how Nabonidus made a strong point of the dream in which he saw Nebuchadnezzar. Dreams figure in the authentic records of Mesopotamia from the earliest times, forming an integral part of the kings' actual accounts of their own reigns.[33] It is quite wrong to write off all dreams as apocryphal accretions. Even if ancient rulers invented the dreams, they were accepted by the people as one of the ways in which the gods spoke to men. Hence the many references to dreams in the context of Babylonia are quite in keeping with the facts of the case.

Up to the present the enigmatic figure of "Darius the Mede" in Daniel (5:21; 6:1-28; 9:1; 11:1) is quite unknown to the archaeologist. Concerning this man W. F. Albright wrote, "The elusive problem of Darius the Mede remains exactly as puzzling as ever; it certainly cannot be solved merely by hypercriticism."[34] Perhaps we have to do here with a title.

One of the texts of Nabonidus found at Haran and dated to 546 B.C. refers to the "King of the Medes."[35] This statement opens up the whole question afresh. D. J. Wiseman asks whether this phrase may not have been another name for Cyrus.[36] Certainly the people of Haran spoke of the king of the Medes in 546 B.C. But by this time there was no such king, his place having been taken by Cyrus the Persian who went on to conquer Babylon. Wiseman suggests that we should translate Daniel 6:29 as "in the reign of Darius, even in the reign of Cyrus the Persian."

We have already referred to the place of Belshazzar in the closing days of the Chaldean rule in Babylon. The writer was correctly informed in this matter. The relationships beween Nabonidus and his son and the achievements of each have been made the subject of a valuable piece of research by R. P. Dougherty in his book *Nabonidus and Belshazzar*, which contains a wealth of valuable material about these times.[37]

The story of the three young men who were thrown into a fire because they refused to worship the image of the king (Dan. 3) reminds us of the large brick kilns outside the city where Nebuchadnezzar's workmen baked bricks for his

---

33. C. Gordon, *Introduction to Old Testament Times* (Ventnor, 1953), pp. 66f.

34. W. F. Albright, *JBL* (Dec., 1949), p. 375. Cf. H. H. Rowley, *Darius the Mede* (1953); J. C. Whitcomb, *Darius the Mede* (Grand Rapids, 1959).

35. See p. 197.

36. D. J. Wiseman in D. W. Thomas (ed.), *Documents from Old Testament Times* (London, 1958), p. 83; D. J. Wiseman et al., *Notes on Some Problems in the Book of Daniel* (London, 1965), pp. 9-18.

37. R. P. Dougherty, *Nabonidus and Belshazzar* (New Haven, 1929).

buildings. Some of these have been uncovered in excavations. A strange comparison with this very incident comes from the days of Rim Sin, a former king in these lands (1750 B.C.). This king once decreed concerning four men of Larsa: "Because they threw a young slave into an oven, throw ye a slave into a furnace." Although the precise significance of this decree is not clear, E. G. Kraeling remarks about this incident, "Clearly, that sort of thing was nothing new in Babylonia."[38]

While these items do not settle the date of composition of the book of Daniel, they show that the author was in possession of a good deal of authentic background material. Archaeological research can do much to establish the value of the background material appearing in an ancient document such as this.

THE EXILES LOOK HOMEWARD

Ezekiel the prophet had spoken of days of restoration and had told the people of his version of the valley of dry bones (Ezek. 37). Earlier still the prophet Jeremiah had spoken of restoration after seventy years (Jer. 25:12) under the kings of Babylon. Magnificent passages in the latter part of the book of Isaiah gave strong hope of restoration. Here, too, Cyrus was referred to as the Lord's shepherd, the Lord's anointed (Isa. 44:28; 45:1). As the years went by, and more especially as the progress of Cyrus the Persian was witnessed, there must have been a spirit of keen anticipation among those exiles who still held to the faith of their fathers. The Lord was about to turn again the captivity of Zion (Ps. 126). No longer need the exiles sit down and weep by the waters of Babylon (Ps. 137). To the exciting story of Cyrus and his decrees which granted freedom to all the exiles, we now turn.

38. E. G. Kraeling, *Bible Atlas* (Chicago, 1956), p. 323.

11

THE RETURN OF THE JEWS FROM EXILE

THE fall of Babylon in 539 B.C. ushered in twenty-five years of significant history for the Jews. After the restoration of their Temple in 516 B.C. or early in 515 B.C. we enter upon a period of comparative silence. But these early days were vital in setting the pattern for much of the subsequent history of the Jews. In actual fact considerable numbers of the exiles did not return from Babylonia and those who did were faced with tremendous hardships in their own land. There were droughts, there were enemies on every hand, the land to which the Jews were returning had been devastated and required much attention before it would yield the fruits of the field, and finally heavy taxation was exacted by the Persian overlords. By perhaps March, 515 B.C., the Temple was completed in Jerusalem. This gave to the returning exiles a tangible focal point in their national life. There is a large amount of archaeological material referring to these days, far more indeed than there is for the subsequent centuries.

THE DECREES OF CYRUS

The book of Ezra opens with an account of the decree of Cyrus which allowed the exiles to return to their land:

> Thus saith Cyrus king of Persia, The Lord God of heaven hath given me all the kingdoms of the earth; and he hath charged me to build him an house at Jerusalem, which is in Judah. Who is there among you of all his people? his God be with him, and let him go up to Jerusalem, which is in Judah, and build the house of the Lord God of Israel, (he is the God), which is in Jerusalem (Ezra 1:2, 3).

There is an alternative form of this decree in Ezra 6:3-5.

Historians of a former day approached these simple biblical statements with suspicion.[1] Some writers argued that we had no evidence that Cyrus made a decree of this kind, much less that he paid any sort of honor to the God of Israel. He was a Persian who worshipped Persian gods and could hardly be expected to pay honor to the God of the Jews. We no longer raise questions of this kind since we have given due weight to important documents from the days of Cyrus which show us that he was a master of propaganda and knew how to exploit every occasion to his own best advantage. A study of the so-called Nabonidus Chronicle, of the famous Cyrus Cylinder, and of the verse account of Nabonidus helps a great deal in understanding the true state of affairs at the time.

The Nabonidus Chronicle referred to in our previous chapter[2] was almost certainly prepared under the direction of Cyrus. We have seen how it tells us of the last years of Nabonidus and of how he neglected his duties to the gods in Babylon. It is clear that Nabonidus in a last panic gathered many gods into Babylon as a sort of protection in his time of desperation. It was all to no avail. The chronicle tells us that the noble Cyrus was welcomed into the city with real joy.

1. W. O. E. Oesterley and T. H. Robinson, *A History of Israel* (Oxford, 1932), Vol. II, pp. 75, 81.
2. See above, p. 198. See also J. B. Pritchard, *ANET*, p. 305.

The so-called Cyrus Cylinder relates the Persian king Cyrus' capture of Babylon without a battle, his return of prisoners (including Jews) to their own countries, and his restoration of treasures to the temples from which they came. The nine-inch, baked clay cylinder from Babylon is inscribed in cuneiform and is dated 536 B.C. (British Museum)

In the month of Arahshamnu, the third day, Cyrus entered Babylon, green twigs were spread in front of him... the state of peace was imposed upon the city.... From the month of Kislimu to the month of Addaru, the gods of Akkad which Nabonidus had made come down to Babylon... returned to their sacred city....[3]

It is evident from this document that Cyrus had a policy of returning the gods to their own homes. This fact is borne out by a study of the important Cyrus Cylinder, which was especially prepared for the occasion. The document, which is really a baked clay cylinder, begins with a strong piece of propaganda in which the new king shows how he has the approval of the gods. After some broken lines in the record it goes on to say:

... the correct images of the gods he removed from their thrones, imitations he ordered to place upon them.... he interrupted in a fiendish way the regular offerings.... the worship of Marduk, the king of the gods, he changed into an abomination, daily he used to do evil against his city.... Upon their complaints the lord of the gods became terribly angry.... he scanned and looked through all countries, searching for a righteous ruler willing to lead him [Marduk] in the annual procession. Then he pronounced the name of Cyrus, king of Anshan, declared him to become the ruler of all the world.... Marduk the great lord, protector of his people, beheld with pleasure his [Cyrus'] good deeds and his upright mind and ordered him to march against Babylon.[4]

This must have been of tremendous value in establishing the prestige of the new king in the eyes of the Babylonians. Here then was the legitimate king of the region, who had the approval of the gods. Cyrus wisely entered Babylon without destroying the city and gave careful instructions to his troops to respect the people and their property. The story is told in considerable detail on the cylinder. More was needed, however, in order to secure the goodwill of the people, and especially of those who were slaves in that land. It would be wisdom indeed to free all captives and restore them to their homes. This Cyrus did. The decree reads:

As to the inhabitants of Babylon who against the will of the gods (...) I abolished the corvee [yoke] which was against their social standing. I brought relief to their dilapidated houses, putting an end to their main complaints.[5]

It is not hard to see in these words the intention of the king that enslaved peoples should be freed, although it must be admitted that these words might have applied only to the local Babylonians. Later on in the document, however, we have a possible reference to the return of exiles of various kinds to their lands:

3. *Ibid.*, p. 306, col. 2.
4. *Ibid.*, p. 315, col. 2.
5. *Ibid.*, p. 316, col. 1.

I also gathered all their former inhabitants and returned to them their habitations.[6]

Concerning the treatment of the gods we have some clear statements. The gods were to be returned to their homes and restored to their temples, which were to be repaired:

I returned to the sacred cities on the other side of the Tigris, the sanctuaries of which have been ruins for a long time, the images which used to live therein and established for them permanent sanctuaries. I also gathered all their former inhabitants and returned to them their former habitations. Furthermore I resettled on the command of Marduk, the great lord, all the gods of Sumer and Akkad whom Nabonidus has brought into Babylon. . . . May all the gods whom I have resettled in their sacred cities daily ask Bel and Nebo for a long life for me. . . .[7]

It was clearly the policy of the Persian ruler to allow freedom of worship. It is to be noticed that although Cyrus was not a worshipper of the gods of Babylon, he knew how to make a show of honoring them in order to win the hearts of the Babylonian people. We need not conclude that because he spoke in terms such as we read in this document he necessarily worshipped the gods of Babylon.

In the light of material like this we may conclude that Cyrus prepared similar documents for other people. In the case of the Jews there were no images to be restored to the Temple, but there was a Temple to be rebuilt and sacred vessels to be returned. It is sheer hyperskepticism to deny that Cyrus granted to the Jews privileges similar to those that were allowed to other people. We argue that the brief decrees in the book of Ezra are extracts from longer decrees issued for the Jews by the great king. We need not pay particular attention to the fact that Cyrus seems to pay honor to the God of the Jews. He probably paid no more respect or worship to this God than he did to others.

That Cyrus did in fact restore temples is borne out by some of the inscriptions found in excavations. Thus, at Uruk the excavations of E. Heinrich, H. Lentzen, and others showed that the sanctuary of Ishtar was rebuilt by Cyrus, who left inscribed bricks on which this claim was made.[8] At Ur also, although inscribed bricks show that some restoration was done by the former ruler Nabonidus, it is of special interest to us to find that Cyrus himself authorized and completed a great deal of restorative work in the sanctuaries of Ur.[9] Both inscribed bricks and an important baked clay cylinder found near the great ziggurat refer to this fact.

Further information along this line is obtained from a baked clay tablet in

6. *Ibid.*, p. 316, col. 2.
7. *Ibid.*, p. 316.
8. R. P. R. de Vaux, "Les décrets de Cyrus et de Darius sur la reconstruction du Temple," *RB* (Jan., 1937), p. 33.
9. *Ibid.*, p. 34.

the British Museum, unfortunately badly damaged, which presents in verse form the information contained in the Nabonidus Chronicle.[10] We now know it as the "Verse Account of Nabonidus." It was evidently prepared by the priests of Babylon, and gives in panegyric form an account of the victories of Cyrus. Despite the gaps we can still read that Cyrus, after the capture of Babylon, was occupied with sacred works. He multiplied the offerings to the gods and prostrated himself before them. He restored the gods and the goddesses to their sanctuaries and sent back the people with them.

There can be no doubt that Cyrus showed a great deal of tolerance toward the various religious groups in the community. It is against the background of these facts that we must read the decrees of Cyrus found in the Bible. Quite clearly there is every reason to regard the biblical accounts as authentic. W. F. Albright has written, "The substantial historicity of the edict of Cyrus in 538 has been confirmed by modern archaeological discoveries."[11]

One further point is relevant to our discussion. The two accounts of the decree of Cyrus in the Bible are in two different languages. The passage in Ezra 1:2-4 is in Hebrew, and the passage in Ezra 6:3-5 is in Aramaic. This fact may well be significant because on the one hand Persians used Aramaic in their official and international documents, and on the other hand it seems clear that they often used the local languages for the promulgation of information in given areas. In Ezra 6:2 there is a specific term used, *dikronah*, which we now know to have been an Aramaic term for an official memorandum "which recorded an oral decision of the king or other official and which initiated administrative action. It was never intended for publication but solely for the eye of the proper official, following which it was filed away in government archives."[12] This will explain why the document was later found in the official archives at Achmetha or Ecbatana (Ezra 6:2).

The Hebrew document of Ezra 1 would refer to information for local consumption. It was a proclamation in Hebrew, possibly to be made by the royal heralds, and it was addressed to those who claimed to be worshippers of Yahweh, God of heaven. Precisely the same sort of thing happened elsewhere in Persian times, as we know today from documents brought to light by the archaeologists in which the wishes of the Persian king were made known to the people in written form in their own tongue. For example, there are records from Egypt, not precisely from the days of Cyrus, but from the days of his successor Darius, who instructed the Egyptians in matters affecting their religion. He sent a message to the satraps (governors) of Egypt to assemble the wise men, priests, and scribes to undertake the publication of the ancient laws of Egypt, as they

---

10. J. B. Pritchard, *ANET*, pp. 312-315.
11. W. F. Albright, *The Biblical Period* (Oxford, 1952), p. 49.
12. G. E. Wright, *Biblical Archaeology* (London, 1957), p. 200.

Gold model (fifth century B.C.) of a four-horse Persian chariot. The high chariot, with wheels approximately as tall as a man, was developed by Sennacherib (705– 681 B.C.). (British Museum)

affected in particular the Pharaoh, the temples, and the people. Again, there are inscriptions in the local Egyptian script referring to the work of Darius in restoring temples and the like.[13] There are also several references to the beneficent acts of the Persian kings in the general area of Asia Minor. The names of these rulers were long remembered in these areas, and one notable inscription found near Magnesia in Asia Minor, written in Greek, refers to a letter from Darius to his local satrap, expressing grief that damage had been done to his reputation because the satrap had charged impost on sacred vessels of the god Apollo. These cases point to the possible use of local scripts and writings in certain cases where the Persian king wished to express his will.

In the light of all this evidence there seems no reason to doubt that the decrees of Cyrus recorded in the Bible give the substance of the originals. In any case, much of the background we have been able to discover from archaeological research lends support to the biblical picture. Thus it was that Jews who lived in Babylonia found themselves in the year 539 B.C. in the happy position of being able, if they so desired, to return to the land of their fathers.

13. R. P. R. de Vaux, *op. cit.*, p. 40.

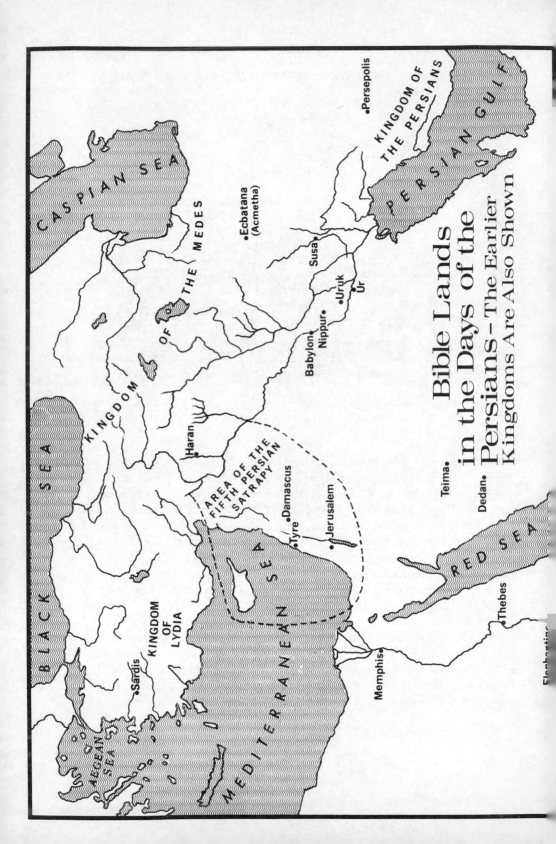

Bible Lands
in the Days of the
Persians – The Earlier
Kingdoms Are Also Shown

THE LAND OF JUDAH AT THE TIME OF THE RETURN

It has been pointed out more than once in recent years that at the time of Nebuchadnezzar's final assault on Judah in the years 587–586 B.C. there was considerable destruction in all the cities of Judah. W. F. Albright has written in this connection:

> A fair number of towns and fortresses of Judah have now been exca-vated in whole or in part; many other sites have been carefully exam-ined to determine the approximate date of their last destruction. The results are uniform and conclusive: many towns were destroyed at the beginning of the sixth century B.C. and never again occupied; others were destroyed at that time and partly reoccupied at some later date; still others were destroyed and reoccupied after a long period of aban-donment, marked by a sharp change of stratum and by intervening indications of use for non-urban purposes. There is not a single case known where a town of Judah proper was continuously occupied through the exilic period.[14]

The destruction does not seem to have extended to the former territory of Israel. We have evidence, based on excavations, that towns north of Jerusalem were occupied throughout the sixth century. In particular the town of Bethel, which really lay outside Judah proper, in the area of Benjamin, was occupied till about 500 B.C., when it was destroyed. The reason for its destruction is still unknown. Further north, towns like Samaria, Megiddo, and Tell en Nasbeh, whose biblical name is not now known, were all occupied in the sixth century. All of this points to the fact that Nebuchadnezzar confined his destruction to the area of Judah, although, as the quotation from Albright shows, he ravaged that land thoroughly.

It seems evident, therefore, that when the Jews returned from their exile they found little in the way of towns, houses, or farms awaiting them. It has been suggested that only one other period in the history of the land showed such a tragic picture, and that was before the days of Abraham, at the close of the Early Bronze Age.

The actual area occupied by the returning Jews was a small one. Its limits can be partly worked out from the material supplied in the lists given in Ezra 2 or in Nehemiah 7. It extended from Bethzur, which is just north of Hebron, to a point not far north of Jerusalem, perhaps twenty-five miles from north to south along the central ridge. Nehemiah 7:66f. gives a population of just under 50,000.

Were it not for the generous attitude of Cyrus and his successors, we may well wonder how the returning Jews survived. Hostile neighbors were likely to cause trouble, and the burden of a land which had lain waste for over half a century was a big one. It was to this task that the returning exiles now set their hands.

14. W. F. Albright, *Archaeology of Palestine* (London, 1956), pp. 141f.

A BRIEF REVIEW OF THE KINGS OF PERSIA UP TO 500 B.C.

In order to obtain a correct perspective for our study, we should now give some attention to the story of the Persian rulers and their methods of government during these years, since these facts are important for our understanding of the biblical narrative.

The first of these rulers was Cyrus. Already in 549 B.C. he had united the peoples of Media and Persia under his rule, and by 546 he had subdued Croesus, the king of Lydia. In 539 B.C. he entered Babylon, which he was to rule till 530 B.C. We think of him today as the founder of the great Persian Empire. In order to govern his great domain he established twenty provinces called satrapies, each ruled by a satrap (protector of the kingdom). These officers were kept under his eye by means of his personal secretaries, financial officers, and generals, who owed allegiance directly to him although they served in the capitals of the satraps. The vast expenses of such an empire were raised from taxation, which was often unkind. This taxation was to be a source of trouble to the people in Judah, who, as subjects of the Persian rulers, had to pay their share. There are biblical references to this burden of taxation, for example in Nehemiah 5:4.

In the year 530 B.C. the great Cyrus was killed in battle, fighting some tribal peoples to the northeast of his land. His son Cambyses rescued his body and buried him in a tomb that was already prepared and which can be seen today, although it has since been plundered.

Cambyses had helped his father to govern Babylon and was an experienced ruler. During his short reign he was able to conquer Egypt, and by 525 Memphis, the capital of Egypt, was in his hands. We remember this king in Jewish history because of his kindness to the Jewish settlement far down the Nile at Elephantine. Here there was a military post manned by Jews to protect the southern borders of the land. We have no idea of the origin of the Jews here, but they had a temple erected for worship. When Cambyses destroyed the local temples of the Egyptians, he spared the temple of the Jews, a fact which is mentioned in important documents from a later day to which we shall refer later.[15] When the task in Egypt was completed, Cambyses set out on the return journey. As he reached Mount Carmel in Palestine, he heard that a usurper had risen up in Persia and claimed his throne. Whether due to shock or, as some claim, by his own hand,[16] he died there.

In the service of Cambyses was a younger relative, Darius by name. He left Palestine at once and organized opposition to the usurper. Before the year 522 had passed, the usurper Bardiya, whose real name was Gaumata, was slain.[17] Meantime, revolts broke out all over the empire and Darius began a struggle for

---

15. See below, pp. 243–246. See also J. B. Pritchard, *ANET*, pp. 491f.
16. Herodotus iii.62f.
17. The original Bardiya was a brother of Cambyses but was executed for rebellion. Gaumata, a Magian, claimed to be this Bardiya, whose death was never announced.

Cylinder seal (right) and impression showing Darius I on a lion hunt; note how the human figures and lions tower over the horses. The cuneiform inscription gives Darius' name and his title, "The Great King," in three languages—Old Persian, Elamite, and Babylonian. The agate cylinder was found at Thebes, Egypt, and is dated ca. 500 B.C. (British Museum)

recognition. After two years he was able to subdue all his opponents and rule supreme. He commemorated his success by having a mountainside smoothed off and a huge inscription carved on its face, with a picture of himself placing his foot on the head of one of his conquered foes. This inscription is still to be seen at Behistun. Darius had a long reign, lasting till 486 B.C., during which he did much to reform the laws of Persia and to extend his domains. It was he who built the first canal to join the Mediterranean Sea to the Red Sea.[18] He also undertook the invasion of Greece, but was defeated at the battle of Marathon in 490 B.C. His work as a builder is seen in palaces from his time which have been excavated in Babylon, Susa, and Persepolis, although his successors extended his building program considerably. Finally, we remember him as an outstanding financier who standardized the weights and measures of Persia, developed the coinage, which in his day was of comparatively recent invention, and began to interfere in the commercial life of the people.[19] Some economists say that owing to the government interference price levels rose with a jump at the start of the reign of Darius and contributed to the end to the economic disintegration of the great empire.[20] Numerous documents of the period found in excavations show the extent to which the king was taking an undue share of the profits of the traders.[21] This led to price rises and to the distress of the poor people. We have traces of this trouble in the Bible, for example in Nehemiah 5:1-4.

18. A. T. Olmstead, *History of the Persian Empire* (Chicago, 1948), p. 145.
19. F. A. Banks, *Coins of Bible Days* (New York, 1955), p. 16. A. T. Olmstead, *op. cit.*, pp. 186f.
20. A. T. Olmstead, *op. cit.*, pp. 193f.
21. *Ibid.*

THE RETURN OF THE EXILES

The Bible has two lists which give the composition of the group that finally left Babylonia to return to Judah, one in Ezra 2 and one in Nehemiah 7. These lists differ slightly from one another, and various attempts are made to explain this. Many writers are inclined to think that the lists refer to the state of affairs at the time when the story in Ezra and Nehemiah was finally committed to writing.[22] More recent study has sought to show that the difference between the two lists can be explained best in terms of slight scribal variations in lists which were compiled from an actual original which made use of a numerical notation such as we have found in several Aramaic documents from Persian times. This system of notation, which was widely used both among the Persians and among the later Nabataean and Palmyrene scribes, consisted of a series of strokes and other special marks which could lead to minor scribal variants. It is suggested that the Jews themselves had a similar system and, indeed, there is a hint of this on some of the ostraca from Samaria dating back to the eighth century B.C. One writer has said:

> As for the lists in Nehemiah 7 and Ezra 2, while at first glance these textual numerical differences may seem detrimental, actually they greatly enhance the value of the lists, as they bring out much of their real nature and age—remains of ancient census lists made by the build-ers and supporters of the restoration and reform sometimes called "the Second Temple," documents vested with reality and antiquity by the very blemishes and signs of use they exhibit.[23]

It seems clear that the returning company of Jews wished to remain exclu-sive and required that a man should have his name on the official list before he could gain recognition in the community. For this reason many of the local people were excluded (Ezra 4:1, 2).

It is evident from documents unearthed at Nippur that many Jews did not return at this time.[24] Those that did were led by Sheshbazzar (Ezra 1:8, 11). This man had a Babylonian name, perhaps Sin-ab-usur or Shamash-ab-usur, but there is some dispute as to who he was. There is a name like this among the sons of Jehoiachin (Jeconiah) in the list in I Chronicles 3:17, 18, Shenazar, and it has been thought that the strangeness of the name caused scribal confusion. It is not at all impossible that in 538 B.C. there should be a son of Jehoiachin alive. He had five sons in 592 B.C. according to tablets found in Babylon, and they could not have been very old at the time of the return.[25] There may well have been a son still alive aged sixty or so.

22. W. F. Albright, *The Biblical Period*, p. 62.

23. H. L. Allrik, "The Lists of Zerubbabel (Nehemiah 7 and Ezra 2) and the Hebrew Numeral Notation," *BASOR* (Dec., 1954), p. 27.

24. G. E. Wright, *op. cit.*, pp. 205f.

25. J. B. Pritchard, *ANET*, p. 308, col. 2.

On the other hand, some writers have held that we may have here a Babylonian official in Persian employ to whom was entrusted the task of leading the Jews home.[26] Another Persian official, Mithredath, handed to him the sacred vessels of the Temple (Ezra 1:8), and presently the party set out for their homeland. In the subsequent story, the Bible tells us only of the work of Zerubbabel (Zer-babil, "offspring of Babylon") and Jeshua the priest. What happened to Sheshbazzar we do not know. Perhaps he was frustrated by the groups that later troubled Nehemiah, or perhaps his task was only of limited duration and having completed it he returned to Persia. In any case, Zerubbabel and Jeshua alone feature in the Bible story.

This Zerubbabel had a Babylonian name, but he was the son of Jehoiachin's eldest son Shealtiel. It was these two men, Zerubbabel and Jeshua, who led the national life. Although their first aim was to build the Temple, they were sidetracked and did little about it till the days of Darius.[27] They seem to have done some preliminary work and to have made arrangements to obtain cedar logs from Tyre. At this point we can add an archaeological note. Ezra 3:7 refers to cedar trees being brought by sea to Joppa. It is of real interest to us today to learn that there was a town at the mouth of the little Yarkon River in those days, originally founded about 1200 B.C., but still in use in Persian times. Today it is known as Tell Qasile. It was excavated in part in 1948–1950.[28]

When the time was ripe to take up again the building of the Temple, it was Zerubbabel who was to the fore. In the exciting days that followed the death of Cambyses, the prophets Haggai and Zechariah called on this man, who is described as "governor of Judah" (Hag. 1:14), or as "the Tirshatha" (Ezra 2:63), a Persian word meaning "his excellency" and known from Persian documents of those days. Haggai gave his first message in August 520 and called on Zerubbabel to commence work on the Temple. The foundation was laid and the work began. At once there were local objections from Tattenai, governor of the province "Beyond the River."

This governor is known in a document from Babylon dating from a few years later, actually 502 B.C.[29] The name is also known from a text referring to "Tattenai prefect of Susa."[30] This latter is not the man in the Bible, but the text shows that the name was a common one in those times. E. G. Kraeling has suggested that the name Tattenai may have been confused with Ushtanni, who is known in Babylonian texts as governor of "Babylon and Beyond the River" and whose first recorded date is March 21, 520 B.C.[31]

26. E. G. Kraeling, Bible Atlas (Chicago, 1956), p. 329.
27. The writer is well aware of the many unsolved problems relating to the foundation of the Temple.
28. B. Maisler, "The Excavation of Tel Qasile," BA (May, 1951), pp. 43ff.
29. E. G. Kraeling, op. cit., p. 331.
30. Ibid.
31. Ibid.

The objections of Tattenai led to the search for the original memorandum of Cyrus to which we have already referred.[32] This was found in the archives at Ecbatana (the biblical Achmetha, Ezra 6:2). Permission being granted to continue, the work went on and was finally completed in March, 515 B.C. (Ezra 6:15). Some have seen in the willingness of Darius to accede to the request of the Jews a desire on his part to win over yet another part of his domains. The work of the prophets Haggai and Zechariah fell at the time when Darius was just recovering from the revolts of recent days. Perhaps indeed Zerubbabel was a loyal supporter of the new king at first. There is more than a hint, however, that he allowed himself to become the center of hopes for the restoration of the throne of David (Hag. 2:20f.; Zech. 4:6f.; 6:12f., etc.).[33] The opinion of W. F. Albright is of interest:

> Haggai's second oracle . . . exults in the approaching downfall of Persia and the coming of a new Jewish state; in his fourth oracle (Hag. 2:20–23) dated in December, while the Babylonian rebellion still appeared to be successful, he explicitly declared that the imperial throne would be overturned and implied that Zerubbabel was the Lord's anointed. . . . Whether Zerubbabel died a natural death or was removed, we cannot say; there is not the slightest reason to suppose that he committed any overt act of disloyalty to the crown. . . . evidently the Persian authorities contented themselves with depriving the Davidic family of its political prerogatives, which were turned over to Joshua and his successors. We may safely credit Joshua with political astuteness in the difficult situation in which he found himself.[34]

Unfortunately we have no archaeological evidence about the Temple. If there are remains today, they lie beneath the present ground level. The whole Temple area has suffered greatly through the centuries, and while no doubt there would be much to bring to light if the archaeologists could only excavate on the site where the great Mohammedan mosque now stands, we must await the results of future excavations before we can discover what lies buried there.[35]

It is significant that the state of Judah seems to have been ruled internally by the high priests from this time onward. We know quite a number of the high priests between these days and New Testament times. Perhaps for political purposes the Persians appointed governors, but they seem to have allowed the normal internal affairs of state, like taxation, to be supervised by the high

---

32. See above, pp. 202–207.

33. The prophecies were made in all sincerity and under divine inspiration, but some change in conditions must have led to the postponement of God's purposes. See Jeremiah 18:6–10 for an important principle.

34. W. F. Albright, The Biblical Period, p. 50.

35. K. Kenyon directed a major expedition designed to investigate the area of Ophel, Old Testament Jerusalem, from 1961 to 1968. She discovered a ritual complex, including two stone pillars and a cultic cave dated ca. 800 B.C., as well as a cave dated ca. 700 with 1300 pottery vessels and numerous figurines. See K. Kenyon, Jerusalem: Excavating 3000 Years of History (London, 1967).

priests. That the Persians did allow some sort of priestly rule in their empire is shown by the fact that the priests of Hierapolis in northern Syria were able to levy their own taxes and strike their own coins.[36]

THE PROVINCE OF JUDAH IN 500 B.C.

It is evident, then, that the little province of Judah was closely linked with the great Persian administration from the time of Cyrus onward. In political status it was only a small part of a much larger satrapy. We have seen that the Persians organized their vast domains into large units called satrapies which were ruled by satraps. Persian inscriptions like the great biography of Darius on the rock at Behistun list these satrapies. A. T. Olmstead in his *History of Persia* refers to other lists at various periods in Persian history which make it possible to trace changes in the disposition of these satrapies. Many of these satraps replaced former kings and became little monarchs themselves, and for this reason the Persian authorities needed to keep them in check. These larger units were then divided into smaller provinces, each with its own administrator. One of these satrapies, defined by Herodotus as the fifth, "Beyond the River [Transpotamia]," seems to have been subdivided into several provinces, among them Judah, Samaria, Ammon, Ashdod, and Arabia.[37] The province of Judah was surrounded by these others, whose governors quite naturally viewed any sign of expansion with suspicion. The complete satrapy thus included Syria, Palestine, and other areas to the west of the Euphrates, all united into the one large area of "Babylon and Ebir-nari [Across the River]."[38] We know some of the satraps who ruled this vast area, men like Gobryas and Ushtani (or Hystanes). A. T. Olmstead describes the position of Zerubbabel in this complex system as "only a governor of the third rank." His immediate superior was Tattenai, governor of "Across the River," who in turn was under the authority of Hystanes, satrap of "Babylon and Across the River."[39] In later years, following a revolt in Babylon in 482 B.C., the satrapy "Across the River" was detached from Babylon. This was the state of affairs when Nehemiah was governor, and we shall take up the point again later.

Thus, at the end of the sixth century B.C. there was a little province under the control of the returned exiles, protected by royal decree, but surrounded by hostile neighbors, and opposed even by those Jews who had never gone into exile but who had stayed in the general area to which the exiles returned.

36. W. F. Albright, *The Biblical Period*, p. 55.
37. Herodotus iii.89ff.
38. A. T. Olmstead, *op. cit.*, pp. 56f.
39. *Ibid.*, pp. 138f.

THE PERSIAN PERIOD IN PALESTINE
FROM 500 B.C. TO 330 B.C.

AFTER the building of the temple the Jews entered on a period of history which is for us today obscure, to say the least of it. The darkness is penetrated at one or two points only, notably in the days of the governor Nehemiah who rebuilt the wall of Jerusalem. A certain amount of material is available from excavations in towns that were occupied in Palestine during Persian times, and from these we gain some insight into the types of buildings in use, the pottery, the coinage, and in particular the growing influence of Greek culture in the land. But we have no clear idea of the way in which the Persians ruled the land, for we know of only two governors of these times, Nehemiah and Bagoses, although we have some reason to think that the priests did much of the routine work of government, notably in the area of tax collection. Modern archaeological work gives some insight into the neighboring peoples who feature in the biblical narrative. Outside of Palestine we know something about the Jews in Mesopotamia and Egypt, and we shall devote a special chapter to these groups, but it would be well first of all to review the history of the Persians during the period 500 B.C. to 330 B.C. This will provide a good background against which to view the story of the Jews as far as we can reconstruct it today.

PERSIAN KINGS FROM 500 B.C. TO 300 B.C.

At the close of the sixth century B.C. the great Darius was still ruling and was to continue till 486 B.C. We have referred to his attack on Greece and to his defeat at Marathon in 490 B.C. His achievements were great indeed, and his

Bull-headed libation cup (rhyton) in the shape of an animal's horn, a beautiful piece of Persian craftsmanship. Made of silver partially covered with gold foil, it was found in northeastern Turkey and is dated to the fifth century B.C. It calls to mind the words of Neh. 1:11, "Now I was cupbearer to the king." (British Museum)

successor Xerxes I (486–465 B.C.), who had been trained in the art of government by being allowed to rule as viceroy in Babylon, carried on his work. In the light of this experience he was able at a later date to carry through some vital administrative changes in government. His father had commenced to build several great palaces, perhaps the most notable of all being that at Persepolis, but it was left to Xerxes to bring the whole magnificent plan to completion, and to change it in certain respects. He alone seems to have been responsible for the magnificent reliefs, which surpass all the earlier work of his father's craftsmen. He had many military successes in all parts of his own empire despite the fact that he did suffer defeat at the hands of the Greeks in the battles of Thermopylae and Salamis in 480 B.C. and again at Plataea the next year. Perhaps in actual fact these successes of the Greeks were not so great as subsequent Greek writers made them out to be, but they did arouse Greek patriotism and had a tremendous effect on the morale of the Greeks. We know Xerxes best in biblical history from the story of Esther, which took place in the old Elamite town of Susa, conquered by Cyrus, but at the time of the biblical story the site of a beautiful palace built by Darius, and later enlarged and completed by Xerxes. That this monarch lived there for at least some of his reign is evidenced by documents

Darius the Great (522–586 B.C.) moved his capital from Pasargadae to Persepolis, where he began to erect a magnificent group of buildings on a huge artificial platform. The photograph shows the stairway leading to the reception hall, the Apadana; seventy-two columns once supported a roof of 2800 square meters. The reliefs are of tribute bearers and soldiers, notably (by the stairways) the king's guards. (Oriental Institute, University of Chicago)

found in Susa, although there were other palaces, the best loved of them being that at Persepolis.[1]

The next king was Artaxerxes I (465–424 B.C.) during whose reign the famous Nehemiah was governor of Judah and Ezra the scribe was active.[2] Important documents from Egypt and Mesopotamia, dating partly from the reign of Artaxerxes and partly from the reign of his successor Darius II (423–404 B.C.),[3] give us evidence about the Jews for these years. There was a brief period of two years between these two kings, during which Xerxes II (424–423 B.C.) occupied the throne, but this king is relatively unimportant.

The last four kings were Artaxerxes II (404–358 B.C.), Artaxerxes III (358–338 B.C.), Ares (338–336 B.C.), and Darius III (336–331 B.C.). Persia collapsed finally in 331 B.C. before the Greek invader Alexander the Great.

ARCHAEOLOGY AND THE BOOK OF ESTHER

The little book of Esther is placed in the days of Xerxes, whose biblical name is Ahasuerus. It is a puzzling book in some ways because it is difficult to identify

1. A. T. Olmstead, *The History of the Persian Empire* (Chicago, 1948), pp. 230f. and pp. 266f.

2. The writer is not unaware of the problem of Ezra but holds that Ezra and Nehemiah were contemporary. See below, pp. 221ff.

3. Some Egyptian documents came from the reigns of Darius I and Xerxes I as well. See below, pp. 238–246.

This aerial view gives an impression of the vast area covered by the Achaemenian palaces at Persepolis. The city remained the Achaemenian spring capital until Alexander overthrew the Persian empire. (University Museum, University of Pennsylvania)

most of the people concerned from external evidence. The chief characters of the book—Vashti, Haman, and Mordecai—are unknown in nonbiblical history. Excavations, however, as well as general historical evidence make it clear that there is much in the book that shows the writer to have been correctly informed on many of the background details of the story.

The biblical account of Xerxes (Ahasuerus) has been corroborated by historians. The picture given in the book of Esther of a king who was a despot and thoroughly sensuous in character corresponds with the account given by the Greek historian Herodotus.[4] He greatly enlarged his harem at Persepolis, as excavation shows,[5] and became involved in a shameful affair with his brother's wife and later with the daughter as well.

The description of the ornate palace with its bright curtains is quite in the manner of the gaudy palaces of the Persians. Excavations at Susa (biblical Shushan) have yielded abundant evidence of the rich ornamentation of the walls of the palace and of the richly colored glazed bricks used there.[6] This palace, commenced by Darius, was described in glowing terms. It was built of special timbers and adorned with gold, lapis lazuli, turquoise, silver, and ebony, and was erected by men who came from all over the empire.[7]

The story of Esther could well fit into the time of Xerxes, for he reigned for twenty years, and the events of this book do not go beyond the twelfth or possibly the thirteenth year (Esther 3:7, 12). The banquet in the third year may coincide with the great council that Xerxes held before the invasion of Greece, and the four years that intervened before Esther became queen may well fit into the time that the king was absent in Greece (Esther 1:3; 2:16).[8] The standard commentaries on the book of Esther point out that many of the customs referred to in the story are quite in keeping with Persian practice.[9] Thus the arrangements for the banquet (1:6-8), obeisance before the king and his favorites (3:2), belief in lucky and unlucky days (3:7), exclusion of mourning garb from the palace (4:2), hanging as the death penalty (5:14), dressing a royal benefactor in the king's robes (6:8), and dispatching couriers with royal messages (3:13; 8:10) are all customs that are well known from the written records that have come to light.[10] There are, moreover, a number of Persian words in the book, largely from the language of government and trade. All of these factors show that, at the very least, the author of the book of Esther was well informed on numerous matters of Persian practice and Persian life; and while there are difficulties of interpretation and identification still remaining, we may hope to find yet more archaeological evidence to clear up the historical situation. It is risky to adopt the view that has been adopted by many modern writers that the whole story is

4. Herodotus, *The Histories* (London, 1955), pp. 594ff., or Herodotus ix.107ff.
5. A. T. Olmstead, *op. cit.*, ch. 20.
6. *Ibid.*, pp. 166-171. Also R. Ghirshman, *Iran* (London, 1954), pp. 165-167.
7. R. Ghirshman, *op. cit.*, pp. 165f.
8. Herodotus vii.8.
9. For example, L. B. Paton, *The Book of Esther*, ICC (Edinburgh, 1951), pp. 64ff.
10. *Ibid.*, p. 65.

Detail of the Tripylon Relief at Persepolis. Darius sits on his throne, and his son, Crown Prince Xerxes, stands behind him. In front of Darius is a dignitary in Median dress raising his hand to his mouth to show respect. Xerxes is doubtless the Ahasuerus of the book of Esther, while his successor, Artaxerxes, is the king who sent Nehemiah to Jerusalem. (Oriental Institute, University of Chicago)

pure fiction, especially when we have to argue so much from silence, a very uncertain basis for argument in any case.

EZRA THE SCRIBE

The date at which Ezra did his work is not clearly specified in the Bible, which merely says that it was in the seventh year of Artaxerxes the king (Ezra 7:7, 8). The question immediately arises as to whether this was the first or the second king of this name. If it was the first, the date would be 458 B.C., but if it was the second, it would be 397 B.C. The Bible certainly gives us the impression that Ezra preceded Nehemiah. There is little in the way of archaeological evidence to help us solve the question of dating. This is in striking contrast with the case of Nehemiah where we have convincing evidence for a date of 444 B.C. One possible reconstruction which allows of Ezra preceding Nehemiah, and which appeals to the present writer, is as follows:

Artaxerxes I in his seventh year, following the practice of other Persian kings, decided to investigate the religious condition of the Jews in Judah. Such inquiries were not unusual and there is in existence today an important document from Egypt which tells of a similar inquiry into the religious observances of the Jews in Egypt toward the end of the fifth century B.C.:

> To my brethren Yedoniah and his colleagues, the Jewish garrison, your brother Hananiah. The welfare of my brothers may God seek at all times.

Now, this year, the fifth of King Darius, word was sent from the king to Arsames saying, "Authorize a festival of unleavened bread for the Jewish garrison."

So do you count fourteen days of the month of Nisan and observe the passover, and from the fifteenth to the twenty-first of Nisan observe the festival of unleavened bread. Be ritually clean and take heed. Do not work on the fifteenth or the twenty-first day, nor drink beer, nor eat anything in which there is leaven from the fourteenth at sundown until the twenty-first of Nisan. For seven days it shall not be seen among you. Do not bring it into your dwellings, but seal it up between these dates.

By order of King Darius.

To my brethren Yedoniah and the Jewish garrison,

Your brother Hananiah.[11]

In the present instance, Ezra, a Jew living in Persia, was selected by Artaxerxes I because of his reputation in matters of Jewish law, and he was given a strict commission to go to Judah and inquire concerning the way the people obeyed the law of their God. He was to take free-will offerings from the Jews in his own land and have access to government funds if he needed extra money. After inquiry, he was to teach the ignorant, and then enforce the law with penalties (Ezra 7:11–26). He duly arrived in Judah and delivered his commission to the local rulers.

About the same time some illegal building was being carried on in Jerusalem and a complaint went to the king that a wall was being built around the city (Ezra 4:11–16). A prayer recorded from the lips of Ezra makes reference to God giving the people a wall in Judah and in Jerusalem (Ezra 9:9). The next thing we know is that Artaxerxes had forbidden the building of a wall and the work of Ezra was cut short. Ezra did indeed attempt some reforms, but little attention is paid to these in the record and we may conjecture that not much was achieved. Perhaps Ezra was disgraced and his commission taken away because he became involved in the matter. It is here suggested that he went into retirement to reappear when Nehemiah came as governor. If this is not the true picture, then we have to place Ezra after Nehemiah, or at least allow that Nehemiah preceded him to Judah and that he followed a little later. This is the view taken by W. F. Albright, who holds that Ezra came in the thirty-seventh year of Artaxerxes.[12] The fact is, however, that we lack external evidence of an archaeological kind to solve the problem.

NEHEMIAH THE GOVERNOR AND RESTORER
OF THE WALLS OF JERUSALEM

At first reading the biblical records we are in a similar quandary about the date of Nehemiah, for the start of his story is in the twentieth year of Artaxerxes. Now

11. J. B. Pritchard, *ANET*, p. 491.
12. W. F. Albright, *The Biblical Period*, pp. 53f.

The Achaemenian kings Darius I, Artaxerxes I, and Darius II are buried in these rock-cut tombs at Naqsh-i-Rustam near Persepolis. (Oriental Institute, University of Chicago)

is this the first or the second king of this name? The discovery of Aramaic documents at Elephantine[13] in Egypt has placed it beyond all doubt that it is the first of these kings that is referred to in the Bible. The details of this argument will be given in the next chapter, so for the present we shall accept the fact.

It was late in 445 B.C. that Nehemiah learned from his brother Hanani and other Jews who had come from Jerusalem that the situation there was bad. The lack of a wall made attacks from hostile neighbors inevitable. At the time there was a ban on the building of the wall (Ezra 4:17–24). By careful pleading Nehemiah was able to have this order reversed and was himself appointed governor of Judah (Neh. 5:14). Provided with letters to the governors of "Beyond the River," a Persian province (Neh. 2:7, 9), and with a military escort, Nehemiah set out for Judah. Three days after his arrival he went by night on a tour around the city walls. The account of this journey in 2:12–15, together with the accounts of the walls in chapter 3 and 12:31–40, makes a striking picture when compared with the reports of excavations conducted at various points around the walls in recent times. While it is not possible to sort out the picture completely, the disposition of the places mentioned on the eastern side of the city is fairly well agreed upon today. One recent writer said:

> The topographical texts of Nehemiah are likewise of exceptional value, even more so than any passages in Josephus, not only because they present us with a thrice-repeated wall description by an eyewitness more detailed than that of Josephus (Neh. 2:11–15; 3; 12:31–39), but especially because they deal with the city of the Old Testament itself, before as well as after the Exile. When Nehemiah arrived in Jerusalem, Herod's extensive levelling and enlargement operations in the sacred quarter were still far off.[14]

13. For detailed discussion, see below, pp. 238–246.
14. J. Simons, *Jerusalem in the Old Testament* (Leiden, 1952), pp. 437f.

Thanks to the work of Kathleen Kenyon we are now in a position to see some of the archaeological problems more clearly. In the first place, Dr. Kenyon's excavations on the eastern slope of the narrow spur jutting south from the Temple area demonstrated that this area was occupied at the end of the pre-exilic period. Nebuchadnezzar's attack dislodged the stone walls of terraces and houses and covered the hillside with an enormous tumble of stones.[15] This discovery gives point to the statement in Nehemiah 2:14:

> Then I went on to the Fountain Gate and to the King's Pool; but there was no place for the beast that was under me to pass.

The walls that Nehemiah had to inspect were almost certainly along this hilly spur.[16] The King's Pool in this reference is to be identified with the Pool of Siloam or the adjacent Birket el Hamra. When Nehemiah came to rebuild the walls he abandoned the areas of the old town that lay down the eastern slope of the hill and built his wall on the comparatively level crest of the ridge. Dr. Kenyon was able to uncover a part of Nehemiah's wall,[17] which, incidentally, remained the wall of Jerusalem in this area until the destruction of the original city by Titus in A.D. 70, although there were frequent repairs and strengthenings. In the light of these important excavations some earlier volumes[18] that dealt with Jerusalem will need to be modified in some areas, but notably in their references to Nehemiah's wall.

The biblical narrative tells of the completion of the work of rebuilding, a task in which men from various areas played a part. Perhaps the towns referred to in chapter 3, which makes reference to the men of Tekoa, Bethzur, Keilah, Zanoah, Jerusalem, Gibeon, Mizpah, Jericho, and Beth-haccerem, give us the best idea we have of the extent of Judah at the time. By placing these on a map it is possible to see at a glance the area from which Nehemiah drew his helpers.

ARCHAEOLOGICAL LIGHT ON JUDAH'S NEIGHBORS

As Nehemiah began his task he was greatly troubled by the opposition of various neighbors. The most troublesome of these were Sanballat the Horonite, Tobiah the Ammonite, and Geshem the Arab (Neh. 2:10, 19; 4:1, 3, 7; 6:2, etc.) who plotted against Nehemiah, but he was able to frustrate them (Neh. 2:19f.; 4:6).

Archaeological discovery in this century has produced evidence about these neighbors and in the case of Sanballat and Geshem has brought to light some actual written evidence. The name of Sanballat is found on one of the Elephantine papyri dating to the year 407 B.C., which can be shown quite clearly to be

---

15. K. Kenyon, *Jerusalem: Excavating 3000 Years of History* (London, 1967), Plate 9.
16. *Ibid.*, Fig. 6, p. 57.
17. *Ibid.*, Plates 54, 55.
18. E.g. J. Simons, *op. cit.*; L. H. Vincent and A. M. Steve, *Jerusalem de l'Ancien Testament* (Paris, 1954 and 1956), 2 vols.

later than Nehemiah.[19] We shall see that Sanballat had a long life and remained governor in Samaria some years after Nehemiah ceased to be governor in Judah. The name Sanballat is probably a Babylonian name, Sin-uballit (SIN [a deity] has called into life). The man was governor of Samaria under Persian overlordship, but almost certainly he was not a Babylonian. The names of his sons Delaiah and Shelemiah are Hebrew, not Babylonian. Both names include the element IAH, which stood for Yahweh, the name of the God of the people of Israel. It is, however, possible, and even likely, that Sanballat followed a syncretistic kind of religion not unlike the religion of the Jews in Egypt. The Elephantine documents, to be discussed in detail in the next chapter, show us that there were other groups who followed a syncretistic religion not unlike that of the Jews.

The name Geshem is now known from two sources, one being a contemporary inscription found at Hegra in Arabia, and the other found in a temple on the borders of Egypt, belonging probably to Arabs who worshipped there at a time when their influence extended to this point.

At the time of Nehemiah the kings of Dedan were the rulers of a vast area to the east of the Jordan and extending away to the south, and although naturally under Persian domination they had some sort of control over a wide area. They left behind them a variety of inscriptions, one of which reads as follows:

> Niran, son of Hadiru, inscribed his name in the days of Gashm, son
> of Shahar, and Abd, governor of Dedan.[20]

The phrase "Abd [servant], governor of Dedan" is reminiscent of the one in the Bible, "Tobiah, the servant, the Ammonite" (Neh. 2:10, 19). Tobiah is described as "the servant," and the governor of Dedan is "servant." Another feature about the inscription is the use of the word PHT for *governor*. This same word occurs in the books of Ezra and Nehemiah as an element in a proper name, Pahat-Moab.[21] W. F. Albright has suggested that the name, which means "governor of Moab," may well have come from such a governor who gave his name to the family. The word *pahah* would not have been correct until the time of the Babylonians or Persians, since Moab had its own tributary kings till at least 645 B.C.[22] These facts, quite apart from the name Geshem, point to a Persian date for the inscription of Hegra.

Until very recently this reference stood alone, but now we have some most valuable confirmatory evidence from the Arab temple referred to above. On the outskirts of the area, controlled by the kings of Dedan, namely, the eastern Delta region of Egypt, was a temple where offerings were made to the North

19. See below, p. 246.
20. A. T. Olmstead, *op. cit.*, p. 295.
21. Ezra 2:6; 8:4; 10:30; Nehemiah 3:11; 7:11; 10:14. Compare W. F. Albright, *op. cit.*, p. 64 n. 131.
22. W. F. Albright, *loc. cit.*

Arabian goddess Han-'Allat, and in which worshippers had deposited long ago a number of silver vessels, three of which bore inscriptions in Aramaic. The proper names on these are, with one exception, all North Arabic. One of them is of special interest to us because it carries the words "Qainu son of Geshem [Gusham] king of Kedar." These inscriptions are securely dated to the end of the fifth century B.C. by converging lines of evidence. Professor I. Rabinowitz who published the material traces the objects to the Arab shrine at Tell el-Maskhutah (ancient Succoth) in the Wadi Tumilat on the eastern part of the Nile Delta.[23] It is probable that this "Qainu son of Geshem king of Kedar" was, in fact, the son of Nehemiah's adversary since the style of writing points to a date about 400 B.C.

It is becoming increasingly evident that the Arab kingdom ruled over by Geshem was quite considerable and included northern Arabia, old Edom, the Sinai area, part of the Nile Delta, and possibly even a part of southern Judah, where small altars much like those found in southern Arabia have been discovered.[24] This large Arab kingdom was brought under some sort of Persian control and added to the satrap of "Across the River," but its local ruler was evidently allowed to continue as the Persian governor, probably on condition that he paid annual tribute. The discovery in such a context of an inscription such as we have quoted points with some certainty to the son of the biblical Geshem.

The third of Nehemiah's troublesome neighbors was Tobiah the Ammonite. While we have no direct evidence of this man at present, we do have a considerable amount of information about his family. His very name suggests that he worshipped Yahweh: notice the element IAH at the end. His family was of political importance in Transjordan from the fifth century to the second century at least. At the important site of 'Araq el Emir in central Transjordan there are some fine rock-cut tombs, one of which bears the name *Tobiah* deeply cut in the rock, in Aramaic letters of the third century B.C. used during the rule of the Ptolemies in Egypt.[25] In the same region we find the remains of what some writers call a palace and others a mausoleum, built evidently by the last of the Tobiad rulers.[26] We know of an Ammonite governor of this family earlier in the third century B.C., because of a letter which he wrote to an Egyptian official named Zeno employed in the government of Ptolemy II, Philadelphus (285–246 B.C.). The letter stated that Tubias (Tobiah) was sending to Ptolemy a number of animals, including horses, dogs, and camels.[27]

23. F. M. Cross, "Geshem the Arab, Enemy of Nehemiah," BA (May, 1955), p. 47; W. J. Dumbrell, "The Tell el-Maskhuta Bowls and the 'Kingdom' of Qedar in the Persian Period," BASOR, No. 203 (Oct., 1971), pp. 33–44.
24. W. F. Albright, *Archaeology of Palestine* (London, 1956), pp. 143f.
25. *Ibid.*, p. 149.
26. G. E. Wright, *Biblical Archaeology* (London, 1957), p. 204. Cf. W. F. Albright, *Archaeology of Palestine*, pp. 149f.; B. Mazar, "The Tobiads," *IEJ*, Vol. 7 (1957), pp. 137–145, 229–238; C. C. McCown, "The Araq el-Emir and the Tobiads," BA, Vol. 20 (1957), pp. 63–76.
27. G. E. Wright, *op. cit.*, p. 204. See also L. H. Vincent, "La Palestine dans les papyrus ptolémaique de Gerza," *RB* (Apr., 1920), pp. 161ff.

While, therefore, there is no direct evidence at present for the Tobiah of Nehemiah's day, it is clear that there was a Tobiah family in Transjordan in the centuries that followed, and we have good reason to link these later Tobiahs with the man of Nehemiah's time.

SOME ITEMS OF GENERAL CULTURE

Excavations in Palestine have produced a variety of items of general culture which make their contribution to our understanding of these centuries.

We refer first of all to the pottery of the period. There is a distinctive type of pottery for this so-called Persian or Iron III period, as there is for all archaeological periods. But what is of special interest to us is that at this period a considerable amount of very distinctive Greek pottery appeared in Palestine, bearing witness to the growing influence of the Greeks in the eastern Mediterranean lands. It was during the sixth century B.C. that the Athenian and other Greek potters set out to master the art of representing the human figure and its drapery in great detail on their pottery pieces. At first they perfected the art of working black figures on a red background, using a technique that itself was old but was now brought to perfection. About 530 B.C. a new technique appeared in which the potters represented figures in red on a lustrous black background. The Athenians held their art as a secret and attained a brilliance in their vases not equaled elsewhere.

The black-figure ware which has been found in many lands in the East, including Egypt, Syria, and Palestine, argues for Greek trading at some time before 500 B.C. There is also a good deal of red-figure ware now known from excavations, showing that the Greeks were active as traders from the fifth century onward. Actually, once the trading began, it continued on through the centuries, the Greek traders being only the precursors of the Greek conquerors. The excavator of the site of Tell en Nasbeh to the north of Jerusalem has written concerning the presence of Greek pottery in this town as follows:

> In a small hill town, even if it was, or had been, the capital of the minute Persian province of Judah, the presence of such ware is significant, telling of close commercial relations between Attica and Palestine in the period of Athens' greatest glory.[28]

In all, some thirty sherds of Greek pottery consisting largely of Attic black-figure ware, although there was some red-figure ware, were found in this excavation. Greek traders evidently visited this town before 500 B.C.

The most recent work at Shechem has produced evidence of Greek influences in the center of Palestine before 500 B.C. Pieces of Greek black-figure ware, probably of the sixth century B.C., were discovered in one area.[29]

28. C. C. McCown, *Tell en Nasbeh* (Baltimore, 1947), Vol. I, p. 62.
29. E. F. Campbell, *BASOR*, No. 161 (Feb., 1961), pp. 52f.

A beautiful example of Greek red-figure ware. Sherds of both black-figure and red-figure ware were found in various places in Palestine. (British Museum)

Turning to coinage we find further significant material. Coinage as we know it today was probably first used by the kings of Lydia when Croesus, their most famous king, stopped minting lumps of so-called white gold about 550 B.C. and changed over to pure gold coinage. The kings of Persia took the lead from him, and Lydian coins served as patterns for the coinage of Persia. On the golden daric and the silver shekel of the Medes and the Persians appeared the picture of the great king. The Greek colonies of the Ionian isles and of Italy copied the idea, and not long after, Greek traders in the eastern Mediterranean started to make coins. The men of old Greece soon followed suit, although they used silver for their coins because they lacked gold. Significant emblems were used on the coins by many of the Greek states. Aegina had a turtle, and Athens, the home of beautiful vases, had a vase. Later, when the Athenian dictator Peisistratus came on the scene, he used the head of the patron goddess of Athens, Athene, on the front of the coins and a small owl and a twig of olives on the back. The Athenians thought that Athene appeared at times in the guise of an owl, and so they associated this bird with the goddess. The Greek coins were minted in multiples of the drachma.

Both of these latter facts about Greek coinage, namely, that they were minted in multiples of the drachma and that they carried the picture of an owl, are important for our study of the coinage of Palestine in these times. Coins began to appear in Palestine in the fifth century B.C., and excavations reveal that by the third century they had become abundant. W. F. Albright has noted:

> Silver coins, struck in imitation of Attic drachmas, but with the Hebrew or Aramaic inscription *Yehud*, "Judah," are being found in increasing numbers.[30]

In the same discussion this writer observes,

> We have hinted above at the importance of the Attic currency, which became the standard medium of exchange in Palestine more than a century and a quarter before the Macedonian conquest. Attic coins were locally imitated in the second half of the fifth century, and in the following century we find all sorts of barbaric modifications of the figures on the drachma, the owl of Athena being kept until it became unrecognisable.[31]

In the light of these facts it becomes of real interest to discover that several passages in the books of Ezra and Nehemiah, referring to events in the latter half of the fifth century B.C., show that the gifts to the Temple were assessed in terms of coins of some kind (Ezra 2:69; 8:27; Neh. 7:70-72). On any system of dating Ezra and Nehemiah, these passages fit into the fifth century B.C., by which time the drachma standard had already penetrated into other lands besides Greece. It is true that there has been some discussion about the exact nature of this coinage, and the Hebrew word *darkemon* has been variously interpreted as *drachma* or *daric*.[32] In either case, these two standards of coinage were in use at the time, and either would suit the biblical passages.

It is evident from these considerations that the Persians must have granted considerable local autonomy to the Jews, with the right to strike their own coinage. This was not a unique occurrence, for we know today that the priests of Atargatis at Heliopolis in northern Syria received permission to strike their own coinage and to levy their own temple taxes.[33]

Light on the Persian system of taxation comes from a most unusual source. In order to carry out its tremendous program of government the Persians worked out an elaborate fiscal scheme, and taxation was levied in all parts of the empire. We gain a brief glimpse into this program in Nehemiah 5, where we learn that people in Palestine had to mortgage their property in order to meet the requirements of the government. When we come to investigate the methods of collecting taxes we find light from the seal impressions left on the handles of large jars

---

30. W. F. Albright, *Archaeology of Palestine*, p. 143.
31. *Ibid.*
32. Cf. G. E. Wright, *op. cit.*, p. 203, and W. F. Albright, *loc. cit.*
33. W. F. Albright, *loc. cit.*

dating from the fifth and fourth centuries B.C. There are several kinds of seals now known. One type consists of three consonants, YHD, in ancient Hebrew script, together with a small circle in which there is often a cross. This last sign is known from Egypt where it is associated with the letters *lmlk*, meaning "belonging to the king." It was evidently associated in Egypt with some official collection for the king. The letters YHD on the seals found in Palestine signify "Judah," and it is a reasonable conclusion that if at Elephantine in Egypt the symbol of a circle and a cross was associated with the king's portion, it was so in Judah also.

Another group of seals has a circle inside of which is a five-pointed star, between the points of which are the letters YRShLM, which would spell out "Jerusalem" in Hebrew. The writing is again in the old type of Hebrew script. A third group of seals written in a more clearly Aramaic script had only the letters YHD on an oval seal without any decoration. Finally, there is a group of seals mostly from Tell en Nasbeh which carry the letters MTsH, referring possibly to the town of Mizpah.[34] This was evidently an important town in Persian times, for the text in Nehemiah 3:7 may be translated "Mizpah, belonging to the throne of the governor of this Side of the River." The town apparently had some official connection with the satrap of the whole area.

The jar stamps have been found in various places. J. D. Duncan found twenty of them at Ophel (Jerusalem), others were found at Gezer, some twenty-eight others at Tell en Nasbeh. The existence of such a variety of these stamps on the handles of large jars bearing the names of Judah, Jerusalem, and possibly Mizpah, suggests very strongly that there was in use some sort of local method of collecting taxes in kind. Potters were evidently required to make certain jars of standard capacity for the collection of the king's portion.

Until recently architecture and building remains have been poorly understood because of the comparative lack of archaeological data. The later Hellenists, in many sites, destroyed the buildings of the Persian period in order to lay foundations for their own buildings. But in recent years good building remains of the Persian period have been brought to light by Israeli excavators, especially along the coast from Tel Aviv northward, and the picture is becoming much clearer.

At Tell Michel a few miles north of Tel Aviv there was a considerable population in the Persian period and there was probably an anchorage for small ships and boats at the foot of the tell. The lower city spread away to the north.[35]

Further north at Tel Megadim, some 17 kilometers south of Haifa, three strata of the Persian period have been distinguished.[36] A short distance to the south Tel Mevorakh[37] has produced Persian remains which preserved some

---

34. As an abbreviation. See G. E. Wright, *op. cit.*, p. 203; also H. L. Ginsberg, *BASOR*, No. 109, pp. 20f.; N. Avigad, "New light on the MSH seal impressions," *IEJ*, Vol. 8, pp. 113ff.
35. Z. Herzog et al., "Excavations at Tell Michel, 1977," *Tel Aviv*, Vol. 5 (1978), pp. 99–135.
36. M. Broshi, "Tel Megadim," *EAEHL*, Vol. III (1977), pp. 823–826.
37. E. Stern, "Tel Mevorakh," *EAEHL*, Vol. III (1977), pp. 866–870.

Attic pottery. A large building covered the entire mound in the later stages of the Persian period, probably an administrative building.

But there was a Persian presence in several important places. At Abu Hawam, north of Mt. Carmel, a building was discovered facing a main thoroughfare that was more or less parallel to the longitudinal axis of the town. At Shiqmonah,[38] south of Haifa, one section of a dwelling quarter excavated showed houses had been built along two intersecting streets. At Megadim a built-up area bisected a wide, straight road on either side of which were narrow lanes which intersected at right angles. These lanes were further divided into subunits uniform in size and shape. At Acco (modern Acre) good evidence of the Persian period has been unearthed.[39]

One important site in the southern part of the land was Lachish where J. Starcky discovered the remains of an impressive building constructed on the ruins of an earlier Judaean citadel. It was built on an open-court plan approximately 50 by 37 meters, with steps and porticos leading to halls and private quarters. It seems to have been in use from the mid-fifth to the mid-fourth century B.C. It was described by the excavators as the Residency. Like other large buildings found on the top of ancient tells from the Persian period, it represented an administrative center.[40]

Despite these general conclusions, two questions have been raised. The first is a question concerning the occupants of the building. It has been conjectured that we have here one of the residences of the Arab kingdom of which the most famous biblical representative was Geshem.[41]

The other question about the large building at Lachish concerns the date at which the structure was built. It has been assumed that it was built in Persian times. It was certainly used in this period, but some excavators have proposed that the original structure goes back to Assyrian times.[42] For our purpose the building was used in Persian times, either by the Persians or by the local governor who must have been under general Persian control.

Beautiful works of art have been found in some sites. Sir Flinders Petrie discovered a tomb at Tell el Far'ah in the Negeb which contained a beautiful silver bowl and a dipper, the latter having for a handle the figure of an undraped maiden.[43] Art of this kind is known in other parts of the Persian Empire. Other finds of bronze figures of gods and animals bear witness to the well-developed art of the period in some places. The art may not, however, have been the work of

38. J. Elgavish, "Tel Shiqmona," *EAEHL*, Vol. IV (1978), pp. 1101–1109.
39. M. Dothan, "Akko: Interim Excavation Report. First Season, 1973/4," *BASOR*, No. 224 (1976), pp. 1–48.
40. D. Ussishkin, "Excavations at Tel Lachish 1973–1977, Preliminary Report," *Tel Aviv* (1978), pp. 1–97.
41. G. E. Wright, *op. cit.*, pp. 203f.
42. Y. Aharoni, "The Residence," in *Investigations at Lachish, 1973–1977*, in *Tel Aviv*, Vol. 5 (1978), pp. 41f.
43. W. F. Albright, *Archaeology of Palestine*, p. 145.

the Jews themselves, since they normally refrained from representing the form of men and animals in any way at all.

LIGHT ON JUDAH UNDER DARIUS II

Nehemiah left Judah to return to the king in 433 B.C., although he was to go back later and continue his work as governor. We do not know how long he continued in this post, but possibly with the death of Artaxerxes in 423 B.C. he may have been replaced. He was able to carry out reforms and persuade the people to enter into a covenant with God (Neh. 10), in which, among other things, the people agreed to pay an annual contribution for the upkeep of the Temple (Neh. 10:32). A similar payment seems to have been undertaken at Elephantine in Egypt where there was a list of those who contributed to the Temple upkeep.[44] The idea was, of course, very old in Israel, going back to Moses' time.

From the days of Darius II (423–404 B.C.) we have some interesting material on the state of affairs in Judah, with the names of some of the significant people who lived at the time.[45] The information comes from the Aramaic papyri of Elephantine and carries our story down to the close of the fifth century B.C. Before the next century had closed the Persians were overthrown and the Greeks were in the ascendancy. We are now in a position to turn to the fortunes of the Jews in lands outside Palestine, and to study the remarkable documentary evidence that has been brought out of the earth by the modern excavator in both Mesopotamia and Egypt.

---

44. A. Cowley, *Aramaic Papyri of the Fifth Century B.C.* (1923), pp. 65–73.
45. See below, pp. 238–246.

13

THE JEWS OUTSIDE PALESTINE
IN THE FIFTH CENTURY B.C.

THERE were many Jews living outside Palestine in the fifth century B.C., partly as a result of enforced exile and partly because of voluntary migration. We know of several occasions in Bible history when the people of Israel were taken into captivity. Even before the collapse of the northern kingdom in 722 B.C. there were captives taken from the Galilee area by Tiglath Pileser (II Kings 15:29). When Samaria fell, a further group of exiles was taken (II Kings 17). In the case of Judah, King Manasseh was captured and later released, but we may conjecture that some Jews accompanied him into exile (II Chron. 33:11). Then came the various visits of Nebuchadnezzar (II Kings 24:1, 2; 24:10–16; 25:1–21; Jer. 52:31), which led to the exile of other groups of Jews. It would be impossible today to estimate the total number of people of general Israelite stock who eventually reached Mesopotamia.

But other lands such as Egypt had their complement of exiles from Palestine.[1] One wonders whether Pharaoh Shishak just before 900 B.C. took any captives to Egypt (I Kings 14:25). Certainly Pharaoh Necho, just before 600 B.C., took King Jehoahaz to Egypt (II Kings 23:34), and we may believe that he took also some of his subjects. It is not unlikely that after Nebuchadnezzar's first visit to Jerusalem in 598 B.C. Pharaoh Hophra encouraged the Jews to rebel against the Chaldeans. An inscription of one Nesuhor, a prince under Hophra, tells of Syrians, Greeks, and Asiatics at Elephantine, and it is possible

---

1. E. G. Kraeling, *The Brooklyn Museum Aramaic Papyri* (New Haven, 1953), pp. 41–48, discusses the origin of the Jewish colony at Elephantine.

that there were Jews among these also. A further group of Jews, among whom was the prophet Jeremiah (Jer. 41–44), reached Egypt after the fall of Jerusalem in 586 B.C., although, unlike the exiles to Babylon, these came voluntarily and settled in the Delta area (Jer. 43:7). An interesting message is recorded in Jeremiah 44 in which the prophet addressed remarks to all the Jews in Egypt, both to those at Tahpanhes, Noph, and Migdol, all of which are in the northern part of the land, and to those in the country of Patros, the region of southern or Upper Egypt. From this it would appear that at the time of Jeremiah there were Jews in both northern and southern Egypt.

Without doubt the people of Palestine were to be found in other areas, too, in the post-exilic period, and we shall not be surprised if future research reveals this to be so. Against the background of the exile and dispersion of the people of Palestine, we can understand why it is that modern archaeologists have discovered important evidence of Jewish colonies in both Babylonia and Egypt during the present century.

THE DEVELOPMENT OF ARAMAIC AS AN INTERNATIONAL LANGUAGE

Before we discuss the Jewish colonies of Egypt and Babylonia it will be wise to give a brief review of the ways in which the Aramaic language came into prominence until it eventually became the medium of international correspondence in Persian times.[2] A group of people that may be regarded as one of the less important groups in the East, and which never rose as a people to the status of an empire, nevertheless gave to the great conquerors of their day a language and a script which provided them with the means of communication with their vast empire.

The Aramaeans are known from early times, possibly as early as 2000 B.C., when there is evidence of them in southern Mesopotamia.[3] The Assyrian inscriptions refer to them in 1320 B.C., and after the tenth century B.C. there is an abundance of written material in Aramaic. Certainly in the ninth, eighth, and seventh centuries B.C., and from then onward, there is a wide range of material from diverse regions in the general area represented today by Syria. This indicates that it was possible to write standard Aramaic from the first half of the ninth century B.C. We may say that before the little Aramaean states were finally destroyed by the Assyrians, their language had attained such maturity that not only did it survive, but it was actually able to impose itself on the conquerors. From the ninth and eighth centuries onward the Assyrian scribes needed to know Aramaic because of their dealings with the Aramaeans. The Bible in II Kings 18:26 makes reference to the fact that the Jewish leaders in

2. A. Dupont-Sommer, Les Araméens (Paris, 1949), gives a good outline in ch. 6.
3. A. Dupont-Sommer, "Sur les débuts de l'histoire araméenne," Congress Volume (Copenhagen, 1953), pp. 40f.

Aramaic was a widely used language and eventually became the lingua franca *of the Near East. There are Aramaic inscriptions on both of these sculptures from Hatra, a small kingdom of the first and second centuries A.D. located fifty kilometers northwest of Asshur. Below is a bas relief of an eagle, the patron of the armies of Hatra, and of a military standard. At right is a statue of Princess Washfari (or Sapphira), King Sanatruq's daughter, wearing an ornate headdress, a long robe, and several necklaces. (Consulate General, Republic of Iraq)*

Jerusalem invited the Assyrians to speak to them in Aramaic: "Speak, I pray thee, to thy servants in the Syrian language [Aramaic]; for we understand it."

That Aramaic was known in Assyria is shown by a long letter written on a piece of pottery (an ostracon) in the days of Ashurbanipal, about 650 B.C. There are in addition standard weights in the shape of a lion from the ancient site of Nimrud marked with the names of Shalmaneser V, Sargon, and Sennacherib, and bearing some marks in Aramaic. At Nineveh the excavations brought to light numerous contracts dating from the seventh century B.C., written in the laborious cuneiform script, but carrying also a short summary in Aramaic to facilitate classification.

Two reasons for this widespread use of Aramaic may be suggested. It was a language that had a simple alphabet in contrast to the syllabic cuneiform (wedge-shaped) script of the Assyrians and others. It was also the language of the virile Aramaeans, thousands of whom had been taken captive through the centuries. Men of business began to use the script and the language, and once this step had been taken, progress was rapid.

Throughout the seventh century B.C., long Aramaic inscriptions were made in Syria proper. When the Chaldeans took over after the Assyrians, they, too, knew Aramaic, as we know from numerous cuneiform tablets from the days of Nebuchadnezzar and Nabonidus, which carry notes in the Aramaic script, although the bulk of the tablets is written in cuneiform. There was clearly a complex linguistic situation in which Aramaic took its place alongside Akkadian.

A most interesting document from Egypt dating to the early years of the sixth century B.C., perhaps about 586, is written in Aramaic and is addressed to the Pharoah by a Phoenician king named Adon who asked for help against the king of Babylon.[4] Evidently the Phoenician prince believed that the Egyptian scribes could read Aramaic.

When Cyrus took over Babylon in 539 B.C. and the whole Chaldean empire fell, Aramaic became the official language of Persian diplomacy. Under Darius I the empire spread from India to Egypt, and in order to keep in touch with this vast area, Aramaic was used as the one language that would facilitate international contacts. It will suffice to state here that Aramaic documents from Persian times are known in abundance and have been found in almost all the provinces of the great empire from Egypt to India.[5]

A note of caution should be added here. We have good evidence that the Persians at times used local languages along with Aramaic.[6] In Asia Minor there are inscriptions in Greek, including two stelae on the Bosporus, one in Greek and one in cuneiform, which Herodotus says were erected by Darius. In Egypt a set of laws was drawn up in demotic, the script of the common people, and correspondence between a satrap and the priests of Khnum was in demotic also. So it seems that there was flexibility in practice.

According to Esther 1:22, 3:12, and 8:9, Xerxes issued edicts to each of the peoples in its own tongue. Although this was evidently done at times, the

4. H. L. Ginsberg, "An Aramaic Contemporary of the Lachish Letters," BASOR, No. 111, pp. 24f.

5. These are listed in A. Dupont-Sommer, Les Araméens, pp. 79–102.

6. A. T. Olmstead, History of the Persian Empire (Chicago, 1948), pp. 116, 297. Also R. P. R. de Vaux, "Les décrets de Cyrus et de Darius," RB (Jan., 1937), pp. 38–41.

tremendous importance of Aramaic cannot be overlooked. We shall see in this chapter that the Jewish colony at Elephantine in southern Europe used Aramaic a great deal during the fifth century B.C.

THE JEWISH COLONY AT NIPPUR IN BABYLONIA

In 1889 an American excavation conducted by the University of Pennsylvania began excavations in the ancient site of Nippur to the south of old Babylon.[7] In the northwest area of the ruins the excavators discovered a remarkable collection of baked-clay tablets in a room about eighteen feet by nine feet. There were some 730 tablets in this room comparable in quality of writing and appearance with those found in the library of the great Assyrian ruler Ashurbanipal. These tablets were dated to the reigns of Artaxerxes I (465–424 B.C.) and Darius II (423–404 B.C.), but there was one tablet also from the reign of Artaxerxes II. The cache turned out to be the archives of a family of Babylonian businessmen, the Murashu family.

At the time of the discovery, tablets from this period were rare, and the find created a great deal of excitement because it gave a remarkable insight into the business methods of those years. For the most part the tablets are plain commercial documents, contracts, receipts, lists of witnesses, letters, and the like. Much of the business was concerned with matters of agriculture, lands, crops, workmen, canals, public works, cattle, tools, vines, and trees. Payment was made by weighing out silver or occasionally gold.

The Murashu family ran a sort of banking business for exchange of moneys and for payments at a time when a new system of taxation had come into force in Persian lands.[8] Introduced by Xerxes, its full rigor was experienced under Artaxerxes I. In many areas in Mesopotamia agricultural lands were held by what was called "bow" tenure, that is, the owners were obliged to furnish a bowman for the armed forces. This was an ancient custom, and as the years went by it became possible to commute the service to a money payment. With the rise of a new class of Persian officials, much of the land passed into the hands of the Persians by a clever trick. The former holders of "bow" lands, no longer required to send a bowman to the army, but required now to pay a money equivalent, often had to borrow money at forty percent per annum from such profiteers as the Murashu family. Their pledge lands were then worked by those rogues for their own advantage, until the title was completely lost to the original owners. When additional fields fell into the hands of the state, because owners were unable to pay the taxes, there were corrupt officials who leased these lands to the same dishonest moneylenders. We have already referred to the passage in the

---

7. See above, pp. 188f.
8. A. T. Olmstead, *op. cit.*, pp. 299, 356, *passim.*

book of Nehemiah where some of the people complained that they were unable to help in the building of the walls because of the claims upon them for money and the necessity for them to devote all their time to working their fields.

> We, our sons, and our daughters, are many; therefore we take up corn for them, that we may eat, and live. Some also there were that said, We have mortgaged our lands, vineyards, and houses, that we might buy corn, because of the dearth. There were also that said, We have borrowed money for the king's tribute, and that upon our lands and vineyards (Neh. 5:2–4).

In the troubled days following the death of Artaxerxes I the Murashu family needed to gain the goodwill of the new king, whoever that might be. When finally Darius II emerged supreme, Enlil-nadinshum, the head of the firm, made a trip to greet his new master and to see that the privileged position of the Murashu family was maintained. He evidently succeeded. Documents show that in the years that followed the Murashu sons acquired "bow" lands on an unprecedented scale. It would seem, however, that at last the authorities caught up with the rogues and after 417 B.C. the firm suddenly disappeared. It has been suggested that the royal commissioners finally ran the villains to earth, recovered the crown lands, and punished the wrongdoers.

We have given this detail in order to underline some of the problems that confronted the people under the Persian administration, and to stress the way in which the small farmers were exploited by unscrupulous officials and bankers.

But there is another point about the archives of the Murashu bankers. These bankers recorded a great variety of names in their receipts and contracts. It is clear that they did business with many different peoples, Persians, Medes, Chaldeans, Aramaeans, and—what is of special interest to us—Jews, who seem to have been free citizens by then. There is a considerable number of Jewish names in the documents, pointing to the fact that many of the exiles did not return to Palestine but remained in the land, following the advice of Jeremiah (Jer. 29:1–7) to build houses and to seek the welfare of the city to which they had been exiled. Many of the names have the element YAH in them, like Yahulamu, Dadiya, Hananiah, Gedaliah, and Pedaiah. Other well-known Jewish names occur, such as Gadalyama, Ahiyama, Haggai, Benjamin, Natunu, Shabbata, and Mordecai. Over sixty Jewish names are known from the days of Artaxerxes, and over forty from the time of Darius II. It is of some interest to discover that the name Mordecai was especially common in the days of Artaxerxes I. It was, of course, in the time of his predecessor Xerxes that the Bible places the story of Esther and the Jew Mordecai.

LIFE IN "YEB [ELEPHANTINE] THE FORTRESS"

There was a contrast between this settlement at Nippur in Babylonia and that at Elephantine in Egypt. The Nippur residents were part of a community that was engaged largely in agriculture and commerce, whereas the Elephantine colony had no agricultural pursuits to speak of, their means of livelihood being trade, shipping, stone quarrying, guarding the border, and attending to the taxes on goods that passed through this frontier post. In other words, the Elephantine colony was a military and administrative post.

The Aramaic texts of Elephantine speak of "Yeb the Fortress," and of "Syene the Fortress." Yeb was situated on a narrow island in the Nile, opposite modern Assuan, and Syene was on the site of Assuan itself. Syene was regarded as the southern limit of Egypt, and the phrase "from Migdol to Syene" is one that is known in the Bible (Ezek. 29:10; 30:6). In 1893 Charles Wilbour, an American traveler, acquired some valuable Aramaic papyri while visiting Assuan. A few years later, in 1904, Lady Cecil and Sir Robert Mond, two English visitors, bought some more, while yet others fell into the hands of German scholars. By 1914 a sizeable number of these had been published and the world was given a remarkable glimpse into the life of a Jewish colony on this island in the Nile in the period 500 to 400 B.C. The documents were written in Aramaic on papyri which, thanks to the dry climate of Egypt, had been preserved all these years. They consisted of deeds, contracts, and letters, both private and official. The translation of these documents enabled the scholars to form an idea of how the affairs of daily life were conducted and by what laws the people of this colony were governed.[9]

All transactions were safeguarded by agreements, and contracts were drawn up in proper manner, attested by witnesses, and then rolled up and sealed. Finally a note was added to the outside of the document to identify it. The procedure is not very different from that followed by Jeremiah in the purchase of his field (Jer. 32:8–14), and is basically the Babylonian method which was adopted by the Persians. Most of the documents at Elephantine carry two dates, one in Egyptian style and one in Babylonian style, so that we have no doubt about the date at which they were written.

Marriage contracts, as we might expect, are numerous and show that marriages were generally arranged between the bridegroom and someone acting for the bride. It was usual for the groom to give a bridal gift. In case of a divorce (which seems to have been rare, to judge from the few documents referring to it), the husband lost his marriage gift. It was possible for the wife also to sue for divorce. One woman whose name was Mibtahiah was involved in more than one marriage.

Slavery was known in Yeb and slaves were bought and sold, or perhaps inherited. One poor female slave, with three sons, had her children divided on the death of her master. There is, on the other hand, a case where a slave was freed and seems to have become the heir of his master.

9. Discussions and translations are available in J. B. Pritchard, ANET, pp. 222f., 491ff.; E. G. Kraeling, op. cit.; and A. Cowley, Aramaic Papyri of the Fifth Century B.C. (Oxford, 1923).

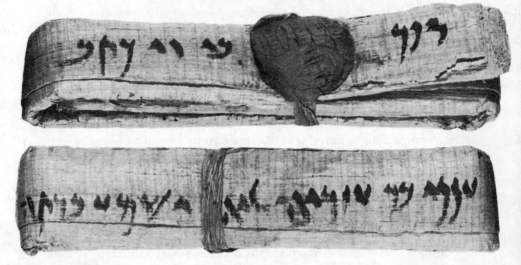

Folded and sealed contracts found at Elephantine, Egypt. They were labeled on the outside for quick identification. The Aramaic words (transliterated) on the top document are spr bi zi ktb, *"letter concerning a house, written by. . . ." (Brooklyn Museum)*

Many of the documents deal with loaning and borrowing, and it is evident that both men and women were able to engage in business. The interest rate on loans was high, as much as sixty percent in some instances, with the threat that if the sum were not repaid the interest would be added to the capital and the same rate of interest charged. Modern wives will be interested in the case of a husband who used his wife's money and had to write out a promissory note to repay within a month. To the lady's credit it should be added that she charged no interest. Other business contracts deal with all sorts of things. One case is recorded where two men signed a receipt for a load of barley they received from a boatman and promised to deliver it to a certain company of soldiers.

Real estate transactions were common. The Jews could buy and sell houses and make legal transfer of gifts of houses and lands. Daughters seem to have been specially favored as the recipients of houses, but more particularly on the occasion of marriage.

Litigation was common in Elephantine for all kinds of reasons. It is clear that Jews could go to law in civil matters, and the case would be heard before the Persian-Egyptian courts, although in internal matters affecting the Jewish community the case was dealt with by the priests. Typical civil cases were disputes about land, boundaries, possession of stock, and stealing.

Regular correspondence was sent and received by the people in the colony.

Letters generally began with salutations to the temple of the deity, followed by the name of the addressee, the name of the writer, and the wish that God might permit them to see the face of the addressee in peace. After all these formalities came the formal requests, some of which are very modern. One man asks a friend to visit him; another complains that since his friend came to live in Syene he had not seen him; yet another sends greetings from several friends. So the simple matters of common life are discussed. Generally the letters were written on papyrus, but some were written on broken pieces of pottery (ostraca).

Among the most interesting of the papyri are several that consist of little more than lists of people. One contains the names of those who contributed gifts to the temple at Yeb. There are 123 names on the list, many of them being women, and it may be regarded as a sort of "Who's Who" of the colony of Yeb. The correspondence relating to government affairs, and especially the important letter addressed to the governor of Judah, requires a special discussion.

Glimpses into the Persian government that was in existence in Egypt at the time are also to be gained from these papyri.[10] Thus the satrap at the time of Xerxes was Achaemenes. His successor, who features frequently in the documents and who functioned under both Artaxerxes I and Darius II, was Arsham (Greek, Arsames). In matters of government there were various departments, each of which had a presiding officer assisted by a group of colleagues. At the head of the chancery from which the orders of Arsham were issued was a chancellor, who is called in Aramaic be'el te'em, which is precisely the name found in the Bible in Ezra 4:9 for Rehum, who is there associated with a number of other officials, "the scribe and the rest of the companions." It was this group that took action as a body against the builders of the wall of Jerusalem early in the reign of Artaxerxes I. It is of interest also to learn that at Elephantine there was another Rehum, who occupied much the same sort of post. In the provinces, the head man was a pekid or "officer," a title known both in Persian contexts and in the Bible (Esther 2:3; Neh. 11:9, etc.) and which had a variety of connotations.[11] It is clear that the Persians in Egypt used peoples of various nationalities in this and similar posts. In the letter addressed to the governor of Judah, the term is peha, which is also a biblical word. Other Persian titles that appear either here at Elephantine or elsewhere occur in the Bible. A common Persian title for "treasurers," gizbarayya, does not happen to occur in the Elephantine texts, but it is found in the Bible in Ezra 7:21. The list in Ezra 4:9, which commences with Rehum and goes on to speak of the Dinaites, is really referring to the "judges." The Aramaic texts before us throw a great deal of light on the function of these "judges" in a typical Persian colony. All of these insights into Persian methods of administration add to our understanding of the biblical records, for time and

10. E. G. Kraeling, op. cit., pp. 27–40.
11. Hebrew pakid, used in Genesis 41:34; Jeremiah 20:1; II Chronicles 24:11; Judges 9:28, etc.

again we discover that the Bible has used a title that has a specific Persian connotation.

THE RELIGION OF THE JEWISH COLONY

The Jews in Egypt still worshipped Yahweh, the God of Israel. They built a temple for worship on the island of Yeb, and contributed to its upkeep. They observed the feast of unleavened bread, for we learn from a document dated 419 B.C. that Darius the king had sent to Arsham the satrap a letter ordering the Egyptian Jews to celebrate the feast from the fifteenth to the twenty-first of Nisan. While there is no reference to the Passover as such, it is likely that the Jews observed this also. There are one or two texts that show that the Sabbath was observed also. For example, one sentence on an ostracon reads: "Tie up the ass tomorrow on the sabbath lest he stray."

It is not certain that the Jews of Elephantine had copies of the Jewish Scriptures with them. There are some sentences in the papyri that suggest that they had parts of Deuteronomy, and perhaps of Genesis, but this is not beyond doubt.[12] The only literary piece that we know for certain they possessed was the story of Ahikar, an ancient worthy who had various exciting adventures and acquired a good deal of sound wisdom which he passed on to his son. The story comprised a piece of wisdom literature rather like some of the literature of the Bible and the sacred books of other peoples.[13]

We cannot, of course, argue from silence and conclude that the Jews here had no biblical literature simply because no pieces of the Bible have been found. It may be one of the accidents of preservation that it is chiefly documents of a business character that have been found.

It is to be further noted that in the temple of Yahu (Yahweh) sacrifices were offered. Reference will be made below to the letter addressed to the governor of Judah in which it is pointed out that when this temple at Yeb was destroyed, it was no longer possible to offer meal offerings, incense, or burnt offerings. Two priests are mentioned as well as a servant of Yahu, which indicates that there was evidently a well-organized ritual in use at the temple of Elephantine.

One disconcerting feature of the Jewish religion at Yeb is the fact that evidently some kind of syncretism was tolerated. The long list of contributors to the temple of Yahu indicates that of the total sum collected, certain moneys were earmarked for Eshem-bethel and 'Anat-bethel. The distribution was as follows: Yahu, 246 shekels, Eshem-bethel, 140 shekels, and 'Anat-bethel, 240 shekels.[14] The element "bethel" in the latter two names frequently occurs as the name of a god from the seventh to the fourth century B.C. in Canaanite-

---

12. E. G. Kraeling, op. cit., pp. 97–99.
13. J. B. Pritchard, ANET, pp. 427–430.
14. W. F. Albright, Archaeology and the Religion of Israel (Baltimore, 1956), p. 169.

Aramaean contexts. A third name that has a divine connotation, Herem, is found on other documents from Elephantine. The conclusion of W. F. Albright, whose discussion we have followed here, is as follows:

> There can, accordingly, be no reasonable doubt that we are confronted with Aramaic syncretism, arising about the seventh century B.C. in Jewish circles which were under strong pagan influence.[15]

In another place the same writer discusses the possibility that these names may represent substitutes for the name of God:

> The three divine names Eshem-bethel, Herem-bethel, Anat-bethel (Anat-Yahu), meaning respectively, "Name of the house of God" (God), "Sacredness of the house of God," and "Sign(?) of the house of God" would reflect pure hypostatizations of deity. . . .[16]

Possibly the same happened here as in later Judaism, where a fence was built around the holiness of God by substituting words denoting aspects or qualities of God, such as Divine Wisdom, or the Divine Word, or the Divine Presence, for the name of God. There remains, however, something of uncertainty about the exact nature of the religion of Elephantine. We naturally think of the picture of the religion of the Jews in the years just before and just after the exile in Judah itself. Indeed, at various times syncretism was very serious in both Judah and Israel and was strongly assailed by more than one prophet. If that happened in the homeland, there is no reason why it should not have happened in a foreign land like Egypt.

Such divergences from the official orthodox view of the priests in Jerusalem would not be tolerated by them for a moment, and it was unthinkable that there should be a second temple beside the one in Jerusalem. This comes out clearly in the letter which we now take up for discussion.

LETTER TO THE GOVERNOR OF JUDAH
FROM THE PEOPLE OF YEB

One of the most striking of the letters found among the Aramaic documents at Yeb was one dated 407 B.C. It was a petition to the governor of Judah to assist in the rebuilding of the temple in Yeb. The circumstances seem to be these. At some earlier time, even before the days of Cambyses, the Jews had built a temple in Elephantine.

> Our forefathers built this temple in the fortress of Elephantine, back in the days of the kingdom of Egypt, and when Cambyses came to Egypt

---

15. *Ibid.*, p. 171.
16. W. F. Albright, *From the Stone Age to Christianity* (New York, 1957), p. 373.

he found it built. They knocked down all the temples of the gods of Egypt but no one did any damage to this temple.[17]

When Darius II came to the throne after violent measures, his brother rose against him and there were uprisings in many of the provinces, such as Asia Minor, Media, and Egypt, in the years 410 to 408 B.C. It is possible to deduce from the documents available that, whereas the Jews were formerly in the service of the Egyptians and served them loyally, they were now in the service of the Persians and served them loyally too. In the troubles of these years, when the satrap Arsham was recalled for consultation with Darius II at the start of his reign, the local Egyptians took the opportunity to attack the Jews. There was conspiracy, with the local officials, Widrang (Vidarang), the local Persian chief, and his son co-operating with the Egyptians, probably for personal gain.

In the month of Tammuz, in the fourteenth year of King Darius, when Arsames departed and went to the King, the priests of the god Khnub, who is in the fortress of Elephantine, conspired with Vidarang, who was commander in chief here, to wipe out the temple of the god Yaho from the fortress of Elephantine. So that wretch Vidarang sent to his son Nefeyan who was in command of the garrison of the fortress of Syene this order: "The temple of the god Yaho in the fortress of Yeb is to be destroyed."[18]

The temple was duly razed, its pillars of stone, its five gateways, and its room of cedar-work were destroyed, and fire set to the ruins. The basins of gold and silver and other articles in the temple were taken off. Subsequently, after a long period of fasting and praying to Yaho, the God of heaven had allowed them to have some cause of rejoicing over their enemy, for the Persians had duly punished and demoted him.

The next part of the story concerns the letter which was written by the Jews of Elephantine to the priests in Jerusalem. This letter, though no longer in existence, is referred to in the letter to the governor. There was no answer to this, so the people wrote to the governor himself, and this is the letter we now have. Its main purpose is to ask the governor Bagoas (Bigvai) to give some help in the rebuilding of the temple in Elephantine since the Egyptians "do not allow us to build."

Your servants Yedoniah, and his colleagues, and the Jews, the citizens of Elephantine, all thus say: If it please our lord, take thought of this temple to rebuild it, since they do not let us rebuild it. Look to your well-wishers and friends here in Egypt. Let a letter be sent from you to them concerning the temple of the God Yaho to build it in the fortress of Elephantine as it was built before.[19]

17. J. B. Pritchard, *ANET*, p. 492, col. 1.
18. *Ibid.*, col. 1.
19. *Ibid.*, col. 2.

If Bagoas would do this they offered to pray for him, and to offer meal offerings and incense and sacrifice to Yaho. They assured him that merit would be stored up before Yaho by this act, greater than the merit of those who sacrificed the value of one thousand talents.

Two other important facts are given in the letter. First, these Jews of Elephantine stated that they had written to the high priest in Jerusalem, Johanan, and his colleagues the priests, to Ostanes (Ustan), the brother of Asani, and to the nobles of the Jews. To this letter there had been on reply. Secondly, they stated that they had written to Delaiah and Shelemiah, the sons of Sanballat the governor of Samaria.

These two facts are most significant, for they give us a glimpse into Judah and Palestine at the close of the fifth century B.C. We learn that Bagoas was governor, Johanan was high priest, and Sanballat was still alive, although his two sons were of some importance, owing no doubt to the age of their father. It was useless for the people of Elephantine to ask further help from the religious leaders at Jerusalem, for that door was evidently closed. It has been argued by some scholars that the Jerusalem priests regarded the Jews in Egypt as semi-heretical, and therefore did not encourage them in their apostasy.[20] If that was so, the only hope of help for the Jews at Yeb was to work through the Persian political leaders, Bagoas and Sanballat.

The outcome of this letter is full of interest. Request was made that Bagoas should write to the Jews in Egypt and inform them of his plans to help. What happened was that the emissary brought back some verbal information.

> Memorandum of what Bagohi and Delaiah said to me. Memorandum. Let it be an instruction to you to say in Egypt before Arsham concerning the altar house of the god of heaven which in Yeb the fortress was built formerly before Cambyses, which Widrang, the evil-doer did cast down in the year 14 of Darius the king, that it should be rebuilt in its place, as it was formerly, and that meal offerings and frankincense should be brought upon that altar corresponding to what formerly was done.[21]

It is not clear just how the Jewish colony in Egypt stood under the protection of the governor of Judah, but he agreed that they should go to Arsames and report these facts. It is interesting to note that the new temple was to be a place where the only offerings were to be the non-blood offerings. This has led some writers to suggest that the governor of Judah may have consulted the priests in Jerusalem, as well as the nobles, before giving his opinion. In the end it seems that the temple in Elephantine was finally rebuilt. One document dated to 402 B.C., in referring to a certain house that changed ownership, located it on the

---

20. Logically, of course, other answers may be given. The writer assumes that the worship in Jerusalem, despite certain defects, was essentially true to the divine intention in that age.

21. E. G. Kraeling, op. cit., p. 106.

west of the temple of Yaho, which suggests that the temple and the cult were still in existence then.

This is the last we hear of the Jewish colony. Persian control in Egypt ceased just at the turn of the century.[22] The Jewish colony "which burst mysteriously into the historical picture with the coming of Cambyses, disappears from it equally mysteriously a few years after the eclipse of Persian rule."[23]

THE DATE OF NEHEMIAH

The material in the papyri from Elephantine enables us to date Nehemiah very firmly in the reign of Artaxerxes I. The high priest referred to in the papyri is Johanan, who, according to Nehemiah 12:22, was the second high priest after Eliashib, the priest referred to in the days of Nehemiah. Again in Nehemiah 12:10, 11 we have a list which places Johanan (or Jonathan) after Eliashib. Another significant reference is to be found in Josephus, who speaks of an officer of the Persians, Bagoses, and a high priest named John (Johanan).[24] According to this reference, Bagoses, living in the days of Johanan, must have ruled after Nehemiah. Bagoses is the governor referred to in the Aramaic letter we have just considered from the year 407 B.C. Evidently the Sanballat referred to is the same man whom we meet in the days of Nehemiah, but now grown older. We are led to the conclusion that Nehemiah lived before 407 B.C. Since he went to Jerusalem in the twentieth year of King Artaxerxes, we look for a king of this name who ruled prior to 407 B.C. This is, of course, Artaxerxes I, who reigned from 465 to 425 B.C., which means that Nehemiah's arrival in Jerusalem is to be dated in 444 B.C. In a most exciting way, the discovery of some Aramaic papyri in Egypt, hundreds of miles away from Palestine, enables us to give an exact date to an important Bible character.

After the close of the fifth century B.C. we enter upon a period of great obscurity for the Jews. Yet there were important things happening all around them which had a vital bearing on their future history. Thanks to archaeological research we can pierce the darkness just a little.

HEBREW PAPYRI FROM SAMARIA

A remarkable collection of papyri, evidently from Samaria, came to light in 1962.[25] Ta'amireh Bedouin discovered the documents in a cave in a desolate area north of Jericho in the Wadi Daliyeh. The papyri turned out to be documents from the close of the Persian period in Palestine and ranged in date from

22. *Ibid.*, pp. 111–119.
23. *Ibid.*, p. 115.
24. Josephus, *Antiquities* XI.vii.1.
25. A preliminary report was made by F. M. Cross, "The Discovery of the Samaria Papyri," *BA*, Vol. XXVI, No. 4 (Dec., 1963), pp. 110–121.

375 B.C. to 335 B.C., that is, over a period of forty years. The papyri are all legal or administrative in character. One of the first pieces of writing investigated carried the words

. . . . iah, son of (San)ballat governor of Samaria.

Another carried the words,

. . . . this document was written in Samaria,

along with the names of officials before whom the document was written,

(before) Jesus son of Sanballat (and) Hanan, the prefect.

Yet another document referred to a slave named Nehemiah who seems to have been bought or sold for thirty pieces of silver.

In fact the finds consisted of a group of papyrus rolls rolled up and sealed. On at least one of the seals the ancient Hebrew script was used. The documents proper were written in the later Aramaic script, the script that is still used in Hebrew Bibles and in Modern Hebrew.

Later study has revealed some interesting facts. Wherever the opening or closing formulae of the documents are preserved we are informed that the documents were written in Samaria. The names are mixed. The majority of them preserve the element Yah or Yahu, but others carry names that include pagan divine elements: Qos (Edomite), Sahar (Arabic), Kemosh (Moabite), Baal (Canaanite), and Nabu (Babylonian). These names suggested a very mixed population in the Samaria area.

A number of dates recur on the documents. The earliest comes from the days of Artaxerxes II (404–358 B.C.). The latest document is dated to March 18th, 335 B.C. (our dating). Several documents come from the 350's, including one dated to March 4th, 354, written "before Hananiah Governor of Samaria," evidently one of the Sanballat family of whom we first hear in the days of Nehemiah (Neh. 4:1, 7; 6:1).

As to contents some of the documents refer to dealings with slaves, either purchase or manumission. Others deal with real estate transactions, loan agreement, settlement of broken contracts, divorce, etc.

The circumstances that brought these documents to the cave where they were found are a matter for speculation. But we may suspect that some of those who dwelt in the Samaria area fled the city before the advance of Hellenistic forces, taking with them precious documents. They found shelter in a cave but eventually were discovered and slain. A great number of skeletons—male, female, young, and old—were found in the cave when it was excavated.

From the viewpoint of palaeography these papyri give a range of documents covering most of the fourth century B.C. They are written in the Aramaic script in use during this century. Some of the seals carried the old Hebrew script.

Although the contents of the documents were meager and rather commonplace they throw welcome light on a still obscure segment of the history of Palestine. There is probably no period so poorly known as the fourth century B.C. But these papyri may now give us a sequence of governors—Sanballat I, Delaiah son of Sanballat, Sanballat II, Hananiah son of Sanballat II, and Sanballat III.[26]

26. *Ibid.*, p. 120.

14

THE COMING OF THE GREEKS

THE fourth century B.C. was to witness the collapse of Persian power in the East and the rise of the Greeks. At the close of the fifth century the Persian ruler was Artaxerxes II (404–361 B.C.), whose reign was not without merit, although he lost control in Egypt following the revolt of his brother Cyrus. The famous Greek expedition in which the Greek writer Xenophon took part contributed to the Persian loss of Egypt. Thirty years after the death of Artaxerxes II the great Persian Empire collapsed. But before the final collapse Artaxerxes III (Ochus), a brutal man, had a measure of success and was able to restore some of the lost fortunes of the Persians. He recovered Egypt in 342 B.C. and was able to quell revolts in the general area of Phoenicia. There are hints in some ancient records that the Jews were involved in these revolts and that some of them were exiled to the area of the Caspian Sea.[1] The last Persian king, Darius III, was faced with the impossible task of opposing the might of Alexander the Great. By 331 B.C. the Persians were no more and the East fell into the hands of the Greeks. In this chapter we shall follow the fortunes of the Jews in Palestine in the period 331 B.C. to 63 B.C., during which Greek rulers controlled the land, and at the end of which Palestine fell into the hands of the Romans.

BRIEF HISTORICAL OUTLINE, 331 B.C. TO 63 B.C.

Alexander the Great, son of Philip of Macedon, was born in the year 356 B.C. At the age of twenty he came to the throne of Macedon on the assassination of

1. For example, the Chronicle of Eusebius.

249

his father. The various states around Macedonia seemed to think that the treaties with Philip ended on his death, but they were to learn that the young Alexander was as strong as his father. Very soon he subdued all these and decided on an invasion of Persia. By 331 B.C. he was master of the East. Yet his life was to ebb away in June 323 B.C. before he was thirty-three years old. Almost at once his empire was divided between his generals. The senior general Perdiccas tried to hold the empire together and the various generals were assigned to satrapies. We are especially interested in Ptolemy, who went to Egypt, and Seleucus, who went to Babylon. But the scheme did not work and before long war broke out. There was fighting for several years, but by 315 B.C. four leaders had emerged. Ptolemy Lagi ruled in Egypt, the most compact of the four kingdoms. He was assisted by General Seleucus, who had been forced out of Babylon by the second leader, Antigonus, who ruled in Syria and central Asia. Then Cassander held Macedonia, and Lysimachus held Thrace. When Antigonus tried to exert greater claims in the Palestine area, he came into conflict with Ptolemy and Seleucus, and in 312 B.C. these two defeated him at Gaza and obtained control of Palestine and parts of Syria. Seleucus seized this moment to

Portrait of Alexander the Great on a silver drachma. (Oriental Institute, University of Chicago)

The discovery of this statue of Hermes, the Greek god of travelers, at Nineveh is evidence that Greek influence reached far and wide in the ancient world. Paul was worshipped as Hermes by the crowds at Lystra in Asia Minor (Acts 14:8–18). (Consulate General, Republic of Iraq)

dash across the desert to Babylon and to reinstate himself in his old satrapy. This was the commencement of the Seleucid dynasty. Eleven years later Antigonus was again defeated and Seleucus extended his boundaries to the north and established his capital at Antioch. The final outcome of all this strife, as far as Palestine was concerned, was that from now on the Ptolemies and the Seleucids were to strive for the possession of the Holy Land. For the first hundred years till 198 B.C., Palestine was ruled by the Ptolemies, but after this it passed into the hands of the Seleucids and remained, nominally at least, a Seleucid possession till the Romans took over the land in 63 B.C.

We can distinguish three periods in the Seleucid rule: (1) from 198 B.C. till 175 B.C., a period of undisputed Seleucid rule; (2) from 175 B.C. till 135 B.C., the period of the Maccabaean struggle; and (3) from 135 B.C. till 63 B.C., the period of nominal Seleucid rule during which there was a great deal of real independence for the Jews. With the coming of the Romans in 63 B.C. Jewish independence was finally lost.

We have some valuable archaeological evidence for the years 400 B.C. to about 50 B.C., and even if it is not great in quantity, it does help to fill out the written records.[2] The latter part of the period is better supplied with such evidence than the earlier.

EDOMITES, IDUMAEANS, AND NABATAEANS

During the three centuries under consideration, the history of the Jews, though incomplete in many places, touches again and again on the Edomites, now known as Idumaeans, and a newer group called Nabataeans. Archaeological work in Transjordan has given some additional information about the Edomites during these years. It will be remembered that at the time of the fall of Judah in 586 B.C. these people exploited the situation in southern Judah and invaded the area. Some written evidence about early Edomite pressures in southern Judah has come from the recently discovered Arad ostraca. One of the letters discovered in Arad refers to preparations for an Edomite attack, evidently in the years preceding Nebuchadnezzar's first campaign.[3] These same Edomites were to be overwhelmed in their own homeland by other Arab groups before the end of the fifth century. Excavations at the old port of Ezion Geber, which was originally founded by Solomon, have produced seal impressions from City IV which contain names that are clearly Edomite.[4] But by the fifth century ostraca carry names that are Arab in character.[5] We may conclude that with the rise of the Arabs belonging to the group that produced the Geshem of Nehemiah's day, the

2. W. F. Albright, *Archaeology of Palestine* (London, 1956), p. 147.
3. See above, p. 159.
4. N. Glueck, "The Topography and History of Ezion Geber and Elath," BASOR, No. 72, pp. 11f.
5. N. Glueck, "Ostraca from Elath," BASOR, No. 80, pp. 3–10.

Edomites lost much of their power. Many moved to Judah, while others were absorbed. In southern Judah they lived on and became known as the Idumaeans. We have valuable evidence about them here from some tombs found at Marisa which date to the middle of the third century B.C. These will be described in some detail later.[6] A variety of inscriptions, containing many names, indicates that Edomites lived alongside other types of people, such as the Phoenician settlers. For the most part the names are recorded in Greek, but there are some in Aramaic, among which there are those with the divine element *Qos*, the name of the chief god of old Edom. Interestingly enough, Josephus refers to the husband of Salome, the sister of Herod, as "Kostobaros, an Idumaean by birth . . . whose ancestors had been priests of Koze, whom the Idumaeans had formerly worshipped as a god."[7]

In due course the Arab group that replaced the Edomites was itself replaced by the Nabataeans, who appear first in recorded history in 312 B.C., when Antigonus the Greek decided to attack them.[8] His general actually took the high rock behind Petra, the refuge of the ancient Edomites, but success was short-lived because the troops were wiped out as they were returning home. The researches of Nelson Glueck have shown that the land of Edom had no serious sedentary occupation during the whole Persian period.[9] Then came the Nabataeans, who gave up their own Arabic tongue for Aramaic, as thousands of inscriptions show today, and slowly settled down to build towns and to live an urban life. Petra became their great center, and here they undertook the remarkable task of carving out homes and temples in the red sandstone of the valley. There is much inaccurate talk in some circles where, in order to show how the prophecies that foretold the downfall and desolation of Edom at last came true, pictures of rock-cut dwellings and temples in Petra are shown as Edomite buildings. These structures are undoubtedly Nabataean. The only Edomite site in the area is on the hill behind Petra, where there is evidence of occupation in Edomite times.[10] Of special interest in the Nabataean areas are the "high places" where these Nabataeans offered sacrifices to their gods. These may give some idea of the kind of thing referred to so often in the days of the great prophets of Israel. A great deal of excavation has gone on in Nabataean sites, so that today we know something of the coinage, the splendid pottery, the architecture, and the fortresses erected in strategic places to guard their frontiers. One of their kings, Aretas, is known in the New Testament in II Corinthians 11:32 as the king who controlled Damascus at the time Paul escaped over the wall in a basket.

---

6. See below, pp. 262f.
7. Josephus, *Antiquities* XV.vii.9.
8. Jean Starcky, "The Nabataeans—A Historical Sketch," BA (Dec., 1955).
9. N. Glueck, Reports in AASOR, Vol. 15. Also, *The Other Side of Jordan* (New Haven, 1940).
10. W. H. Morton, "Umm el-Biyara," BA (May, 1956), pp. 26f.

The great high place at Petra. (Eleanor K. Vogel; Department of Antiquities, Government of Palestine)

The Khazneh, a Nabataean rock-cut temple or tomb at Petra in Transjordan. Because of its Greek style, excavators thought that it was built by King Aretas IV ca. A.D. 25, earlier than the other Petra monuments. Compare its size with that of the human figure in the doorway. (Matson Photo Service)

At the period under discussion in this chapter, the Nabataeans were just coming into their own. They were to have dealings with the Greeks, the Maccabees, the Idumaeans, and the Romans before they were finally overcome by the Romans just after A.D. 100.

ARCHAEOLOGICAL EVIDENCE FROM THE DAYS OF THE PTOLEMIES

There were five Ptolemies who controlled Palestine from Egypt in the third century B.C.: Ptolemy I, Soter (323–285 B.C.), Ptolemy II, Philadelphus (285–246 B.C.), Ptolemy III, Euergetes I (246–221 B.C.), Ptolemy IV, Philopater (221–203 B.C.), and Ptolemy V, Epiphanes (203–180 B.C.). There was considerable conflict with the Seleucids during the century when the Ptolemies ruled, and Palestine again became a battlefield over which two empires fought. Under the first of these rulers many Jews were taken to Egypt and forced to live in Alexandria, where Greek soon became their language. Ptolemy II released many of them in view of troubles with the second and third Seleucid rulers, Antiochus I (280–262 B.C.) and Antiochus II (261–247 B.C.). Finally a treaty was made and a marriage arranged between Antiochus II and the daughter of Ptolemy II. This soon failed when the daughter of the Egyptian was murdered, and soon after, his son Ptolemy III waged war on the Seleucid ruler. Further wars followed till finally the Seleucid king Antiochus III, the Great (223–187 B.C.), was able to overwhelm all Egyptian resistance and enter Judaea as ruler in 198 B.C. The story is told in a peculiarly disguised fashion in Daniel 11.

Points of archaeological interest during these years may now be mentioned. We have referred already to the important papyri discovered in Egypt from the archives of Zeno, an official in the government of Ptolemy II.[11] Tobiah, an Ammonite who sent gifts of animals to the Pharaoh, features among these documents, and, as we have seen, the find gives valuable insight into the condition of Transjordan at the time. Another Egyptian papyrus dated to 259 B.C. refers to the purchase of a "Babylonian slave girl" of seven years in Birta of Ammantis, which is identical with the fortress of Tobias. The witnesses to this document are described as "clerechs of the cavalry of Tubias," that is, they were soldier settlers with plots of land. Evidently, then, Tobias had military forces at his disposal and guarded this part of Ptolemy's domains. Perhaps the position of this Tobias under Ptolemy of Egypt was similar to that occupied by his forefather, Tobiah the Ammonite, under Artaxerxes I, the Persian.[12]

Further evidence from Egypt concerns the presence of a sizeable Jewish colony there at the time. Epigraphic evidence from the third century B.C., including

---

11. See above, p. 226. See also C. C. McCown, "The Araq el-Emir and the Tobiads," *BA* (Sept., 1957), pp. 63f.
12. C. C. McCown, *op. cit.*, p. 70.

two Jewish-Aramaic papyri and at least eight ostraca from Edfu in Upper Egypt and from the site known as Zawiyet el-Meitin, all point to the presence of Jews in the land. That there were Jews in the region of Alexandria is clear from the Zeno papyri, which contain Jewish names. To these may be added Aramaic tomb inscriptions from Alexandria and Aramaic writing on coins from Demanhur nearby. The personal names revealed are partly biblical names, partly Aramaic, and partly Greek.[13]

It was during the years of Ptolemy II that, according to the story told in the spurious letter of Aristeas, the king called together Jewish scholars to translate the Torah into Greek for inclusion in the great library that he founded at Alexandria. The names of the men supposed to have been chosen are certainly in line with the names revealed in the epigraphic evidence we have already referred to. While we have none of the original manuscripts of this Septuagint translation into Greek, it is fairly clear that in the period 300 to 250 B.C. the Torah was translated.

One other important find from Egypt from these days is a small piece of papyrus containing the ten commandments in Hebrew, the so-called Nash papyrus.[14] Evidently some of the Jews in Egypt in the third century B.C. could still read Hebrew.

Some of the sites excavated in Palestine have produced coins of this period, and naturally there is an abundance of pottery to show that many sites were occupied. The one group of important monuments of the period is the painted tombs of Marisa in southwestern Judah, the Old Testament Mareshah, and the modern Tell Sandahannah. The tombs, discovered in 1902 by J. P. Peters and H. Thiersch, lay near the tell which represented the most important town in the area. They were originally excavated from the soft limestone rock and painted inside in a most elaborate fashion. Inscriptions and graffiti were scratched on free spaces on the walls in Greek and Aramaic. The personal names were Greek, Phoenician, and Edomite (Idumaean). We are especially interested in the site because Ptolemy II established a Sidonian colony here under an official named Apollophanes, whose epitaph is preserved in one of the tombs. When the tombs were first opened the colors of the frescos on the walls were quite bright, but they have now faded. One tomb had a long procession of animals, some of which were real while others were imaginary. W. F. Albright has suggested that they may have been based on some book of illustrations of wild life sketched from the zoological gardens of Alexandria.[15] The predominance of Greek names on the walls may simply mean that the Phoenicians and the Idumaeans who lived there were Hellenized by that time. One of the tombs had a remarkable painting of tall cressets for carrying torches or lamps. These were painted on opposite piers in

13. W. F. Albright, *From the Stone Age to Christianity* (New York, 1957), p. 349.
14. *Ibid.*, pp. 345, 350.
15. W. F. Albright, *Archaeology of Palestine*, p. 149.

The famous Rosetta Stone, which because of its inscriptions in Egyptian hieroglyphs (top), Egyptian demotic (middle), and Greek gave Thomas Young (1773–1829) and J. F. Champollion (1790–1832) the clues needed to decipher the old Egyptian language. The inscription, a copy of a priestly decree of 196 B.C., concerns a commemoration of the coronation of Ptolemy V Epiphanes and mentions Cleopatra. The black-basalt monument is over a meter high and is named for Rashid ("Rosetta") in Egypt, where Napoleon's soldiers found it in 1799. (British Museum)

the vestibule of one of the tombs and may have represented incense stands, the like of which are known from pictures and from carvings on coins from the general area of Phoenicia. Albright sees in them a possible source of information about the two tall pillars that stood outside the temple of Solomon.[16] The worship of the region was evidently syncretistic, with elements of Edomite, Phoenician, and Greek religion. The town of Marisa was a well-planned town of Greek pattern, with streets at right angles forming blocks of houses.[17] There was a marketplace next to the gate, rectangular in shape, open at one end and with shops on three sides. The material from the tombs in the area gives the impression that this area was thoroughly Hellenized by the middle of the third century B.C. It was this Hellenization that was to lead to much of the Maccabaean trouble in the second century, when the orthodox Jews resisted the changes.

16. W. F. Albright, *Archaeology and the Religion of Israel* (Baltimore, 1956), pp. 144–146; also "Two Cressets from Marisa and the Pillars of Jachin and Boaz," *BASOR* (Feb., 1942), pp. 18f.
17. W. F. Albright, *Archaeology of Palestine*, p. 153.

The town of Bethel at this time shows three phases of occupation between the fourth century and A.D. 70. The first phase covers the Ptolemaic and the Seleucid period down to the reign of Antiochus IV, and it presumably came to an end with the campaigns of General Bacchides about 160 B.C. The coins give the story—there were ten Ptolemaic coins from the years 285 B.C. to 182 B.C. and four coins of Antiochus IV.

The town of Tell en Nasbeh, north of Jerusalem, produced coins of Ptolemy II as well as coins of both earlier and later periods.

The important town of Shechem in central Palestine, which played a prominent part in the earlier history of Israel, was apparently unoccupied between the eighth and the fourth centuries B.C. But toward the end of the fourth century it was reoccupied. Coins of all five Ptolemies have now been found and bear witness to the occupation of the town in the century 300–200 B.C. One small jug unearthed in the Hellenistic area contained thirty-five beautifully preserved Ptolemaic coins, all of them silver tetradrachms. The excavation report reads as follows: "One of Ptolemy I, sixteen, and probably three more, of Ptolemy II; six of them dated to the year of issue; one of Ptolemy III (246–221 B.C.), two of Ptolemy IV (221–204 B.C.); four, and probably eight more, of Ptolemy V (205–181 B.C.). Two of the Ptolemy V coins were dated: one in 198 B.C., and the other in 193 B.C."[18]

ARCHAEOLOGICAL EVIDENCE FROM THE PERIOD 198 B.C. TO 134 B.C.

When the Seleucid ruler Antiochus III entered Palestine in 198 B.C. there commenced an era of great trouble for the Jews. This was aggravated by the fact that some of the Jews were sympathetic to the desire of the Greek rulers to introduce Greek culture throughout the East. When Antiochus was defeated by the Romans in Asia Minor and was required to pay heavy indemnity to them, the Seleucid ruler sought ways and means to raise the money.

This need for money brought conflict with the Jews. There was in Jewish circles a serious tactical struggle going on between groups within the priestly circle, and different parties were contending for the power of the supreme priestly office. One group was inclined to court the favor of the Seleucids by offering money to assist them in their problem. This group was willing, too, to promote Hellenization. Under Seleucus IV (187–175 B.C.), the high priest Onias, representative of the so-called Oniads, and regarded as a worthy occupant of the high-priestly office by the conservative Jews, was made the subject of slanderous reports to the king by the other party (II Macc. 3:4ff.; 4:1ff.). Seleucus did not respond, however. But when he was murdered by the ambitious Antiochus IV (175–163 B.C.), the struggle began in earnest. Antiochus had

18. E. F. Campbell, "The Third Campaign at Balatah (Shechem)," *BASOR*, No. 161 (Feb., 1961), p. 44.

been taken as a hostage to Rome as a boy and had learned the ways of Rome. He had also learned to fear Rome. Anxious to obtain more funds, he responded to the appeal of one Jason to remove Onias. Jason promised the new king rich gifts of money and a vigorous promotion of Hellenization in Jerusalem (II Macc. 4:7ff.). So Onias was removed and Jason appointed in his stead. Three years later a certain Menelaus offered still larger sums, Jason was removed, and Menelaus was appointed in his place. The appointment of the high priest had been taken over by a pagan ruler, much to the offense of the pious Jews. When in 169 B.C. Antiochus invaded Egypt, and it was reported that he had been killed, the exiled Jason seized Jerusalem and the office of high priest and banished Menelaus. When Antiochus, very much alive, returned, he forcibly replaced Menelaus and at the same time took valuable treasure from the Temple in Jerusalem. He himself entered the Temple, an act of desecration in the eyes of the pious Jews. A year later, during a renewed campaign in Egypt (168 B.C.), he was ordered to leave Egypt by the Roman representative Popilius Laenus and to abandon all designs on Egypt. Perhaps in spite, he gave orders for his officer Apollonius to make a surprise attack on Jerusalem. Many Jews lost their lives and much damage was done. This was followed by repressive measures. Antiochus forbade the Jews to read their Scriptures and to practice their religion. Worst of all, he desecrated their Temple and offered pagan sacrifices there. Then he set up a fortress near the Temple, often referred to in the books of Maccabees as "Akra," a veritable symbol of foreign domination. Its position is not known with certainty today, although archaeological and topographical considerations suggest the southeast hill on the ridge south of the sanctuary.[19]

The Jews could bear the insults no longer and rebelled under the family of the Hasmoneans, whom we know as the Maccabees, a name given to one of their leaders and possibly derived from a Hebrew word meaning "hammerer." From 168 B.C. till 142 B.C. the Jewish patriots waged incessant war aginst their enemies, being led at first by the aged Mattathias, and then in turn by his three sons, Judas (166–160 B.C.), Jonathan (160–142 B.C.), and Simon (142–134 B.C.).

Judas was able to defeat a number of Seleucid armies, and by the end of 165 B.C. the Jews were allowed to return to the Temple and were granted religious freedom. But they wanted political liberty too, and the war went on. To strengthen the hand of the Jews, Judas built forts, one of the most interesting of which was the fort at Bethzur to the south of Bethlehem. By 161 B.C. this was taken by the Seleucid general Bacchides, who destroyed it and rebuilt it on the site to a Greek plan.

When Judas was slain in battle, Jonathan took his place. Before his death he was able to consolidate the position of the Jews greatly. He was actually appointed high priest by a usurper of the Seleucid throne to whom he gave support.

19. J. Simons, *Jerusalem in the Old Testament* (Leiden, 1952), pp. 144ff.

This usurper, Balas by name, made many concessions, and when he died and a new king took control in Antioch, Jonathan besieged Jerusalem, which was in the hands of the Seleucids. The price of lifting the siege was a lightening of taxation and the granting of certain areas near Samaria to Jonathan. When further troubles in Antioch brought a change in Seleucid policy, Jonathan supported another rebel named Tryphon, and proceeded at once to Bethzur, the Seleucid fortress, and took it. But Tryphon was afraid of Jonathan and had him trapped and imprisoned. The leadership then passed to his brother Simon. Before long Simon had captured Gezer, another Seleucid stronghold, and had taken the fortress in Jerusalem itself. The Jews were so pleased at these successes that they accepted Simon formally as high priest, even though he was not of the correct family. Simon also gained recognition by the Roman Senate of the day, but he met his death by treachery at the hands of his son-in-law. It was under Simon that the Jews emerged again into real independence. The family to which he belonged, the Hasmoneans, was now both the ruling family and the high-priestly family. Civil and religious authority was vested in them. This had its problems, but from 142 B.C. to 63 B.C. the Jews preserved their independence, even though the Seleucids at times endeavored to exert control over them. The Jews had a strong desire to recover lands lost to their enemies, and the Seleucids made one or two abortive attempts to regain control of the Jews. But before we take up that story, we shall collect the archaeological data for the period 198 B.C. to 134 B.C.

Our information comes from the excavation of several important sites, among which Bethzur, Samaria, Marisa, and Gezer feature as especially valuable. We must remember that the Greek conquerors, in pursuance of their Hellenizing policy, built towns all over their domains. In Palestine several towns were repeopled and numbers of Greek colonists settled there. Thus Samaria was repeopled by colonists from Macedonia, and coastal towns like Gaza, Askelon, Caesarea, Dor, and Ptolemais became Greek cities. East of Jordan there were numerous Hellenized towns, and in the mountain areas such places as Bethshan (Scythopolis) and Gezer became Greek cities in addition to Samaria. The Ptolemies had previously been active in Transjordan where Amman had been renamed Philadelphia by one of these rulers.

Reference has already been made to the ruins at 'Araq el Emir in Transjordan, where the rock-cut tomb of one of the Tobiads carries an inscription in Aramaic. The building in the vicinity, called by some a mausoleum and by others a palace, was built in a vigorous Hellenistic style with carved lions and Corinthian capitals. More recently it has been argued that we have here the remains of a fortress. It was built of huge blocks of limestone and was set upon a slight elevation, surrounded by a small lake, and almost completely surrounded by walls.[20] This whole building is probably to be referred to the time of Hyr-

20. C. C. McCown, op. cit., pp. 66, 68.

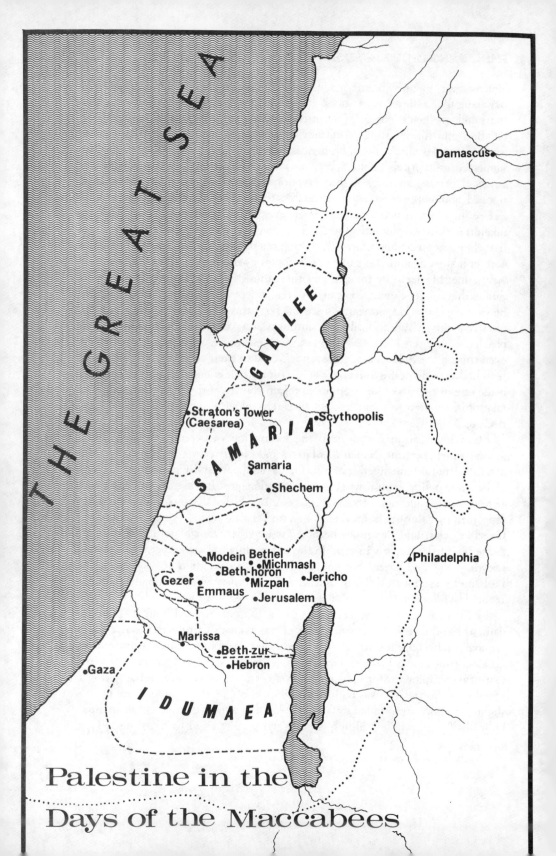

THE GREAT SEA

Damascus•

GALILEE

•Straton's Tower
(Caesarea)

SAMARIA

•Scythopolis

Șamaria

•Shechem

Modein Bethel
•Michmash
•Beth-horon
Gezer• Mizpah
Emmaus •Jericho
•Jerusalem

•Philadelphia

Marissa•
•Beth-zur
•Hebron

•Gaza

I D U M A E A

Palestine in the
Days of the Maccabees

canus, the last of the Tobiads, for Josephus described the layout in great detail and credited it to Hyrcanus who, he says, lived across the Jordan and built this remarkable place for himself.[21] If that is so, the building would date from about 175 B.C., just before the days of the Maccabees.[22]

The town of Bethzur is full of interest because it provides a fascinating correlation between the documentary evidence and the excavated evidence. It was the scene of several battles during the Maccabaean wars. The earliest town here was probably built during the Persian period as a protection for the Jews against the Idumaeans. In the days of the Ptolemies it was a prosperous place, to judge from the range of coins found in the excavation. Fifty-two coins from the days of the first six Ptolemies were brought to light, the earliest dating to 252 B.C. and the latest to 210 B.C. There were other coins found at the site, but they tell a different story.[23] There were in all nearly three hundred coins found in the excavation, but the greater part of them come from the days of the Seleucids and the Maccabees. In detail, the story is as follows. There were 126 coins of Antiochus Epiphanes (175–163 B.C.), none from his successor, five from Balas (150–145 B.C.), thirteen from Demetrius II (145–139 B.C.), ten from Antiochus VII (139–129 B.C.), only two Seleucid coins from the years 125–121 B.C., but sixteen Jewish coins from the days of John Hyrcanus the Jewish ruler (134–104 B.C.). This story in coins tells us that Bethzur was occupied in the days of Antiochus IV, with a decline in occupation between 160 and 145 B.C. There was a revival, then, from 145 B.C. till late in the reign of John Hyrcanus. After about 100 B.C. the coin story ceases.

On the summit of the mound of Bethzur the excavators discovered the foundations of a large fortress which gave evidence of three periods of occupation. The first, built in the days of the Ptolemies, was almost completely destroyed and rebuilt into a much larger fortress. It can be attributed to Judas Maccabeus, who built it between 165 and 163 B.C. Soon after, it was captured, destroyed, and rebuilt on a Hellenistic plan by the Seleucid general Bacchides about 161 B.C.[24] The archaeological picture thus follows closely the literary picture.

The coin story shows a gap in occupation again till 145 B.C., which takes us to the days of Jonathan and Simon, when the fortress again fell into the hands of the Jews.

One interesting sidelight on the excavations in Bethzur is that there was a sizeable collection of jar handles from large wine jars that normally came from Rhodes, and which have become known as Rhodian jar handles. Each of these bears the name of the potter or magistrate for the year. The presence of so many

21. Josephus, Antiquities XII.iv.11.
22. W. F. Albright, The Archaeology of Palestine, pp. 149f.
23. O. R. Sellars and W. F. Albright, "The First Campaign of Excavation at Beth-Zur," BASOR, No. 43, p. 10.
24. W. F. Albright, The Archaeology of Palestine, pp. 151f.

of these here testifies to a Greek garrison in the town, and as G. E. Wright says, "They certainly preferred this imported wine to the native product of the local vintage."[25]

Our next site, the town of Gezer, was finally taken by Simon. It was in a strategic position, guarding the approaches to Judaea from the west and commanding the great coast road. From the literature we learn that the town was taken after a desperate struggle and the heathen population deported and replaced by Jewish colonists. Then Simon "made it stronger than it was before and built therein a dwelling place for himself" (I Macc. 13:43–48). An important inscription found in the debris reads, "Pampras says: May fire overtake Simon's palace."[26] The most recent excavations of Gezer have uncovered a substantial second-century B.C. stratum in which house walls of fine masonry and courtyards equipped with large mortars and ovens were revealed. Down the slopes of the mound fine terrace walls well laid out were discovered in an area quite close to the modern surface of the tell. The excavators expect to discover a considerable portion of the Hellenistic city in this area. The characteristic Hellenistic pottery, including some fine red-glazed wares that can be dated elsewhere to about 175–150 B.C., helps to date this area.

This Pampras—the name is Greek—was probably one of those dispossessed by Simon, and left a curse scratched on a wall.

Ruins at Gezer were interpreted by R. A. S. Macalister as a Maccabaean castle, but more recently Y. Yadin has shown them to be the remains of a Solomonic gate.[27] However, the Maccabaean town has been exposed and among other interesting features in the town was a building which seems to have been a town bathhouse. It was built of stone lined with cement, with benches around the walls, a drain beneath the floor, and a heating room at one end. It is possible, however, that the building was some sort of industrial plant.

We have already made reference to the town of Marisa, the site of Moresheth-gath of the Old Testament (Josh. 15:44; Mic. 1:15; Jer. 26:18, etc.).[28] Excavations produced Ptolemaic coins, showing occupation at that time. During the days of the Seleucids the town was in the hands of these hated foreigners (II Macc. 12:32ff.), until it finally fell into the hands of the Jews during the reign of John Hyrcanus, about 110 B.C.

An interesting aspect of the town of Marisa is the plan of the city. A Greek architect named Hippodamus from the town of Miletus on the southeast coast of Asia Minor had proposed a city plan during the fifth century B.C. which became popular. Even today we refer to the Hippodamian city plan. Basically the streets of the city were laid out in regular rectangles with streets intersecting at right angles. Adequate spaces were left for open marketplaces and assembly areas.

25. G. E. Wright, *Biblical Archaeology* (London, 1957), p. 209, col. 1.
26. R. A. S. Macalister, *Gezer*, Vol. I, pp. 212f.
27. Y. Yadin, "Solomon's City Wall and Gate at Gezer," *IEJ*, Vol. 8, pp. 80ff.
28. See above, pp. 252, 255.

Marisa provides an excellent example of a town laid out originally according to Hippodamian principles, although it suffered some distortion later in the Hellenistic period. It seems clear that this city plan became popular in Palestine also. Excavations in a number of towns of the Hellenistic age both along the Mediterranean coast and in the hinterland have produced evidence of the fact. No doubt as excavations continue further evidence will become available. Marisa provides one of the best examples.

Another feature of Hellenistic towns in Palestine is their distinctive pottery. The town of Marisa provided a rich repertoire of pottery including numerous undamaged Rhodian jars as well as 328 Rhodian jar handles, many of them carrying a seal impression and covering a range in time from the third to the end of the second century B.C. The total repertoire of Hellenistic pottery is sufficient to make possible the drawing up of a very useful compendium of this pottery arranged in chronological order for the period 200 B.C. to A.D. 70.[29]

Samaria was an important town during the Greek period, and there are several indications of Greek occupation here. Some two thousand Rhodian jar handles, for example, are a strong testimony to the presence of Greek soldiers.[30] In the actual building remains we may refer to the fine Hellenistic wall built astride the earlier Israelite wall, and especially the magnificent round towers which are dated nowadays to the time of Alexander the Great who settled Greek colonists there. His representative Perdiccas is said to have rebuilt Samaria.[31] He repaired the old Israelite walls and strengthened them by these round towers. There is a line of walls built around the summit of the mound about four meters thick, which is dated about 150 B.C. and points to the time of the Maccabaean troubles. The town of Samaria fell finally to the sons of John Hyrcanus, when a ditch and a double line of walls were built around the city to starve the people out. All relief from Syria was cut off, and Samaria returned at last to Jewish hands in 107 B.C.

The town of Shechem suffered violent destruction during the course of these years, and this may have been the work of John Hyrcanus in 107 B.C. A coin of Antiochus VIII dated about 121-120 B.C. and another from 112-111 B.C. point to an occupation of Shechem extending into the period of Jewish freedom which preceded the Roman occupation.[32] The excavations of G. E. Wright and others in the years 1956 to 1962 have provided additional details about Shechem in Hellenistic times.[33] From the wide range of coins uncovered, one from the reign of Alexander the Great (*ca.* 333-323 B.C.), and many from those of Ptolemy I to Ptolemy V, it is clear that Shechem was occupied during

29. P. W. Lapp, *Palestinian Ceramic Chronology, 200 B.C.-A.D. 70* (New Haven, 1961).

30. G. E. Wright, *op. cit.,* p. 209.

31. W. F. Albright, *The Archaeology of Palestine*, p. 150.

32. G. E. Wright and L. E. Toombs, "The Third Campaign at Balatah (Shechem)," BASOR, No. 161 (Feb., 1961), pp. 45f.

33. G. E. Wright, *Shechem, the Biography of a Biblical City* (London, 1965).

Round tower (center) and walls of the Hellenistic second defense system, which replaced the Israelite inner wall around the summit of Samaria. (Bastiaan VanElderen)

the Greek period. It was in the days of Ptolemy V that Palestine fell to the Seleucid rulers. Numerous coins bearing the reigns of these kings from Antiochus III (223–187 B.C.) onward have been found to mark the Seleucid age. The latest of these comes from about 110 B.C. It seems clear that Shechem suffered greatly at the hands of the Greeks, but when the hue and cry quieted down Shechem was rebuilt and refortified. The excavators recognize four strata of occupation between this reoccupation and the final abandonment of the city about 110 B.C., although the last two cities were unwalled.

Contemporaneous with this last period of Shechem's life was a temple on Mt. Gerizim, and it may have been that John Hyrcanus (134–104 B.C.) brought an end both to the temple and to the city of Shechem, both of which represented a challenge to the authority centered in Jerusalem.

EVIDENCE FROM THE PERIOD 135 B.C. to 63 B.C.

When Simon was foully slain at the instigation of his son-in-law, his son John Hyrcanus, who was governor at Gezer, came at once to Jerusalem and took over control of the government. In 130 B.C. he was attacked by the Seleucid ruler Antiochus VII, who was making a bold bid to regain control over Judaea. He actually succeeded momentarily and took John Hyrcanus off to Mesopotamia to war against the Parthian hordes who were becoming a menace at this time. Very soon Antiochus died and John was free. He returned to Jerusalem and reigned for thirty years, during which time he extended the boundaries of Judaea greatly. He was able to take Shechem, subdue the Samaritans and the Idumaeans, and, as we have seen, retake Samaria by the hands of his two sons. He was keen to proselytize neighboring peoples and forced many to be circumcised. He was high priest as well as ruler and offended many by his carelessness in the priestly office and by his political ambition. He offended such new groups as the Pharisees, for example. In order to provide some protection against the Seleucids he strengthened the links with Rome. His reign saw the start of tension between two groups that we later know as the Pharisees and the Sadducees.

John's successor was his son, who took the title "king" but reigned only one year as Aristobulus I. It was a busy year, and he kept his brothers out of the way by casting them into prison. On his death in 103 B.C., his brother Alexander Jannaeus (103–76 B.C.) succeeded him and married his widow, much to the disgust of the pious groups. He turned out to be an ambitious and successful ruler, but he was cruel and unpopular. Although he extended the boundaries of Judaea still further to the east of Galilee and into Philistia and central Transjordan, he had serious clashes with the religious groups, especially with the Pharisees. It was in this general period that the sect of Qumran, to be discussed in the next chapter, founded their monastery in the wilderness near the Dead Sea. Before Alexander died he advised his wife to divide the priestly and the kingly functions. This she did, ruling the country herself as Alexandra (76–67 B.C.), and having her son Hyrcanus appointed high priest. Her younger son Aristobulus was bold and enterprising and quite unlike his weak and irresolute brother Hyrcanus. But Aristobulus was restrained for the time being. When Alexandra died in 67 B.C. she left the Hasmonean dominions to the dissensions of her two sons. At first Hyrcanus was both king and high priest. But Aristobulus refused to submit. He collected an army and defeated the army of Hyrcanus at Jericho. Following this, much of the army of Hyrcanus joined him. He then proceeded to Jerusalem where he shut up Hyrcanus and forced him to surrender. Hyrcanus gave up both the throne and the high-priesthood and retired to private life in Jerusalem. There might have been peace had not Antipater, the governor of Idumaea, espoused the cause of Hyrcanus and intrigued with the Nabataean king. Hyrcanus was persuaded to leave Jerusalem and go to Petra, to Aretas the king of the Nabataeans. Aretas then led his army against Aristobulus in Judaea and defeated him in battle. He was finally besieged in Jerusalem. In such circumstances Pompey the Roman general, at the time in Syria, who had been approached by both parties, took the initiative, postponed his projected attack on the Nabataeans, and proceeded to Jerusalem. The outcome was that Aristobulus was taken to Rome, Hyrcanus was allowed to remain as high priest and was given the title of ethnarch, while the wily Antipater continued as an agent of the Romans, in the capacity of an adviser, until he was murdered in 43 B.C.

These years, from the accession of John Hyrcanus to the conquest by the Romans, have left some archaeological material. The town of Bethel was occupied during this period and has yielded coins of John Hyrcanus, Alexander Jannaeus, and later rulers, but a lack of coins from the time of Herod suggests a period of non-occupation.

Tell en Nasbeh tells a similar story, as far as the Hasmonean period is concerned, although it was occupied in Herod's time and produced some Herodian coins. One of the greatest hoards of coins yet found in Palestine comes from Joppa where, in 1949, some 851 coins of Alexander Jannaeus were unearthed, all of them of one type, bearing the inscription "Alexander, King." There was evidently a mint at Joppa which supplied coins for Alexander.[34]

The final collapse of Samaria came during these years, and other towns, like Marisa and Bethshan, fell to the Hasmonean kings. We have reviewed the archaeological material for these towns above. One general feature for the three towns, Bethzur, Gezer, and Marisa, is that the series of Jewish coins comes to an end about 100 B.C. The reason is not clear, but it may mean that soon after the aggressive policy of Alexander Jannaeus (103–76 B.C.) these towns were abandoned because it was no longer necessary to maintain garrisons at these points.[35]

It is of considerable interest to us to follow the story of the coins of the Hasmonean rulers through these years. A letter from a Seleucid ruler, referred to in I Maccabees 15:6, tells how Simon was given leave to coin money. There is some debate about whether coins that have been found are really to be attributed to Simon or not. One recent writer suggests that it was only after the death of Antiochus VII in 129 B.C., when the Seleucid power in Palestine was finally broken, that Maccabaean coinage began to be minted.[36] It is clear that John Hyrcanus (134–104 B.C.) did make coins, using as symbols on their face flowers, fruit, stars, anchors, and such items as would not offend a people that held to the divine authority of the second commandment. On the reverse side he commonly used the cornucopia, the pomegranate, and a wreath, with the inscription in archaic Hebrew letters reading "John the High Priest and the Community of the Jews." One of the common coins was the tiny bronze *lepton*, which was made in Judaea more than any other coin. It is the widow's mite; its value was one four-hundredth part of a shekel.

Alexander Jannaeus had the title "King" put on his coins, and used Greek letters on some of them as well as the old Hebrew letters. His symbols were the palm, the lily, the pomegranate, the cornucopia, and the wheel. By the time of

34. A. Kindler, "The Jaffa Hoard of Alexander Jannaeus," *IEJ*, Vol. 4 (1954), pp. 170ff.
35. W. F. Albright, *The Archaeology of Palestine*, pp. 153f.
36. L. Kadman, "The Hebrew Coin Script," *IEJ*, Vol. 4, p. 150.

Hyrcanus II (63 B.C. ff.) the coins bear only the title "High Priest," but by then the Romans were in control. The last of the Hasmoneans was Antigonus, who seized the throne in 40 B.C., at the time when the Roman Empire was in a turmoil. In the years immediately preceding the appointment of Herod as king, Antigonus actually had coins minted with the title "King Antigonus" on one side and the words "Mattathias, the High Priest and the Community of the Jews" on the other. These coins were significant because they give us the Jewish name of Antigonus. They were, however, poor coins, being seriously adulterated, with twenty-seven percent copper, thus reflecting the deterioration due to Roman extortions and continual warfare. The symbols on these coins were the usual ones, but in addition we now find for the first time the seven-branched candlestick that was to become so common in later synagogue art.

We might be permitted to make one concluding remark to this chapter. It is that although the archaeological evidence, apart from the magnificent finds at Qumran and in other areas nearby, is by no means spectacular, our knowledge of these times is provided by a good deal of written evidence for most of this period, particularly for the latter part, thanks to writers like Josephus. To a large extent Greek remains lie near the surface of the mounds and tells of Palestine, and have either eroded away or have been removed for the buildings of the Romans, Arabs, and later builders. Nevertheless, such material as is available is of considerable value in supplementing the written records.

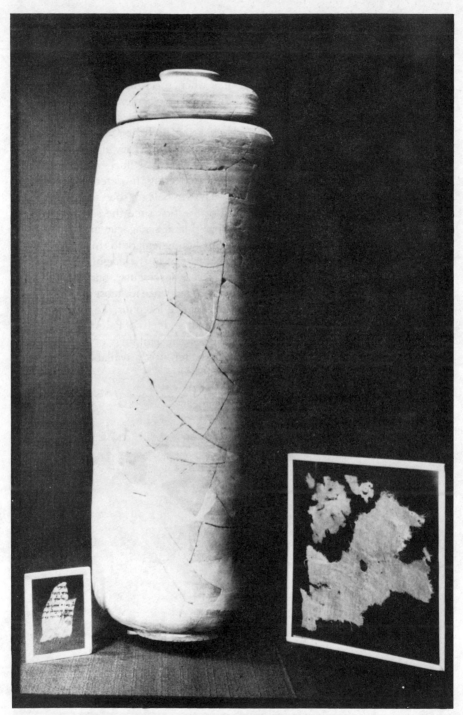

From left to right are fragments of the Dead Sea Scrolls (nonbiblical Hebrew text), a jar that held scrolls, and linens that wrapped them. (Oriental Institute, University of Chicago)

15

THE RELIGIOUS COMMUNITY OF
QUMRAN

It was during the Greek period we have been discussing that a remarkable community of Jews settled in the barren hills to the west of the northern end of the Dead Sea. The sect flourished here from the last part of the second century B.C. until about A.D. 70, living, so it seems, partly in a monastery whose remains have now been excavated, and partly in the caves nearby. Valuable manuscripts were left behind by these people, to be discovered in recent years and thus to provide the world with what is in some ways the most spectacular archaeological discovery of our times.

When Muhammed ed Dhib, a young Bedouin shepherd, threw a stone into a small circular hole in a cliff in these hills bordering the Dead Sea, and heard something crack and break, he could have had no idea of the train of excitement he was to set in motion in the lands far away to the west. He had discovered a treasure trove of ancient manuscripts the like of which had never been found before and which was but the prelude to yet other discoveries of a similar kind. Since that first exciting discovery in perhaps March, 1947, each year has brought to light yet more amazing discoveries. Now that we have the story unfolded, at least in part, we can reconstruct the setting with some clarity. We shall do this in order to make the significance of the find clearer.

HELLENIZATION AND THE PIOUS JEWS OF THE SECOND CENTURY B.C.

In our last chapter we outlined the growth of the Greek influence in Palestine to the point where it led to a Jewish revolt. It was an influence that began back in

269

the fifth century B.C. when Greek traders visited the land and Greek influences in agriculture, coinage, pottery, art, thought, ways of living, indeed in nearly every aspect of life, were imbibed by the people of Palestine. Then came the days of the Ptolemies and the Seleucids, who had the specific intention in most cases of Hellenizing the East. The Jews themselves were divided in their reaction to these influences, for, although on the purely cultural level Greek ways might be acceptable, there were dangers for the spiritual life of the Jews. Acceptance of Greek influence in some areas was likely to lead to repercussions in other areas, and perhaps finally to a destruction of the Jewish way of life which, after all, was based on the very law of God. Pious men who became known as the Hasidim banded together to resist these sinister influences. When Antiochus IV (Epiphanes) came to the Seleucid throne in 175 B.C. he, too, had the policy of Hellenizing the East and so providing a unifying force for his empire. Because of this he soon interfered with the legitimate priesthood of the Jews, replacing the descendant of Zadok by Menelaus, who was sworn to assist the progress of Hellenization. Antiochus finally decided to prohibit the distinctive features of the Jewish faith, and this led, as we have seen, to the Maccabaean revolt. Many Jews were slain, others resisted by fighting back. It was 142 B.C. before the pagans were finally driven out by the efforts of the Maccabaean leaders. At first these leaders were supported by the Hasidim, who were anxious above all else to secure religious liberty, but once this had been obtained they were not at all interested in the political aspirations of the Hasmonean family and they withdrew their support. A particular evil from their point of view was that the Hasmonean family had taken the position of high priest as a gift from the pagan Seleucid rulers and had then endeavored to combine with it political ambitions. When finally Aristobulus I took the title "king," and Alexander Jannaeus seemed to go into the depths of wickedness, many of the Hasidim seem to have organized themselves into a group to resist such evils. From such a setting the Pharisees were to emerge. One of the groups found a leader whom they called the Teacher of Righteousness,[1] withdrew into the wilderness of Judaea, and organized themselves into a religious community in the region of what we know today as Wadi Qumran.

There are perhaps some elements of conjecture in the story as we have outlined it here, but it is essentially correct. Archaeologically some important points have been established. The record of coins found at Qumran starts with the coins of John Hyrcanus (134–104 B.C.), and it continues until the time of Antigonus (40–37 B.C.). There is a break at this point, with a lack of evidence from the days of Herod the Great, but the story resumes in the reign of his son Archelaus (4 B.C.–A.D. 6), and carries on till about A.D. 70, when there is another break. Finally, there are some coins from the period A.D. 132–135.

1. Or "Right Teacher." See T. H. Gaster, *The Scriptures of the Dead Sea Sect* (New York, 1956), p. 5.

It appears that the site was abandoned about 37 B.C. for a reason that is not yet known. An earthquake did considerable damage to the building in 31 B.C., but after Herod's death the people returned and stayed then till A.D. 70. At that time the Romans finally devastated the place. It was at this period, when the Roman legions were moving toward Qumran, that we think the inhabitants hid their precious documents in the caves nearby, hoping to return later. But they never did. Who occupied the site in the days of the second Jewish revolt is not certain, although the coins from A.D. 132–135 suggest an occupation of some kind. Although this strange community had come to an end, the nature of the people and of their beliefs and hopes was carefully portrayed for us in their documents.

WRITTEN TREASURES FROM THE CAVES OF QUMRAN

The first cave that was entered produced a number of amazing documents, some of which were acquired by the Syrian monks in Jerusalem, and others by the Hebrew University of the State of Israel. The main documents were a complete roll of the book of Isaiah, a second roll of Isaiah complete from chapter 41 onward but with fragments of earlier chapters, a commentary on the first two chapters of Habakkuk, the Rule of the Community, an expanded Aramaic paraphrase of Genesis 5 to 15, a book now known as the *Wars of the Children of Light Against the Children of Darkness*, and a book of Thanksgiving Psalms.

These finds were startling enough (they may be read about in some of the excellent accounts now available), but they were only a start.[2] The cave from which these original documents came was subsequently discovered in January, 1949, by trained archaeologists, and a systematic search was undertaken by experts in February to March, 1949. Unauthorized persons had been there before them and had disturbed the cave greatly, but many fragments were found on the floor of the cave, including scraps of Genesis, Leviticus, Deuteronomy, Judges, Samuel, Isaiah, Ezekiel, and Psalms. There were also portions of commentaries on Micah, Zephaniah, and Psalms, all in very fragmentary form, and some pieces of other books, such as the Book of Noah, the Book of Jubilees, and the Testament of Levi.

Toward the end of 1951 the Bedouin discovered a second cave containing yet more fragments, which they sold to the Museum in Jerusalem. At once an expedition of scholars set off to search the area. They were able to investigate forty caves. It was in March, 1952, that pottery of the type found in the first cave was found in several others, pointing to occupation by the same people at about the same time. Two of the caves, Cave 2 and Cave 3, contained fragments

2. F. F. Bruce, *Second Thoughts on the Dead Sea Scrolls* (Grand Rapids, 1956); M. Burrows, *The Dead Sea Scrolls* (London, 1956); C. T. Fritsch, *The Qumran Community* (New York, 1956); Y. Yadin, *The Message of the Scrolls* (London, 1957); J. M. Allegro, *The Dead Sea Scrolls* (London, 1957).

The caves in the cliffs near Wadi Qumran have proved to be veritable storehouses of archaeological treasures. Cave 4, pictured here, yielded many fragments of manuscripts that came from the library of the Qumran monastic community. (Bernard W. Anderson, Understanding the Old Testament [Prentice-Hall, 1957], by permission).

The entrance to Cave 1. (Photo by the author)

The author standing beside the entrance to Cave 1. Note the circular hole through which a Bedouin shepherd threw a stone that broke a jar and thus led to the discovery of the ancient manuscripts.

of the Old Testament, but Cave 3 yielded strange inscribed copper rolls, which were subsequently found to contain mysterious lists of treasures and the places where they were buried.

Cave 4 was the most startling of all in some respects, for here in September, 1952, the archaeologists cleared a cave that had been disturbed by the Bedouin. It contained many thousands of pieces representing over three hundred books, biblical and nonbiblical, including every book in the Old Testament except the book of Esther. Commentaries on Psalms, Daniel, and some of the Minor Prophets were represented, as well as hymns, apocryphal and apocalyptic writings, and fragments of other books known from Cave 1.[3]

Cave 5 was found in September, 1952, also, but the archaeologists themselves were the discoverers this time. It yielded a good harvest of fragments of nonbiblical works, as well as some phylacteries.

Cave 6, high up in the cliffs behind the settlement, had some pieces of manuscripts, but the most interesting item here was a fragment of a work known as *The Damascus Document of the Sons of Zadok*, which was discovered earlier in this century in an old synagogue in Cairo. It is evident that the Qumran people knew this writing and had a copy of it in their library.

3. The contents of the various caves can be found in *RB* for the years 1953ff. See also F. F. Bruce, *op. cit.*, p. 31, and J. M. Allegro, *op. cit.*, pp. 35–40.

Caves 7 to 10 were found by the archaeologists, but contained very little material. Then, early in 1956, Cave 11 was discovered by the Bedouin.[4] It contained material comparable in quality to that found in the first cave, including a small roll of Psalms, many pieces of the *Apocalypse of Jerusalem*, an Aramaic Targum of Job, and two copies of the book of Daniel already known in fragment form from Caves 1, 4, and 6.

In addition to the work in the caves near Qumran, the excavation of the ancient ruin which represented the original monastery of the sect was undertaken. The work began in November, 1951, and soon it revealed a connection between Cave 1 and the ruins when a jar of the same type as was found in the first cave came to light, along with pottery and coins of the first century A.D. In the spring of 1953, 1954, 1955, and 1956 this work went on. The excavations revealed a building that had experienced three periods of occupation. Its dimensions and plan are now known.[5] Pottery and coins assist in dating the periods of occupation. The building had a water supply which came in by way of a conduit from springs in the hills behind. A considerable number of cisterns and more shallow receptacles for holding water links up with statements in the writings which show that these people laid a great emphasis on ritual washings. One room in the monastery was evidently the scriptorium where the scrolls were written, for here were found the remains of benches where men sat, and even two of the inkwells. The whole building was a complex one with many rooms. It was here that the members of this strange community lived and worked to produce the manuscripts and rolls found in the caves.[6]

Quite apart from the finds directly connected with the Qumran community, there were important discoveries in other areas of the wilderness of Judaea. As early as January, 1952, there was a six-week campaign of excavation in the Wadi Murabba'at, eleven miles to the south, which produced evidence of occupation in the Chalcolithic Age (before 4000 B.C.), the Middle Bronze Age (2000–1550 B.C.), the Iron Age (1200–550 B.C.), and the Roman period. In all, four caves were investigated. The texts, coming mostly from the second cave, were of various types. One nonbiblical text in Hebrew was written over an earlier text, probably in the centuries B.C., while other texts came from the post-Christian centuries. Some fragments of Genesis, Exodus, Deuteronomy, and Isaiah were from the first and second centuries A.D. Included among the finds were also a complete phylactery, several ostraca, and a sensational find of two letters of the leader of the second Jewish revolt of A.D. 135, the well-known Bar Kochba, whose real name, as revealed by the letters, was Simon ben Kosebah. In the same

4. Editorial in *Evangelical Quarterly* (Oct.–Dec., 1957), pp. 193f.
5. The overall area was some 260 feet square.
6. Details are to be found in J. T. Milik, *Dix ans de découvertes dans le désert de Juda* (Paris, 1957), pp. 41–44, and diagram 3. See also R. de Vaux, "Fouilles au Khirbet Qumran," *RB* (Jan., 1953), pp. 83–106.

The ancient ruins of Qumran on the northwest shore of the Dead Sea. An Essene-like community lived here at the beginning of the Christian era. (Bernard W. Anderson, Understanding the Old Testament [Prentice-Hall, 1957], *by permission)*

caves were fragments of Latin and Arabic manuscripts. None of these finds is to be related in any way to the Qumran material.

Further discoveries at the end of 1959 brought to light yet other letters of Bar Kochba. Reports from Jordan led the Israeli Department of Antiquities to undertake careful investigations in caves to the north of Masada, with the result that a variety of objects was discovered including jugs, bowls, jars, cloth, food, but in particular a bundle of papyri and wooden slats all carrying writing. These proved to be letters written either by Bar Kochba or by his secretary to some of his officers, Jehonathan and Masabala, at a time when Bar Kochba was still commanding his forces. Evidently these two men took the precious documents with them to the cave where they were found.[7]

In yet another area, in the Wadi en Nar, which is the extension of the Brook Kidron, a ruined site was investigated in February to April, 1953. It yielded fragments of Greek New Testament texts, as well as Syro-Palestinian and

---

7. Y. Yadin, "New Discoveries in the Judean Desert," BA (May, 1961), pp. 34-50.

One of the most startling finds in the caves was a complete scroll (and also a partial scroll) of the book of Isaiah. The scroll is made of pieces of leather sewn together with linen thread. (American Schools of Oriental Research)

Arabic texts. The place was formerly an early Christian monastery, now known as Khirbet Mird.

As a result of all this searching and excavation, scholars have an embarrassing wealth of material which will occupy them in close study for many years to come. Not only do the finds throw light on the remarkable religious community of Qumran, but they also give valuable information about the thought of those times, the character of the Hebrew text, the background to the ferment of biblical interpretation in which our Lord Jesus Christ preached and in which the Christian Church was formed, as well as insight into various aspects of the history of those times. We shall comment briefly on some of these items, indicating the lines which should be followed by the thoughtful reader.

THE CHARACTER OF THE QUMRAN COMMUNITY

The written material discovered in the caves, and especially the *Manual of Discipline*, or the *Rule of the Community* as some writers now call it, enables us to obtain a fairly clear impression of the basic ideas, the constitution, and the practice of the community.[8]

In the difficult days of the last part of the second century B.C. the pious group of Jews represented here was convinced that the end of this wicked age was at hand and that the days of judgment spoken of by the prophets of the Old Testament were about to commence. The very site of the monastery was at the point where the river described in Ezekiel 47 entered the Dead Sea. In such perilous times this society believed that God still had a remnant of faithful people who were in the line of the faithful remnants of past days, but that this one was the final one. The people of Qumran used names for themselves which remind us of the names of God's covenant people in the Old Testament, such as "the Elect," "the Saints of the Most High," "the Sons of Light," "the Holy People," "the Poor of the Flock," and "the Community of Israel and Aaron." As members of the covenant they believed that they were already in possession of the law of God, but they desired to live by its precepts. Their great aim was to study the Torah in order to discover its true interpretation along lines of procedure that had been given to them by the Teacher of Righteousness (or Right Teacher),[9] who had set out for them the way of holiness and had shown them how to live and to serve God in such momentous days. They now awaited the dawning of the Messianic age in which there would be a new Jerusalem and a new Temple, where worthy sacrifices would be offered by a worthy priesthood. Until that day dawned, this community of God's elect was required to devote itself to the law of God, to submit to the discipline of the sect, and even to be prepared to suffer as an atonement for the sins of Israel that had gone astray. Indeed, they would make atonement for the whole earth and thus bring wickedness to an end.

The community was organized rather like a medieval monastery, with members composed of both the priests (sons of Zadok) and laity. At the head of the hierarchy stood the priests, who were supreme in all matters doctrinal and economic, and after them the Levites, the elders, and the rest of the people. The laity was divided into groups of thousands, hundreds, fifties, and tens, and the priests had authority over them in matters of law and property. Yet all members of the community were allowed to vote on matters of law and property in the general assembly, which was conducted according to certain fixed rules. The priests in the assembly took their places first, then the elders, then the rest. No one was allowed to speak while his brother was speaking, and the supervisor who presided gave each man a clear opportunity to speak.

There was another important group, the council, a sort of supreme court,

8. Simple outlines are to be found in F. F. Bruce, *op. cit.*, pp. 99-111; T. H. Gaster, *op. cit.*, pp. 1-28; and G. Vermes, *The Dead Sea Scrolls in English* (London, 1962).

9. F. F. Bruce, *The Teacher of Righteousness in the Qumran Texts* (London, 1957), has an excellent summary of present knowledge about this figure.

comprising twelve men, of whom three were priests, all skilled in the law, "to guard faithfulness in the land."

It seems that there were organized cells of this sect wherever ten men were found belonging to the order. Of these, one needed to be a priest who was able to interpret the law to them at any time of day or night, so as to preserve harmony.

It was not easy to become a member of this community. A man had to volunteer, and to agree to live by the regulations of the sect. He was first examined by the overseer as to his intelligence and character. After a time he appeared before the "many" and was examined. He was then required to serve a full year of probation during which he did not share either in the wealth of the community or in the purificatory rites. At the end of the year he was examined again, and, if accepted, he deposited his property with the overseer and was allowed the next year to share the purificatory rites of the group, but not its communal meal. When finally he was accepted, he surrendered all his property, which was included in the common fund, and after confession and the reciting of blessings and curses by the priests, the applicant became a full member of the covenant community. He swore to follow the law of Moses, to live by it, and to shun all evil men and their ways.

Communal life was expressed in various ways. The two principal rites were baptism and the communal meal, and in these all members had a part. There were many occasions on which members of the sect had to carry out ritual washings, not only at their initial baptism but also on various other occasions which required outward lustrations. The community did not regard these washings as in themselves a substitute for purity of heart, for several portions in their writings insist on inward purity as the only way to win divine approval. The outward washing was only the symbol of inward cleansing.

The communal meal was another occasion where the whole group acted in unison, and where "all are to dine together, worship together and take counsel together."[10] When they ate, the priest occupied the first place, and after that the members sat in their orders. Before meals, which evidently had a sacramental character, the priest gave thanks. In other ways, too, the society was communal. Much work, covering a great variety of occupations, had to be done in order that the group could gain its daily bread. The excavations revealed the potters' corner and the room where the scribes worked, and it is believed that there is evidence of farming activity also in the area.

To these men time was a sacred trust from God, and there were set times for prayer and meditation as well as for work. Throughout the night some of the men were engaged in the study of the Torah, the law of God, in three shifts. Wherever ten men were gathered, one of them devoted himself exclusively to the study of the law.

10. T. H. Gaster, op. cit., p. 49; Manual of Discipline, col. vi, lines 2, 3.

Terra-cotta and bronze inkwells from the scriptorium at Qumran. (Israel Department of Antiquities and Museums)

There were penalties imposed on those who broke the laws and offended in matters of community discipline. These were mainly exclusion from the fellowship and reduction of the food ration. Details can readily be found in the *Manual of Discipline.*

It would appear that women as well as men might be admitted to the community, and that marriage and family life were not discouraged. The graves in the area give evidence of the presence of women in the community, for a number of female skeletons were found and there are references in the documents to both women and children. The sect often took children in from outside and trained them along with other children for a period of ten years; after this the young adult could apply for membership in the society, for which he was eligible at the age of twenty, admittance generally coming after examination and probation. Charles T. Fritsch has given an excellent summary of the character of the Qumran sect.

> The Qumran sect was a monastic community whose members practiced the common life according to strict regulations; it was a covenant community which lived according to the requirements of the New Covenant; it was a sacramental community in that every phase of life was lived in accordance with the divine ordinances; it was a priestly community in that its life was directed by priests, or sons of Zadok; it was a Bible-centered community, where the Scriptures were read and

studied day and night, and where Biblical texts were continually copied by members of the group; and finally, it was an apocalyptic community, waiting expectantly for the quick overthrow of evil and the establishment of God's kingdom here on earth.[11]

We may suspect that the first settlers at Qumran believed the end to be very near, and no doubt they thought the time had come when the Romans came to the land in 63 B.C., for it seems certain that the Romans feature in their writings as one of the factors in the final victory. However, for a reason that is not clear, they vacated their settlement for some years and departed to "Damascus," returning after the death of Herod to await the time of the end. During these years John the Baptist was declaring that the time had come, and that Jesus Christ was the Messiah. This teaching did not influence the Qumran sect, and they were still in their monastery in A.D. 68 when the Roman armies began to quell the revolt of the Jews, who were led by the more violent elements of the nation, anxious to hasten the downfall of the Romans. In the reprisals that followed, the whole of Judaea was subdued and the Qumran settlement was destroyed. In a sense the end had come, but not in the way for which the community had hoped.

THE QUMRAN APPROACH TO THE OLD TESTAMENT

The Qumran community believed that God had given them special insight into the meaning of the Old Testament Scriptures, which were interpreted so as to enable the readers to see in the Scriptures a description of their own times and circumstances. This became evident to modern scholars from the earliest days of the finds, for the commentary on Habakkuk, one of the rolls in the first cave, followed just these lines. The interpreter ignored the historical meaning of the text and read into it the present evil age, so that the text became a source of guidance for the present, an approach not unusual even in our own days. If the reader will take up one of the popular translations of the texts and read the commentary on Habakkuk or Nahum, he will see that the method is to quote the Bible text and then to add the words, "The interpretation of this concerns. . . ."[12] Sometimes the phrase used to introduce the interpretation may differ slightly from this, but the meaning of the passage for "today" is stated after the Bible text in each case.

All of this material is valuable for us today because it throws light on the history of the times. Unfortunately, at the present time we are still in the dark about the meaning of some of the references. For example, reference to the Kittim, which occurs in more than one place, seems to point to the Romans, but there are still some scholars who think differently, and we shall need more

11. C. T. Fritsch, *op. cit.*, p. 75.
12. T. H. Gaster, *op. cit.*, pp. 229–261; M. Burrows, *op. cit.*, pp. 365–370.

information before we can finally decide. When the picture becomes clear, we shall have valuable material for dating the age at which these documents were written. Present indications are that the date of composition was between 135 B.C. and A.D. 70. That this approach to the interpretation of the Old Testament was used quite regularly seems to be implied by the fact that we now have this type of commentary for quite a number of Old Testament books, but notably the prophets.

THE QUMRAN COMMUNITY AND THE MESSIAH

The two centuries before the Christian era were centuries of speculation in many ways, as a study of the apocryphal, pseudepigraphic, and apocalyptic literature of those centuries will show. Such themes as the Messiah, the Day of the Lord, the final judgment, and the lot of the wicked were taken up by many writers, and the Qumran community, born in the midst of this sort of speculation, reflected the discussion of the day. There were, however, some novel ideas. The people believed that things would go on as they were till "the coming of a prophet and the anointed ones [Messiahs] of Aaron and Israel,"[13] and it was these duly anointed persons, one a high priest and one a king, for whom the community waited. Thus, they expected a prophet, a priest, and a king in that day. One document from Cave 4 showed that the teachers of Qumran made use of several passages from the Old Testament to justify their Messianic ideas. Here were collected Deuteronomy 18:18, 19, which refers to a prophet, Numbers 24:15–17, which refers to a king, and Deuteronomy 33:8–11, where Moses pronounced his blessing on the priestly tribe of Levi. The whole society was called "the community of Israel and Aaron," and it evidently expected the two Messiahs to emerge from its own ranks. In another of the documents, the order of precedence of those who sit down at the banquet in the new age is given, and here the Messiah of Israel is subordinate to the priest. We are reminded of the inferior position of the prince in the latter chapters of Ezekiel. It is noteworthy, in the light of these unusual Messianic ideas, that in Christianity the three figures of prophet, priest, and king are united in our Lord Jesus Christ whose Messiahship was achieved through the suffering of the cross.[14]

THE SCROLLS AND THE TEXT OF THE OLD TESTAMENT

Prior to the discovery of these texts, our earliest Hebrew manuscripts were dated about A.D. 900. It has always been the desire of biblical scholars to obtain earlier manuscripts in order to make a comparison with the present-day Hebrew

13. F. F. Bruce, *The Teacher of Righteousness in the Qumran Texts*, p. 77, and *Rule of Community*, col. ix, line 11. Cf. T. H. Gaster, *op. cit.*, p. 58.
14. F. F. Bruce, *The Teacher of Righteousness*, pp. 76–84.

text. In this way they can discover how well the text has been preserved. As a result of these wonderful Qumran discoveries we now have documents as old as 100 B.C., or perhaps even earlier.[15] How do they compare with the Masoretic text which we have in our Hebrew Bible, and which was fixed by the Rabbis according to the tradition (Masorah) which held in the early centuries of the Christian era?

A number of interesting facts has emerged. The most important is that in the main these ancient texts agree fairly closely with the text with which we are familiar. Where they diverge they not infrequently follow the Septuagint text more closely, and this diverges from the Hebrew text in a number of places. It is evident also that there were versions of the Hebrew Bible in existence in those days that differed from both the present Masoretic and the Septuagint texts.

From these discoveries certain facts are clear. It is plain that the Masoretic text, or at least the original form of it, is quite ancient. Although the standardization took place in early Christian times, the process was going on at least in the first century B.C. At the same time it is apparent that the translators of the Septuagint had a slightly different form of the text in Egypt, but it was a form that was not unknown in Palestine, for there is evidence of it in the caves of Qumran. Furthermore, the discoveries of these recent days show that there were still other forms (recensions) of the Hebrew Bible that were current in Palestine in those centuries. It became necessary for the Jews to decide on a standard text for their own use, and this the Rabbis did quite early in Christian times. It is probably because of these different texts that were in use in the days of the early Church that the quotations from the Old Testament occurring in the New Testament are difficult to trace exactly in many cases. Future work on the wealth of manuscript material will do much to show how our Hebrew Bible finally came into its present form.

THE QUMRAN SECT AND THE ZADOKITES

We have already made passing reference to the discovery many years ago, in an ancient synagogue in Egypt, of several fragments of a strange document which belonged to a sect of Jews known as the Karaites. The document was originally written by Jews who regarded themselves as a covenant group. Apparently they had migrated to "Damascus,"[16] where they were organized into a community by a leader called "the Star." The document found in Egypt has been called the Damascus Document or the Zadokite fragment, because of its reference to Damascus and to the sons of Zadok. It gives details of a sect which, in many ways, resembled the sect we have come to know as the Qumran sect. The two

---

15. Ibid., pp. 34, 44; M. Burrows, op. cit., pp. 73–122. A few persistent critics still seek to deny that the documents are pre-Christian and push them into post-Christian times.

16. It is not agreed by all that this term is to be taken literally. See R. North, "The Damascus of Qumran Geography," PEQ (1955), pp. 34ff.

Two leaves of the Damascus Document (Zadokite fragment) (CD 10:123; 11:1–23) outlining the secret Sabbath regulations of the sect. The leaves are from the Cairo Genizah, tenth century A.D. (Cambridge University Library)

lots of written material are related in style and terminology, and the two groups are similar in organization, in structure, and in many of their basic beliefs. Indeed, even before fragments of the Damascus Document were found at Qumran some scholars were postulating a connection between the two groups. The question naturally arose whether the Qumran people knew of the writings of the Damascus group. The discovery of fragments of this Damascus Document in Cave 6 makes it clear that the covenant community at Qumran was in possession of the rules and procedures of the Damascus or Zadokite sect. When a comparison is made between the two groups, it becomes clear that there are differences as well as resemblances. It was easier to enter the Damascus group than to enter the Qumran group, for it was only necessary to take an oath and be enrolled by the supervisor. In the matter of personal goods, too, the Damascus sect had easier rules, for its members were required only to give two days' wages a month to community funds. Again, this group had closer connections with the Temple in Jerusalem, although it was stricter in its observance of many of the requirements of the law than the orthodox Jews of Jerusalem.

It seems that the two communities were closely related, if not identical. However, because of the differences, some scholars think that perhaps they represent two different stages, with the possibility that the Damascus group was the later. We cannot at this stage give a final answer as to the relationships between the two.[17]

THE QUMRAN SECT AND THE ESSENES

Several ancient writers, such as the Roman Pliny and the Jews Josephus and Philo, give a great amount of detail about a sect that was in existence in their time, called the Essenes. Its members were scattered throughout Palestine and were celibates for the most part, although some did marry. They lived a very strict life, and in many ways they conducted themselves like the community of Qumran. They had community meals, devoted themselves to prayer, engaged in ritual washings, were sworn to piety, and in general followed a way of life that reminds us both of the Damascus (or Zadokite) sect and the Qumran sect. Pliny placed them in the Dead Sea area to the north of Masada and Engedi, which would bring them near to, if not actually on, the site of Qumran. Josephus, however, says that they were to be found all over Palestine. There are again many resemblances between the Essenes and the Qumran sect, and also some differences. Some scholars are ready to make an outright identification of the two groups; others feel that this is not warranted at present.[18] The fact seems to be emerging that there were a number of baptist and messianic groups in the Jordan Valley and in the Dead Sea area during the first centuries B.C. and A.D. John the Baptist founded one such group. It will probably turn out finally that all these groups were closely related, and traced their origins back to the same set of circumstances. We propose to regard them, apart from the group of John the Baptist, as basically Essenes.

THE QUMRAN SECT AND CHRISTIANITY

In the excitement of the early days of discovery, before the written materials could be properly assessed, there were those who noticed a number of superficial resemblances between the teaching and the practices of Qumran and those of Christianity. The conclusion was quickly formed that the origins of Christianity were to be sought in this sect. More mature consideration shows that this picture

17. C. T. Fritsch, *op. cit.*, pp. 76–89.
18. F. F. Bruce, *The Teacher of Righteousness*, pp. 112–122; C. T. Fritsch, *op. cit.*, pp. 90–110.

is quite false. There are vast differences between the two systems, and there is no ground at all to think that Christianity is related to the Qumran sect.

The reason for the superficial resemblances in teaching lies in the fact that Christianity touches time and again on the range of thinking of the Jewish people of those days, and offers its own solution. The coming of the Messiah, the significance of the Old Testament for understanding the purposes of God, discussions about the Day of the Lord, the problem of the wicked, and the final lot of the righteous, all of these, and many similar problems that occupied the thinking of the pious men of the times, fell for discussion among the early Christians. The writings of both the Qumran sect and of the early Christians abound in references from the Old Testament, so that similarity in language and theme by no means argues a dependence of one on the other. Both groups go back to the same basic source material in the Old Testament. There are, however, some important things to be said.

In the first place, there is at present no clear evidence of any direct contact between the Qumran community and either the Founder of Christianity or the early Christians. True, such scholars as J. M. Allegro and Professor Dupont-Sommer have argued that in the Teacher of Righteousness we have one who anticipated the teaching, passion, and Messianic claims of Jesus Christ, and that the community of Qumran was a sort of shadow of the Christian Church. These ideas have been popularized by E. Wilson, but they have not met with widespread acceptance.[19] Rather, the majority of scholars have deplored the facile identification that this writer makes on the basis of insufficient evidence. The Teacher of Righteousness did not make Messianic claims for himself, nor did his followers regard him as Messiah, nor do we know how he died.

It would seem quite probable, however, that John the Baptist had contact with the Qumran sect. He lived in the deserts of Judaea when he was young and finally came preaching repentance, separation from this evil age, and the practice of a life of denial, while awaiting the coming of the Messiah whose forerunner he was (Luke 1:76-80; 3:1-8). Much of this teaching is reminiscent of the teaching of Qumran. John also baptized and spoke of judgment, but he never identified himself with the Messiah. He preached to the masses rather than to a select group of people, and when Jesus came, John recognized Him as Messiah, although he still needed to learn the fuller implications of His coming and His ministry (Matt. 11:2-6).

There seem to be many points of contact between John and the Qumran people, but if he ever did belong to the sect, we would have to conclude that he broke with them in order to follow a new path set out for him by God.[20]

When we come to Jesus Himself, we find Him living a life that was very

19. E. Wilson, *The Scrolls from the Dead Sea* (London, 1957).
20. C. T. Fritsch, *op. cit.*, pp. 112-116; F. F. Bruce, *The Teacher of Righteousness*, pp. 128-131; K. Stendahl, *The Scrolls and the New Testament* (London, 1958), esp. the essay by W. H. Brownlee, "John the Baptist in the New Light of Ancient Scrolls," pp. 33-53.

different from that of the covenanters of Qumran. There seem to be many parallels between His teaching and that of the Qumran sect, but this does not mean any more than that He accepted the same Scripture as they did, and lived in days when many were talking about the same great themes. It is a fact that the more we know about the literature and the discussions of these times the more we can place the teaching of Jesus in its setting, and in this regard much can be learned from the Dead Sea Scrolls. But in a thousand ways Jesus Christ was different from the people in the monastery of Qumran, both in His own life and in the peculiar emphasis of His teaching.[21] There is no trace in the teaching of this sect of those great doctrines that make Christianity really distinctive—the Incarnation, redemption through the death of One who was the Messiah, Himself Prophet, Priest, and King of Old Testament expectation, the Son of Man and the Suffering Servant alike.

There are, however, many resemblances in language and in thought between the writings of Qumran and those of the New Testament. This is only natural because the early Christians were showing how it was that Jesus Christ provided the answer to all the hopes, the strivings, and the questionings of those pious souls who, like the covenant community of Qumran, despaired of this present evil age. The last twenty years of scholarly research on these documents have produced some thrilling discussions of the way in which Paul and others took up the challenge of the times, and showed how Christ, the true Messiah, had finally come in the fullness of time to make all things new.[22]

THE IDENTITY OF PEOPLES AND EVENTS IN THE SCROLLS

We have made reference in passing to several persons who appear in the literature of the Qumran sect, but there are others besides these. Such people as the Teacher of Righteousness, the Wicked Priest, the Kittim, a certain Demetrius, king of Greece, and the house of Absalom, all demand an explanation. Then some of the events referred to in the scrolls, such as the reference to the attack of the Wicked Priest who pursued the Teacher of Righteousness to his place of exile on the Day of Atonement, will provide important clues to the true historical situation in which this literature arose. Many writers already feel that the Wicked Priest was Alexander Jannaeus (103–76 B.C.), who clashed with the Jews in his day and slew many. The Jewish rebels did invite Demetrius III, the Seleucid king at the time, to come to their aid, but just who the Teacher of Righteousness was is not at present clear, although suggestions are not lacking. Again, the Kittim would appear to be the Romans.

---

21. C. T. Fritsch, op. cit., pp. 116–124; F. F. Bruce, The Teacher of Righteousness, pp. 131–137. Cf. G. Greystone, The Dead Sea Scrolls and the Originality of Christ (London, 1955).

22. Three important books of essays have appeared in recent years: K. Stendahl, op. cit.; J. Murphy-O'Connor (ed.), Paul and Qumran, Studies in New Testament Exegesis (London, 1968); and J. H. Charlesworth (ed.), John and Qumran (London, 1972).

The fact remains, however, that at present we are uncertain about the identification of many of the people and events referred to in the scrolls. We live in hopes that further research on the Qumran documents or the discovery of more documents will provide the evidence on which we may unravel these puzzles. There is such a wealth of material still being examined, and still more coming to light, that it seems inevitable that we shall soon have a solution to our problems.

It does not seem that the well-known King Herod features at all in the Qumran documents. Yet we have reason to think that he had dealings with the community at Qumran. Archaeological evidence points to the fact that during Herod's time the monastery was deserted. The reason is not known, but it is conjectured that Herod may well have taken a strong dislike to these pious Jews so close to his Jericho palace. The Messianic teachings which they propounded could have been an offense to him and, further, the community seems to have had something of a military significance, to judge from their document *The War of the Sons of Light Against the Sons of Darkness*. If Herod set himself against them, he could do them harm, so it is quite possible that it was during these years that they went to "Damascus," to return after his death. However, here, too, we can do no more than speculate, since in any case "Damascus" may be used in a metaphorical sense, and the *War* scroll may not have referred to physical warfare any more than the Christian hymn "Onward, Christian Soldiers."

It is not without good cause that many have regarded these finds in the Qumran area as the most spectacular archaeological discovery of this age. The documents have widespread significance, touching on the text of both Old and New Testaments, and on the Messianic hopes of the age and the thinking of pious men in the years surrounding the birth of the Christian Church. We feel that here we meet face to face men whose whole being is vibrant with expectation of the coming of Messiah. Even if they were wrong, and even if their interpretations of Scripture were forced and unnatural, they have left for us a strong picture of a hope which only Jesus, the true Messiah, could fulfill. The Messiahship of the Lord Jesus stands out in thrilling contrast to the frustrated hopes of these people. And the story is not finished. We feel that much more light will yet break forth from the writings of this strange community.

16

THE DAYS OF HEROD THE GREAT

WITH Herod's appointment as king by the Romans after the death of Antigonus, the last of the Hasmoneans, in 37 B.C., there was a new order in Judaea. Not being a true Jew, but an Idumaean by birth, Herod was despised by the Jews all his days. His reign was a tragic one and he died without a friend. But because of his tremendous building program, he left behind a great deal of material which is the delight of the archaeologist today. We shall first review the history of the times and then discuss the archaeological discoveries bearing on those days.

HISTORY OF PALESTINE FROM 63 B.C. TO 4 B.C.

In 63 B.C. Pompey entered Palestine and the Holy Land came under the direct control of Rome. This was in many ways an advantage, for it was to give the Jews peace, roads, aqueducts, and many fine buildings. Judaea itself was greatly reduced in size and was included in the Roman province of Syria, with a local governor and Hyrcanus as high priest. Soon after, Scaurus, the Roman proconsul of Syria, had trouble with the Nabataeans, and Antipater, the father of Herod, was able to persuade the Nabataeans to pay tribute and in this way ingratiate himself with the Romans.

Just at this time civil strife, which was to have indirect repercussions on Palestine, was breaking out in Rome. When Gabinius became proconsul of Syria in 57 B.C. he had trouble in Judaea with a Hasmonean rebel, a son of the former Aristobulus. The revolt was quelled and the fortresses of Alexandrium, Hyrcania, and Machaerus were demolished. In the campaign a young Roman named

288

Antony distinguished himself. He met the young Herod and the two became firm friends. Gabinius divided the land into five areas in order to avoid troubles. When he planned an attack on Egypt, Antipater supplied food and water as he passed through Palestine. In 54 B.C., following the success of Gabinius in Egypt, Antipater was able to bring about the collapse of another Jewish revolt by good advice to the rebels. As a reward for his efforts he became, in effect, the ruler of the land.

By this time the Roman world was ruled by a strange alliance of three men (called a triumvirate)—Pompey, Julius Caesar, and Licinius Crassus. In 53 B.C. Crassus met his death and Caesar and Pompey began to fight for supreme power. Caesar won, and by 48 B.C. Pompey was dead. In Palestine, intrigue among the descendants of the Hasmoneans led to serious conflict. The one man who finally profited from it all was Antipater. Whereas formerly he supported Pompey, now he supported Caesar, who at the time was needing help in Egypt. He was able to send three thousand Jewish troops and to persuade other Jews to assist. Hyrcanus the high priest accompanied him to Egypt. Caesar was well pleased and confirmed Hyrcanus as ethnarch of Judaea and high priest, while Antipater was made a Roman citizen and appointed to the position of procurator of Judaea. He proceeded to rebuild the walls of Jerusalem, and to appoint his son Phasael prefect of Jerusalem and his son Herod as governor of Galilee.

At once Herod proved his skill in battle and in the affairs of government. He put an end to banditry in the Galilee area and had the leader, one Hezekiah, and many of his followers executed. In doing this he encroached on the jurisdiction of the Sanhedrin, and was summoned before this august body. He knew very well that he had the strong support of the Syrian governor and could afford to adopt an aggressive attitude in the presence of the Sanhedrin. In the end the Sanhedrin did not sentence him and Herod departed secretly from Jerusalem. He reappeared with a body of troops, wanting to take vengeance on the Sanhedrin, but his father Antipater restrained him and he returned to Galilee. But he had shown that he was a man to be reckoned with, as indeed it turned out. He proceeded at once to report the incident to the Roman proconsul of Syria, who forthwith appointed him governor of Coele-Syria. This greatly increased his power and enraged his enemies.

Then came the assassination of Caesar in March 44 B.C. The Roman senate confirmed the generous concessions Caesar had made to the Jews, but before long the proconsul of Syria, Cassius, an ambitious man, began to press the Jews for money and demanded that Antipater and his sons find it. They submitted, but earned the wrath of the Jews still more, so that when a Jewish conspirator, Malichus, arranged for the poisoning of Antipater, the nation was not grieved. Soon after, Cassius set off to Rome, hoping to gain the supreme place in the empire. Anarchy broke out in Judaea, and Antigonus, the son of Aristobulus and nephew of the high priest Hyrcanus, tried to seize the power; however, he was frustrated for a time.

Eventually Cassius was overthrown, and Antony and Octavian emerged supreme. Antony returned to Asia, where Herod had in the meantime married Mariamne, the granddaughter of Hyrcanus, thus becoming a member of the royal family. When both parties in Judaea appealed to Antony, he favored Herod and Phasael. It was no advantage to Herod, for Antigonus called on the aid of the Parthian invaders from Persia, a great menace to Roman power in the East, and paid them money to invade Judah. This they did, and for the time being the Romans were unable to deal with them. They put Antigonus on the throne, and he ruled from 40 to 37 B.C. This man, as we have seen, had his name placed on coins.[1]

The position of Herod was desperate and he appealed to Rome for help. There were others who were bargaining with Rome at that time, but in the end Rome ignored them all and appointed Herod as king. It took him three years to overthrow Antigonus and to enter into his possessions, but Antigonus was finally taken prisoner and executed. Thus ended the Hasmonean high-priesthood.

Herod's reign can be summarized in three stages.[2] From 37 to 25 B.C. he had considerable strife, with serious domestic trouble, most of which he overcame by executions. When in 31 B.C. Antony was defeated by Augustus, Herod managed to obtain the goodwill of the emperor.

From 25 to 14 B.C. there was peace. During these years Herod's domains were greatly enlarged as a reward for loyal service to Rome. The last years of his life were again dogged by much strife during which he had several of his sons executed. Finally he contracted a disease and died in 4 B.C. at the age of seventy.

HEROD'S BUILDING ACHIEVEMENTS

Herod was one of the most passionate builders of antiquity. Today there is a great variety of ruined buildings to be found in Palestine which date back to Herod's reign. These remains are naturally of great interest to the archaeologist. They may be classified into four groups: the Temple in Jerusalem, other buildings in Jerusalem, buildings in the rest of his kingdom, and buildings in foreign countries.[3]

Herod made use of a particular type of masonry in his buildings which has become known to archaeologists as Herodian masonry. It consists of huge blocks of stone, generally oblong, with a smoothed-out area cut down as a margin all around the outside of the block. Technically this is referred to as a marginal draft. It is quite distinctive and can be easily recognized by the excavator. Much

1. See above, p. 267.
2. S. Perowne, *The Life and Times of Herod the Great* (London, 1956).
3. *Ibid.*; see esp. pp. 18–21, 115–142.

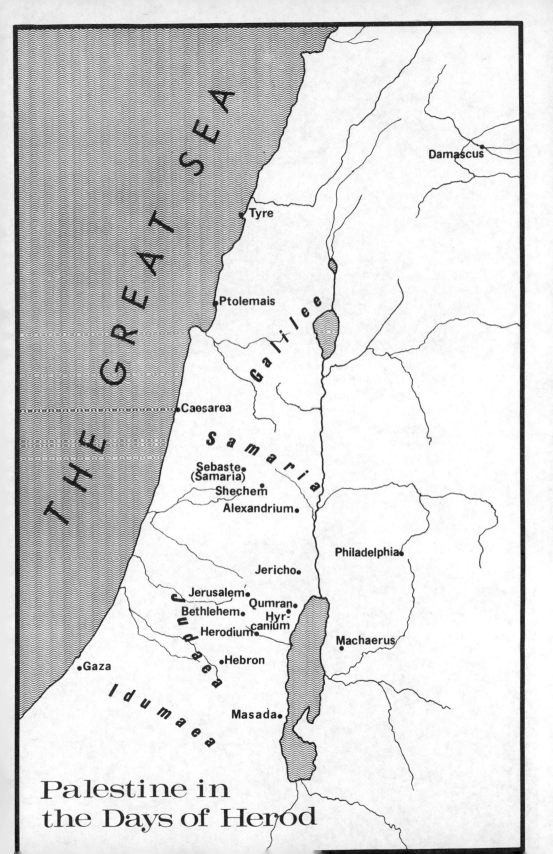

THE GREAT SEA

Damascus

Tyre

Galilee

Ptolemais

Caesarea

Samaria

Sebaste
(Samaria)

Shechem

Alexandrium

Philadelphia

Jericho

Jerusalem

Qumran

Bethlehem

Hyr-
canium

Herodium

Judaea

Machaerus

Hebron

Gaza

Idumaea

Masada

Palestine in
the Days of Herod

The characteristics of Herodian masonry are the immense size of the stone blocks and the so-called marginal draft cut around their facing. The draft is not visible on the pictured stones which form part of a wall near Hebron. (Photo by the author)

The Western (Wailing) Wall (right) of the temple enclosure at Jerusalem contains Herodian masonry. The marginal draft is visible around some of the stones. (Oriental Institute, University of Chicago)

of his building showed a strong Hellenistic influence, and W. F. Albright has described it as the "fullest flowering of the Hellenistic architecture in Palestine."[4]

In the year 19 B.C. Herod decided to rebuild the Temple in Jerusalem. The exact bounds of the Temple as it was when Herod undertook his work are not known. He determined not only to reconstruct the Temple, but also to construct a huge courtyard in which pilgrims could gather. It was necessary to build a platform supported by columns and vaults over a portion of the hill to the southeast where the hill fell away. This area today is called Solomon's Stables, although it was built by Herod. Around the platform a tremendous retaining wall was built, sunk in places into bedrock. As early as 1867 to 1870 Sir Charles Warren excavated around the existing wall down to bedrock. One of the best examples of the typical Herodian masonry is to be seen at the "Wailing Wall," where the huge blocks which make up the wall demonstrate the way in which Herod had his masons do their work. The largest of these blocks is sixteen and a half feet long and thirteen feet wide. In the early part of the last century Edward Robinson found the remains of two arches along the western side which he believed had once belonged to a bridge or viaduct connecting the western hill to the platform. The important excavations that have been carried out around the southwest corner of the Temple area by Professor Benjamin Mazar of the Hebrew University since February 1968[5] have produced an enormous amount of evidence not merely about "Robinson's Arch," but also about a variety of Herodian remains as well as remains from the succeeding centuries.

Robinson's Arch sprang originally from a point quite close to the southwest corner of Herod's huge platform but on the western side. It had been observed by the archaeologist Charles Warren in his explorations in 1867-1870. He had discovered the foundations of a pillar at a distance of 10 meters from the wall and had assumed that here he had identified the first pillar of a series of arches that formed a bridge over the Tyropoeon valley which connected the Temple Mount with the Upper City on the west. That was a view that proved to be wrong, as we shall see. The discovery of the remains of a second arch, "Wilson's Arch," a short distance further along the western wall of the Temple Area then raised the question of whether there were two roads linking the Temple Mount to the Western Hill. Only excavation could unravel the truth about these two arches.

4. W. F. Albright, *Archaeology of Palestine* (London, 1956), p. 154.

5. Several significant articles on these excavations have appeared. Among these the following are important: B. Mazar, "The Excavations South and West of the Temple Mount in Jerusalem: The Herodian Period," *BA*, Vol. XXXIII, No. 2 (May, 1970), pp. 47-60; *The Excavations in the Old City of Jerusalem* (*Preliminary Report of the First Season, 1968*) (Jerusalem, 1969); B. Mazar, "The archaeological Excavations near the Temple Mount" in Y. Yadin (ed.), *Jerusalem Revealed, Archaeology in the Holy City 1968-1974* (1975), pp. 25-35. A valuable general article on Jerusalem in the Second Temple Period is to be found in *EAEHL*, Vol. II, pp. 599-608. See also B. Mazar, "Herodian Jerusalem in the Light of the Excavations South and South-West of the Temple Mount," *IEJ*, Vol. 28, No. 4 (1978), pp. 230-237.

The fact is that Wilson's Arch was indeed the first link in a series of arches which supported a roadway to the Western Hill. This road was 13.4 meters wide and the height of the arches was 23 meters above bedrock. There were some very fine houses on the Western Hill in Herod's days.

The other arch, that is, "Robinson's Arch," proved to be a span supporting stairs which led westward from the Temple Hill downward to a platform from which a second stairway met at right angles and led down to a street below. This means that there was only one roadway leading to the Upper City. This second stairway was somewhat longer. The foundations of several supporting pillars have been excavated.

The excavations revealed a number of other important items. The massive Herodian stones of the huge wall which supported the Temple Area continued

Robinson's Arch (center) juts out of the Western (Wailing) Wall at Jerusalem. The arch formed part of a monumental stairway described by Josephus in his Antiquities *(XV. ix. 5). In front of the wall are remains of the palace complex of the Omayyad Caliphate (seventh and eighth centuries A.D.) (Garo Nalbandian)*

downward. They were all the typical Herodian masonry with its distinctive draft cut around the edge of the stones. At the base of the stairs one street led along the southern side of the great platform wall and another led along the western side. These streets were paved with large, smooth flagstones. The two streets were not level but led to a small series of stairs which raised the street level. At the base of Robinson's Arch several small rooms containing stone vessels, weights, coins, pottery, and the like were found. These were probably shops.

The southern road revealed some remarkable facts. The fine Herodian street with its flagstones was some 6.40 meters wide and led toward the two Huldah Gates referred to in rabbinic writings.[6] There were two of these, the "Double Gate" and the stairway some 64 meters wide, in a good state of preservation. This stairway had been cut into bedrock. It led some 6 meters lower to a fine plaza paved with smooth flagstones, perhaps a gathering-place for pilgrims who would enter the Temple at festival time. This plaza was at a lower level than the southern street with its several stairways which led up from the base of the great flight of stairs leading down from Robinson's Arch. Further along the southern wall there was a second flight of steps leading from the plaza to the Triple Gate. The remains of a large structure between the two stairways revealed a number of pools and cisterns hewn into the rock which may have been places for ritual bathing before entering the Temple precincts.

One of the most interesting finds along the southern street was a number of huge blocks of Herodian masonry evidently cast from the top of the Temple wall at the time of the destruction of Jerusalem in A.D. 70. A fragment of a stone plaque which once carried an inscription in Hebrew was found here. It could be joined to another fragment discovered over a century ago. Even so, it is difficult to read. Another inscription in marble contains only the middle parts of two lines, insufficient to allow a translation. Yet another inscription found among the rubble from the destruction of Herod's temple seems to have fitted into a niche in a large stone which had fallen. Only part of the inscription is preserved, but the words "To the place of trumpeting . . ." are clear. This is thought to have been part of the top cornerstone of the southwestern corner of the Temple Mount, the site of one of four defensive towers, which according to Josephus[7] was the point where the priest would blow the trumpet to usher in the Sabbath. Numerous ornamented architectural fragments from the Herodian period were found among the debris along the Southern Wall.

Of some interest is the Herodian aqueduct which was discovered underneath the pavement along the western wall. This was hewn into rock and covered with vaulted stone slabs. It has been traced for two hundred meters in this area. It links up eventually with a vast water system which brought water

6. *Mishna Middoth* i.3. The reference reads: "the two Huldah Gates on the south, that served for coming in and for going out." See H. Danby, *The Mishna* (1933), p. 590.
    7. *Wars* iv.582.

into Jerusalem from some distance to the south of Jerusalem.[8] The aqueducts near the Temple Area mark only the end point of a system which in Herod's day was about 50 kilometers long.

Something should be said about the buildings on the Western Hill. We know a great deal more about these in the light of excavations which have been conducted in the former "Jewish Quarter" since 1969. The excavators of the Western Hill area uncovered many building remains which have made possible a study of the types and forms of the houses which once overlooked the Temple Mount. The area clearly represented a well-to-do residential area with large houses, frescos, mosaic ornamentations, complex bathing installations, and artifacts of high quality. Three of these houses were given names by the excavators: "The Herodian House" from the second half of the first century B.C., "The Mansion," which was destroyed in A.D. 70, and "The Burnt House," also destroyed with the rest of the city in A.D. 70.

The Herodian House[9] was a spacious building of some 200 meters square. The entire plan is preserved, although some of the details of doorways and walls are lacking. A series of rooms was arranged around a central courtyard in the floor of which four ovens were sunk. A large reservoir which could be approached by a broad stairway was partly vaulted over. There was a second smaller cistern as well. Near the entrance to the reservoir was a stone with a bowl-like depression, probably used for washing the feet prior to going into the pool for water. In the western wall of the house, which still stood at a height of 1.5 meters, there were three large recesses, probably used for household crockery. Indeed, one recess had many broken vessels still in place.

The house was built of both undressed field stones and dressed stone. The walls were plastered and in some rooms the floor also, although the plaster was so thin as to suggest that carpets or mats covered the floors.

The vessels found in the house suggest a degree of wealth. Among these were a fine set of *terra sigillata* ware (a type of pottery covered by a brilliant red glaze), a group of large amphorae bearing Latin inscriptions (which suggests that those who lived in the house drank wine from Italy), and many flasks which were asymmetrical in shape, into which the wine was decanted from the large vessels. The house itself was finally partly demolished and covered over in some sort of replanning of the area. A street paved with large slabs of stone had to be removed before the excavators could investigate the house.

We shall reserve a description of the other two houses till chapter 19 when we are discussing the Jerusalem that Jesus knew.[10] They were in use right up to the fall of Jerusalem in A.D. 70 and so belong more properly to the period

8. J. Wilkinson, "Ancient Jerusalem, its water supply and population," *PEQ* (1974), pp. 33-51.

9. See N. Avigad, *Archaeological Excavations in the Jewish Quarter* (1976), pp. 8-10.

10. See pp. 347f.

following Herod. It is not impossible, of course, that these houses were in use also in Herod's day. As we shall see, they displayed the same grand style.

The Jewish historian Josephus[11] refers to a magnificent royal stoa built by Herod on the western hill. It was possible to reach this stoa by means of a viaduct spanning the eastern slope of the western hill. Robinson's Arch is evidently part of this structure.

It is evident that in this general area the excavators have come upon a very significant collection of Herodian structures. We can be grateful that work is actively proceeding in this fascinating excavation. Unfortunately we have nothing of the Temple left today, although we suspect that if we could clear away the debris under the stone pavements in the old Temple area we might find some traces. We are dependent on the description of Josephus for such details as we have. The Temple was not completed till after Herod's death, as we learn from John 2:20. Possibly the only items we have today coming from the Temple are a complete and a partial inscription in Greek which indicate that one might not penetrate into any of the inner courts on pain of death.[12] The inscription discovered by Clermont-Ganneau in 1871 reads:

> No foreigner may enter within the barricade which surrounds the temple and enclosure. Anyone who is caught doing so will have himself to blame for his ensuing death.[13]

In addition to the important Herodian structures that have been revealed in the excavations near the Wailing Wall, there are various structures around Jerusalem that give evidence of Herod's work, such as the wall around the city in which he built towers, some of which he included as part of his own palace. The words of W. F. Albright give a good summary of the position today.

> Almost the whole length of the Herodian First Wall of Jerusalem can be traced and remains of the Herodian masonry identified. The finest example of Herodian masonry with marginal draft, outside of the retaining wall of the Temple enclosure, appears in the so-called Tower of David at the Jaffa Gate.[14]

The Tower of David was originally known as the Phasael Tower, named after one of Herod's brothers. Of the original tower the main part (21.4 by 17 meters) is still preserved to a height of 20 meters. It is built of large blocks of stone dressed in the standard Herodian style, with margins around the central raised boss. Excavations in the courtyard of this structure revealed that light courses of stone were built on bedrock, then the wall was drawn back a little,

---

11. Josephus, *The Jewish War* XV.ix.3.

12. F. F. Bruce, *Commentary on the Book of Acts* (Grand Rapids, 1954), pp. 433f.

13. Details of the inscription are found in A. Deissmann, *Light from the Ancient East* (London, 1922), p. 80.

14. W. F. Albright, *op. cit.*, p. 154.

and on the resulting base eight more courses were built, the upper ones sloping. This tower was incorporated into the city defenses.

There are other traces of Herodian masonry in the heart of the old city, and these are important in deciding the position of the so-called Second Wall of Herod, which protected the exposed northern side of the city. Two positions are advanced, one of which leaves the Church of the Holy Sepulcher outside the wall, and the other of which leaves it inside.[15] If the site of the Church of the Holy Sepulcher is the authentic site of Calvary, this wall should allow of its being outside the city proper of Herod's day. The matter is by no means settled.

Herod also built a fortress at the northern end of the Temple and named it the Tower of Antonia, after the Roman Antony. This was later to be used by Pilate as his Praetorium. It has been excavated in part in recent years, and a remarkable picture of the area has been brought to light. It contained the Gabbatha, the pavement which formed Pilate's Hall of Judgment, from which Christ was led to the cross (John 19:13).[16] This fortress first served as Herod's palace, but later he built a new palace to the west, in the general area of the Tower of David. On the north side were three towers: Hippicus, named after a friend; Phasael, after his brother; and Mariamne, after his wife. South of these lay the main palace. Of all these, little now remains, for they were destroyed by Titus at the fall of Jerusalem in A.D. 70. However, the so-called Tower of David probably preserves in its substructure part of the fortress of Phasael.[17] It is possible that part of Mariamne was discovered when an Anglican church was being built in 1901, and traces of Hippicus during the excavations of C. N. Johns between 1937 and 1948.

Of the buildings of Herod in other places in his kingdom we have today a great variety of remains available for study. One of the closest to Jerusalem was built about two miles away from the old biblical Jericho, at the place where the Wadi Qilt opens out onto the plain. A good water supply from springs in the wadi made the place a delight. Excavation has been undertaken at this site during recent years from 1949. In 1949 and 1950 the American Schools of Oriental Research uncovered part of a building which had been in use in Herod's day but had been re-used and extended by the later Arabs.[18] More recent excavations from the year 1973 onward have shed new light on the site so that it has become clear that it was originally the winter palace of the Judaean kings from the last of the Hasmoneans to Herod and his successors as well as later. The whole palace site covered an area of about 3 acres. At its center was a building 52 by 48 meters. Herod covered over this building and built a new structure, and

15. G. E. Wright and F. V. Filson, *Westminster Historical Atlas* (London, 1953), p. 99 and Plate XVII, c. See below, p. 362.

16. W. F. Albright, *op. cit.*, pp. 244–246. See below, p. 360.

17. *Ibid.*, p. 154.

18. BASOR (Dec., 1950; Oct., 1951).

in the later years of his reign he decided to enlarge the palace at Jericho. He ended up with a grand complex of sunken gardens, a huge swimming pool, various halls, monumental staircases, numerous other rooms—an altogether grand building. But the full picture has not yet been told because of the limited amount of excavation so far undertaken.[19]

But Jericho was not remote enough for Herod in his solitary moods, so he restored and re-equipped the fortresses of Alexandrium, Hyrcania, Machaerus, and Masada. These were on high, inaccessible peaks, Alexandrium high above the Jordan valley in central Palestine, Masada on the west of the Dead Sea, and Machaerus to the east, each high up and difficult to reach. More recently Masada has been excavated in part, with some striking results.[20] This fortress lay on top of the rock of Masada with a sheer drop of more than 1300 feet to the western shore of the Dead Sea. It had been fortified by others before Herod, perhaps by some of the Maccabees. But the main structures and fortifications that were brought to light by the excavation were the work of Herod the Great. On the steep north face Herod had built a three-tiered palace villa on each of three terraces below the top of the rock. The lower terrace had fine wall paintings and a double colonnade. The middle terrace had a circular pavilion and a colonnade. The upper terrace had a fine semi-circular porch and living quarters. On the top of the plateau were a large bathhouse, vast storerooms, an administrative building, two lesser palaces, and other structures. The edges of the plateau were walled with double walls braced across at intervals with cross walls so that the whole surrounding wall of some 4250 feet consisted of a series of compartments small and large. In addition there were great water cisterns which when full would provide water for a long siege. In fact Masada resisted the Roman attack for three years after the fall of Jerusalem, and fell finally in A.D. 73. Its Zealot defenders died in the midst—men, women, and children. The excavators discovered grim reminders of their last stand in many areas of the fortress.

One of Herod's strangest structures was the Herodium, just south of Bethlehem, where he had an artificial top put on a hill and built there a castle which was reached by two hundred steps cut in the side of the hill. The ruins at the top are still to be seen, and traces of the stairway may still be detected on the side of the hill. Archaeological work carried out at the Herodium from 1962 to 1967 has revealed that the palace here was circular with an outer diameter of 62 meters. At four points north, south, east, and west were semi-circular towers with an average diameter of 15.50 meters. Inside lay a variety of rooms including a

19. E. Netzer, "The Winter Palaces of the Judean Kings at Jericho at the End of the Second Temple Period"; "Preliminary Report of the Joint Jericho Excavation Project," BASOR, No. 228 (1977), pp. 1–13, 15–27.

20. Y. Yadin, Masada, Herod's Fortress and the Zealots' Last Stand (London, 1966); "Masada," EAEHL, Vol. III, pp. 793–815.

Some of Herod's palaces were restored and re-equipped fortresses; one was at Masada, a rocky plateau west of the Dead Sea. This aerial view shows the northern palace (left), which is built on three terraces, the large bathhouse, storehouses, and a quarry. The rectangle at the base of the mound (left, beyond the palace) is the camp from which the Romans beseiged and took Masada from Jewish Zealots in A.D. 70. (Israel Government Tourist Office)

large hall, a smaller hall, and a bath. This palace-fortress was evidently built on the same grand scale as Herod's other palaces.[21]

Herod's work at Samaria must have been among his best. In 27 B.C. he undertook extensive work there. He first of all provided a new city wall, two and a half miles long, with towers at intervals. The chief gateway is still to be seen in ruins, with the two towers on either side. Herod called the new town Sebaste, the Greek name for Augustus, the emperor of the day, to whom this work was

---

21. See note by R. P. V. Corbo on "Gébel Fureidis (Hérodium)," *RB*, Vol. LXXV (July, 1968), pp. 424–428. Cf. *RB*, Vol. LXXI (1964), pp. 258–263; G. Foerster, "Herodium," *EAEHL*, Vol. II, pp. 502–510.

A Corinthian capital found in the ruins of Herod's palace at Masada. (Israel Office of Information)

Part of the mosaic pavement at Herod's palace at Masada. The design has been so damaged that we cannot tell what it represents. (Israel Office of Information)

The many remains at Samaria provide evidence of Herod's building activity. Here is the main gate flanked by two once-elegant towers. (Matson Photo Service)

dedicated. Inside the wall Herod undertook the building of a magnificent temple in honor of Augustus. Built over earlier Israelite structures, it was about 225 feet square and stood on a platform (podium) that was approached by a fine flight of stairs. Today the ruins are the most imposing of all those to be seen in Samaria. The temple was high enough for one to view the Mediterranean Sea on a fine day. But there are other remains of interest in Samaria, such as the stadium, built at the edge of the valley that runs to the north of the town, and enclosed by walls. It was 638 feet long and 190 feet across. Traces of the forum are also to be seen in the heart of the town to the east of the temple.

The town of Caesarea on the coast was another scene of Herodian activity. Here a fine port was constructed during a period of twelve years, from 25 to 13 B.C.[22] A wall, some two hundred feet wide and standing in 120 feet of water, formed the back side of the harbor. It was made of enormous blocks of limestone, some of them fifty feet by ten feet in size, and was furnished with towers here and there. On the shore a town was built with a semicircular wall that enclosed the main public buildings and served to protect them. When Laurence Oliphant visited the area in 1884 he reported that "the old Roman wall could still be traced for a mile and a half enclosing an area strewn with the remains of a theatre, hippodrome, temple, aqueducts and mole."[23] Today this material has

22. Josephus, *Antiquities* XV.9.6; *Jewish Wars* I.21.5-8.
23. S. Perowne, *op. cit.*, p. 126.

Caesarea, a coastal city of Palestine ca. *thirty-seven kilometers south of Mount Carmel, is rich in archaeological material from Roman times and later. This picture shows the Roman hippodrome, an oval arena for horse and chariot races, which is being excavated and restored. (Israel Office of Information)*

largely disappeared, but important archaeological work both on land and in the sea has been undertaken in recent years. Any archaeological work in the sea adjacent to old Caesarea is difficult. But a start has been made.[24] On the land, active excavation has been carried on for many years. Caesarea was, of course, the place where the Roman governors lived from A.D. 6 to 66. Here, too, Paul was tried before Festus and spent two years in prison.

Aerial photography has revealed some important features of this famous town, but exact details of its layout are becoming available year by year. Archaeological work has been carried out by the Italian Archaeological Mission of Milan (which unearthed the impressive Roman Theatre in 1961) and the Hebrew University over several years. The fine Roman aqueduct, of which only a single arch was visible, is now laid bare. When the sand was cleared, a lengthy piece of the original aqueduct was revealed, its arches and conduits well pre-

24. Brief report in *RB* (April, 1957), pp. 243–246, and various specialized discussions in recent issues of *IEJ*. C. T. Fritsch and I. B. Dor, "The Link Marine Expedition to Israel, 1960," *BA* (May, 1961), pp. 50–59.

served. This solid structure brought water to Caesarea from mountain springs to
the north. Ancient synagogues in the area have produced fragments of mosaics,
marble capitals decorated with the menorah (seven-branched candelabrum),
and considerable numbers of coins (one hoard of 3700 bronze coins). Later ruins
from Byzantine, Crusader, and Arab times are also to be found in the area.
These later occupants of Caesarea reused the vast building remains left by
Herod. One of the most fascinating discoveries in the area was a unique inscription bearing the name of Pontius Pilate, the Roman procurator of Judaea at the
time of Jesus' crucifixion. It bears the words . . .]S TIBERIEUM [PON]TIUS
PILATUS [PRAEF]ECTUS IUDA[EA]E. The inscription is very fragmentary
so that the grammar of this section is not clear. But it seems evident that Pontius
Pilate must have been dedicating some structure to Tiberius Caesar with some
such formula as "I dedicate this forum in the name of Tiberius. . . ."[25]

Reference may be made finally to Hebron and its surroundings, where there
are a number of evidences of Herodian building. In the town itself the present

25. This inscription is now on display in the Israel Museum, Jerusalem.

*When Herod received Strato's Tower from the Roman emperor Augustus, he renamed
the city Caesarea to honor the giver, and constructed many new buildings and a seawall
that made the site a port. This huge tower was part of the wall, which enclosed the shore
and extended far and deep into the water. (Israel Office of Information)*

Moslem mosque preserves a very fine example of Herodian masonry. One outer wall is almost completely preserved and gives us an excellent idea of how the exterior of some of Herod's buildings would have appeared. At Ramat el Khalil, two miles to the north of Hebron, there are further examples of splendid Herodian masonry.

We shall not deal in detail with the building program of Herod in foreign lands. Among other gifts to foreign peoples we may note that he endowed Ptolemais (Acre) with a gymnasium, Damascus with a gymnasium and a theater, Sidon with a theater, Byblos with new city walls, Beirut with assembly rooms, temples, cloisters, and marketplace, Latakia with a new water supply, Antioch with a boulevard paved with marble and shaded with cloisters, and other towns with parks. His motive in all these works seems to have been his love for art, which was restricted in Judaea owing to the fact that representations of men and animals were forbidden by the commandments of Moses and, moreover, no inscription could be prepared dedicating an object to a man. Herod wanted to show his gratitude to his friends, too, and there may have been a desire also to commend the Jews in foreign lands. This could be done, he believed, if the ruler of the Jews showed these kindnesses to foreigners.

OTHER ARCHAEOLOGICAL EVIDENCE FROM HEROD'S TIME

The interested student can enlarge his knowledge of the times of Herod in other ways. It is possible, for example, by a visit to the Museum in Jerusalem, to become acquainted with the typical pottery of the times. We have referred to two inscriptions from the Temple, but there are other inscriptions of a secular nature available for study today. Then there is the coinage of the period, with a wealth of interesting history preserved in an incidental way. Herod himself issued coins in bronze, with the inscription in Greek, his symbols being the pomegranate and leaves, the tripod and palms, the eagle, the cornucopia, and three ears of barley. He was wise enough to keep human figures off his coins since this would have been a serious offense in the eyes of the Jews.

In the valley to the east of the present wall of Jerusalem are a number of tombs bearing ancient names. An inscription on one of them, known as the tomb of St. James, mentions several members of the priestly order of Bene Hezir (I Chron. 24:15), three of whom seem to have been high priests in the reign of Herod.[26] The "Pyramid of Zacharias" and the "Tomb of Jehoshaphat" belong to the same period, which Professor Albright holds to be the time of Herod.

Outside Judaea there are the important remains of the Nabataeans, many of which were standing in the days of Herod, just at the close of the Hasmonean era. We have seen how Herod's father was friendly with these people and indeed Herod spent some time with them in his youth. One of the greatest of the kings

---

26. W. F. Albright, *op. cit.*, p. 157.

of the Nabataeans was Aretas IV, who ruled from about 9 B.C. till A.D. 40. It was he who did a great deal to modernize and adorn Petra, playing a similar role in his country to that of Herod in Judaea. Archaeologists distinguish a classical Nabataean period from the first century B.C. to the time of the Roman occupation in A.D. 106. This was well under way in Herod's day, but detailed discussion lies outside the scope of this book.[27]

With the death of Herod in 4 B.C. we are already at the commencement of New Testament times. Jesus was born at the time of the great census which the emperor ordered (Luke 2:1–3) some time before the death of Herod. In Palestine a new arrangement in government followed quickly, and a somewhat different set of circumstances prevailed. To the discussion of that new environment we now turn.

27. J. Starcky, "The Nabateans: A Historical Sketch," BA, Vol. XVIII, No. 4 (Dec., 1955), pp. 82–106.

PART THREE

ARCHAEOLOGY AND THE NEW TESTAMENT

HISTORY OF NEW TESTAMENT TIMES

WE shall first provide a brief historical framework into which the events of the New Testament may be fitted and against which the items that have come to light in excavations may be studied. Only in that way can the excavated materials take on their correct meaning and significance. The story will be taken up to the time of the collapse of the second Jewish revolt in A.D. 135. For ease of presentation we shall break the period into two sections, the first up to the death of Emperor Claudius in 54 B.C. and the second from the accession of Nero to the death of Hadrian.

THE HISTORY OF PALESTINE FROM 4 B.C. TO A.D. 54

When Herod died in 4 B.C., serious problems arose. In his will he had indicated that he wished his son Archelaus to be king in his place. But the people of Palestine had grown weary of the cruelties of Herod. Even before Archelaus visited Rome to have his appointment confirmed, a revolt had to be quelled with some degree of cruelty. Further, there were two other sons of Herod who might press their claims to the succession.[1] In addition, the Jews of Palestine were asking that none of the sons of Herod should be king. The case needed wise handling and, after deliberation, Augustus decided to divide the domains of Herod into three, and to place one son over each part. Herod Archelaus was given the title Ethnarch and allowed to rule Samaria, Judaea, and the northern part of Idumaea; Herod Antipas was given Galilee and Peraea; and Herod Philip

1. See genealogical table, p. 444.

Ruins of the fifth-century B.C. temple of Apollo at Bassae in southwest Acadia, Greece. It was designed by Ictinus, one of the architects of the Parthenon at Athens. (Philip Gendreau)

the area east and northeast of Jordan from the Yarmuk River to Mount Hermon. Thus it came about that in 4 B.C. Palestine had three Herods in place of one.[2] This arrangement continued in the case of Antipas and Philip for the rest of the reign of Augustus, that is, till A.D. 14, and for over twenty years after. In the case of Archelaus, however, a change was made after ten years because he offended the Jews greatly. He divorced his wife and married a woman who had been married twice before, undertook an extravagant building program, and in many other ways created dissatisfaction so that Augustus deemed it wise to remove him. We meet him in the gospel story on the occasion when Joseph and Mary and the child Jesus returned from Egypt. Discovering that Archelaus was ruling, they preferred to go on to Galilee rather than to remain in Judaea (Matt. 2:22).

In place of Archelaus the emperor appointed a Roman procurator who was directly responsible to the emperor himself, but dependent on the governor of Syria for military help and general supervision. Fourteen of these procurators are known for the period up to the fall of Jerusalem in A.D. 70, and three of them are of special interest to readers of the New Testament: Pontius Pilate (A.D. 26–36), Antonius Felix (A.D. 52–59 or 60), and Porcius Festus (A.D. 60–62).

In Roman politics the great Augustus died in A.D. 14 and was succeeded by his adopted son Tiberius, who was to rule till A.D. 37. This emperor was ruling during the period that Jesus was preaching in Palestine and at the time of His crucifixion. It was his "image and superscription" that appeared on the coin given to Jesus that day when the Herodians sought to trap Him (Matt. 22:20). Tiberius was never a popular man and ended life full of suspicion and cruelty. His successor was Gaius Caligula (A.D. 37–41), an amiable man, who won great public support at the start of his reign by granting many concessions to all sorts of people. Very soon, however, he began to show signs of mental disorder and insisted on being worshipped as a god. On one occasion, when Herod Agrippa was visiting Alexandria, some of the citizens tried to compel the Jews to worship the image of Caligula. The Jews appealed to the emperor, but his reply was to order his Syrian representative to set up his statue in the Temple in Jerusalem. The legate delayed to do so, and only the earnest pleas of Agrippa, followed by the death of Caligula soon after, prevented an ugly situation. Toward the end of his life Caligula was quite mad and given up to all sorts of excesses and extravagances. He was finally assassinated by a guard of the palace and was succeeded by Claudius (A.D. 41–54).

What was happening in Palestine in these years? Judaea was governed by the procurators Coponius (A.D. 6–10), Ambivius (A.D. 10–13), Annius Rufus (A.D. 13–15), Valerius Gratus (A.D. 15–26), Pontius Pilate (A.D. 26–36), Marcellus (A.D. 36–38), and Maryllus (A.D. 38–44). It was under Pontius Pilate that Jesus Christ was crucified. In the northeast, Philip ruled as tetrarch

2. See map, pp. 374, 375.

till A.D. 34. His subjects were a mixed lot, largely Greek and Syrian, with a rather small Jewish population. We have every reason to believe that Philip was a good ruler—wise, conscientious, and just. Like the other Herods, he was a builder and is remembered best in this regard for the two towns of Caesarea Philippi and Julias. The first of these (Matt. 16:13; Mark 8:27) was built on the site of the ancient Panias at the source of the Jordan River, and the other on the shores of Galilee close to the older town of Bethsaida. The latter town he called Julias, after the daughter of the Emperor Augustus.[3] It is the old town of Bethsaida, which is known so well in the Gospels (Mark 6:45). Philip himself is mentioned only once in the New Testament, in Luke 3:1. He died in A.D. 34 and his tetrarchy was placed under the governor of Syria until A.D. 37, when it was given by Emperor Caligula to Herod Agrippa I, the extravagant grandson of Herod the Great, about whom we shall comment briefly below.

The third son of Herod the Great, Herod Antipas, figures prominently in the Gospels. He was given the title of Tetrarch of Galilee and Peraea (Luke 3:1),

3. See below, pp. 365f.

This dedication stone from the Roman theatre at Caesarea bears the only extant inscription naming Pontius Pilate. Pilate and the other procurators lived at Caesarea, then the capital of Palestine. (Israel Department of Antiquities and Museums)

two areas which were separated by the Jordan River (see map, pp. 374f.). Peraea lay to the east of Jordan, and Galilee to the west of the lake of the same name. The special area of the Decapolis separated the two parts of his domain but was not under his control. It would seem that of the two parts, by far the less important and the less populated was Peraea, where Machaerus, the strong fortress of Herod the Great, was situated. It was here that John the Baptist was executed.[4] But the main interest for us lies in the area of Galilee where Tiberias, the capital of Antipas, was situated and where the town of Nazareth was to be found. The first capital of Antipas was at Sepphoris, just to the north of Nazareth. This town was ruthlessly destroyed by the Romans in A.D. 6 following a rebellion, after which Antipas decided to move to a new site on the lake. But the new capital was never popular with the Jews because it was built on the site of a cemetery.

We know Herod Antipas, "that fox" (Luke 13:32), best in the New Testament for his murder of John the Baptist and for his association with Pilate in the crucifixion of Jesus (Luke 23:1–12). His marriage arrangements were not savory, for he married the daughter of the Nabataean king and then divorced her to marry Herodias, the wife of his brother. This woman and her daughter Salome joined him at Tiberias, and on one occasion, when John the Baptist rebuked him for his wrong, he cast John into prison. Subsequently, Antipas was induced by his wife and daughter to kill John. The story is given in some detail in the Gospels (Matt. 14:1–12; Mark 6:14–29; Luke 9:7–9). The scandalous infidelity of Herod Antipas toward his wife had serious consequences, for not only did it involve him in a war with the offended Nabataean king, but when Caligula became emperor he deposed Antipas and banished him to Gaul, giving his kingdom to the brother of Herodias, who now became Herod Agrippa I. Thus by the year A.D. 41, the grandson of Herod the Great became king over all the domains once ruled by his grandfather, as well as over some additional areas to the north of Mount Hermon.

Herod Agrippa I was the son of Aristobulus, one of the lesser sons of Herod the Great. Aristobulus had married his cousin Bernice, the daughter of Herod's sister Salome. So Agrippa I was closely linked into the Herodian family tree. He was educated in Rome, and in A.D. 23 returned to occupy a post under Antipas. He soon quarreled with him and fled to Antioch where he had a dispute with the governor, and finally returned to Rome where he became the tutor of the grandson of Emperor Tiberius and also a warm friend of Caligula. He soon found himself in prison for expressing too loudly the wish that Tiberius might die so that Caligula could become emperor. When the emperor died in A.D. 37, his friend Caligula, now the occupant of the imperial throne, released him and appointed him king of the former tetrarchy of Philip, which for three years had been under the care of the governor of Syria. To this area was added the territory

---

4. Josephus, *Antiquities* XVIII.v.2.

of Abilene to the north of Mount Hermon. As we have seen, Agrippa was able to restrain Caligula from offending the Jews by setting up his image in the Temple in Jerusalem. When Herodias, Agrippa's sister, the wife of Herod Antipas, saw the honors bestowed by Caligula on her brother, she planned to gain some for her husband and urged him to ask the emperor to grant him the title of king. Accusations of plotting were laid by the representatives of Agrippa, and Antipas was banished and his domain added to those of Agrippa in A.D. 39. The final stage in Agrippa's progress toward the possession of the domains of his grandfather came when, following the assassination of Caligula, he supported the candidature of Claudius as the new emperor. When this came about and things settled down, Claudius confirmed all the other appointments which Agrippa filled, and then added to his domains Judaea and Samaria.

Agrippa took up his residence in Jerusalem and worshipped regularly at the Temple, suppressing all attempts to introduce pagan images or practices into the synagogues. As a strict Jew he soon came into conflict with the Christian Church, then in its infancy, and executed James and imprisoned Peter (Acts 12:2-4). When Peter escaped by divine intervention, Herod ordered the execution of the guards (vv. 11-19). He did not reign long over his large kingdom and met his death at Caesarea on the coast where he had gone to attend games in honor of the emperor. As he sat there in all the splendor of his royal garments, flatterers declared that he was a god. He died shortly afterward (A.D. 44). The story in Acts 12:21-23, which is closely paralleled by that in Josephus, suggests that his death was an exceedingly painful one.[5]

His son Herod Agrippa II was only seventeen at the time and was regarded as too young to take over the responsible task of governing so great an area. Palestine returned to the control of the procurators. Six years later, in A.D. 50, following the death of his uncle, the king of Chalcis, a territory to the north of Abilene, the young Agrippa became the new king. This office carried with it the right to appoint the high priest of the Temple in Jerusalem. A few years later Agrippa II was transferred to the former territory of Philip and ruled over lands to the east and northeast of Galilee, as well as the area of Abilene. His domains were enlarged still further by Emperor Nero in A.D. 54 by the addition of other areas in the region of Galilee and some areas in Peraea. Agrippa retained his position till his death, toward the close of the first century.

Emperor Claudius ruled till A.D. 54. His reign was significant for the Christian Church, for it was really under his rule that the great period of missionary expansion in the early Church began, with the missionary journeys of Paul as a central feature. Under Claudius, Jews were persecuted in Rome because of riots that broke out there "at the instigation of one Chrestus." Possibly Chrestus was the leader of the riots, but many commentators are convinced that the riot was caused by Jews who objected to the preaching of early Christian

5. Josephus, *Antiquities* XIX,viii.2.

Tiberius Claudius Nero Germanicus, emperor of Rome A.D. 41–54. Influenced by his supporter Herod Agrippa, Claudius at first allowed the Jews to observe their own laws and customs but later expelled them from Rome. (British Museum)

missionaries in Rome.[6] In any case, the Jews were expelled, and we learn from Acts 18:2 that among these were Priscilla and Aquila, who were to become pillars of the church in Ephesus.

FROM A.D. 54 TO A.D. 138

Claudius was succeeded by Nero (A.D. 54–68), under whom Christian expansion continued. Later there was some persecution, in Rome at least, when Nero laid the blame for the great fire at the door of the Christians. It was during his reign that Paul had his trials in Palestine under the procurators Felix and Festus, and finally met his death in Rome, probably in A.D. 67.

6. F. F. Bruce, *The Book of Acts* (Grand Rapids, 1954), p. 368.

After Nero was slain at his own request, in order to avoid capture by the army, there were three short reigns in the years A.D. 68–69, namely, those of Galba, Otho, and Vitellus. Then Vespasian became emperor and ruled from A.D. 69 to 79. At the time of his appointment he was in Palestine quelling the Jewish insurrection that had broken out in A.D. 66. When the army heard of the death of Nero, they proclaimed Vespasian emperor, and he had to hasten back from Palestine to Rome to secure his emperorship. The task in Palestine was left to his son Titus who, after some delay, took Jerusalem in A.D. 70 but was cleaning up pockets of resistance in the country areas till A.D. 73. He eventually succeeded his father but had only a short reign of just over two years (A.D. 79–81). The remaining emperors that interest us are Domitian (A.D. 81–96), Nerva (A.D. 96–98), Trajan (A.D. 98–117), and Hadrian (A.D. 117–138). It was under this last-named emperor that the second Jewish revolt broke out in A.D. 132, led by Ben Kosebah (Bar Kochba).

Palestine was ruled by the procurators from A.D. 44 onward. Things moved along reasonably well at first, and Cuspius Fadus (A.D. 44 to perhaps 46) and Tiberius Alexander (perhaps A.D. 46–48) had no serious troubles. But from then on the Jews became increasingly troublesome, and under Cumanus (A.D. 48–52) riots broke out in Jerusalem and Samaria. Felix (A.D. 52–60), who had married Drusilla, the sister of Agrippa II, was suspicious of further troubles, and when Paul was sent to Caesarea by the officer of Jerusalem following a disturbance, Felix retained Paul in custody (Acts 21:27–24:27). He was succeeded in 60 (or perhaps 59) by Porcius Festus before whom Paul made his defense and appealed to Caesar (Acts 25:1–12). The narrative in Acts 25:13–26:32 refers to the occasion when Agrippa II, in company with his sister Bernice, visited Caesarea to welcome Festus to his new office. The new procurator, who found Paul something of a problem, called in Agrippa to advise him. Paul had appealed to Caesar, who at that time was Nero. It was not strange that in the early years of Nero Paul should appeal to him, for in the years A.D. 54–59 his administration was good, at any rate in the provinces, and there was little sign then of the persecution of the later years of his reign. It is clear from the narrative in Acts that Agrippa II, though a faithful Jew outwardly, had little knowledge of the deeper spiritual meaning of the faith he professed.

From the time of Festus the situation in Palestine grew worse. Trouble continued to brew during the procuratorship of Albinus (A.D. 62–64), but in the days of his successor Gessius Florus (A.D. 64–66) the whole thing flared up. At first Herod Agrippa II tried to advise the Jews against the rebellion, and Florus tried to use his power to quell the revolt. The Roman legate in Syria sent troops to assist but, after initial success, the Roman contingents were defeated, and the Jews, encouraged by this, rose all over the country. The rebels held several of the strong fortresses built by Herod the Great, such as Herodium, Machaerus, and Masada, but it soon became evident that there was division in their own ranks. The historian Josephus, for example, was sent early to lead the

Jews in the Galilee area, but had to compete with a certain John Giscala. When Josephus was captured by the Romans, he became a supporter of the Roman cause and sought to induce his fellows to surrender. Other cases of division in the Jewish ranks are well known.

Emperor Nero sent his general Vespasian to carry out the Roman counter-attack, and he was able to subdue the Galilee area by A.D. 67 and then move down into the center and finally overrun Samaria. By A.D. 68 only the area around Jerusalem was still in Jewish hands, apart from a few of the fortresses. Before Vespasian could complete the capture of Jerusalem, Nero had died and Vespasian had been proclaimed emperor by his troops. He did not pursue the

The Arch of Titus at the entrance to the Forum in Rome; part of the Colosseum is in the background. Titus and his father Vespasian erected the arch to commemorate their victory over the Jews and the fall of Jerusalem in A.D. 70. (Italian State Tourist Office)

A panel inside the Arch of Titus depicts a triumphal procession of Roman soldiers, who carry off the table of showbread, trumpets, and the seven-branched candlestick from the temple in Jerusalem. (Metropolitan Museum of Art)

subjugation of Palestine till he was secure in his imperial position and then, in A.D. 70, his son Titus took up the task and completed it. He was aided in the latter stages of the war by a considerable amount of quarreling and division among the Jewish leaders in Jerusalem. Once the Holy City fell, this meant the effective end of the struggle and the few remaining outposts were sealed off and finally taken. The stronghold of Masada held out till A.D. 73. Titus commemorated the victory by building an impressive arch in Rome, which is still to be seen. On the inside of this he portrayed his soldiers carrying off sacred vessels from Jerusalem, and the seven-branched candlestick can be easily discerned in the sculptured picture. Jerusalem itself was systematically destroyed and the Temple left in ruins. Archaeological work shows us today just how effective was the destruction of Jewish buildings throughout the land.

It was in the wars of these days that the remarkable monastery of the exclusive sect of the Essenes[7] that lived near to the Dead Sea, in the region of

7. Scholars are more and more inclined to accept the Qumran community as an Essene group, though opinions still vary. Essenes, Zealots, and Pharisees have all been suggested. See above, p. 284.

the modern village of Qumran, was destroyed. In the panic that attended the approach of the Romans, the members of this community hid their precious documents in caves in the hills about their monastery; and it was here in 1947, and in the following years, that the now famous Dead Sea Scrolls were found.

For all practical purposes the Jewish people of Palestine were defeated with the capture of Jerusalem in A.D. 70. But they were a resilient people and were to stage another revolt in the days of Hadrian (A.D. 117–138). Outside Palestine, urged on by some messianic hope, the Jews of Mesopotamia, Cyprus, Egypt, and Cyrene rose in revolt in A.D. 115 in the reign of Emperor Trajan (A.D. 98–117). The uprising was put down with excessive cruelty, and not without much bloodshed on both sides. In Palestine itself, the so-called second Jewish revolt broke out in A.D. 132 and lasted till 135. The leader was a certain Ben Kosebah, formerly known as Bar Kochba, "Son of the Star," who was held by many people to be the Messiah according to Numbers 24:17. Hadrian had issued a decree forbidding circumcision and ordering a temple of Jupiter to be built on the site of the Temple. This was a most grievous offense to the Jews and they rebelled. The revolt was finally quelled, and Hadrian carried out his plan to rebuild Jerusalem as a pagan city, which he called Aelia Capitolina. He forbade the Jews to enter the city at all, on pain of death, and they did not come to Jerusalem again for centuries, at least in any considerable way, although there was a relaxation of the decree sometime later. But in point of fact, the Jews did not again exercise any sort of political control over this land till the setting up of the modern state of Israel in very recent years. Reference has already been made to the valuable documents from the days of Bar Kochba, comprising some actual letters from this leader of the Jews, and some others from his secretaries and scribes.[8] One of the Aramaic contracts was dated "in the third year of the liberation of Israel by the hand of Simeon Ben Kosebah."

Other evidence from the days of the Jewish revolt is to be found on the coins of the Jews. Both in the revolt of A.D. 66–70 and in that of A.D. 132–135, the independent coins that were struck refer to the "Year of Redemption." It was not to be redemption but, rather, defeat and scattering. For the present purpose we must conclude our story at A.D. 135.

8. See above, p. 275.

18

ARCHAEOLOGY
AND THE ROMAN OCCUPATION
OF PALESTINE

THE New Testament story is set in the context of the Roman world of the first century A.D. An understanding of that world is necessary for an appreciation of the meaning of the New Testament writings, for these are full of allusions, not only to the history, but also to the customs and culture of the times. The most important influence in our period is the Roman one, and we shall attempt in this chapter to present several important aspects of that culture, especially as it is revealed by the excavations. But there were other influences at work in the first century, some of which had been effective for several centuries, and we should mention these briefly by way of introduction.

SOME CULTURAL ELEMENTS IN THE BACKGROUND OF NEW TESTAMENT PALESTINE

When the Roman armies entered Palestine in 63 B.C. and introduced Roman rule into the land, they found a people there who had been subjected to a wide variety of influences through the centuries past.

Quite basic in the life and outlook of the Jews was their own faith, which by New Testament times found expression in two ways. They were still able to worship in the Temple with the full range of priestly services, sacrifices, and rituals which had long been associated with their religion. Alongside the Temple worship was the worship in the synagogues, which was based rather on the teaching of the law, and where no sacrifice was offered. A Jew with any degree of

319

piety at all was given careful instruction in his faith from boyhood, and the worship of the one true God was fundamental to his whole view of life. Any thought of polytheism or of idol worship was anathema to him, and while some Jews are known to have been careless in their observance of the requirements of the law, the majority were rigid in their ways and were offended by any suggestion of introducing pagan procedures or compromise of any sort.

A second element, and in many ways one of the strongest, is the Greek. We have seen in an earlier chapter that Greek influence in Palestine began as early as the fifth century B.C.,[1] and well before the Christian era Greek motifs in architecture and art were widespread in Palestine. With the coming of the Romans this did not die, for they, too, owed much to the Greeks. As we have seen, the days of Herod the Great, a lover of Greek culture, witnessed "the fullest flowering of Hellenistic architecture in Palestine."[2] The remarkable tombs opposite the southern end of the Temple area on the east side of the Brook Kidron are now all assigned to the first century B.C., when Greek influence was strong. In addition, the Greek language was well known in the commercial world, and although the ordinary people of Palestine spoke Aramaic, Greek was the *lingua franca* of the East and there would be many in Palestine who knew the language. Greek literature and Greek thought, too, had left their mark on some of the more educated groups.

Reference should also be made in passing to cultural influences from further east. The Persians, and later the Parthians, had made some impact on the culture of Palestine over the years in art, architecture, thought, and religion. The worship of the god Mithras came from lands to the east of Palestine and in due course became popular among the Roman soldiers.

By the first century A.D., however, a culture had emerged that we now distinguish as Graeco-Roman. It took over certain elements from the past and combined these with new tendencies. Building showed points of comparison with Roman architecture while preserving elements of Greek influence. Among these was a fine large building at Jericho which was clearly Roman, as shown by its ruins, although in the structures behind the facade there were discernible some Greek influences. The specifically Roman aspects of this composite culture may be noted in a wide variety of objects used in everyday life such as pottery pieces of various kinds, whether for domestic or for artistic purposes, glass, metal objects, mosaics, coins, and the like. These can be compared with material found in other contexts outside Palestine, and the Roman character demonstrated. In addition to these material items we know that there were influences in law and government, and to some slight extent in language. There are, for example, a considerable number of Latin inscriptions which show that for certain official purposes this language was used.

1. See above, pp. 249-251.
2. W. F. Albright, *Archaeology of Palestine* (London, 1956), p. 154. See above, pp. 290-305.

Ruins of a Roman temple in Baalbek (ancient Heliopolis), Lebanon. It dates from the first century A.D. (UNESCO/P. A. Pittet)

Detail of a sculpture found in the Roman ruins at Baalbek, Lebanon. The scene apparently depicts Neptune and his wife Salacia, deities of the sea. (UNESCO/ P. A. Pittet)

It is not our purpose in this book to follow up all these cultural influences, but to concentrate on the clearly Roman material, which was so much a part of the daily life of the people in the first century when the Christian Church was born.

COINAGE OF THE PERIOD 4 B.C. TO A.D. 135

Coins play a very important part in dating the material remains that come to light in an excavation, but they tell us a great deal more, as we shall see. It was probably about the seventh century B.C. before coins as such came into general use.[3] By Roman times they were widely used. They are found in excavations because the people who used them often dropped them (as we do) or stored them in some corner of their house so that we often find caches of them. Sometimes they are found in the ruins of buildings that were once shops or places of trade. At times they were in the clothes of people who were killed in their homes in war, earthquake, or fire. Indeed there are countless reasons why the coinage of

3. See pp. 228f.

These Roman columns found in Ashkelon have been erected in the city's Antiquities Park. (Israel Office of Information)

the day might have been left behind in the buildings now brought to light by excavators.

Today there is a surprising variety of coins available for the student of the New Testament.[4] Roman coinage was introduced into Palestine by Pompey in 63 B.C., but Greek or Hellenistic coinage, which had been in use over the years, persisted. In addition, the Jews themselves minted their own coins, so that the coin picture is a complex one. In the New Testament we have references to coins that were originally Greek and to others that were Roman. The English translation is not always helpful and the same word is used at times for different coins. Some attempt to preserve the Greek or Roman names seems to be warranted.

There are five pieces of money of Greek origin referred to in the Gospels. Two of these, the "talent" and the "pound" or *mina*, were really weights of silver, although golden "talents" and *minas* were known in the world of that

4. Good reviews are obtainable in F. A. Banks, *Coins of Bible Days* (New York, 1955); A. Kindler, *Antiquity and Survival* (Jerusalem, 1957), Vol. II, pp. 225f.

time. The talent is referred to in Matthew 18:24. The "pound" or *mina*, a silver weight, is mentioned in Luke 19:13f. Both of these were weights and no coins. The other three pieces were definite coins. One, called the "silver piece" in the New Testament, was really the silver *drachma* (Luke 15:8, 9). Another was the *didrachma*, which is the "tribute money" referred to in Matthew 17:24. It was a silver coin. The "piece of money" or *stater*, referred to in Matthew 17:27, was a silver coin known as the *tetradrachm*. Attempts to give an equivalent in the money of today are doomed to failure because of the frequent changes in the value of money.

In addition to these coins there were others of Roman notation, the "penny" or *denarius*, a silver coin (Matt. 18:28; 20:2, 9, 10, 13; etc.), the "farthing" or *quadrans*, a bronze coin (Matt. 5:26), and another coin called a "farthing" in the English version of the New Testament but known to the Romans as the *as* or *assarion* (Matt. 10:29; Luke 12:6). Finally there was the tiny bronze coin, the "mite" or *lepton* (Mark 12:42), worth a very tiny amount indeed, only a fraction of a cent in modern currency.

The Romans reserved the right to mint silver coinage but allowed the local mints to make bronze coins. In the excavations we find coins of both types but naturally far more bronze coins than silver ones. There were Roman bronze coins too, but the great majority of the bronze coins found are local.

Strictly, the Roman silver coins constituted Judaea's principal monetary standard, and among these the silver denarius, coined in Rome, was the best known. It was the silver denarius of Tiberius Caesar that Jesus held in His hand on the day when the Herodians sought to trap Him (Matt. 22:19–21). This coin carried the head and superscription of the emperor, which read "TI. CAESAR DIVI AVG. F. AVGVSTVS" on the side where the head of the emperor was impressed, and on the other side "PONTIF. MAXIM." In translation this means "Tiberius Caesar, Augustus, Son of Divine Augustus," and "Pontifex Maximus." The Jews were never happy about the emperor worship that the Romans practiced and stubbornly resisted the growing cult of the emperor. For official purposes the Jews were forced, of necessity, to use the coins of Augustus as well as those of Tiberius, his stepson, who was identified as "son of the deified Augustus." So the coin that the Herodians handed to Jesus was full of meaning for them and for Him. "Whose is this image and superscription?" He asked. They replied, "Caesar's." To this He replied, "Render therefore unto Caesar the things which are Caesar's; and unto God the things that are God's," by which He indicated that what was stamped with man's image belonged to man, especially if man made a special claim to it as did Tiberius. This did not, however, prevent men from giving to God the things that were His.

One of the Roman bronze coins was the *dupondius*, which pictured Livia, the wife of Augustus, who was reputed to be a woman of great beauty. She divorced her first husband in order to marry Augustus. She had two sons by her first marriage, one of whom was to become the next emperor. There was some-

The "penny" brought to Christ by the chief priests and scribes was probably the silver denarius of Tiberius, emperor A.D. 14-37. The enlarged obverse shows the image and superscription of Tiberius; on the reverse is his mother, Livia, as Pax (Peace), seated and holding a scepter and branch. (British Museum)

thing uncanny about the way "fate" disposed of the relatives of Augustus in order to make the succession of Tiberius possible, and many suspected the beautiful Livia without being able to prove anything. We have the picture of this notorious woman today, as well as that of her illustrious husband, on the coins of the time. The handsome head of Augustus reminds us of the Caesar in whose reign "there went out a decree that all the world should be taxed" (Luke 2:1). It was this decree that brought Joseph and Mary to Bethlehem where Jesus was to be born.[5]

The locally minted coins that interest us may be divided into three groups: (a) those of Herod and his descendants, (b) those of the procurators, and (c) those from the free cities that evidently held a charter to mint coins.

The coins of Herod the Great were still in use at the beginning of our period. He was the first of the Jewish rulers to drop Hebrew from the inscriptions on the coins and to use Greek. In general, he did not provoke the Jews by using symbols on his coins that would offend them by defying the second commandment, and he confined himself to such symbols as the pomegranate and leaves, the tiara and palm leaves, and the tripod and palm leaves, although on one of his small coins he did make use of an eagle. The normal inscription on the face (obverse) of the coin was "King Herod." His sons Herod Archelaus (4 B.C. to A.D. 6) and Herod Antipas (4 B.C. to A.D. 39) followed the example of their father and used neutral symbols, but Herod Philip (4 B.C. to A.D. 34) minted coins that were completely pagan in character and carried on them the image of the emperor on one side, and such symbols as a temple on the other. His domains were, of course, predominantly Greek, and this would account for his use of pagan symbols.

With the accession of Agrippa I to the throne in A.D. 37 the people of Judaea, after some thirty years of rule by procurators, returned to a king of their own race. He used non-Jewish symbols on the coins, apparently without any

Bronze coin of Herod the Great, king of Judaea at the time of Christ's birth. The obverse shows a tripod with a bowl; the Greek inscription (transliterated) is Basileos Erodou *("King Herod"). The reverse shows an incense burner between two palm branches. (British Museum)*

Coin of Herod Philip the Tetrarch (4 B.C.–A.D. 34) showing the head of Augustus (obverse) and the temple built by Herod to honor Augustus (reverse). (British Museum)

embarrassment, and quite freely represented the head of the emperor on the obverse, and on the reverse (the secondary side of the coin) such items as the Greek city goddess, pagan temples, the king and his chariot, a man with a scroll, the king's son and his horse, and the king offering sacrifice. One of his coins carried the words "King Agrippa the Great, Lover of Caesar" on one side, and on the other, the city goddess holding a cornucopia and leaning on the rudder of a boat. The inscription on the reverse was "Caesarea on the Sea." Such coins as these must have caused offense to pious Jews. For us their great value lies in the fact that they preserve the picture of Agrippa. In defense of his practice, it should be said that his coins were probably intended for the use of the pagan population in his domains, for he did issue other coins with neutral symbols such as the umbrella and ears of barley, meant to emphasize the dignity of the kingdom and the prosperity of his domains.

Herod Agrippa II (A.D. 50 to about A.D. 100) issued many coins during his long reign of which there are very many in existence today. On some of his early coins he left his portrait as a young man, but on others he placed the bust of a goddess. One of his coins was a victory coin, issued after the victory of Rome over the Jews in A.D. 70, and shows Agrippa as a vassal king subordinate to the Romans. It had a humiliating intention, no doubt, and was probably issued under instruction from the Romans.

The coins of the procurators from A.D. 6 onward in Judaea are well represented. In general these men did not offend the Jews and confined themselves to neutral symbols such as the ear of barley, the palm tree, the olive branch and cornucopia, the grape leaf and tendril, and so on. Only the fifth procurator, Pontius Pilate, offended the Jews with pagan symbols on the coins. All these procurators' coins were really imperial coins although they were struck locally, and inscriptions on them referred to the emperor or to his family. No reference to the procurator is made on the coins, and they can be assigned to the year of a

Bronze coin (A.D. 29/30) of Pontius Pilate, procurator of Judaea at the time of the crucifixion. The obverse shows three ears of grain, the central one upright and the others drooping. The reverse shows a vessel resembling a simpulum, a ladle used in rituals to pour wine into a cup. (British Museum)

given procurator only on the basis of dating material that refers to the emperors. Some of the best known of these coins come from the days of Coponius (A.D. 6–9), Valerius (A.D. 15–26), Pilate (A.D. 26–36), and Felix (A.D. 52–59). Typical of the dating material to be found on the face of these coins is that on a coin of Pilate, a tiny *lepton* in fact, which reads "Tiberius Caesar" on the obverse and carries the symbol of an augur's wand, and on the reverse has a wreath surrounding the date LIZ, which indicates Year 17 of this emperor, that is, A.D. 30–31.[6] The symbol used in this case was one of those which were offensive to the Jews because augury was forbidden among them (Deut. 18:10f.).

We need not enter into details about the coins from the independent cities. These have been found from a wide variety of places such as Askelon, Antioch, Tyre, Damascus, Sidon, Byblos, Gadara, Seleucia, Berytus (Beirut), Gaza, Cyprus, and Caesarea.

The tiny coin, the *lepton,* is of special interest to the Bible reader. It was first minted, it seems, in the days of the Maccabees and was worth about one four-hundredth part of a shekel. Since it was so tiny and worth so little, great care was not taken in stamping it out, and the pattern is quite often incomplete, although there are enough of these coins known to be able to arrive at the typical patterns on them. Some even had an inscription. These tiny coins are known for the reign of Herod the Great, Herod Archelaus, Procurator Valerius, and Procurator Pilate. They must have been made in very great numbers, for even today they are to be found in great quantity in excavations. It was two of these coins that the widow threw into the box in the story in Mark 12:41–44, for which she earned the praise of the Lord Jesus. The same coin featured also in His remarks to the hypocrites when He made reference to the hard judge who would exact the "very last mite" in his judgment (Luke 12:58f.).

We have referred to the unfortunate translations of the Greek words for coins in the New Testament. Some writers have urged that we ought to translate these terms by English words that bear a close resemblance to the Greek, or even by transliterations. Thus for "penny" we might use *denarius,* for "piece of silver" the correct word, either *stater* or *drachma,* and for "farthing" either *assarion* or *quadrans.* At times, however, there is not much help even in the Greek form of the word, as, for example, in the narrative where we learn of the bribe paid to

6. L = year (Egyptian); I = 10 in Greek notation; Z = 7 in Greek notation.

Silver coin of the first Jewish revolt (A.D. 66–70). The obverse shows a cup and is inscribed "Year 1" and "Shekel of Israel." The reverse shows a three-budded pomegranate branch and is inscribed "Jerusalem [the] Holy." (British Museum)

the Roman soldiers to keep them quiet after the resurrection. This was to be "large money" (Matt. 28:12). Does this mean large in amount, or large in size of the coins? If the latter, then perhaps we should think in terms of one of the big silver coins such as the *tetradrachm.* [7] The thirty pieces of silver that were taken by Judas were of the same kind (Matt. 27:5). Their total value in modern currency could hardly be more than a few pounds, small reward for treachery so base and so far-reaching.

The special coins which the Jews struck at the time of their two revolts in A.D. 66–70 and A.D. 132–135 are of some interest. Fully persuaded that the days of deliverance or redemption had come, they minted shekels and half-shekels in silver, as well as other coins in bronze, which told of their hopes. The symbols were all neutral and included palm trees, citrons, baskets, bundles of twigs, the vine and grape, a chalice, and so on. Typical of the coins issued at the time of the first revolt was the silver shekel that carried on the obverse a chalice and the words in ancient Hebrew script "Shekel of Israel, I," and on the reverse, "Jerusalem Holy," written around three pomegranates. There was also a bronze coin which bore on its face a bundle of twigs between two citrons and the words "Year 4," while on the back was a chalice and the words "For the Redemption of Zion." Five years can be distinguished on these coins, which would be the years A.D. 66 to 70. The coins discovered at Qumran[8] and at Masada[9] are of particular importance for the story of the first Jewish revolt. The coin record at Qumran continues till the third year of the revolt. Thereafter Roman coins tell their story. At Masada one of the rooms in the surrounding wall produced seventeen silver shekels strewn over a small area of the floor in one corner of the room. They were in good condition and carried the words *Shekel Israel* and *Jerusalem the Holy.* Hebrew letters on them date them to year one, year two, year three, year four, and year five. Until this discovery there were only six "year five" coins in existence, but three of these rare coins were found here in a systematic archaeological excavation and in a stratum that may be dated accurately to the time of the first Jewish revolt. Year five was, of course, the year in which Jerusalem fell. Masada held on till A.D. 73, although no more coins were

---

7. F. A. Banks, *op. cit.*, pp. 89f.
8. See pp. 270f., 336.
9. See p. 331.

minted after A.D. 70. When the Jews were finally defeated, the Romans commemorated their victory by a special series of coins which we now call the *Judaea Capta* coins. They were struck in Rome, as the letters "S.C." ("with the consent of the Senate") indicate, and show the head of Emperor Vespasian surrounded by his titles on the obverse, and on the reverse a woman, representing Judaea, sitting under a palm tree with a Roman soldier on guard over her. The caption reads *Judaea Capta*. It was a humiliating experience and resulted in the placing of a heavy tax on the Jews for some years. When eventually this was eased in the days of Emperor Nerva (A.D. 96–98), another bronze coin was struck by the Romans.

The second Jewish revolt of A.D. 132–135 produced a second lot of coins rather like those of the first revolt. In the early days of the revolt the leader, Ben Kosebah (Bar Kochba), took Roman coins and over-stamped them with his own markings. Later on he issued what has been described as the "finest set of coins ever issued by any Jewish authority."[10] Among these we may refer to the silver *tetradrachm*, with a star above the Temple and the name "Simon" on the face, and a citron and bundle of twigs, with the words "For the Liberty of Jerusalem" on the back. The silver *denarius* had a wreath and "Simon" on the front, and a jug and palm with the words "Year 2 of the Liberty of Israel" on the back. Simon is described as "Prince of Israel" on some of the coins. Another name on these coins is "Eleazar the Priest." Romans commemorated the quelling of the revolt in A.D. 135 with the issue of a special coin depicting the emperor with a pair of oxen plowing the boundaries of a new town. That town was Jerusalem, renamed Colonia Aelia Capitolina, and thenceforth a pagan Roman colony.

It is evident from this brief study of the coins of these years that there is much to be learned from them about the history of the times. But they have a most important part to play also in the dating of the remains found by the excavator; and since they are found by the hundreds, and even thousands, in Palestine, it is obvious that their discovery in an excavation is hailed with enthusiasm by the archaeologist. There are certain limitations in their value for dating, for they often continued in use for many years after the death of a king. Again, some coins were struck in considerable numbers and would have a better

10. A. Kindler, "Coins as Documents for Israel's Ancient History," *Antiquity and Survival*, Vol. II (1957), p. 235.

Silver tetradrachm of Bar Kochba, the leader of the second Jewish revolt (A.D. 132–135). On the obverse are a four-columned temple containing law scrolls and the inscription "Simeon"; on the reverse are a palm branch and citrus and the inscription "Deliverance of Jerusalem."

chance of survival than those which had a limited minting. However, where supplementary evidence is available, they are useful for dating. One or two illustrations of their value in dating ancient remains will now be given.

When the large building in Roman Jericho was excavated in 1951, the question of date naturally arose.[11] Coins found in the debris provided helpful clues and enabled the archaeologists to give a range of years during which the site was in use. The report reads as follows:

> The earliest coins found were those of Herod I of which there were eleven. Twenty-seven bore the stamp of Archelaus; six were Herod Agrippa coins; and five were identified tentatively as belonging to one or another of the Procurators. Two of the Archelaus coins were found directly on major walls of the building. The presence of these forty-nine coins, dating from the century covering the last third of the first century B.C. and the first two-thirds of the second century A.D., with the largest number from the time of Archelaus at the midpoint of this span, would seem to point to a major occupation at the time of Christ and perhaps to the construction of the building within this period.[12]

Coins also give the clue to the period of occupation of the Qumran monastery once occupied by the exclusive Jewish sect that awaited the coming of the Messiah. The coin record starts with John Hyrcanus (135–104 B.C.), and continues without a break till Antigonus (40–37 B.C.). There is only one coin from the days of Herod the Great, but the coin story starts again with Archelaus in 4 B.C., and from then on there is a continuous series of coins till about A.D. 68, including six from Archelaus, three from the procurators under Augustus (A.D. 6–14), seven from the procurators under Tiberius (A.D. 14–37), a coin from Tyre dated A.D. 29, twenty-three from Agrippa I (A.D. 37–44), five from the procurators under Nero (A.D. 54–68), and eleven struck by the Jews during the first two years of the war.[13] The record ends in A.D. 68, although there were a few coins which represent the occupation of the site by a Roman garrison from A.D. 70 onward, say from the end of Nero's reign (A.D. 68) to the reign of Titus (A.D. 79–81). A single coin of Agrippa II found outside the building is not very significant, as it might have been dropped there after the destruction of the building. After a gap there are a few coins from the time of the second Jewish revolt.

From this collection we conclude that the monastery at Qumran was founded sometime before 100 B.C., deserted in the days of Herod the Great, occupied again in the days of Archelaus and then on till the defeat of the Jews in A.D. 70, with a short occupation by a Roman garrison after that, and finally a brief occupation at the time of the second revolt.

    11. See pp. 341ff.
    12. J. B. Pritchard, "The 1951 Campaign at Herodian Jericho," BASOR (Oct., 1951), pp. 14f.
    13. F. F. Bruce, Second Thoughts on the Dead Sea Scrolls (Grand Rapids, 1956), p. 49.

A third illustration comes from Masada, which we have just discussed. The fact that coins from each year of the revolt up to year five were found at Masada suggests that this fortress was in contact with Jerusalem till quite late, that is, till A.D. 70. Masada did not fall till A.D. 73, and the Roman legions were evidently not able to prevent the distribution of such coins. L. Kadman has recently written, "There can be no doubt that the three coins of Masada were found on the spot where they had dropped from the hands of the Jewish defenders of the fortress, nearly 1900 years ago."[14]

INSCRIPTIONS AND WRITTEN RECORDS

One of the most important of these is a Greek inscription found by Clermont Ganneau in 1871 and now housed in the Istanbul Museum.[15] It contains seven lines written in Greek capitals and was evidently once placed in the precincts of the Temple to warn Gentiles to keep away from those areas which were reserved for Jews only. One translation of the text reads:

No Gentile may enter inside the enclosing screen around the Temple. Whoever is caught is alone responsible for the death which follows.

The inscription was found some fifty meters from the Temple area, but it is agreed that it is ancient and must have come from the Temple. It is of special interest in the light of the statement in Acts 21:28 where Paul was accused by the Jews of bringing Greeks into the "holy place":

This is the man that teacheth all men everywhere against the people, and the law, and this place; and further brought Greeks also into the temple, and hath polluted this holy place.

A second fragmentary example of this inscription was found in 1935 in the course of excavations being conducted by the Department of Antiquities of Palestine not far from St. Stephen's Gate, in the midst of debris.[16]

Another inscription of great interest was found by R. Weill in the excavations at the southern end of Ophel in 1913–1914, but not published till 1920. It is part of a synagogue inscription, the oldest yet known in the whole of Palestine and dating from before A.D. 70.[17] The inscription refers to the building of a synagogue by a certain Theodotus. The complete text reads:

Theodotus, son of Vettenus, priest and synagogue-president, son of a synagogue-president and grandson of a synagogue-president, has built

---

14. L. Kadman, "A Coin Find at Masada," *IEJ*, Vol. VII, No. 1, pp. 61f.
15. W. F. Albright, *Recent Discoveries in Bible Lands* (New York, 1955), p. 112. See also A. Parrot, *Le musée du Louvre et la Bible* (Paris, 1957), pp. 142f.
16. A. Parrot, *op. cit.*, p. 144. Also J. H. Iliffe, "The Thanatos Inscription from Herod's Temple," *Quarterly of the Department of Antiquities of Palestine*, Vol. VI (1937), pp. 1-3; and *Museum Catalogue, Palestine Archaeological Museum*, p. 28.
17. W. F. Albright *op. cit.*, pp. 172f.

In this Greek inscription, uncovered in Jerusalem, "Theodotus, son of Vettenus," tells that he built a synagogue and a hostel for travelers. Dated before A.D. 70, the synagogue inscription is the oldest found in Palestine. (Israel Exploration Society)

the synagogue for the reading of the Law and the teaching of the commandments and [he has built] the hostelry and the chambers and the cisterns of water in order to provide lodgings for those from abroad who need them—[the synagogue] which his fathers and the elders and Simonides had founded.[18]

It has been argued that the name Vettenus shows that Theodotus was the son or grandson of a Jewish freedman from Italy who had received his name from the family of the Vetteni (gens Vettena or Vettia), a well-known Roman family. It was a common custom for the freed slave to take the family name of his liberator. The original Jew may have been taken captive to Italy in an earlier day, perhaps in the time of Pompey. Interest in the inscription grows when we read in Acts of a synagogue of the freedmen in the time of Stephen, in whose days "there arose certain of the synagogue which is called the synagogue of the Libertines [Freedmen]" (Acts 6:9).

The men of this synagogue were strongly opposed to Stephen and the new faith, as we learn from the narrative in Acts 6. We may conjecture that the

18. W. F. Albright, *Recent Discoveries in Bible Lands* (New York, 1955), p. 112.

synagogue in question was founded some time early in the first century at the time when Christ lived in Nazareth.

There are a few other inscriptions that date from the first century A.D. which are of no direct interest to the student of the New Testament, although all material of this age from Palestine is of indirect value because it helps build up the total picture. One such inscription scratched in the plaster of a wall at Sebastia (Samaria) reads: "May Martial the learned master and all his friends be remembered by Kore [Persephone]."

The goddess Kore was popular at Samaria in the Roman period and a statue of her, found there some years ago, is on display in the Museum in Jerusalem (Jordan).[19]

Another type of inscription is found on pottery items used in building. A great number of these has been found in Palestine. They are of many kinds—roof tiles, drain pipes, tiles to cover drains, floor tiles, and so on. Some carry the name of the maker of the tile, or the name of the legion or detachment that constructed the building where the object was used. The language on these tiles is regularly Latin. A very common inscription is that of the tenth Roman legion, which was long in Palestine, from the time of Nero till the third century, although other legions feature as well. The complete text on the tiles of the tenth legion reads, *Legio Decima Fretensis*. The adjective *Fretensis* was attached to the tenth legion in memory of some great event in its history, possibly its participation in a battle near the straits between Italy and Sicily in 36 B.C. in the army of Octavian. The word *fretensis* is the genitive of the Latin *fretum*, meaning "sea." It is known that the tenth legion took part in this battle. Quite regularly the tiles bear the words "LEG.X.FRE" or "LEG.X.F." Because this legion made up the garrison of Aelia Capitolina when the pagan colony was founded at Jerusalem by Hadrian after the second Jewish revolt, many of the excavations in Jerusalem have yielded tiles of the tenth legion. One inscription tells a story that must have been repeated many times over. It speaks of a soldier of the tenth legion who died on garrison duty in Palestine. The inscription, which is to be seen today in the Museum in Jerusalem (Jordan), reads: "D M L MAGNIUS FELIX, MIL LEG X FRET, B TRIB MIL ANN XVIII VIX XXXIX." The translation is: "Sacred to the memory of L. Magnius Felix, a soldier of the tenth legion, the Fretensis, who was an orderly to the tribune, served eighteen years, and died aged thirty-nine."[20]

Numerous other Roman inscriptions are scattered up and down Palestine. Typical of these are the inscriptions associated with the high-level aqueduct at Caesarea. A number of these have been left by the Roman legions who undertook public works at Caesarea.[21] The tenth legion participated in work on the

19. *Palestine Archaeological Museum Gallery Book*, pp. 55f.
20. A. C. Bouquet, *Everyday Life in New Testament Times* (London, 1953), p. 26.
21. A. Negev, "The High Level Aqueduct at Caesarea," *IEJ*, Vol. XIV, No. 4 (1964), pp. 237-249.

aqueduct as the following inscription shows: IMP CAESAR TRAIANUS HADRIANUS AUG FECIT PER VEXILLATIONE LEG X FRTEN, that is, "Emperor Trajan Hadrian Augustus had (the aqueduct) constructed by a detachment of the Tenth Legion Fretersis."[22] Other legions like the sixth and the second were also involved in building at Caesarea and left inscriptions. Finally, reference should be made to the numerous Roman milestones left in Palestine by the Roman road makers which often carry Latin inscriptions. Some of these are found in Transjordan on the road leading south from the area of modern Amman to the Gulf of Aqaba.

Further discussion of Roman inscriptions lies outside the scope of this book. But they bear eloquent testimony to the presence of the Romans in Palestine both before and after New Testament times.

We have already referred to the remarkable finds of manuscripts in the caves of the Dead Sea area. Some of these come from the later period of the Qumran sect and so fit into our period. There are others which have been found in caves further south which have no connection with the Qumran settlers. Among these were the two letters of Ben Kosebah already mentioned. We shall reserve a fuller discussion of material like this to a chapter on manuscripts.

TOMBS

Tombs and graves of Roman times have provided some most important material concerning the origins of Christianity. As a general rule in the ancient world, once a grave was sealed up, the likelihood was that it would remain intact through the centuries and objects placed in it would be preserved whole, though there was always the chance of tomb robbers breaking in. In an open city small objects of pottery or glass were likely to be broken as a result of war or earthquake or fire. The grave or the tomb, then, where objects were not normally disturbed, is of particular interest to the excavator. Here he will usually find pottery pieces, glass and metal objects, coins, inscriptions, and graffiti (writing that is scratched on a surface but not cut deeply), and in the case of large tombs, certain architectural features. These larger tombs provided for the burial of a number of people. They were entered by a comparatively small opening which could be closed by rolling a stone in a groove across the entrance. After each burial the large stone was rolled across the door and the tomb sealed up until the next burial. Some of these stones, which are still to be seen in parts of Palestine, were so big as to require the effort of more than one man to move them. Such a discovery explains the concern of the women who came to the sepulcher where our Lord was buried. Joseph of Arimathaea "rolled a great stone to the door of the sepulchre" (Matt. 27:60), and later the angel came and "rolled back the stone from the door" (Matt. 28:2). Other passages in the Gospels which refer to the

---

22. This inscription is on display in the Israel Museum in Jerusalem.

A typical Palestinian tomb with a circular stone door. (École Biblique, Jerusalem; R. deVaux, O.P., Director)

rolling of the great stone from the door are Mark 15:46; 16:3f.; Luke 24:2; John 11:38, 39, 41; 20:1. Even comparatively small tombs had this rolling stone, but single graves were normally carved out in the rocky hillside and the body interred there.

Inside the larger tombs there were many rooms with shelves on which rested small ossuaries (stone caskets containing the bones of the departed). These ossuaries were normally made of limestone and were beautifully decorated. Quite often they carried a brief inscription naming the departed person. The practice was to collect the bones of the dead person after the flesh had decayed and place these in the ossuary in the family tomb. In this way several generations could be accommodated. Today there are some hundreds of these ossuaries known, and inscriptions in Aramaic and Greek have added a good deal to our knowledge of names and of family and social organization. Thus the typical names of Palestine in the first century A.D. are now well known. Such a name as "Jesus [Jeshua], son of Joseph," is actually known from one of these ossuaries. Other common names are Simon, Judas, Ananias, Lazarus, and among the names of the women are Martha, Elizabeth, Salome, Johanna, Sapphira, Maryam (Mary), and Apphia. It is of real significance to the New Testament scholar to discover that the names of the New Testament are the common names of the day. Even such a

Aramaic epitaph of King Uzziah of Judah, inscribed in square Hebrew letters on a marble plaque. The combined evidence of the Bible and Josephus indicates that Uzziah was originally buried outside the city because he was a leper but that his bones were transferred during the Second Temple period, the date of this inscription. (Israel Museum, Jerusalem; photo by David Harris)

title as "Teacher" or "Rabbi" occurs on these ossuaries, for a certain Theodotion is referred to as *didaskalos,* the common name for "teacher" in the Gospels.

One of the most fascinating inscriptions investigated in recent times was evidently associated with a burial, although it had become dissociated from its grave. It read, "Hither were brought the bones of Uzziah, king of Judah—do not open." Supposedly the original tomb contained the bones of this great king, and this inscription was prepared when the tomb was discovered in the first century A.D. Whether this was so or not we cannot now say, but the inscription was in Aramaic of the time of Christ and was neatly inscribed on a slab of stone.[23]

Some of the large tombs in the Kidron valley must be dated to the first

23. W. F. Albright, *Archaeology of Palestine,* pp. 159f.

century A.D. even though the names that are now attached to them refer to such famous men as Absalom and Jehoshaphat. Other rock-cut tombs are to be found in many places around Jerusalem. One in the Hinnom valley shows early Roman influence in architecture, and is dated to the period before A.D. 70. The impressive Tombs of the Kings, first cleared in 1850 and 1863 by de Saulcy, represent the tomb of Queen Helena of Abilene and her house. She was converted to Judaism in A.D. 48 and migrated to Jerusalem some twenty years before the Jewish revolt. The sarcophagus of the queen and an inscription in Hebrew and Syriac are to be seen in the Louvre in Paris today.[24] This particular tomb was of the catacomb type and contained several rooms underground. It is entered by a small opening which can be closed by rolling a large circular stone, set in a groove, across it.

While there are many Jewish tombs in the ancient cemeteries around Jerusalem, it has been pointed out that after the first Jewish revolt in A.D. 66–70 things were not at all easy for the Jews in the Jerusalem area, and after the second revolt in A.D. 132–135 the Jews were forbidden even to come into the area of the Holy City. Hence it is likely that most of the tombs and ossuaries in the area preceded the fall and destruction of the city and the Temple in A.D. 70.

There is always the chance that archaeologists may find the graves of some of the early Christians in the cemeteries around Jerusalem. As early as 1873 the French scholar Clermont Ganneau reported the discovery of a burial chamber on the Mount of Olives containing some thirty ossuaries, on one of which was the name Judah, and a cross with arms of equal length. The name Jesus occurred also, in association with a cross. At the time of the discovery these were taken as being Christian ossuaries of the second century or later, for it was held that Christian Jews would have come under the general ban in the Jerusalem area after A.D. 135, and in any case it was held that the sign of the cross was late. In 1945 the late Professor E. L. Sukenik learned of a tomb that had been discovered in the Jerusalem suburb of Talpioth.[25] The tomb was carefully excavated by the Museum of Jewish Antiquities and was discovered to be a room some eleven feet square with a courtyard in front. The ossuaries had been placed as usual, in narrow tunnels running off from the main room. Some of them were removed by the workmen who found the room, and eleven others were removed by the archaeologists. Pottery pieces such as lamps, the character of the lettering on the ossuary inscriptions, and a coin of Agrippa I dated A.D. 42–43 found in the tomb, all combine to give a date not later than the middle of the first century A.D. for the final use of the tomb. Of considerable interest to us is the fact that five of the ossuaries carry inscriptions, three in Aramaic, belonging to Simeon

24. A. Parrot, op. cit., pp. 139f.
25. E. L. Sukenik, "The Earliest Christian Records," AJA (Oct.–Dec., 1947). See also A. Parrot, Golgotha and the Church of the Holy Sepulchre (Eng. trans., London, 1957), pp. 113–116.

Barsaba, Miriam daughter of Simeon, and Mat' (an abbreviation for Mattathias), and two Greek inscriptions which are harder to interpret, although
there is no doubt that the name of Jesus appears on each, followed in one case by
the word *Iou* and in the other case by the word *Aloth*. One of these was written
in charcoal and the other cut into the limestone with a sharp instrument. The
two words *Iou* and *Aloth*, according to Sukenik, are typical of exclamations
found in other Greek funerary inscriptions and express the idea of misfortune or
lamentation. *Iesou Iou* means literally, "Jesus woe," and *Iesou Aloth*, "Jesus
Aloth" (probably another word for lamentation).

Yet another recent discussion[26] of these words offers the suggestion that
"woe" is to be interpreted as a cry to the risen Christ—"Jesus, help!" The word
Aloth is regarded as derived from the Hebrew root "to rise," and is translated,
"Jesus, let [him who rests here] arise." If this interpretation is correct, we have
here two prayers addressed to Jesus Christ as the living, risen Lord—a remarkable testimony to the early Church's faith in Jesus as the risen Lord. In addition
to these words there were crosses on the second of the caskets, drawn in charcoal, in the center of each side. The fact that there were two of these side by side
in the same tomb, each with the name Jesus, led Sukenik to suggest that here we
have Christian burials in which the name of Jesus is invoked in the hour of grief.
The crosses he regards as quite deliberate "pictorial expression of the crucifixion
tantamount to exclaiming, 'He was crucified.' "

Sukenik even made bold to suggest from the names inscribed on the other
ossuaries, namely Simeon Barsabas and Miriam daughter of Simeon, that we may
have discovered the burial tomb of a Christian family, and he speculated as to
whether it might be the same as the one referred to in Acts 1:23 where "Joseph
called Barsabas" was one of the possible candidates of the apostolic band. Again,
a certain "Judas named Barsabas" was one of the disciples sent to Antioch with
Paul and Barnabas after the great Council of Jerusalem (Acts 15:22). There may
be something of speculation in this last suggestion, but it indicates the sort of
material that is available for the study of Christian origins. And it could be that
Sukenik is correct in his speculations!

However, an alternative explanation rejects Sukenik's view and sees in the
words *Aloth* and *Iou* proper names. *Aloth* is a complete name and *Iou* is taken to
mean either Jehu or an abbreviated form of Judas (Ioudas). The readings of the
two inscriptions would then be: *Jesus, son of Judas*, and *Jesus Aloth*, or *Jesus, son
of Aloth*. These inscriptions, like the others in the same tomb, merely identify
the dead as in other ossuary inscriptions. Hence, there is nothing among the
finds in the Talpioth tombs that can be related to the early Christians of
Jerusalem.[27]

26. B. Gustafsson, "The Oldest Graffiti in the History of the Church?", *New Testament
Studies*, Vol. III, pp. 65-69.
27. John P. Kane, "By No Means 'The Earliest Records of Christianity'—with an Emended
Reading of the Talpioth Inscription IESOUS IOU," *PEQ* (July–Dec., 1971), pp. 103-108.

Another fascinating group of fifteen ossuaries was found in 1968 in three burial caves at Giv'at ha-Mivtar, Jerusalem. Thirteen were filled to the brim with human bones and two only partly. It is calculated that some thirty-five skeletons were housed in these ossuaries. Evidence of death by violence was found in five cases—two by burning, one by arrow wound, one by a blow by a mace, and one by crucifixion. The latter example is of considerable interest. Crucifixion was common both before and after Jesus' time, and many thousands of both Jews and Gentiles suffered this death. But here is a specific case. The man was in his middle twenties. His name, according to the inscription on the ossuary, was Yohanan ben Hezq'el. He was crucified with the aid of three nails, one driven through each wrist and a third driven through both heels together. This latter nail was still in its original position as it had bent when it had hit a knot in the olive wood cross. The nail was seventeen to eighteen centimeters long, that is, about seven inches. The man must have been placed with a small wooden support for his buttocks, his knees drawn up and one knee overlapping the other so as to place one foot over the other and enable the one nail to be driven through the two feet at once. In addition both the shin bones had been smashed by a severe blow. The whole discovery suggests an agonizing death.[28] The procedure is reminiscent of that described in John's Gospel (19:31-34).

POTTERY, GLASSWARE, AND METAL OBJECTS

We turn now to a brief discussion of the typical pottery, glassware, and metal objects for the years under discussion. The New Testament refers to quite a variety of household vessels, among which we might mention waterpots at Cana (John 2:6), pots and cups to be washed before eating (Mark 7:8), oil vessels and lamps (Matt. 25:4), a vessel for vinegar (John 19:29), platters (Matt. 23:25; Luke 11:39), and so on. Excavations have turned up a great variety of pottery in Palestine, some intact, but a large amount broken in pieces (sherds). A visit to the Palestine Archaeological Museum (in Jordan)[29] or to the Museum in Jerusalem (Israel) will convince the student that there is an abundance of material for study. The ordinary domestic pottery, such as cooking pots, lamps, oil bottles, jugs, juglets, cups, bowls, beakers, dishes, indeed the whole range of household pottery, can be seen and studied quite readily. A great deal of this comes from the tombs of the period and is therefore quite unbroken.

Of special interest is a type of red glazed ware very widely used all over the Roman world, the so-called *terra sigillata* (literally, "ornamented earth"). This is not the best name for it, for the name infers that the pottery bears a pattern stamped into it. While this is often so, it is not always so, for much of the pottery

28. N. Haas, "Anthropological Observations on the Skeletal Remains from Giv'at ha-Mivtar," *IEJ*, Vol. XX, Nos. 1-2 (1970), pp. 49-59 and Plates 22-24.
29. *Palestine Archaeological Museum Gallery Book*, Persian, Hellenistic, Roman, and Byzantine periods (Jerusalem, 1943), pp. 28-71.

is plain, particularly in Palestine. In general this pottery was the "best china" of the Roman world at the time it was in use. It derived originally from Hellenistic pottery and was made in Asia Minor at Pergamum and Samos (hence it is often called Samian ware), as well as in many centers throughout the empire. Some of the potters in Italy exported the ware all over the Roman world, as can be seen from the trademarks and potters' names stamped into the interior of the vessels. The same maker's marks are to be found in places as far apart as Britain and Transjordan. The shapes, the decoration, and the potters are so well dated that it is possible to use this material for a rough dating of a building or a tomb. Among the stamped ware found in Palestine there are pieces from Gaul, from Arretium and Puteoli in Italy, and from kilns in the East.

Some of the most interesting pottery from the Roman period was discovered in first-century houses on the Western Hill in Jerusalem. One group of plates, bowls, and jugs is quite impressive in its fine forms and deep red slip. One of the jugs was shaped like vessels made of metal and was a fine example of its type. Such pottery was luxury ware, and was not found in every household.[30] Actually there is some suggestion that this pottery was locally made and should be called eastern *terra sigillata* ware. It was present in the Jewish Quarter houses which date to the first century B.C., although it seems to be lacking in the buildings destroyed in A.D. 70.[31] The greatest concentration of *terra sigillata* ware so far discovered occurred in the Hellenistic stratum of Tell Anafa in Upper Galilee.

The typical Roman lamps of the day occur in great numbers and show a gradual change in type as the years advance. Experts in the story of the lamp can give a good estimate of the age of a lamp from its shape.[32] Patterns such as animals, human forms, fruit, leaves, geometrical designs, and the like were quite regularly worked into the lamps. In the years after the birth of the Christian Church specifically Christian motifs were commonly molded into the lamp. Among these were the fish, the lamb, the vine and grapes, the cross, and the loaf of bread.

When we come to interpret some of the New Testament references to lamps, we are sometimes at a loss to know what is meant by the Greek word. It is obvious that if we are ever to know what was intended, we shall have to call in the aid of the archaeologist. The Greek word *lampas* is used for "lamp" in Matthew 25:1-8, Acts 20:8, and Revelation 4:5 and 8:10, and the word *luchnos*, translated "light," is used in Matthew 6:22, Luke 11:34, 12:35, John 5:35, II Peter 1:19, and Revelation 21:23. Some of these may be torches, and others the small terra-cotta lamps so common in the excavations. We await more information on the subject but meanwhile feel that we have in the material from the tombs of Palestine the kind of evidence that will provide the answer.

---

30. N. Avigad, *Archaeological Discoveries in the Jewish Quarter of Jerusalem, Second Temple Period* (Jerusalem, 1976), p. 21 and Plates 4, 27.
31. *Ibid.*
32. F. W. Robins, *The Story of the Lamp* (London, 1939); H. Menzel, *Antike Lampen*.

Roman glassware is well represented in Palestine.[33] Much of it today has a beautiful multicolored sheen, but this is due to chemical changes that have taken place through the centuries. Glass manufacture came late to Italy from the East, but it then received a certain uniformity of treatment and shape which became known all over the empire. However, each area produced its own glass and developed characteristics of its own. Excavations in the Jewish Quarter of Jerusalem brought to light a remarkable collection of glass.[34] Below the paved street which covered the Herodian House[35] a complex of reservoirs and baths was brought to light. One of the reservoirs had been filled with many fragments of broken glass. Among them were hundreds of fragments of hemispherical and conical bowls made in molds. Others were blown glass. It would seem that this area was a dump for some local factory. The presence of molded glass and blown glass at the one place may point to a transitional phase in the technique of making glass vessels. The discovery of almost one hundred coins of Alexander Jannaeus (103-76 B.C.) points to the fact that glass blowing was known in the land about the middle of the first century B.C. Glass production continued into the Roman period.

Various pieces of bronze ware have also been discovered, such as lamps, jars, bowls, cosmetic boxes, cooking pots, buckets, tools of various kinds such as knives, forks, and shovels, ornaments such as pins and brooches, and other items for household use and grooming. It is outside the range of this book to give further detail, but it is now possible for the student of the times of Christ to publish a book in which considerable detail is collected about the ordinary items of everyday life.[36]

ROMAN BUILDING REMAINS

When the American Schools of Oriental Research began to excavate among the ruins of Roman Jericho in 1950, they soon discovered evidence of the Roman influence in architecture. The upper layers of the debris that covered what was once a Hellenistic tower, and also the remarkable facade to what may have been a palace in its day, gave evidence of Roman influence. A particular type of construction, made by setting small square stones into plaster so as to give the appearance of a net (called technically *opus reticulatum*), was found in several places.

Subsequent work has shown a large palace from Herodian times with many indications of the influence of Roman building methods. The local method of building with mud bricks on top of foundations of rubble stone was integrated

33. *Palestine Archaeological Museum Gallery Book*, pp. 47-53. P. P. Kahane, "Some Aspects of Ancient Glass from Israel," *Antiquity and Survival* (1957), pp. 208f.
34. N. Avigad, *op. cit.*, p. 23.
35. See above, p. 296.
36. A. C. Bouquet, *op. cit.*; see also G. E. Wright, *Biblical Archaeology* (London, 1957), pp. 239-244.

with the Roman technique of cement covered with *opus quadratum* and *opus reticulatum*. These were peculiar Roman styles of setting small square stones into plaster so as to give the appearance of a net, a type of construction found in excavations in Italy in such places as Rome, Pompeii, Tivoli, Palestrina, etc. The first excavator of Roman Jericho wrote in his report as follows:

> Indeed one might say that here in New Testament Jericho is a section of Rome that has been miraculously transferred on a magic carpet from the banks of the Tiber to the banks of the Wadi Qelt.... If this masonry were in Italy, it would not be later than the reign of Tiberius, as there is no brick of any kind used.[37]

The large building unearthed in 1951 whose overall size was 88 meters long and 47 meters deep[38] was called "gymnasium" by the excavators. It was built by Herod as a winter palace during the first years of his reign. There were other evidences of Roman influence in the shape of Roman baths, in particular the clear remains of a hot room (caldarium) with several of the small pillars which once supported the floor of the room. Heat circulated under the floor and around the walls, and water dashed on the floor produced a sort of steam bath.[39]

Coins suggest that this building was in use in the days of Herod the Great, Archelaus, and Agrippa, which brings it into the time of Christ. It is quite possible that our Lord knew this very building. No doubt it was known to Zacchaeus the tax-gatherer (Luke 19). It is evident that the builders of Herod and his successors here were influenced, at least in part, by the Romans.

Other sites where traces of buildings of the first century are to be found include all those where there are still good Herodian remains, such as Caesarea,[40] Herodium,[41] Masada,[42] Hebron,[43] and Samaria.[44] But there is a comparative dearth of Roman remains from the first century A.D. apart from the Herodian structures. A closer study of the various excavation reports will provide material.

Of a less spectacular nature are the remains of the Roman encampments and siege walls, and these are to be found in various places, some of the best of which are at the foot of Masada[45] and at Bittir,[46] the scene of the last stand by Ben Kosebah in A.D. 135.

37. J. L. Kelso, "The First Campaign of Excavation in New Testament Jericho," *BASOR* (Dec., 1950), p. 19.

38. J. B. Pritchard, "The 1951 Campaign of Herodian Jericho," *BASOR* (Oct., 1951), p. 10. See also *AASOR*, Vols. XXXII and XXXIII.

39. J. B. Pritchard, *The Excavation at Herodian Jericho, 1951* (New Haven, 1958), pp. 10–12, Plates 7–9. Cf. Y. Yadin, *Masada, Herod's Fortress and the Zealots' Last Stand* (London, 1966), pp. 75–85.

40. See above, pp. 302–304.

41. See pp. 299f.

42. See p. 304.

43. See pp. 300–302.

44. See pp. 300ff.

45. Y. Yadin, *op. cit.*

46. W. F. Albright, *Archaeology of Palestine*, p. 166.

The later period of Roman rule in Palestine provides much more material for our study. These ruins come from a period outside the one to which we have confined outselves, but in passing we may notice that there are fine ruins at Jerash (old Gerasa), dating from the days of Trajan onward, that is, from the period of the Roman expansion into the province of Arabia. Trajan erected a great monumental arch here in A.D. 115, and Hadrian likewise in A.D. 130. Other buildings here date from the later second and third centuries. The rest of the towns in the Decapolis region, that famous area where independence was given to ten Greek cities, also have Roman remains. We may refer to Scythopolis (Bethshean), Pella, Gadara, and Philadelphia (Amman) (see Matt. 4:25; Mark 5:20; 7:31). Samaria, too, has good Roman remains of a later time, including the fine Roman basilica dated about A.D. 180 to 237. A discussion of Jerusalem itself will be taken up in the next chapter, since it will involve our taking notice of a number of important topographical items and seeing them in the light of the New Testament.

These ancient Roman steps lead down from the probable site of the Upper Room on Mount Zion to the city of David (the Lower City of Jesus' Jerusalem). (Garo Nalbandian)

ROMAN ROADS IN PALESTINE

The general outline of the road system in Palestine is well known today, and maps are available.[47] Inscriptions on milestones have been a great help in determining the roads through the land, although it must be agreed that there may have been more roads than the milestones indicate, since the preservation of a milestone is a matter of chance. We are further assisted in our study by the discovery of the remains of Roman camps and by small pieces of roads, which point to a connection with a larger network.

It seems clear that in the time of Christ the great Roman road system had hardly begun in Palestine. We believe that the earliest road followed the coast, and already in the days of Nero it ran from Antioch to Ptolemais (Acre), as we learn from inscriptions. South of this, although the inscriptions are all later than A.D. 200, it is thought that the road probably ran on to Egypt. Josephus refers to the road surveyors in the Roman army of Vespasian at the time of the first revolt.[48] Such milestones as we have, however, seem to point to a date after A.D. 70 for the Roman expansion of the road system. This would mean that in the time of our Lord the roads were very poor, and passable only in dry seasons.

With the Jewish revolt the situation changed and the Romans, in order to face the possibility of new revolts in Palestine, had to give thought to new roads. The setting up of the tenth legion in Jerusalem seems to have led to the construction of a road to connect Jerusalem with Caesarea, the administrative center. One milestone that can be read was found three miles north of Jerusalem and came from the days of Nerva (A.D. 96–98). Four other milestones, not now decipherable, were found near Gophna on the shortest route between the two towns.

All the evidence points to the fact that the road system of Palestine was not completed till well into the second century. Even the road from Jerusalem to Jericho (Luke 10:30f.), which can be traced today, goes back only to the first Jewish revolt about A.D. 68–70, though no doubt it followed, in large part, the earlier road.[49]

Thus in Jesus' day, although travel was free and constant between all parts of Palestine, it was along old, rough roads which were not passable all the year around.

47. M. Avi-Yonah, "Map of Roman Palestine," *Quarterly of the Department of Antiquities, Palestine,* Vol. V, pp. 139ff. Also F.-M. Abel, *Géographie de la Palestine* (Paris, 1938), Vol. II, pp. 222–231.

48. Josephus, *Wars* III.vi.2.

49. R. Beauvery, "La route romaine de Jérusalem à Jéricho," *RB* (Jan., 1957), pp. 72f.

THE JERUSALEM THAT JESUS KNEW

MOST readers of the New Testament would feel that the pride of place among towns that Jesus knew should be given to Jerusalem. In actual fact Jesus spent far more time away from Jerusalem than He did in it. But it was here that He questioned the doctors when He came up with His parents as a boy (Luke 2:41–50). Here, too, He cleansed the Temple (John 2:13–16), healed the man who had been ill for thirty years (John 5:1–16), spoke to the Jews at the Feast of Tabernacles (John 7), asserted His deity at the Feast of Dedication (John 10:22–30), and finally passed through those tragic days that led up to the cross. It was in Jerusalem that He rose from the dead and appeared to the friends and disciples. Here, too, the Christian Church was born (Acts 1, 2). Hence, though the actual known visits to Jerusalem are few, the impression left by the fourth Gospel is that Jesus was there frequently. These visits were in every case important ones. With tragic irony Jesus told the Pharisees that "it cannot be that a prophet perish out of Jerusalem" (Luke 13:33). With that, He indicated one important feature about the city. Modern archaeology has given us important information about the town of those days, and if it has not solved all our problems, it has pointed the way to a solution of some of them. There must be a great deal of valuable information yet to be taken from the earth under the modern city. It has been occupied through the ages and is today heavily populated in the vital areas so that excavation has been difficult, if not impossible. Rebuilding operations in the old Jewish Quarter have provided an opportunity to investigate important areas on the Western Hill inside the old walled city.

Such operations commenced soon after the conclusion of the 1948 war. The

Jewish Quarter lies further west from Professor Mazar's excavations.[1] Here during the years 1969-70 important finds were made in five different areas. There are further remains from the Herodian age, including many fragments of colorful painted frescoes, an incised menorah (seven-branched candelabrum) that gives a new understanding of the way these were made, many stamped tiles of the *Legio X Fretensis*, earlier levels of the Hasmonean, late Hellenistic, and Iron II periods, along with many small remains like pottery, many stamped jar-handles, lamps, etc. One of the most significant finds was a short section of wall that dates to the Iron II period, as we have seen.[2] Small finds in the area suggest a date in the seventh century B.C. The wall was some six to seven meters thick (about eighteen to twenty feet) and would appear to be a part of the city wall of those days. It indicates an expansion of the city boundaries to the west of the Temple.

It may be that we have now discovered evidence of the *Mishneh* (second quarter) of the Old Testament (II Kings 22:14; Zeph. 1:10; Neh. 11:9). The unusual thickness of the wall is reminiscent of Nehemiah's "Broad Wall" (Neh. 3:8; 12:38). If this were indeed the western wall of the city of Hezekiah's time, we could understand better how it was that he brought water into a pool within the city (II Kings 20:20; II Chron. 32:2-4, 30).

The discovery in this Jewish Quarter of a pre-exilic city wall, of a Herodian house, of numerous architectural items, of a Byzantine church and bathhouse, of numerous small inscriptions, and of many small items of archaeological significance after a couple of years' work holds out great hope of other important discoveries in the area.

Some reference should be made to two of the houses from the first century A.D. The excavators refer to these houses as "The Mansion" and "The Burnt House."[3]

The "Mansion" was over 600 square meters in size. Here rooms were arranged around a central courtyard which was paved with flagstones and had an opening to a cistern. On the western wing of this house were two rows of interconnected rooms the walls of which still stood 3 meters high and were built of large dressed blocks. These had been ornamented with colored frescos. In one large room, perhaps the reception room, the plaster resembled Herodian masonry in appearance. One room had a mosaic floor partly preserved, while another room had frescoed walls preserved to a height of 2.5 meters with ornamentation in red and yellow not unlike the style one finds in Pompeii. A fine mosaic of a schematic six-petalled rosette in black and red formed the floor of a small bathing area. From the courtyard two stairways led to a lower level on which were several rooms. This lower story had a considerable number of

1. See pp. 293ff.
2. See p. 165.
3. N. Avigad, *Archaeological Discoveries in the Jewish Quarter of Jerusalem* (Jerusalem, 1970), pp. 11-13.

The Old City of Jerusalem as seen from the Mount of Olives to the east. At left, within the wall, is part of the Dome of the Rock, the mosque built on the site of the Temple; at right is the Golden Gate, now closed. (Trans World Airlines)

stepped pools covered by vaulted masonry as well as deep cisterns and storerooms. This large "house" is unique both in size and splendor and may have been the home of some noble Jerusalemite family.

To the north of the "Mansion" was the "Burnt House." It was in a street where there were several such houses, all of which had been burned. Only some 55 square meters of this house remained in the basement area. There was a kitchen, a bathing pool, and four rooms. Many stone vessels—cooking pots, amphorae, vases, bowls, cups, mortars and pestles, querns, and stone weights—were preserved. Many coins from the period of the Roman procurators, around the time of the first Jewish revolt, were found in the area of these houses.

One of the more fascinating finds was a seven-branched candelabrum (menorah) some 20 centimeters high (about 8 inches) and incised on a fragment of plaster. It was incomplete, but the central short stem with its long extension formed one of the seven branches and the three branches on the right were all ornamented in a stylized fashion. This is one of the earliest depictions of the seven-branched candelabrum in the Temple, and it was incised on the wall of a house at a time when the actual menorah was still in use in the Temple only a few hundred meters to the east of the house.[4]

THE GENERAL TOPOGRAPHY OF JERUSALEM

Through the centuries the disposition of the town of Jerusalem has altered. One structure, however, has remained in the same location since Solomon's day. That is the Temple. At various times the site of the town in relation to the Temple has altered. In the Old Testament period it lay to the south and west, while in the New Testament it expanded more to the west and to the north.

Jerusalem is situated in the central highlands some thirty-three miles from the Mediterranean Sea and fourteen miles west of the north end of the Dead Sea. Immediately to the east of the city is the Kidron valley, which separates the Mount of Olives from the ridge on which Jerusalem proper stands. On the western side of the Temple area in New Testament times was a smaller valley, the Tyropoeon valley, which joined the Kidron valley at the southern end of the Temple ridge. To the west of the Tyropoeon valley is a larger plateau which falls away fairly steeply to the south and west into what was formerly known as the Valley of Hinnom. The small Tyropoeon valley thus divided the Jerusalem area of Jesus' day into two parts, of which the western part was the greater. The Old Testament settlements were on the Temple ridge, which has been variously known as the Jebusite city, the city of David, Zion, and Ophel. Today these sites would be placed to the south of the Temple area. Indeed archaeological work has revealed the exact site where the former city stood on the area south of the

4. *Ibid.*, p. 26 and Plate 2.

present walls.[5] By the time of Christ the city had spread rather to the west, and this southern part of the ridge was little used. At one stage it was cut down by the Hasmonean (Maccabean) rulers so as not to be higher than the Temple site.

The only two springs of any value in the whole area lie on the eastern side. These are Gihon and En-rogel. With the shifting of the city to the west, arrangements had to be made to bring water into the city by aqueduct or to store it in cisterns. Pontius Pilate (A.D. 26-36) constructed an aqueduct for this purpose, although there is some evidence that he may have repaired an old one.

On the north side of the city there were no deep valleys so that the defense of the city called for strong walls on this side. In the course of the centuries there were at least four of these. On the other sides of the city defense was not so difficult because of the deep valleys, although walls were built nevertheless.

HEROD'S JERUSALEM

From the days of the Maccabean revolt on, Jerusalem had suffered a great deal, and even as recently as Pompey's day the walls had been breached. But Herod with his typical massive masonry repaired the walls and erected new buildings. After his extensive building projects there were few changes for many years.

Let us take a quick look around the city of Herod, starting from the west side of the walls at a point overlooking the Valley of Hinnom. As we have seen,[6] Herod built a fortified palace at a point where there were gates in the city wall. He erected three towers named Hippicus, Phasael, and Mariamne—after a friend, a brother, and his favorite wife. Part of one of these, probably the tower of Phasael,[7] has survived through the centuries and today forms part of the so-called Tower of David. Excavations by C. N. Johns between 1934 and 1940 established the fact that this tower was built on a foundation of massive stones, weighing up to ten tons, with an average weight of five tons. It was set into a still older wall underneath. At this point the wall curves south, and it is now agreed that we can fix the northwest corner of Herod's city here. It is possible to trace the remains of the so-called first wall of Jerusalem from here in a line running due east to meet the west wall of the Temple enclosure. Josephus described this wall as follows: "That wall began on the north at the tower of Hippicus and extended as far as the Xystus [a court for games] and then, joining to the council house, ended at the west cloister of the Temple."[8]

But there was a second wall, described by Josephus in these words: "The second wall took its beginning from that gate which they called Gennath which

5. G. E. Wright and F. V. Filson, *The Westminster Historical Atlas to the Bible* (London, 1957), p. 105; B. Mazar, "Jerusalem," *EAEHL*, Vol. II (1976), pp. 580-591; Y. Yadin, *Jerusalem Revealed* (Jerusalem, 1975), art. by B. Mazar, "Jerusalem in the Biblical Period," pp. 1-8.

6. See p. 297.

7. W. F. Albright, *Archaeology of Palestine* (London, 1954), p. 154; G. E. Wright, *Biblical Archaeology* (London, 1957), p. 222.

8. Josephus, *Wars* V.iv.2.

Aerial view of Jerusalem from the south. In the center is the Moslem Dome of the Rock on the Temple Mount; beside the mount runs the Valley of Kidron. At the bottom of the picture is the Valley of Hinnom (Gehenna). Use the map on page 356 to identify other points of interest. (Matson Photo Service)

belonged to the first wall; it only encompassed the northern quarter of the city and reached as far as the tower of Antonia."[9] This description gives the start and the end of the wall, but does not describe the portion in between. The tower of Antonia can be identified, but the gate of Gennath is not known. Consequently there has been a great deal of discussion about the position of this wall. Its exact location is not merely of academic interest, for our identification of the precise position of Calvary is affected by the decision reached. If the Church of the Holy Sepulcher today occupies a site that was originally outside the city wall, then there may be some reason to accept it as marking the place of Calvary. If, on the other hand, the site was inside the wall in Jesus' day, then the church is not on the site of Calvary. In Jesus' day the second wall was the outside wall of the city. Subsequently there were two other walls outside this one, that is, to the north. There was a wall built by Agrippa in about A.D. 42 of which traces

9. *Ibid.*

Part of the old wall around Jerusalem. The masonry of the upper part is evidence that Herod probably built the wall. (Philip Gendreau)

are now known, and later still the wall of Hadrian, built about A.D. 135 in the approximate position of the present north wall of the old city.[10] We shall not discuss these two walls further but shall return in due course to the wall of Jesus' day when we seek to identify the site of Calvary.

We have already discussed briefly[11] the results of recent archaeological work in the area west and south of the southwest corner of the Temple platform. Professor B. Mazar, N. Avigad, and others have brought to light the remains of buildings of the Herodian and first-century period which we have already described.[12] These structures were, of course, close to the Temple area.

Continuing our excursion around the city of Jesus' day, we proceed eastward from Herod's towers to the Temple area, crossing over the roadway that linked the Western Hill to the Temple area at Wilson's Arch. Without referring to the Temple area proper we go to the north side of the Temple enclosure where

10. G. E. Wright and F. V. Wilson, *op. cit.*, p. 107; M. Avi-Yonah, "Jerusalem of the Second Temple Period," in Y. Yadin (ed.), *Jerusalem Revealed*, pp. 9–13. Note the map on p. 10.
11. See pp. 293–297.
12. *Ibid.*

Herod rebuilt a fortress that formerly gave protection to the Temple. Extensive excavations in this area by Père L. H. Vincent in recent years have given us the probable outline of the fortress. It evidently had towers at the four corners and was joined to the Temple area by raised roadways. There must have been some space between the fortress, known as Antonia, and the Temple, for the Jews cut away the roads at the time of the first Jewish revolt and engaged in fighting in this area. [13] In our Lord's time there was a Roman garrison here, however, which kept guard over the Temple in case of troubles at the time of the feasts. It was to this "castle" that Paul was taken when he was rescued from the Jewish mob on the day he was accused of bringing a Gentile into the Temple precincts (Acts 21:27-40, esp. v. 34). Some modern scholars think that this is the place of the trial of Jesus before Pontius Pilate. [14] We shall take up the point later in some detail. But it is of interest to note that Père Vincent found here in the excavations a stone pavement which seems to have been the court of Antonia and which he affirms was the "Pavement" of John 19:13.

To the south of Antonia was the great Temple area and the Temple proper. This must be regarded as the highlight of Herod's work. [15] While we do not know precisely how much of the Temple built by the returning exiles in 520-516 B.C. was used again by Herod, it seems clear that the various wars had brought the existing Temple to a place where extensive repair was needed, and Herod undertook this. At the same time he enlarged the courts and beautified the whole area. The work began in 20-19 B.C. and, although the essential construction was finished in a year and six months, [16] the over-all work of beautification went on till A.D. 64. In Jesus' day the Jews could say, "forty and six years was this temple in building" (John 2:20). These words, spoken in A.D. 27, are important in deciding the date of Jesus' ministry.

Josephus again is our chief source of information. [17] He claimed that the court of the Temple was twice the size of the earlier Temple, an arrangement that was made possible by cutting into the rock on the hill Bezetha to the north and building up the embankment to the south. Excavations on the south wall in 1867-68 showed that there was a difference of forty-seven meters between the rock on which the foundation was laid and the level of the inner court at the southeast corner, and thirty meters at the southwest corner where today we have the famous Wailing Wall. Here fourteen courses of the large Herodian masonry were visible before recent excavations began. Now quite a number more of these have been brought to light. A point has been reached where the large stones with finely cut marginal drafts give way to the same large stones but with rather

13. Josephus, *Wars* VI.i.7. See also *Antiquities* XV.xi.4.
14. L. H. Vincent and W. F. Albright, among others. See below, pp. 360f.
15. A. Parrot, *The Temple of Jerusalem* (London, 1957), pp. 76-100.
16. Josephus, *Antiquities* XV.xi.1-6.
17. *Ibid.*

Model based on Michael Avi-Yonah's design of the Jerusalem Temple built by Herod. The Court of the Gentiles is outside the wall. The gate (Beautiful Gate?) in that wall leads into the Court of the [Israelite] Women, which contains rooms where lepers stood and storage rooms. On the steps of the Nicanor Gate (center, smaller structure) the priests blew the trumpets. Beyond that gate are the Court of Israel (men only) and then the Court of the Priests, which held the altar of burnt sacrifices. The tall structure is the holy of holies, which could be entered only by the high priest and only on the Day of Atonement. (W. S. LaSor)

rougher finish. These, no doubt, were not meant to be seen originally and were covered over with fill.[18] Perhaps it was the sight of great blocks of stone like these in some of the buildings that made one of the disciples in the Temple area say to Jesus, "Master, see what manner of stones and what buildings are here!" To this Jesus replied, "Seest thou these great buildings? There shall not be left one stone upon another, that shall not be thrown down" (Mark 13:1f.). In the destruction under Titus, the Temple buildings were in fact destroyed, but these retaining walls were left.

The great courtyard was entered by eight gates, two on the south, four on

18. See pp. 293ff. and picture, p. 294.

the west, one on the north, and one on the east. The four gates on the west led to the western city, but passers to and from them had to cross the Tyropoeon valley by bridges or aqueducts. In recent times excavators have shown that the so-called Wilson's Arch was one of the supporting arches for a roadway that crossed from the Temple area to the Western Hill.[19] The so-called Robinson's Arch supported a staircase which led down from the Temple area to the street below.[20] A gate leading into the Temple area on the west side today, and known as the Gate of the Cahin (Bab es-Silsile), probably marks the position of the old Coponius Gate.

On the east side of the courtyard in the direction of the Kidron valley there was but one gate, probably on the site of the present Golden Gate. In its present form it is Byzantine in origin, although it is thought that its substructure dates from the days of Herod. Both Josephus and the Mishna know of only one gate in the east side of the city, and it is possible that the gate that Jesus entered on Palm Sunday stood at this point, or not far from it (Mark 11:11; Matt. 21:10; Luke 19:28-48). This was the most direct route from Bethany to the Temple.

The excavations of Professor B. Mazar on the southern side of the Temple enclosure have provided us with a very good picture of the entrance to the Temple on this side. A worshipper would either move along a narrow road which followed the southern wall from the southwest corner or move on to a fine plaza and proceed up an impressive flight of stairs to enter the Temple enclosure at one of the so-called Huldah Gates. He would then find himself in the Royal Porch.[21]

Josephus had much to say about the porticoes and the courts of Herod's Temple. Within the walls of the Temple area there were rows of pillars, four on the south and two on each of the other sides. As one passed through one of the eight doors, he came into the large open courtyard known as the Court of the Gentiles. On the south was the Royal Porch, and on the east was Solomon's Porch. It was in Solomon's Porch that Jesus walked at the feast of the dedication referred to in John 10:22f. (see also Acts 3:11; 5:12).

The extreme southeastern part of the Temple area is described by Josephus as follows:

> While the valley was very deep and its bottom could not be seen, if you looked from above into the depth, this further vastly high elevation of the cloister stood upon that height, insomuch that if anyone looked down from the top of the battlements, or down both those altitudes, he would be giddy, while his sight could not reach to such an immense depth.[22]

---

19. See p. 293.
20. B. Mazar, "The Archaeological Excavations near the Temple Mount," in Y. Yadin, *Jerusalem Revealed*, pp. 25-40.
21. This area has been discussed already on p. 295. Note the plan of the area on p. 256.
22. Josephus, *Antiquities* XV.xi.5.

The corner referred to in this passage was probably the "pinnacle of the temple" mentioned in the story of the temptation (Matt. 4:5).

The Court of the Gentiles provided a place for non-Jews to gather. Somewhere in this court the moneychangers did their work, and it was probably a thoroughfare for people passing through the city, from east to west or from north to south. When Jesus cast out those that sold and bought in the Temple area, He forbade that "any man should carry any vessel through the temple" (Mark 11:15f.). Josephus refers to the prohibition against Gentiles passing out of this court behind the balustrade which set off the area where Jews were permitted. He spoke of "a stone wall for a partition with an inscription which forbade any foreigner to go in under pain of death."[23] We have already referred to the discovery of two of these inscriptions.[24]

Finally there was the inner area of the Temple precincts. As one entered through the Gate Beautiful, he would first reach the Women's Court, the furthest point to which women might go. Here the poor widow brought her mites (Mark 12:41–44). After this came the Men's Court, raised somewhat above the Women's Court and entered by seven gates, three on the north, three on the south, and one into the Women's Court. Then came the Priests' Court, where sacrifices were offered on the altar of burnt offering, and finally the Temple proper, with its porch, its Holy Place, and its Most Holy Place. This inner sacred place must have been a most ornate building with its white stone embellished with gold. The people of the day used to swear by the gold of the Temple (Matt. 23:16).

The medieval Jewish scholar Maimonides, drawing on information culled from the Jewish Fathers in the Mishna, the Talmud, and other writings, adds a number of other details about the Priests' Court. He describes the large altar where sacrifices were offered and the ramp leading up to it, the rings to which the animals for sacrifice were tied, the flaying tables and other items associated with the sacrifice, the Chamber of Hewn Stone in the right-hand corner of the court where lots were drawn before the sacrifice and where the Benediction was said afterward, and the House of the Hearth just west of it where the priests on duty spent the night. No doubt remains of these items lie beneath the modern pavement. It may be a long time before excavations will be undertaken in the Temple area.

It is natural to ask how much of all this remains today for the archaeologist to study. The answer is that very little can be studied firsthand. We gain a lot of information from Josephus, some from the New Testament, and a little from the archaeologist. The difficulty arises because the whole area where the Temple once stood has been held sacred down the centuries. After the fall of Jerusalem in A.D. 70 the buildings were destroyed. In the years that followed a variety of

---

23. *Ibid.*
24. See above, pp. 331f.

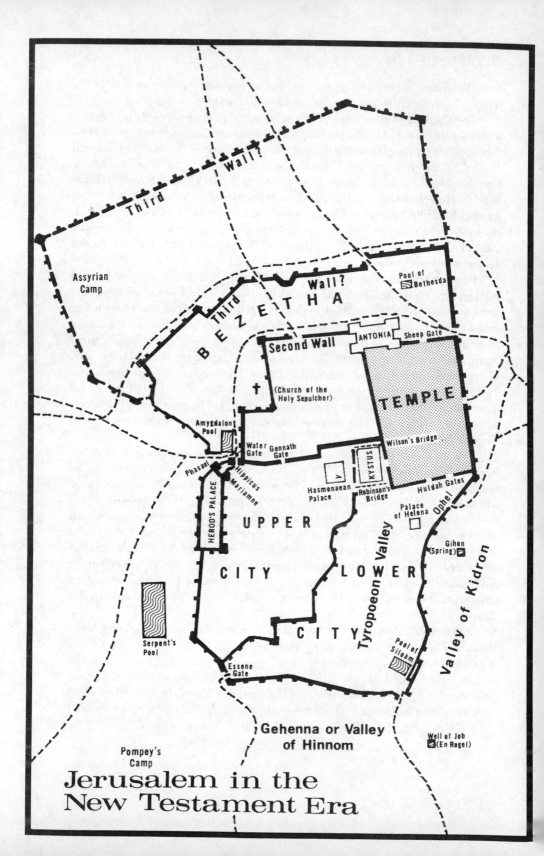

Jerusalem in the
New Testament Era

structures has appeared on this site, including Christian churches and a mosque, which still stands today. The whole area is a sacred site to the Moslems nowadays, and although much valuable information surely lies buried beneath the surface, we are unable to excavate. For the present at least we must be content to remain in comparative ignorance about what lies beneath the present ground level.

The visitor to Jerusalem in Herod's day would see other items of interest, among which would be a theater, an amphitheater, and a hippodrome. These catered to the dramatic and athletic interests of the people. Other buildings are mentioned by Josephus, such as the palace of the Hasmoneans and the meeting place of the Sanhedrin. Then there were impressive tombs to be seen on the east side of the Kidron valley. In the valley itself were the springs of Gihon and En-rogel. Other important pools of water were to be seen in the city, such as the pool of Bethesda. To complete the picture, the houses of the ordinary people were scattered throughout the city and its environs. This was the town that Jesus knew so well.

JESUS IN JERUSALEM

It is a well-known fact that John, of all the Gospel writers, emphasized the ministry of Jesus in Jerusalem. Indeed, John says very little about the ministry in Galilee, although he does not altogether neglect this. We are concerned to indicate where modern archaeology has given some light on the Gospel narratives.

Much of the material in the Gospels is concerned with happenings in the Temple. With the aid of Josephus and modern interpretations of his descriptions, we can picture many of the incidents reported. Thus the presentation of the baby Jesus (Luke 2:22) probably took place at the door leading from the Women's Court into the Men's Court. It is not easy to decide where Jesus as a boy of twelve sat and asked questions of the doctors (Luke 2:46–50), but it was probably somewhere in the Outer Court, the place where public instruction was often given. The Temple features in the temptation story, and we have already referred to the pinnacle (Matt. 4:5; Luke 4:9).[25] The cleansing of the Temple took place in the Court of the Gentiles (Matt. 21:12f.; Mark 11:5; Luke 19:45f.; John 2:14–16). Perhaps trading and business were carried on in the Royal Porch at the south end of the great enclosure. On one of these occasions Jesus forbade people to make the courtyard a thoroughfare (Mark 11:16).

After the early ministry in Jerusalem Jesus went to Galilee, but returned to Jerusalem for a "feast" of the Jews, probably the Passover. It was on this occasion that He was present at the Sheep Gate near the pool of Bethesda and healed a man who had been sick for thirty-eight years (John 5:1–15). Some writers argue

25. See p. 355.

that we have some archaeological information on this site today. Some ancient manuscripts read Bethzetha instead of Bethesda. The word Bethzetha recalls the name of the district of Bethzatha to the north of the second wall.[26] There is some reason to believe that the pools in the property of the monastery of St. Anne, in the area of old Bezetha, represent the waters in question. Painstaking work has been done here by the White Fathers in ancient pools now many feet below ground level. The remains of pillars around the area point to the "porches" of John 5:2. Père L. H. Vincent and N. van der Vliet agree with the identification.[27] There were, in fact, two pools roughly rectangular in shape but not exactly so, the smaller approximately 160 by 130 feet and the larger 160 by 200 feet. The pools stood beside each other and were surrounded on all sides by colonnades. Counting the two long sides and the three shorter cross sides, there were five colonnades in all.[28]

More recently R. de Vaux and P. Rousée have extended the excavations into other Roman and later Byzantine remains.

As we move along in the chronological order of our Lord's life,[29] we come to the later Judaean ministry where Jesus had many contacts with the Temple. He was there at the Feast of Tabernacles (John 7:10-52) and appeared first on the fourth day (v. 14) and again on the last day, making a special appeal to the people. This was the occasion of the ceremony of offering up the golden vessel of water brought from the pool of Siloam. He declared that in Himself alone there was a source of living water. The pool of Siloam is quite well known today. It is the termination of an important conduit that brought water from the spring Gihon (the Virgin's Spring) into the heart of the city of David. Probably the conduit that still exists was cut by King Hezekiah (II Kings 20:20). It was in this tunnel that the famous Siloam inscription was found in 1880.[30] The man born blind whom Jesus healed was sent to wash in this same pool of Siloam (John 9:7).

Jesus was in the Temple again at the Feast of Dedication, walking in Solomon's Porch (John 10:23). It was winter, according to John, and perhaps Jesus joined the people on the eastern side of the great courtyard in order to seek some sunshine and shelter from the winds. In any case, He spoke concerning His oneness with the Father and offended the Jews greatly. After His Peraean ministry, He returned to Jerusalem for the last time. It was on this occasion that He made His triumphal entry into the city (Matt. 21; Mark 11). We have suggested that He entered the city by the eastern gate which stood at the site of the present

26. There is a textual problem here and the strength of this argument depends on the choice of Bethzatha as the true reading.

27. N. van der Vliet, *Sainte Marie, où elle est née, et la piscine probatique* (Paris); E. G. Kraeling, *Bible Atlas* (New York, 1956), pp. 392f. Cf. *RB* (1957), pp. 226-228.

28. J. Jeremias, *The Rediscovery of Bethesda* (Louisville, 1949)—note the reconstruction on p. 26; J. Finegan, *The Archaeology of the New Testament* (Princeton, 1969), pp. 142-147.

29. We follow A. T. Robertson, *A Harmony of the Gospels* (London, 1922).

30. See above, p. 153; J. B. Pritchard, *ANET*, p. 321.

A colonnade-surrounded pool of Bethesda, one of two discovered in modern times. The Bethesda pool in New Testament Jerusalem was located north of the Sheep Gate in the Bezetha district (see map). By that pool Jesus healed an invalid who had long lain there hoping to be cured by the waters (John 5:1-9); the name Bethesda probably means "house of mercy." (W. S. LaSor)

Golden Gate.[31] There followed the second cleansing of the Temple, which, we hold, followed the pattern of the first (Matt. 21:12f.; Mark 11:12-18; Luke 19:45-48). It was at this last period of His life that the Pharisees and the Herodians tried to involve Him in criticism of Caesar in the matter of tribute money.[32] During these days, too, He commended the poor woman in the Temple as she offered her mites (*lepton*),[33] placing them in the offering box in the Women's Court (Mark 12:41-44).

The day of our Lord's crucifixion drew on apace. He spoke of His coming death and of the destruction of Jerusalem and the Temple. He was going out of the Temple when one of His disciples drew attention to the great stones of the building. It was then that He prophesied that there would not be left one stone standing upon another (Mark 13:1f.).[34]

Then came Gethsemane. The site of the final hours of prayer is not known

31. See above, p. 354.
32. See above, p. 324.
33. See above, pp. 324, 327.
34. See above, p. 353.

with certainty, although it was across the Kidron valley on the side of the Mount of Olives. There are today several rival sites for the place. The confused visitor will be shown the scene by the Roman Catholics, the Greeks, the Armenians, and the Russians. The oldest tradition places the scene on the ground now occupied by the Tomb of the Virgin. But the fact is that we have no clear information, archaeological or historical, which will allow precise identification.

It is not any easier to identify the scenes of the last hours of Jesus on earth, although the visitor to Palestine will be shown a bewildering variety of places. There is more than one proposed site for the prison of our Lord (the house of Caiaphas), the place of the trial, Calvary, and the "garden tomb." For some of these sites there is some archaeological information that may finally prove to be of value.

The first place for which some scholars appear to have some solid grounds is the site of the Praetorium where Jesus was tried. After the arrest in the garden of Gethsemane, Jesus was examined by the high priest Annas (John 18:13), then by Caiaphas and the Sanhedrin (Matt. 26:57-68; Mark 14:53-56; Luke 22:54-71; John 18:24). Finally, in a formal way, after dawn, the Sanhedrin condemned Him (Matt. 27:1f.; Mark 15:1; Luke 22:66-71). In this context Peter's denial and the remorse of Judas are set. Then came the first appearance before Pilate (Matt. 27:2, 11-14; Mark 15:1-5; Luke 23:1-5; John 18:28-38), who called in Herod Antipas,[35] the ruler of Galilee where Jesus belonged (Luke 23:6-12). A second time Jesus was sent to Pilate, who slowly, reluctantly, and in fear surrendered Him to be crucified.

It is in connection with this trial before Pilate that important statements are made in the New Testament text, especially in John's Gospel. After surrendering Jesus to the Jews, Pilate "brought Jesus forth, and sat down in the judgment seat [Greek bema] in a place that is called the Pavement [Greek Lithostrotos], but in the Hebrew, Gabbatha" (John 19:13). The Hebrew word means literally, "ridge or elevated terrain."[36] Hence a search has been made for a rocky pavement that might be associated with some of the buildings where Pilate would be likely to be at the time. For a considerable time there has been a debate about the location of the Praetorium referred to in Mark 15:16, to which Jesus was led after Pilate had condemned Him. Some argue that the Praetorium was the place where Jesus stood, and feel that it was more likely the palace of Herod than the barracks of Antonia.[37] The argument has taken on new interest following the work of the Dames de Sion and the Franciscans of the Convent of the Flagellation in the area just to the northwest of the present Temple area.[38] Here, in the position of the former tower of Antonia, a large Roman pavement has been discovered under the so-called Ecce Homo arch, occupying not less than

35. See above, pp. 309, 311f., 325.
36. W. F. Albright, Archaeology of Palestine (London, 1956), p. 245.
37. G. E. Wright and F. V. Filson, op. cit., p. 106.
38. Le Lithostrotos, with a foreword by L. H. Vincent, 1933.

twenty-five hundred square meters. This pavement was the court of the tower of Antonia and stood on the rocky elevation which rose above the surrounding terrain. It might well be called *Gabbatha*. It is worth mentioning that the Ecce Homo arch in the vicinity was built over this pavement long after it had been buried under the ruins of Antonia, in the time of Aelia Capitolina. The arch does not therefore belong to the pavement. According to W. F. Albright, "the location of the Lithostrotos has been settled by the brilliant investigations of L. H. Vincent, utilizing both the outcroppings of rock in the region of the Tower of Antonia [at the northwestern end of the Temple enclosure] and the excavations carried on quietly for many years by the Dames de Sion and the Franciscans of the Convent of Flagellation."[39] Of passing interest are the patterns scratched in the stones of the pavement in more than one place. These represent the play board for a popular game played by the Roman soldiers on duty.

While this evidence seems convincing, there are those who feel that it is not final. It is argued that while no pavement has been found in the area of Herod's palace, there may well have been one there. When Pilate came from Caesarea to Jerusalem at the time of the Passover, he would be more likely to stay at the palace of Herod than in Antonia. Josephus tells us of a later occasion when the procurator Florus sat in judgment before Herod's palace.[40] There was evidently a judgment seat (*bema*) set up there for Herod to carry out his own ordinary judicial functions. Hence the entrance to the palace could well have been the Praetorium on that occasion. In this opinion the Roman Catholic scholar R. P. P. Benoit shares, against some of his colleagues.[41] Other competent scholars agree, among whom are E. G. Kraeling[42] and G. E. Wright.[43] If this latter opinion is correct, then the traditional *Via Dolorosa* cannot be the path taken by Jesus from Pilate's residence to the cross. When Jesus went to Herod Antipas (Luke 23:7), He would then have gone in the opposite direction, moving from Herod's palace toward Antonia, but stopping perhaps at the place of the Hasmoneans. L. H. Vincent's reply to all this is that Antonia may well have been Herod's early palace that kept its name.[44] No final conclusion is yet possible, but in the discussion we have looked at important material which will surely help in the final solution, even if it only helps to eliminate unsound suggestions.

The site of Calvary and the tomb where Jesus was buried present us with another difficult problem. A great deal turns on the position of the second wall of the city, for the crucifixion took place outside this wall. Traditionally, the present position of the Church of the Holy Sepulcher marks the site of Calvary, and the tomb must be close by. If this tradition is correct, then the wall of the

39. W. F. Albright, *op. cit.*, p. 245.
40. Josephus, *Wars* II.xiv.8.
41. R. P. P. Benoit, "Prétoire, Lithostroton et Gabbatha," *RB* (Oct., 1952), pp. 531f.
42. E. G. Kraeling, *op. cit.*, pp. 405f.
43. G. E. Wright and F. V. Filson, *op. cit.*, p. 107.
44. L. H. Vincent, "Le lithostrotos évangélique, *RB* (Oct., 1952), pp. 513f.

city must have passed to the east of the church so as to allow it to be outside in the days of our Lord.

As we have seen, the start and finish of the second wall are defined by Josephus.[45] The end of the wall was at the tower of Antonia. This is well marked. But the start of the wall at the gate Gennath is not known. According to some writers, this gate was between the towers of Hippicus and Phasael. But in fact four courses have been proposed for this second wall, and none of them is finally acceptable to all scholars.

In our discussion, the map on page 356 should be followed.[46] The shortest wall suggested leads west from Antonia and turns south to meet the first wall halfway between Herod's Temple and the palace. This would allow the Church of the Holy Sepulcher to be outside the wall. There are traces of Herodian masonry along this course, but their meaning is not clear, and in any case the area enclosed seems to be very small and leaves outside the wall the small hill on which the Church of the Holy Sepulcher stands. It has been argued that this would be a strange arrangement for fortification purposes, which was the reason for building the wall in the first place. An enemy on this small hill would have a distinct advantage in siege warfare.

A second proposal is to follow this same line to a point just south of the church, and then to assume a turn to the west. Finally the wall turned south to meet the first wall near Herod's palace. This suggestion has the weakness of the first one in regard to defense, and is rejected by many writers.

The third proposal allows for the wall to swing to the north from Antonia and then to circle south to Herod's palace. The difficulty here is that there is some evidence that the wall did in fact start in a westerly direction from Antonia, rather than toward the north. But such a wall would include the church and thus bring the traditional site of Calvary inside the walls.

The fourth suggestion for this second wall follows a line west from Antonia and then swings in a half-circle to include the Church of the Holy Sepulcher before it meets the first wall at the palace of Herod.

In the absence of serious excavation in the area of the Church of the Holy Sepulcher it is difficult to arrive at a final decision. The opportunity for some work was afforded to Kathleen Kenyon in 1963. In the heart of the Old City a small area belonging to the Order of St. John in the vicinity of the Church of the Holy Sepulcher became available for excavation.[47] The area proved to be nothing more than a deep hole that had been filled with debris. After fifteen meters of digging, bedrock was reached. Eleven meters of the excavated material proved to be only some filling debris. This consisted of large quantities of debris from the seventh century B.C. and the first century A.D. There was no indication at all

45. See above, p. 356.
46. We follow the notation of G. E. Wright and F. V. Filson, *op. cit.*, Plate XVII, c.
47. K. M. Kenyon, "Excavations in Jerusalem, 1963," *PEQ* (Jan.–June, 1964), pp. 7–18, esp. pp. 14–16.

that regular stratified remains existed in the area. Dr. Kenyon concluded that the site represented an ancient quarry that had been filled in at the time when Hadrian built Aelia Capitolina on the ruins of Old Jerusalem in A.D. 135. Evidently a hollow area had been filled with material dug from other areas that contained only material from the seventh century B.C. and the first century A.D. In that case the area that was excavated seems to have been a quarry that the emperor caused to be filled so as to be able to extend his new city in this area. Now quarries lie outside city walls and not inside. The site lies due south of the Church of the Holy Sepulcher, which must likewise have been outside the walls. This does not, of course, prove that the Church of the Holy Sepulcher is, in fact, on the site of Calvary, but it does show that the Church site lay outside the walls in the first century A.D. and hence its claim to be the authentic site of Calvary is enhanced.

As to the site of the tomb, it was evidently close to the place of the crucifixion according to John, who wrote, "Now in the place where he was crucified there was a garden; and in the garden a new sepulchre, wherein was never man yet laid" (John 19:41). Those who contend that the Church of the Holy Sepulcher gives us the site will show a tomb within the precincts of the church. But this lies under the same kind of doubt that attaches to the site of Calvary.

A popular alternative site for Calvary and the tomb was taken up by General Gordon in 1883 when he saw a peculiar skull-like formation in the rocks to the north of the present wall. The rocky hill above was identified with Calvary and a tomb in the vicinity was taken as the garden tomb. More careful archaeological investigation shows that there are other tombs in the area which are Byzantine (fifth and sixth centuries). But there is no convincing evidence at all that Gordon's Calvary and the tomb have authentic value. The tomb may indeed be as late as the third or fourth century A.D.[48] The setting is, however, a beautiful one and has often been an inspiration to the casual visitor. But in archaeological matters we cannot be moved by mere sentiment.

We feel that the ancient city of Jerusalem has many secrets yet to be given up to the archaeologist and the scholar. It is tantalizing to the New Testament scholar to think of the many problems whose solution lies beneath the soil of Old Jerusalem. With the progress of the years and the need to rebuild parts of the Old City, we may expect valuable information to come to light. Meanwhile we are grateful for the light we have.[49]

---

48. J. Finegan, *Light from the Ancient Past* (Princeton, 1946), p. 240; *The Archaeology of the New Testament*, pp. 173f.

49. In recent years two important works have been written that present to the student a wealth of valuable information about the city where Jesus gave much of His teaching and where He died and rose again: J. Simons, *Jerusalem and the Old Testament* (Leiden, 1952); H. Vincent and A. M. Steve, *Jerusalem de l'Ancien Testament* (Paris, 1954). The recent excavations of Israeli archaeologists B. Mazar and N. Avigad have provided important modifications to these two works.

FIRST-CENTURY TOWNS IN PALESTINE AND SYRIA

THOUGH Jerusalem occupied pride of place among the towns of Palestine in Jesus' days, we must remember that the events of the New Testament took place in a wide variety of towns stretching from Palestine to Italy. In Palestine itself many towns are mentioned. For many of these we have information from excavations, although there is a vast field of research still open for the archaeologist. Considerable uncertainty still obtains in numerous areas, but the combined results of excavations and literary records provide the student with valuable insights. We shall confine our attention in this chapter to the towns of Palestine and Syria.

TOWNS IN PHOENICIA AND IN THE DOMAINS OF HEROD PHILIP

Phoenicia was ruled by the Roman governor of Syria. Three of its towns are of interest to the New Testament student—Tyre, Sidon, and Ptolemais (Acre).

There are several references to Tyre in the New Testament. Jesus Himself was once in "the coasts of Tyre and Sidon" (Matt. 15:21–28; Mark 7:24–30), and the people of the region came to see Him (Mark 3:8; Luke 6:17). It is not clear that He Himself was in the town, though it is not impossible. A woman from this area, the Syro-Phoenician woman, was treated kindly at His hand when her daughter was healed. Tyre itself was an ancient town. Formerly the town was divided between the island and the mainland, but following the attack of Alexander the Great in which two causeways were built out to the island, the two areas became joined. Since about 1860 when Ernest Renan began some excavations at Tyre a considerable amount of archaeological work has gone on at this important site. Systematic excavations were commenced by Maurice Chéhab, the Director General of Antiquities of Lebanon, in 1947. In subsequent years the Byzantine and Roman levels of Tyre have been laid bare. These proved to be so important that Roman Tyre is to be preserved for future generations to see. Earlier occupations are to be investigated in other areas.

The site has produced a wide variety of coins and inscriptions, a fine street bordered by porticoes over five meters wide, many fine green and white marble columns, remains of some of the mosaic streets that were mentioned by Roman writers as a special feature of Tyre, the remains of several large buildings, considerable quantities of crushed murex shells from which dye was extracted, a hippodrome, an important cemetery containing fine sculptured sarcophagi, and other features too numerous to mention. The excavation continues year by year. It is clear, however, that the Roman city of Tyre was worthy of the title conferred by the Emperor Hadrian, "metropolis of Phoenicia."[1]

Just to the north of Tyre lies the town of Sidon. Here, too, remains of Roman times have been found. A considerable range of tombs and sarcophagi has been found in the area behind the modern town which provides valuable information about Roman times.

The town of Ptolemais (Acco) features only in the story of Paul's journeys (Acts 21:7). It was the end point of the Roman road from the north in the days of Nero, as we have already seen.[2] It, too, had a long history. Excavation in the area has shown a range of occupation from early Canaanite times through Roman times up to the modern period. In 39 B.C. Herod landed here and began his campaign of conquest of the territories that the Romans had given him. Under Nero (A.D. 54–68) Ptolemais became a Roman colony where soldiers discharged from the third, fifth, tenth, and twelfth legions were settled. This is known from coins struck in honor of the event. During the first Jewish revolt (A.D. 66–70) the people of Ptolemais were hostile to the Jews. Christianity reached the city during Paul's third missionary journey (Acts 21:7). There was a Christian bishop named Clarus here in A.D. 190. Some areas in the vicinity of the modern town are currently being excavated by Israeli archaeologists with important results. Important tombs from the Hellenistic and Roman periods have been known for many years.

In the domains of Herod Philip we have the important towns of Caesarea Philippi and Bethsaida. The former of these was the scene of Peter's great confession (Matt. 16:13–20; Mark 8:27–30). The town was formerly known as Panias, but in 3 B.C. Herod Philip named it Caesarea Philippi (Philip's Caesarea), in honor of Augustus. After the defeat of the Jews in A.D. 70, the

1. See N. Jidejian, *Tyre through the Ages* (Beirut, 1969), pp. 84–113, for a brief outline of the Roman period. References to excavation reports occur here. Some fine photographs are to be found also.

2. See above, p. 344.

This cave at Caesarea Philippi (a city at the base of Mount Hermon) housed a shrine that was dedicated to Pan in New Testament times and possibly to Baal-gad or Baal-hermon in Old Testament times. From the cave issues the Nahr Banias, one of the four sources of the Jordan River. (W. S. LaSor)

name reverted to Panias, which eventually became Banias, its name today. There are ruins in the area, but the most spectacular of them date from the Middle Ages when Crusaders and Moslems fought in the region. Medieval walls and towers are to be seen today on the heights above the modern village, but it is thought that they are built over the site of the ancient acropolis of Roman times. Herod Philip permitted pagan shrines in the area for his predominantly Greek population. The remains of a grotto carved out of solid rock in honor of Augustus—a shrine to Pan, the Roman nature god—may still be seen. Greek inscriptions in the area dating to the days of Agrippa tell of an altar dedicated to the Nymphs. But there has been little serious archaeological work in the place, though it appears to be full of promise.

There is a problem associated with the town of Bethsaida. It seems likely that Philip built his capital a short distance to the north of the old town and called it Julias, in honor of the daughter of Augustus. No excavation has been done in the area (which probably marks the site of Julias), but we feel fairly certain that the old town of Bethsaida is represented by an area known as Khirbet el 'Araj. E. G. Kraeling, in his *Bible Atlas*, writes as follows:

[A traveller at the site] had an unusual opportunity to examine the stratification there when the wall of a cistern that workmen were constructing for his host, collapsed. There was an upper layer of about twenty inches composed of alluvial sand; below that was a layer of about six inches with sherds of the Roman period down to about 250 A.D. He mentions the typical red-coloured ones and the painted jar-handles. Another layer of alluvial sand of twelve to fourteen inches lay above the next lower stratum of twelve inches. This last layer he confidently assigned to the time of Christ, for from it he was able to extract four lamps and eleven small coins showing three ears of grain on one side; these he asserts were minted in the time of Pilate (26–36 A.D.). He notes that the stratum in question was destroyed by fire, and finds therein a remarkable vindication of Jesus' woe over Bethsaida (Matt. 11:21). In any case the situation observed here warrants further investigation.[3]

TOWNS IN GALILEE AND PERAEA, THE DOMAINS OF HEROD ANTIPAS

Archaeologically we are not much better off here than in the case of the towns already mentioned. The most important cities were in the area to the west of Jordan. There was little of importance in Peraea.

Capernaum (literally "Village of Nahum") features a good deal in the Gospels. Jesus began His ministry here after the temptation (Matt. 4:13–16). Here, too, He healed many, including the centurion's servant and Peter's wife's mother (Matt. 8:5–17; Mark 1:21–34; 2:1–12); and here the incident of the fish and the tribute money took place (Matt. 17:24ff.). It was on the way to Capernaum that the dispute as to who should be the greatest took place (Mark 9:33–37), and nearby Jesus walked on the water (John 6:16–21). Here He gave some of His most profound teaching, for example, the instruction about the bread of life (John 6:32–35), but He also delivered woes against the same proud city (Luke 10:15).

For a number of years there has been a dispute about the exact location of the town, and more than one site has been suggested,[4] but the area of Tell Hum (an Arabic form of a Jewish name Tanhum) is now widely accepted. The original name Capernaum has now been confirmed by an Aramaic inscription found by the late Professor Sukenik in excavations in an old synagogue at Hamath Geder near the mouth of the Yarmuk River, where persons who presented gifts are recorded, among them one Dositheus of Capernaum (Kephar Nahum).[5] The ruins of Capernaum are spread over an area of about a mile along

---

3. E. G. Kraeling, *Bible Atlas* (New York, 1956), pp. 388f.
4. S. L. Caiger, *Archaeology and the New Testament* (London, 1948), p. 83.
5. E. G. Kraeling, *op. cit.*, p. 377.

The magnificent ruins of the synagogue at Capernaum (Tell Hum) attract many visitors. Dating from the third century A.D., the synagogue is not the one in which Jesus taught (Mark 1:21) as was formerly thought, although the site may be the same. (Israel Office of Information)

the shore of the lake. Up to the present there has been little in the way of excavation at the site except in the case of the fine, partly ruined structure that represents an ancient synagogue. It has been for many years in the custody of the Franciscan monks and has been preserved by them and in part restored. This ancient synagogue was formerly thought to be the building referred to in Luke 7:5, but more mature judgment has led to the conclusion that the present ruins are later than the time of Christ. Very likely they were built on the site of the earlier synagogue, but no excavation has been done under the present remains, and indeed none is likely to be done, since no one would wish to destroy the present magnificent ruins in order to find the foundations underneath. Some excavation has, however, been done alongside the synagogue which has thrown important light on structures of the early Christian period in the area.

The first work was done here as early as 1905 by the German archaeologists Kohl and Watzinger. Since then the Franciscan monks have carried on the work. It is now clear that the structure is a third-century building, made of white limestone, which must have been brought into the area, for the native stone here is black basalt. The present ruins reveal a building of the basilica type. Originally it had a stairway leading up to the four-columned front where there were a large central door and two smaller side doors. Inside there were nine columns on each side, and five at the rear. The main hall was more than seventy feet long and fifty feet wide. There were galleries for women at the back, and a courtyard on the east side. The carved stone work scattered about the area gives a good idea of the decoration of the typical synagogue of the day, with ornamentation showing seven-branched candlesticks, vine leaves and grapes, palm trees, eagles, doves, all sorts of animals, especially lions, and a wide variety of geometrical patterns. Among the items scattered about were some that carried inscriptions to show that they had been presented by individuals. One such fragment of a pillar carried the name of Zebida bar Jochanan (Zebedee the son of John).[6] This was quite a regular practice among the Jews, and some valuable information has come from such inscribed items donated to synagogues.

We notice in passing that the existing ruins of synagogues in Palestine are all later than the first Jewish revolt. It would seem that the destruction of the synagogues was carried out systematically by the Romans. The oldest trace of such a building seems to be the inscription found in Jerusalem referring probably to the synagogue of the Freedmen.[7] There are several in Galilee but none of them can be dated earlier than the end of the second century A.D. To this earlier period belong the synagogues at Capernaum, Chorazin, and Kefr Bir'Im.[8] What is probably a synagogue of the time of Herod the Great has now been found at Masada, the great fortress of Herod overlooking the Dead Sea.[9] This synagogue was in use in Herod's time. It had a small anteroom and a main room, with columns along its southern, western, and northern sides. When the Zealots occupied Masada some time prior to its fall at the hands of the Romans, they added benches on three sides, tore down the walls separating the anteroom to enlarge the main room, and left a small anteroom in one corner of the new structure. Fragments of the scrolls of Ezekiel and Deuteronomy and some important ostraca were found in the debris.

Not far from Capernaum was Chorazin, which was associated with Bethsaida in our Lord's warning of judgment (Matt. 11:21-23; Luke 10:13-15). The position of Chorazin is marked today by Keraze, two miles to the north of Capernaum. Here, too, we may see the impressive remains of a synagogue, but, unlike the one at Capernaum, this is built of the black basalt which abounds in the area. Like its neighbor it dates from the late second or early third century A.D., and shows the same rich ornamentation. There was evidently a new and

---

6. J. Finegan, *Light from the Ancient Past* (Princeton, 1946), p. 227; *The Archaeology of the New Testament* (Princeton, 1969), pp. 50-53.

7. See above, p. 332.

8. J. Finegan, *The Archaeology of the New Testament*, pp. 58, 59.

9. Y. Yadin, *Masada* (London, 1966), pp. 180-191.

A close-up view of a symbolic motif (possibly of the holy ark, or perhaps of a carriage) on the white stones of the synagogue at Capernaum. Other stones are decorated with geometric designs, seven-branched candlesticks, plants, or animals. (Israel Office of Information)

more liberal attitude toward art by the third century, for these synagogues depict animals and human beings, motifs forbidden by the second commandment.[10]

One of the very interesting features of this synagogue is the seat of honor set in the end of the building, facing the congregation. Here sat honored visitors or elders who might minister to the people. It is thought that we have in this an example of the "seat of Moses" referred to in Matthew 23:2.[11] It was cut into solid basalt and was provided with a back rest and decorated arm rests, and carried an inscription which read, "May Judan son of Ishmael be remembered for good, who made this portico and its staircase. As his reward may he have a share with the righteous."[12] The man referred to here was the donor of the seat. One other such seat is known from Hammath, south of Tiberias.[13] Perhaps the

10. E. L. Sukenik, *Ancient Synagogues in Palestine and Greece* (London, 1934), pp. 57–61.

11. G. E. Wright and F. V. Filson, *Westminster Historical Atlas* (London, 1958), p. 60. See also I. Renov, "The Seat of Moses," *IEJ* (1955), pp. 262f.

12. E. G. Kraeling, *op. cit.*, p. 378.

13. G. E. Wright and F. V. Filson, *op. cit.*, p. 60.

synagogue that Jesus knew at Capernaum had such a "seat of Moses" and carried the name of the centurion who built it!

The area of Capernaum and Chorazin brings to mind the story of the feeding of the five thousand. While it is outside our period, it is of some interest to note that an ancient Christian church, excavated at Tabghah on the lakeside between Capernaum and Tiberias, has a very fine floor mosaic on which is represented a basketful of loaves and two fishes beside it, illustrating no doubt the famous miracle. One tradition is that Jesus preached the Sermon on the Mount to the people on the little hillside nearby. We cannot be sure of this, but the whole area is full of rich association, and almost any place in the region might have witnessed the ministry of our Lord.[14]

The town of Tiberias lay further south along the lake. In its day it was an important town,[15] and no doubt much lies buried here for our investigation. Since 1955 excavations in some ancient baths produced evidence from the days of Herod Antipas, whose capital was here.[16] The region has remains extending through to the tenth century A.D., and it is felt that even if the town has today little of the glory of the past, there may well be a story awaiting the excavator. Tiberias is mentioned only once in the New Testament (John 6:23).

To the west of Galilee lay the towns of Nazareth, Cana, and Nain. The geographical position of these can be determined today fairly easily, although our archaeological knowledge of them is limited. In a more general connection G. E. Wright and F. V. Filson have remarked that "it is gratifying to find that we can identify the main sites of Jesus' life and ministry. The birthplace, Bethlehem, and the childhood residence, Nazareth, are certainly known. Concerning the Sea of Galilee, Cana, Nain, Capernaum, and Chorazin, there can be no reasonable doubt."[17]

While this statement is true in regard to geographical position, we are in difficulty about the identification of the details of the towns. Thus Nazareth is a town that is full of traditional churches and other sites. The visitor is shown the Church of the Annunciation, the workshop of Joseph, the table of Christ, and so on. There is no solid evidence for any of these. Perhaps the one authentic item is the village well where Mary drew water, for it is the only well in the area. An ancient synagogue, now restored as a church, may possibly provide a link with early times. But the simple fact is that Nazareth has little of a reliable nature to offer us today. Indeed, some writers suggest that the Nazareth of the New Testament may actually have been a short distance from the modern town.[18]

14. J. Finegan, The Archaeology of the New Testament, pp. 48f.
15. See p. 312.
16. Articles in RB (Jan., 1956), p. 97; (Apr., 1957), p. 258.
17. G. E. Wright and F. V. Filson, op. cit., p. 94.
18. E. G. Kraeling, op. cit., pp. 358–360.

Nazareth in Galilee was the village where Jesus grew up and lived until His public ministry. This scene must show many places where He walked. (Israel Office of Information)

Cana is to be identified with the modern Khirbet Qana (John 2:1, 11; 4:46). There are remains of the third century A.D. here, but on the hill behind the village potsherds of the time of Christ and of the early Christian period are scattered about.[19]

Nain likewise may be identified today with a village that carries the same name. There is some evidence that excavation for the foundation of houses being built here disturbed ancient Roman remains.[20]

The other part of the domains of Herod Antipas lay in Trans-Jordan. At the extreme south of the area, on the edge of the Nabataean kingdom, was the fortress of Machaerus, situated on an isolated hill and surrounded by a wall. It was first built by Alexander Jannaeus, but was razed by the Romans in 63 B.C. Herod the Great rebuilt it between 25 and 13 B.C. Later it came into the territory of Antipas, and here, according to Josephus, John the Baptist met his

19. F.-M. Abel, *Géographie de la Palestine* (Paris, 1938), Vol. II p. 413.
20. E. G. Kraeling, *op. cit.*, p. 380.

death.[21] The town is not mentioned in the New Testament. Today there is a considerable area of ruins awaiting serious excavation.

TOWNS IN THE PROCURATORIAL PROVINCE OF JUDAEA

At the time of Christ this province included Samaria and extended from north of Caesarea on the coast to below Hebron. It included important towns, such as Samaria, Shechem (Sychem or Sychar), Jericho, Bethlehem, Jerusalem, Samaria, and a number of smaller places like Joppa, Lydda, and Bethany.

Caesarea on the Mediterranean was the administrative center of the Roman government. Philip preached here (Acts 8:40), and Paul was imprisoned here. Here, too, Cornelius lived (Acts 10), and Peter preached (Acts 11:11; 12:19). The town remained important into the Middle Ages and is mentioned in several writings of that time.[22] Until very recent times this important site was neglected, but now a new interest is being taken in the old town. Since 1961 serious archaeological work has been conducted at Caesarea by the Italian Archaeological Mission of Milan as well as by the Hebrew University and others like the American Schools of Oriental Research. Some discussion of the finds has already been given.[23]

An excellent glimpse into one facet of Roman culture has come from the excavation of the hippodrome at Caesarea in 1973-74. The arena was about 90 meters wide and 450 meters long and resembled in size the hippodromes at Tyre and elsewhere. It was functioning at its peak in the second century A.D. when the Christian movement was already well launched. But two coins of Herod Agrippa (A.D. 42-43) and a coin of Felix the Procurator (A.D. 54) found in the foundation soil that was used to level the arena before the structures were built, would suggest that the work was begun before the first century had run its course.[24] It is not our intention to describe the excavations at Caesarea any further, but they are important if we want to gain an understanding of the nature of the town in which Paul made his defense before Felix and Agrippa (Acts 25:4, 6-12, 13-27; 26:1-32).

Samaria is a town that has been excavated in some detail in recent times.[25] In the New Testament it does not feature a great deal, although the district is important. Philip preached here (Acts 8:5), and Simon the sorcerer came under the sound of the gospel. God blessed the ministry of Philip so that many believed. A woman from the same district met Jesus at the well (John 4), and early

---

21. Josephus, *Antiquities* XVIII.v.2.

22. A. Reifenberg, "A Study in the Decline of a Town," *IEJ*, Vol. I, No. 1, pp. 20ff.

23. See above, pp. 302f.

24. J. H. Humphrey, "A Summary of the 1974 Excavations in the Caesarea Hippodrome," *BASOR*, No. 218 (Apr., 1975).

25. The complete report has been published by the Palestine Exploration Fund (1958), as *Samaria-Sebaste*, Vol. III.

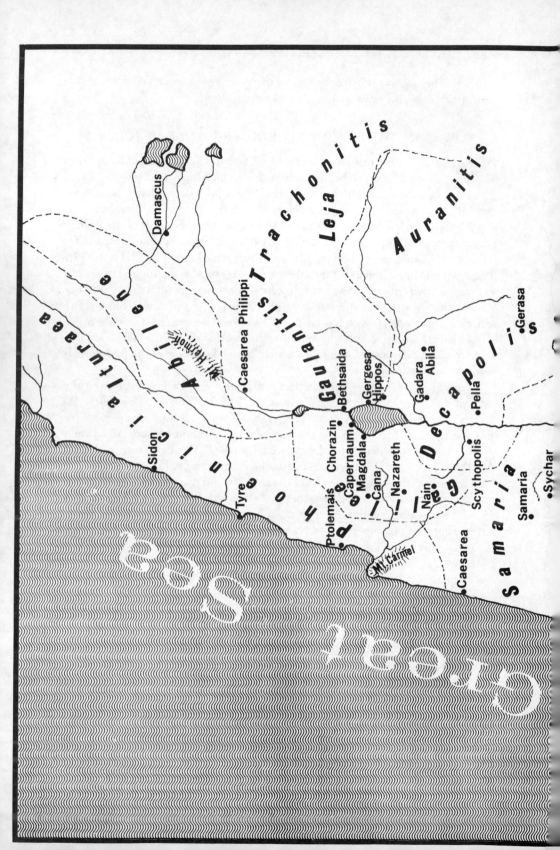

Palestine in the Time of Christ

Remnants of Roman columns near the seawall of Caesarea. (Israel Office of Information)

Christians preached here with some success (Acts 1:8; 8:4–6). Paul's conversion brought peace to the new churches in the area (Acts 9:31). There is no indication that Jesus Himself was ever there. It was a strongly Hellenized city, and Jesus' work lay chiefly among the Jews.

The nature of the city in the days when Herod the Great sponsored a building program is now well understood. As we have seen,[26] he built a temple for Augustus over the site of the palace of the earlier kings of Israel, and erected a stadium and forum in the town. The city was extended again toward the close of the second century and in the early third century A.D. A great basilica here later became a Christian church. But there are not the same sacred memories attaching to Samaria as there are to many other towns.

26. See above, pp. 301f.

The great stairway of the temple that Herod built for Augustus at Samaria. Herod renamed the city Sebaste (Greek for "Augustus") to honor the Roman emperor. (J. Eijckeler)

In recent years the Department of Antiquities of Jordan and the British School of Archaeology in Jerusalem have continued excavation work here. In campaigns in 1965 and 1966 the Department of Antiquities of Jordan undertook further work in the area of the theater and was able to add further details to the picture known since 1933. Many of the remaining structures date to the Hellenistic period, and some of them to the fourth and fifth centuries A.D. Yet Herod is known to have been active in Samaria and the excavators have been searching for substantial Herodian remains in the theater area. Up to the present little of importance from Herod's day has been found. Perhaps the existing facilities were adequate for his purpose.

A campaign conducted by the British School in 1968 outside the palace areas and mainly in the residential areas has brought to light evidence of the domestic buildings of the Roman period dating to the first century A.D. It seems clear that a great deal of the masonry used in these buildings was robbed from the previous Hellenistic buildings.

The town of Shechem, with a history reaching back into pre-patriarchal times, has more recently been suggested as the town referred to in John's Gospel as Sychar. It is called Shechem in the old Syriac Gospels, and this points to a corruption of an original *Sycem* to *Sychar*. But the identification is not finally secure despite the suggestion of W. F. Albright.[27] The most recent excavations at this site indicate that this town came to an end somewhere about 100 B.C.[28] The coin record for the Hellenistic city is quite strong up to about that point. If the indications are supported by subsequent excavations, then the old site known today as Tell Balatah ceased to be occupied before Roman times, and we shall need to look elsewhere for the *Sychar* of New Testament times. The late G. E. Wright, who gave a lot of attention to Shechem in recent years, reported that there were occasional Roman coins in the debris but thought these were probably from a Roman village near the spring below the present village of Balatah.[29] It seems therefore that we must await further evidence about the village known to Jesus.

In recent years a lot of excavation has been carried on in the Herodian and Roman town of Jericho. Reference has already been made to the excavation of Herodian buildings at Jericho.[30] After Herod's death and the transfer of power to Roman procurators, Jericho declined since it did not seem to have had any special attraction for the Roman governors. Most of the area surrounding the site gradually returned to desert. But there was some occupation there. The remains of a fine house from the second century A.D. were found over the ruins of Herod's palace in one area. This house had been burned in a major conflagration, perhaps during the Bar Kochba revolt. Jericho the garden city, which was inhabited by tens of thousands of Jews during the days of the Second Temple, probably shrank after the fall and destruction of Jerusalem in A.D. 70 to a much smaller town.[31] In Jesus' day Jericho was still an important town and was the scene of several New Testament happenings such as the healing of the two blind men (Matt. 20:29ff.), the healing of blind Bartimaeus (Mark 10:46ff.), and the incident in which Zacchaeus the tax-gatherer was converted (Luke 19:1–10).

There is strong circumstantial evidence that the modern village of Bethlehem represents the birthplace of Jesus. There are very early traditions attaching to the town and there are ancient building remains as well. As early as the time of Justin Martyr (about A.D. 150), the tradition that a certain cave was the place where Jesus was born seems to have been established. Other writers of antiquity state that the cave of the nativity was desecrated by Hadrian and was used by a cult of the god Adonis about A.D. 140. Jerome, the early Christian

27. W. F. Albright, *Archaeology of Palestine* (London, 1956), p. 247.
28. G. E. Wright, "The Second Campaign at Tell Balatah (Shechem)," BASOR (Dec., 1957), p. 28.
29. *Ibid.*, p. 26; J. Finegan, *The Archaeology of the New Testament*, pp. 34f.
30. See pp. 298f.
31. E. Netzer, "The Winter Palaces of the Judean Kings at Jericho at the End of the Second Temple Period," BASOR, No. 228 (Dec., 1977), pp. 1–13. Note p. 12.

A peaceful scene near Bethlehem in Judah, with part of the city in the background. Fertile fields, fig and olive orchards, and vineyards surround the city. (Trans World Airlines)

writer and translator of the Bible, who lived toward the close of the fourth century, is believed to have done some of his work here. In any case, he spoke of the restoration of the sacred place by the Emperor Constantine (A.D. 323–337), who cleared away the last traces of paganism and built a church over the cave.[32]

The present Church of the Nativity built on this site has undergone consid-

32. E. G. Kraeling, *op. cit.*, pp. 361f.

erable rebuilding, notably in the sixth century. The original church was built by Constantine, though little remains of the original structures within the later buildings still standing.[33] One enters the cave by a set of steps leading down below floor level to a grotto some thirty-three feet long and thirteen feet wide. There is little doubt that this is the cave known to the Christians in the fourth century, and no doubt the tradition goes back further. But we have no archaeological evidence before about A.D. 325. Tradition is not always wrong, and we have come to look behind tradition for elements of truth. But we still lack clear evidence that here we have the authentic birthplace of Christ. Nearby is a "shepherd's field" that lends an air of verisimilitude to the picture, but even here the tourist is shown at least two such fields, so that we have to rest content that Christ was born somewhere in the area, without knowing exactly where.[34]

Bethany was a village known to our Lord. It lay a little to the southeast of Jerusalem and was the place where Jesus was anointed by the woman with the alabaster box of ointment and where He raised Lazarus from the dead (John 11). It is mentioned in the Passion narratives (Mark 11:1; 14:3) and is described by John as "fifteen furlongs" (literally, *stadia*), or half an hour's walk, from Jerusalem. In the Syriac version of the New Testament it is written as Beth 'Anya, which may be the short form of Beth Ananiah (Neh. 11:32). Today there is a little village called El Azariyeh ("place of Lazarus"), and just to the west of this is a small hill where cisterns and Jewish tombs have been discovered.[35] Close to the present village is the traditional tomb of Lazarus; and even though a church was built here about A.D. 380, looking back perhaps to an earlier tradition about the burial place of Lazarus, there is no clear evidence that we have here the authentic site of Lazarus' tomb. The church has been excavated in recent times. All we can allow is that we probably have here the general position of the village of Bethany. Bethphage was not far away, most likely to the northwest, but there is no certainty about its position either.

Other towns of interest in the area of Roman Judaea, such as Joppa, Lydda, Emmaus, Hebron, Gaza, Askelon, and Azotus, are of interest but must be studied in a fuller work than this.

THE POPULATION OF PALESTINE IN THE TIME OF JESUS

Various peoples were to be found in the Holy Land in our Lord's day: Jews, Greeks, Phoenician-Canaanites, and smaller numbers of other peoples. The Jews, or, more correctly, the descendants of the Israelites, were well scattered through many areas. The Greeks, who had been brought to Palestine following the conquest of Alexander the Great, had established colonies in many places

33. R. W. Hamilton, *The Church of the Nativity, Bethlehem* (Jerusalem, 1947), pp. 91–96.
34. S. L. Caiger, *op. cit.*, pp. 77f.
35. E. G. Kraeling, *op. cit.*, pp. 393f.

The traditional tomb of Lazarus near the modern village of Bethany, which is ca. *one kilometer from Jerusalem. (Religious News Service)*

but chiefly in the center and in the areas around Galilee. In the south were the Idumaeans, the old Edomites, now partly mixed by intermarriage. Herod and his father and grandfather were of this stock. Across the Jordan, in addition to the Greek population and the admixture of Arabs, was the important, and now strong, kingdom of the Nabataeans, who occupied the areas south of Peraea. Their capital was at Petra.

We have seen that Herod Philip ruled a largely Greek population and that even in Galilee and in Samaria there were many Greeks. The most interesting area is that of the Decapolis (ten cities). The name occurs in the New Testament in Mark 5:20. Its origin goes back to the early days of the Romans in Palestine. Following the expansion of the Seleucid (Greek) rulers and their tremendous building program, the area to the east of Jordan became dotted with cities. With the restoration of the Jewish state under the Maccabees, the independence of these towns was threatened. When Pompey visited the area in 63

B.C., he saw that these Greek towns could be useful to Rome. He therefore confined the Jews in Trans-Jordan to a narrow strip along the Jordan and gave to the Greek cities their independence. Towns like Jerash, Gadara, Philadelphia, Scythopolis (Bethshean), Hippos, Abila, and some to the north, including Damascus, were numbered among the cities of the Decapolis. Roman remains exist in some of these, and a place like Jerash even today has a magnificent amount of material for the archaeologist.[36] A considerable amount of work has been done here, as we have seen.

To the northwest of Palestine lived the Canaanite-Phoenician population, the traders of the day. Many of them came into Palestine, and some at least had dealings with Jesus. In religion they were still polytheists as they had been for centuries. They provided a splendid mission field for the early preachers of the gospel who went to their lands and established the Christian Church.

Finally we refer to the Nabataeans who defied all conquerors till the Romans finally overcame them in A.D. 106.[37] Their greatest king was Aretas IV (9 B.C.–A.D. 40), who at the time of our Lord held places like Damascus under his sway. Paul in Damascus had an adventure with the "governor under Aretas,"

36. W. F. Albright, *op. cit.*, pp. 168–170.
37. J. Starcky, "The Nabataeans, a Historical Sketch," BA (Dec., 1955).

A view of modern Damascus, Syria. This religious and cultural center was first mentioned in a sixteenth-century B.C. Egyptian text and has been part of many empires. On the site of the central building, the Omayyad Great Mosque, once stood the Church of St. John the Baptist (fourth to eighth centuries) and before then a temple of the storm-god Hadad. (UNESCO/P. A. Pittet)

who sought to take him, and Paul had to escape over the wall in a basket (II Cor. 11:32, 33). The Nabataeans chose as their capital the mountain retreat of Petra[38] and carved out of the rock magnificent buildings of all kinds—temples, houses, shops, tombs, and so on. Their architecture shows Greek and Roman influence. Excavation here and in other sites has given us a good picture of their culture. They were polytheists, manufactured splendid pottery, and were good builders. They controlled and exploited the trade routes leading from the Arabian peninsula to the lands along the Mediterranean Sea. It was a Nabataean princess who was the first wife of Herod Antipas. His divorce of this woman in favor of the notorious Herodias caused a war with the king of the Nabataeans. The fortress of Machaerus stood at the southern boundary of the domains of Antipas as a protection against the Nabataeans.[39]

As we leave our brief survey of the towns and peoples of the Palestine that Jesus knew, we have the impression that we are still comparatively ignorant of many of the details about them. There is strong hope that the picture will be enlarged in the future. Active excavation is going on in many sites in Palestine and in the very places mentioned in the New Testament narratives. The subject is by no means exhausted and holds out much promise for future study.

38. W. F. Albright, op. cit., pp. 160–165.
39. See above, pp. 288, 312, 345, 372.

21

LUKE THE HISTORIAN

At the close of the nineteenth century extreme critics like F. C. Baur could argue that statements in Acts "can only be looked upon as intentional deviations from historic truth in the interest of the special tendency which they possess."[1] Such extremists compelled special study of Acts, with the result that it is widely agreed today that in this book we can see the hand of a historian of the first rank. Much of the credit for this change is due to the efforts of W. M. Ramsay, whose patient work proved that F. C. Baur and his school were wrong. Ramsay wrote a series of volumes to establish his point, among which *St. Paul the Traveller and the Roman Citizen and The Bearing of Recent Discovery on the Trustworthiness of the New Testament* are the best known. In the former of these books Ramsay made the following statement:

> I may fairly claim to have entered on this investigation without prejudice in favour of the conclusion which I shall now attempt to justify to the reader. On the contrary, I began with a mind unfavourable to it, for the ingenuity and apparent completeness of the Tübingen theory had at one time quite convinced me. It did not then lie in my line of life to investigate the subject minutely; but more recently I found myself brought in contact with the book of Acts as an authority for the topography, antiquities and society of Asia Minor. It was gradually borne in upon me that in various details the narrative showed marvellous truth. In fact, beginning with the fixed idea that the work was essentially a second-century composition and never relying on its

---

1. Quoted by A. T. Robertson in *Luke the Historian in the Light of Research* (Edinburgh, 1920), p. 1.

A covered market street in Damascus, Syria. Paul stayed in this city after being converted during his journey there, and was lowered in a basket over its walls to escape from the Jews who wanted to kill him. (UNESCO/P. A. Pittet)

evidence as trustworthy for first-century conditions, I gradually came to find it a useful ally in some obscure and difficult investigations.[2]

If we ask what it was that produced this radical change of opinion in Ramsay, the answer is largely that archaeological investigation demonstrated that the historical, geographical, topographical, and political atmosphere of the books Luke and Acts as a whole, and of Acts in particular, suggests a close knowledge of the first century A.D. On many of the pages of his writings Ramsay pays glowing tribute to the sound historical sense of Luke, whom he describes as "among the historians of the first rank."[3]

SOME MATERIAL FROM LUKE'S GOSPEL

It is evident that the writer of this Gospel is interested in placing events he narrates in the context of history, because he keeps on giving historical landmarks. It was in the "days of Herod, the king of Judaea," that Zacharias the priest learned from the angel about the birth of a son (Luke 1:5). It was in the days of "Caesar Augustus, that all the world should be taxed; and this taxing was first made when Cyrenius was governor of Syria" (Luke 2:1f.). "In the fifteenth year of the reign of Tiberius Caesar, Pontius Pilate being governor of Judaea, and Herod being tetrarch of Galilee, and his brother Philip tetrarch of Ituraea and of the region of Trachonitis, and Lysanias the tetrarch of Abilene, Annas and Caiaphas being the high priests," John the Baptist began to preach (Luke 3:1f.).

Such statements as these are open to archaeological and historical investigation. Herod reigned from 37 B.C. to 4 B.C. This gives a date before 4 B.C. for the birth of John the Baptist and Jesus Christ. There is no difficulty about these facts, but some interesting points are raised in Luke 2:1f. where reference is made to the census of Augustus, and to Cyrenius. First of all, "all the world" in verse 1 is not meant to be taken literally. It refers to the Roman world of those times. Nor does the passage require that a single census was to be held at one time, but rather that the world "should be enrolled." Ramsay pointed out that Luke used the present tense deliberately and meant "that Augustus ordered enrollments to be regularly taken."[4] This interpretation is according to the strict and proper usage of the present tense. What Augustus did was to lay down the principle of systematic "enrollment" in the Roman world, not to arrange for the taking of one single census.

This enrollment was the "first enrollment when Quirinius was governor," and is thus to be distinguished from the later census referred to in Acts 5:37. The point may be raised as to whether there is evidence that Augustus did in fact have an arrangement for such a system of enrollment. Here we have a good deal

---

2. W. M. Ramsay, *St. Paul the Traveller and the Roman Citizen* (London, 1897), pp. 7f.
3. *Ibid.*, p. 4.
4. W. M. Ramsay, *Was Christ Born at Bethlehem?* (London, 1898), pp. 123f.

Bust, made of fine Greek marble, of Augustus Caesar, A.D. 14. At the time of Jesus' birth Augustus decreed "that all the world should be enrolled [taxed]" (Luke 2:1). (British Museum)

of material on hand. Clement of Alexandria (A.D. 155–220) spoke as though he knew of such a system and said that it began with the census at the time of the birth of Christ. It is established that in the later empire there was a cycle of fourteen years between enrollments; and in Egypt, at any rate, there is documentary evidence, in the form of actual census papers, for enrollments in A.D. 90, 104, 118, 132, and on till 230.[5] Ramsay speaks of census records for A.D. 34 and 62, and indirect references to the censuses of A.D. 20 and 48. There is no reference extant to a census in A.D. 6, which would be the one in Acts 5:37, but presumably it took place. The one before this would be 8 B.C. E. M. Blaiklock in his *Pathway* book quotes a notice from A.D. 104, which reads as follows:

> Gaius Vibius, chief prefect of Egypt. Because of the approaching census it is necessary for all those residing for any cause away from their own districts to prepare to return at once to their own governments, in order that they may complete the family administration of the enroll-

5. A. T. Robertson, *op. cit.*, pp. 123ff., summarizes the data in a handy form.

ment, and that the tilled lands may retain those belonging to them. Knowing that your city has need of provisioning, I desire. . . .[6]

This document shows that the enrollment was by households. Even if there is no direct evidence of such an enrollment in Palestine, the picture from Egypt provides good circumstantial support that this kind of thing went on in the Roman world. If it happened in Egypt, which was under Roman rule, we might expect that the same thing would occur in Palestine. Professor Blaiklock, in the same chapter, adds other illustrations of documents found in Egypt, one being lodged by a woman in Egypt on the occasion of the census in A.D. 48.

The question of the exact date of the decree in Luke 2 is raised because on several grounds the birth of Christ seems to be about 7–6 B.C.[7] The census cycle would give a date of 8–7 B.C. Ramsay argued that the situation in Palestine and Syria at the time may well have caused some delay in Herod's kingdom.[8]

We raise finally a question about Quirinius (Cyrenius). According to Josephus, this man was governor of Syria in A.D. 6 when a census that angered the Jews was taken. The Greek word translated "governor" in Luke 2:1 may not, however, carry precisely the same idea as our word. Its basic idea is that of "oversight," and this may take on various forms. It is now clear from inscriptions that Quirinius had authority of some kind on two occasions in Syria, though the office was not the same. One inscription tells us that P. Sulpicius Quirinius duumvir was engaged in war in Syria sometime before 6 B.C.[9] F. F. Bruce believes that "there is substantial evidence that Quirinius held such a post at an earlier time, probably between 10 B.C. and 7 B.C. when, as extraordinary imperial legate in the province of Syro-Cilicia for military purposes, he commanded an expedition against the Homanadenses, a mountain tribe of Asia Minor."[10] Ramsay found an inscription to this effect at Antioch of Pisidia. Luke does not say that Quirinius himself held the census which took place at the time of our Lord's birth, but only that it was while he was governor. He was actually fulfilling an extraordinary function alongside the regular governor, who at that time was Sentius Saturninus (8–6 B.C.). The precise identification of Quirinius is difficult and no solution offered is free of difficulty. The problem can hardly be solved without the discovery of fresh evidence. Clearly, Luke intended to recall an enrollment for the purposes of taxation in the Roman style. This took place during the reign of Herod as part of the general policy of Augustus in regard to taxation.[11]

The third reference we have noticed in Luke 3:1 gives yet another attempt

6. E. M. Blaiklock, Out of the Earth (Grand Rapids, 1957), p. 14.
7. A. J. Maclean, "Chronology of the New Testament," Hastings' Dictionary of the Bible (Edinburgh, 1954), pp. 133ff., gives five converging lines of evidence for this date.
8. W. M. Ramsay, op. cit., pp. 174f.
9. A. T. Robertson, op. cit., p. 128.
10. F. F. Bruce, Are the New Testament Documents Reliable? (Grand Rapids, 1946), p. 85.
11. I. H. Marshall, The Gospel of Luke (Exeter, 1978), pp. 100–104, gives a comprehensive discussion of the various solutions that have been offered in regard to Quirinius. Cf. B. Reicke, The New Testament Era (London, 1969), pp. 134–137.

to date an event by reference to persons who lived at the time. Ancient historians used different methods to fix their dates and quite often made no attempt to be as exact as we are today. Here in Luke 3:1 seven synchronisms are given to establish the time when the ministry of John the Baptist began. A difficulty has been imagined in the mention of Lysanias, who is here named as tetrarch of Abilene (west of Damascus), in the fifteenth year of Tiberius (A.D. 27-28). The only Lysanias of Abilene known from ancient history died in 34 B.C. Josephus refers to his father Ptolemais as ruler of a state, which included Abilene and whose capital was Chalcis. He supported Jewish nationalists against the Romans in 49 B.C. Lysanias, the son, followed his father's policy, but was finally put to death by Antonius in 34 B.C. After this there is little known about Abilene till A.D. 53.[12] Josephus tells us that this area was added to the kingdom of Agrippa II by the emperor Claudius. In this later reference there is a mention of Lysanias. Josephus says concerning Abilene that "this had been the tetrarchy of Lysanias."[13] A second and later Lysanias was postulated for a time, but there are now two inscriptions which refer to such a man so that his existence is no longer a matter of speculation. In one of these he is coupled with a certain Zenodorus and is called "tetrarch." In the other we have a record of the dedication of a temple "for the salvation of the Lords Imperial and their whole household, by Nymphaeus a freedman of Lysanias the tetrarch."[14] The "Lords Imperial" was a joint title given to the emperor Tiberius and his mother Livia, the widow of Augustus, so that the date of the inscription may be fixed between A.D. 14, the year of Tiberius' accession, and A.D. 29, the year of Livia's death. The reference to Lysanias in Luke 2:1 is therefore strongly supported by archaeological evidence.

Alfred Plummer, whose commentary on Luke was written in 1913 when much of this evidence was unavailable, remarked then that "the accuracy of Luke is such that we ought to require very strong evidence before rejecting any statement of his as an unquestionable blunder."[15] This statement is in strong contrast with the statements of numerous New Testament scholars of the last part of the nineteenth century, thanks to the discoveries of the archaeologists and the careful research of scholars such as Sir William Ramsay.

ACTS IN THE LIGHT OF ARCHAEOLOGY—PAUL'S FIRST MISSIONARY JOURNEY

The accuracy of Luke shows up particularly well in the book of Acts. Ramsay's *St. Paul the Traveller and the Roman Citizen* is devoted largely to an account of the journeys of Paul and the archaeological material bearing on them. Since Ram-

---

12. J. M. Creed, *The Gospel According to St. Luke* (London, 1950), p. 308.
13. Josephus, *Wars* XX.vii.1.
14. J. M. Creed, *op. cit.*, p. 309; I. H. Marshall, *op. cit.*, p. 134; E. Schürer, *The Jewish People in the Time of Jesus Christ (1885-1891)*, Vol. I, pp. 567-569.
15. A. Plummer, *St. Luke*, ICC (Edinburgh, 1913), p. 50.

say's day we have additional information from excavations and documents unknown to him. There is more reason than ever to conclude with Ramsay that

> Luke is a historian of the first rank; not merely are his statements of fact trustworthy; he is possessed of the true historic sense; he fixes his mind on the idea and plan that rules in the evolution of history, and proportions the scale of his treatment to the importance of each incident. He seizes the important and critical events and shows that true nature at greater length, while he touches lightly, or omits entirely, much that was valueless for his purpose. In short, this author should be placed along with the very greatest of historians.[16]

Our method of treatment will be a chronological one. We shall proceed through the book of Acts in order, commenting on the narrative with archaeological material as we go.

We commence with Acts 11:27-30 where there is a reference to the "great dearth throughout all the world" which came in the days of Claudius Caesar. Ramsay collected evidence to show that this famine is "singularly well attested."[17] Suetonius speaks of *assiduae sterilitates*, causing famine prices under Claudius; and Dio Cassius and Tacitus refer to two famines in Rome, implying famines in the Mediterranean area, for Rome received her grain from overseas. Eusebius speaks of famine in Greece, and an inscription points to famine in Asia Minor. It seems clear that the reign of Claudius (A.D. 41-54) was marked by a succession of bad harvests which caused serious famines in various parts of the empire.[18] It was this famine that stirred up Christians in Antioch to send help to the poor Christians in Jerusalem, and Paul went on his second visit to this great city about A.D. 46, bearing a gift. It is known that others helped the poor of Jerusalem at this time, for example, Queen Helena of Abilene, who bought corn in Egypt and figs in Cyprus, and sent them to Jerusalem. Josephus dates this event in the days of Cuspius Fadus (A.D. 44-46) and Tiberius Julius Alexander (46-48), procurators of the time.[19] This visit of Paul is probably the same as that referred to in Galatians 2:1ff. It was by revelation (cf. Acts 11:28 and Gal. 2:2), and the friends of Jerusalem asked that they go on remembering the poor (Gal. 2:10).

With chapter 13 we come to that portion of Acts which concentrates on the life and work of Paul. It must have been in about A.D. 46 that the church of Antioch "separated Paul and Barnabas for the work" and sent them off on the first missionary journey. They left Seleucia by boat to go to Cyprus. Today the ruins of the old port of Seleucia, founded originally by Seleucus, the first

16. W. M. Ramsay, *The Bearing of Recent Discovery on the Trustworthiness of the New Testament* (London, 1915), p. 222.
17. W. M. Ramsay, *St. Paul the Traveller and the Roman Citizen*, pp. 48f.
18. F. F. Bruce, *The Book of Acts* (Grand Rapids, 1954), p. 243.
19. Josephus, *Antiquities* XX.ii.5 and v.2.

Port of Antalya (biblical Attalia) on the southwest coast of Asia Minor. Attalos, the king of Pergamum, founded the walled city in the second century B.C., and his heirs bequeathed it to Rome. From there Paul and Barnabas sailed to Antioch. (B. K. Condit)

Seleucid king, in 301 B.C., lie scattered along the shore and for some distance inland. Very little excavation has been done here, but there is a splendid opportunity for someone to undertake this task. The travelers landed in Cyprus, an island of great importance for many centuries past, but annexed by Rome in 57 B.C., and attached to the province of Cilicia in Asia Minor in 55 B.C. In 27 B.C. it became a separate province governed by a legate. Then, in 22 B.C., Augustus handed it over to the Senate and it was administered by a proconsul. Thus, in the course of thirty-five years it had four types of Roman government. Unless Luke were well acquainted with the facts there was plenty of occasion to make a mistake. A certain amount of excavation work has been carried out at Seleucia, but there is a vast area of ruins here awaiting a concerted archaeological investigation. However, in verse 7 he gives to the ruler of those times the correct title of "deputy" (Greek anthupatos translates the Latin proconsul).

Salamis and Paphos, mentioned in the narrative, are both places in which, although some excavation has already been undertaken, there is an excellent opportunity for further work.

Mound of Kerti Huyuk in south-central Asia Minor, identified as ancient Derbe. Paul visited this Lyconian city on his first and second missionary journeys and possibly on his third; he won many converts here. (Bastiaan VanElderen)

In Paphos the missionaries met the proconsul Sergius Paulus. There is a good possibility that the name of this man has been found on an inscription in Cyprus. Ramsay refers to such an inscription found at Soloi on the north coast dated "in the proconsulship of Paullus."[20] One of the officers of Claudius in Rome, the "curator of the Tiber," was a man named Lucius Sergius Paullus,[21] and it is quite possible that he went afterward to Cyprus as a proconsul.

One of the interesting suggestions of Ramsay is that some of the family of this Sergius Paullus later became Christians. He advanced epigraphic evidence for this suggestion.[22] Another item in this passage which possibly follows Roman usage is the reference to Paul's names in verse 9. Roman citizens had three names—a praenomen, a nomen, and a cognomen. Luke here gives only one of these names, Paulus, the cognomen. Luke, being a Greek, probably did not bother with other names. On the other hand, we may have here an example of the Jewish custom of an alternative Jewish name.

Leaving Cyprus, Paul and Barnabas went to Pamphylia in Asia Minor and then struck inland to the southern parts of the large Roman province of Galatia,

20. W. M. Ramsay, *St. Paul the Traveller and the Roman Citizen*, p. 74.
21. F. F. Bruce, *op. cit.*, p. 264.
22. W. M. Ramsay, *The Bearing of Recent Discovery on the Trustworthiness of the New Testament*, pp. 150f.

which had been formed in 25 B.C. It was divided into a number of regions such as Pisidia, Isauria, Phrygia, and Lycaonia.[23] It seems that there were two regions known as Lycaonia, one in Galatia (Lycaonia Galatica) and one further east belonging to an independent kingdom (Lycaonia Antiochiana). The town of Antioch mentioned in verse 14 is called by Strabo "Antioch near [or toward] Pisidia." It was the center of the region known as Galatic Phrygia and was the chief civil and military center of that part. An inscription found here some years ago speaks of a "regionary centurion," evidently a military officer charged with special duties in the area.[24] Hence Luke in Acts 13:49 quite accurately refers to preaching taking place in all the "region" round about.

The result of the preaching of the Word in the synagogue was that "almost the whole city" returned on the next Sabbath to hear. The local Jews stirred up strife. Luke mentions that the women had a share in this, and Ramsay points out that whereas this kind of thing would be unthinkable in Athens or an Ionian city, it was in accord with the custom in these inland cities.[25] So the missionaries moved on to Iconium, a town in the same region politically, but on the eastern edge of Galatic Phrygia. Actually the boundary here was a little artificial, and Iconium was quite near to Lystra, so that the two towns had close commercial relations. This fact is evident from Luke's comment in Acts 16:2. After more troubles in Iconium, Paul and Barnabas moved on to another "region," crossing over the boundary between Phrygia Galatica and Lycaonia Galatica. Ramsay confessed that it was the discovery of this fact of geography that led to his "first change in judgment" about the book of Acts, which he had hitherto regarded as of uncertain value.[26] The Greek writer Xenophon in 401 B.C. referred to Iconium as a Phrygian city, and there is both literary and epigraphic evidence to show that it remained a Phrygian city till A.D. 295.[27] While it was thus linked with Lystra and the towns of Lycaonia for commerce, it was in fact politically in Phrygia. This fact appealed greatly to Ramsay since it showed that Luke was accurately informed on such a precise detail.

The description in Acts 14:6 is entirely correct. There was a region here consisting of two large towns, Lystra and Derbe, and the area round about. Both towns lay in Lycaonia Galatica. To these strategic cities Paul and Barnabas came to preach. Lystra had become a Roman colony in the time of Augustus in A.D. 6, and lay eighteen miles from Iconium, which was in Phrygian Galatia. Paul healed a crippled man here, and won the admiration and worship of the local population who came out with offerings and garlands as to gods, and cried out in the local dialect. Inscriptions show that Latin was the language of the colonists,

23. W. M. Ramsay, *St. Paul the Traveller and the Roman Citizen*, p. 104.

24. *Ibid.*, p. 103.

25. *Ibid.*, p. 102.

26. W. M. Ramsay, *The Bearing of Recent Discovery on the Trustworthiness of the New Testament*, pp. 35f.

27. F. F. Bruce, *op. cit.*, p. 288.

but evidently the local people still spoke their own dialect, especially when they were excited.[28] There do not seem to be inscriptions in this local dialect, so perhaps there was no written language.

The mention of the two gods, Mercury and Jupiter, leads us to ask why these two were chosen out of all the possible gods in the pantheon. The names in the Authorized Version of the Bible are Latin and differ from the Greek forms of the names, Hermes and Zeus, which occur in the Greek New Testament. At Sedasa, near Lystra, two inscriptions have been found.[29] One, dating from the middle of the third century A.D., records the dedication to Zeus of a statue of Hermes by men with Lycaonian names. The other mentions the "priests of Zeus." A stone altar, also found near Lystra in 1926, and dedicated to the "Hearer of Prayer [presumably Zeus] and Hermes," makes it clear that these two gods were linked in the worship of the people in this area.[30] Zeus was the head of the pantheon and Hermes was his herald. It is evident that when Paul and Barnabas came to Lystra, Paul was the active one and was thought to be Hermes the messenger, while Barnabas appeared more like Zeus who sent Hermes about his affairs.

Paul and Barnabas then moved on to Derbe and finally retraced their tracks to Antioch in Syria to report to the Church. So ended the first missionary journey.

PAUL'S SECOND MISSIONARY JOURNEY

The great Council of Jerusalem met in the period between Paul's first two journeys. In the years between, Paul wrote his letter to the Galatians, whom he had visited.[31] It was the remarkable events of the first journey, and the conversion of the many Gentiles, that required the Church to state its policy. This was done at the Council of Jerusalem. Then Paul and Barnabas were ready to set off again to visit the churches they had founded in Galatia. As things turned out, Paul took Silas, and Mark accompanied Barnabas (Acts 15:36-40). This must have been in A.D. 49 after an interval of teaching at Antioch.

Traveling this time overland, Paul and Silas passed through the province of Syria and Cilicia, a single Roman province (15:41), and then came to the province of Galatia. The book of Acts does not refer to this as such, but merely to the region of Derbe and Lystra. There is a precise touch here in 16:2, where Timothy is spoken of as "well reported of by the brethren that were at Lystra and Iconium." These two towns were, as we have seen, in different regions politically, but closely related economically, and it would be more likely that a man

---

28. *Ibid.*, p. 291; E. M. Blaiklock, *Cities of the New Testament* (London, 1965), pp. 31-34.
29. *Ibid.*
30. *Ibid.*, p. 292.
31. New Testament scholars still argue as to whether Paul's letter to the Galatians was written to the churches around Antioch in the south, or to churches further north. English scholars on the whole accept the "South Galatian" theory, which is the view of the present writer.

would be better known in them than in Lystra and Derbe. Ramsay notes that "this is true to the facts of commerce and intercourse."[32]

The geographical information is continued in 16:6, which refers to the crossing of the boundary of a new region. The Greek text describes it as "Phrygia and the Galatian territory" (or possibly, "the Phrygian and Galatian territory"). This is a composite phrase for a single district. Actually old Phrygia was now divided by the Romans into a Galatian and an Asian portion (see map, p. 404). Mysia (v. 7) was a region of Asia, Bithynia (v. 7) a province, and Macedonia (v. 9) the first province of Europe to be visited by the missionaries. In all of this, Luke's information is quite consistent with what we know about the geography of this part of the Roman empire in the first century A.D. from a study of ancient documents. And so to Philippi and the evangelization of Europe!

Archaeological work has made an important contribution to our understanding of the story of Paul's visit to Philippi (Acts 16:12–40). Philippi came under Roman control in 168 B.C. After a battle in which Antony and Octavian defeated Brutus and Cassius in 42 B.C., veterans of the battle were allowed to settle here and to form a Roman colony, and other Roman citizens came later. The Greek text refers to it as a *colonia*, which is correct. One other feature about this city is that it is described here as "first." There are inscriptions extant which show that some cities in Asia, Bithynia, and Macedonia had such a title. Acts 16:12 is a much discussed text, but it is evidently based on fact.[33] The point of discussion turns on the exact meaning of "first," but while scholars decide the true interpretation, the fact remains that this title "first" was used.

Verse 13 in the Authorized Version should be changed to read, "we went forth without the gate by a river side," which is in close accord with the facts of archaeology. From 1914 to 1938 French archaeologists worked in Philippi. In the course of uncovering the old Roman road that ran through the town, they discovered the foundations of a great arched gateway at the northwest edge of the town through which the old road passed.[34] The only watercourse in the region that is worthy of the name of river adjoins this road at only one place, a little more than a mile to the west of the city limits. The topography of Acts is thus quite accurate. The missionaries would in fact have gone "without the gate to the river side." We judge that we have here the exact spot where the gospel was first proclaimed in Europe.

A woman named Lydia, a seller of purple dye, was converted here, and a damsel was delivered of a demon. This caused an uproar, and Paul and Silas were dragged into the marketplace (Greek *agora*). This site has been exposed by the excavations.[35] It followed the usual pattern of a Roman forum with a platform to

32. W. M. Ramsay, St. Paul the Traveller and the Roman Citizen, p. 179.
33. F. F. Bruce, op. cit., p. 330; E. M. Blaiklock, op. cit., pp. 39–44.
34. W. A. McDonald, "Archaeology and St. Paul's Journeys in Greek Lands," BA (May, 1940), p. 20.
35. Ibid.

the north, where cases were heard, and a large open square surrounded by important buildings. Paul and Silas appeared before the "magistrates" (Greek *strategoi*, v. 20). There were various kinds of magistrates and the Greek term here is normally used for the Latin magistrate, the *praetor*. In Roman colonies the magistrates were normally not *praetors* but *duumvirs*. We need not conclude that Luke has erred here, for these officers often took the more dignified title *praetor*, according to Cicero, one of the writers of the time.[36] This is no doubt what happened here. In any case Paul and Silas were beaten with the attendants' (*lictors'*) rods and cast into prison, where the jailor was converted in the night. The next day the magistrates sent to the "sergeants" (Greek *rabdouchoi*; lit. "rod bearers," the equivalent of *lictor*) to release them. Learning that Paul and Silas were Roman citizens, who were exempted from flogging and all degrading forms of punishment, the Roman magistrates were full of confusion and urged them to leave, which they did, passing through the city gate and traveling westward along the Egnatian Way, of which remains have now been discovered.

The next town for which we have some information is Thessalonica (Acts 17:1-9). Little in the way of excavation has been done here, for modern buildings cover the site of this ancient town. There are, however, a number of monuments of late Roman and early Christian times still standing. One important item bears on the days of Paul, and is connected with the reference to the "rulers" (v. 6) before whom Jason and the brethren were brought after the uproar. Jason had received Paul and earned the wrath of the Jews. The Greek word for "ruler" here is *politarchos*. It is now known to have been used particularly in Macedonian towns, although it is not yet known elsewhere in Greek literature. There are extant today some nineteen inscriptions ranging from the second century B.C. to the third century A.D. where the title is used, and in the majority of cases the reference is to magistrates of the Macedonian cities, although a few refer to other cities. Of the Macedonian examples five refer specifically to Thessalonica, which seems to have had five politarchs at the beginning of the first century B.C. and six in the following century.[37]

Paul left Silas and Timothy in Macedonia and went on alone to the province of Achaia in which lay the important towns of Athens and Corinth. There have been excavations in both of these towns and the archaeologist's spade has again produced considerable material for the student of the New Testament.

While Paul waited in Athens for his friends (they joined him after a few weeks in Corinth, Acts 18:5), he was able to look around this famous city with all its beauty of architecture and sculpture. Although the heyday of Athens in sculpture, literature, philosophy, and oratory had been the fifth and fourth centuries B.C., she was still unsurpassed, and the Romans, who had considerable respect for its culture, gave Athens a certain freedom. Much of the beautiful

36. F. F. Bruce, *op. cit.*, p. 335.
37. *Ibid.*, p. 344; E. M. Blaiklock, *op. cit.*, pp. 45-49.

A Greek inscription, once part of the Gate of Vardar at Thessalonica, listing six rulers of the city, or "politarchs." Luke in Acts 17:16 correctly designates officials of Thessalonica by this Macedonian title. (British Museum)

sculpture and architecture, however, was for the honor of the gods, and this offended Paul. He "disputed in the synagogue with the Jews, and with the devout persons, and in the market daily" (v. 17).

In this statement there are two items of interest. First, excavations have brought the marketplace (Greek *agora*) to light, and it is possible today to draw a fairly complete plan of it.[38] Secondly, there is a keen observation hidden away here that reveals close knowledge of local customs. Ramsay pointed out that "in Ephesus, Paul taught 'in the school of Tyrannus'; in the city of Socrates he discussed moral questions in the market place. How incongruous it would seem if the methods were transposed."[39]

The Areopagus mentioned in verse 19 was where Paul was taken by the philosophers. This was an ancient court which met on a small rocky hill just at the foot of the great Acropolis and almost due west. The Acropolis itself was formerly the site of the fortress which protected the town. It was a striking, rocky hill which rose high behind Athens. According to tradition this little hill was the place where Ares, the god of war, stood trial for slaying the son of the sea god, and thereafter this rocky eminence served as the meeting place of the most ancient court and council of Athens. There were two white stones here, on one

38. O. Broneer, "Athens, City of Idol Worship," BA (Feb., 1958), p. 17; E. M. Blaiklock, *op. cit.*, pp. 54–55.
39. W. M. Ramsay, *St. Paul the Traveller and the Roman Citizen*, p. 238.

The Acropolis at Athens, which has temples on top and the odeum (theatre or concert hall) of Herodes Atticus (ca. A.D. 160) at its base, is one of the most impressive sights in Greece. Many of the large buildings, including the Parthenon (center), were built during the Golden Age of Pericles (fifth century B.C.). (Ewing Galloway)

of which the defendant stood and on the other the prosecutor. In Paul's time the Areopagus had control over teachers like Paul who were expounding a new philosophy. By then, however, much, if not all, of the judicial authority had been lost, and its power lay chiefly in matters of religion and morals. Ramsay refers to the occasion when the Roman Cicero persuaded the Areopagus to invite a certain Cratippus, a philosopher, to lecture in Athens.[40] Paul was invited by this august body to come to the little hill to expound his philosophy, and in verses 22 to 31 we have a summary of his address.

Archaeological comment may be made on two items in Paul's address. The reference to the Athenians being "too superstitious," or preferably, "very reli-

40. *Ibid.*, p. 247.

gious," is better understood in the light of our knowledge of the very great number of temples and religious statues and images that were to be seen in the city. Other writers, like Sophocles, Pausanias, and Josephus, were similarly impressed.[41] The extant remains of temples and religious sculptures certainly support Paul's remark. The great Acropolis, on which stood the Parthenon, was covered with a variety of temples and shrines, many of which can still be seen even though they are in a state of ruin.[42]

The other item on which we should comment is the reference to the altar with an inscription, "To the Unknown God." That such altars were known in Greece, and in particular in Athens, is borne out by two writers of ancient times. Pausanias, who lived in the second century A.D. and traveled widely, observed in his description of Greece that at Athens there were altars of gods called "unknown." Again Philostratus in the early third century spoke of Athens "where even unknown divinities have altars erected to them."[43]

As a result of Paul's preaching some believed, including a woman called Damaris. Ramsay suggests that this woman may have been foreign, perhaps one of the educated foreigners who were common in Athens. "It was possible in Athenian society for a woman of respectable position and family to have opportunity of hearing Paul."[44] This may be true, though it is not entirely clear, for she may have been one of the "God-fearers who heard him in the synagogue."

The last great town Paul visited on this journey was Corinth (18:1-17). He stayed here a year and six months "teaching the word of God among them." This was probably about A.D. 51. At that time Corinth was the commercial and political center of the Roman province of Achaia and therefore a strategic center from Paul's point of view. A strange occurrence made it possible for the archaeologists to work in old Corinth. In 1858 an earthquake in the region caused most of the survivors to abandon the old site and move three or four miles away. In 1896 the Greek government gave a permit to the American School of Classical Studies to excavate, and since that day an enormous amount of information has been accumulated.

The city of Corinth had been badly damaged by the Romans in 146 B.C., though not completely obliterated. Remains of the earlier city, such as the great columns of the temple of Apollo, have been discovered. Julius Caesar refounded the city as a Roman colony, and it made rapid strides in prosperity. It became the capital of the Roman province of Achaia in 27 B.C.

Paul met a Jewish couple, Aquila and Priscilla, shortly after his arrival and discovered them to be of the same trade as himself. They became friends. These two had come from Rome on the occasion of the expulsion of the Jews from that

41. F. F. Bruce, op. cit., p. 355.
42. W. A. McDonald, "Archaeology and St. Paul's Journeys in Greek Lands, Part II, Athens," BA (Feb., 1941). See also O. Broneer, op. cit.
43. F. F. Bruce, op. cit., p. 355.
44. W. M. Ramsay, St. Paul the Traveller and the Roman Citizen, p. 252.

Doric columns, the most primitive of those extant, on the archaic Temple of Apollo (sixth century B.C.) at Corinth, Greece. Seven of the original thirty-eight columns survive; they are seven meters tall and two meters in diameter. The temple stands in the only part of the city not destroyed by the Romans in 146 B.C. (Allen Myers)

city by Emperor Claudius. We have referred to this event already and to the uncertainty attaching to the name *Chrestus* in the account of Suetonius.[45] It is quite possible that we have here a reference to troubles caused by the Jews at the time of the introduction of Christianity to Rome. The passage in Suetonius reads: "Because the Jews at Rome caused continuous disturbances at the instigation of Chrestus, he [Claudius] expelled them from the city."[46]

Paul, as usual, preached to the Jews, whose synagogue is mentioned in verse 4. That there was a synagogue somewhere in the city is evidenced by the discovery of a long block of stone which was evidently the lintel of a doorway. Seven Greek letters were still visible, "GOGEEBR." An attempted restoration is "[SUNA]GOGE EBR[AION]," which means "Synagogue of the Jews."[47] This piece was dated by Deissmann at between 100 B.C. and A.D. 200, although some writers do not allow that it is pre-Christian. W. A. McDonald argues that it was actually after Paul's time. "The careless style of lettering indicates that the inscription, and presumably the synagogue to which it belonged, is considerably later than the time of St. Paul. But it is reasonable to conclude that both this and the earlier one, in which the Apostle 'reasoned every sabbath, and per-

---

45. See above, p. 313.
46. Suetonius, *The Twelve Caesars* (Harmondsworth, 1958), p. 197.
47. A. Deissmann, *Light from the Ancient East* (London, 1927), p. 16.

suaded the Jews and the Greeks' (Acts 18:4), were located in this area. No existing foundation has yet been convincingly associated with this lintel."[48]

Paul's two friends Titus and Timothy (v. 5) now joined him, and the work of preaching went on. In time, however, trouble began according to the usual pattern, and Paul was brought before Gallio, the "deputy of Achaia" (v. 12). The date of spring A.D. 52 can be given with considerable accuracy from the reference to Gallio. Paul was thus in Corinth from autumn A.D. 50 to spring A.D. 52. Certain pieces of information link together very neatly in this connection.

Gallio is described as the "deputy" (Greek *anthupatos*), that is, *proconsul*, in Latin. The first question we ask concerns the precise nature of the governor of Achaia. Ramsay gives the facts as follows: "Achaia was governed by a proconsul from 27 B.C. to A.D. 15 and from A.D. 44 onwards. It was a province of the second rank and was administered by Roman officials after holding the praetorship, and generally before the consulship."[49] So Paul gives the correct title for Gallio.

Next, what can be discovered about this Gallio? There was a Gallio, son of the elder Seneca (about 50 B.C. to A.D. 40) and brother of the younger Seneca the philosopher (about 3 B.C. to A.D. 65). He was adopted by the rhetorician Lucius Junius Gallio, and took his name. He was renowned for his amiable character and his wit. An inscription, found at Delphi in central Greece, records a proclamation of the emperor Claudius sometime early in A.D. 52, which mentions that Gallio was proconsul of Achaia[50] and suggests that he had been appointed to the office earlier, perhaps in A.D. 51. Seneca mentions that Gallio caught fever in Achaia and took a cruise. He was later in Rome, but perished finally with Seneca and other members of his family in the days of Nero's purges.[51] All of which shows again that Luke was well acquainted with the facts of the case.

Paul was taken to the "judgment seat" (Greek *bema*). The position of this in the marketplace in Corinth is now known. It was situated near the center of the Agora, along a magnificent terrace dividing the lower area on the north from the upper area on the south. There was a structure here which was really an outdoor speaker's stand. It originally had an outer coat of marble, traces of which remain and indicate the richness of its decoration. Flanking the *bema* at the level of the lower Agora were waiting rooms with mosaic floors and marble benches on each side.[52]

48. W. A. McDonald, "Archaeology and St. Paul's Journeys in Greek Lands, Part III, Corinth," BA (Sept., 1942), p. 41.

49. W. M. Ramsay, St. Paul the Traveller and the Roman Citizen, p. 258; E. M. Blaiklock, op. cit., pp. 56–61.

50. A. Deissmann, Paul (London, 1926), pp. 261ff., esp. p. 272.

51. F. F. Bruce, op. cit., pp. 373f.

52. O. Broneer, "Corinth," BA (Dec., 1951), pp. 91f.

Remains of the shops and monuments that lined the agora (marketplace) of Corinth. In the background is the Acrocorinth, a mountain on which stood the Temple of Aphrodite, where cultic prostitution was practiced. The city of Paul's day was populated by Greeks, Romans (who first settled in Corinth when Julius Caesar made it a Roman colony in 46 B.C.), and Jews. (Ewing Galloway)

Gallio quickly decided that the matter was purely one of a difference in interpretation between groups of Jews and dismissed the case. The mob, sensing the insult to the Jews, took occasion to beat up their leader in a sort of anti-Jewish demonstration. Gallio ignored this (v. 17), and Paul rejoiced in the "freedom of speech which the imperial policy as declared by Gallio seemed inclined to permit." So says Ramsay, and adds, "The action of Gallio, as we understand it, seems to pave the way for Paul's appeal a few years later from the petty outlying court of the procurator of Judaea, who was always much under the influence of the ruling party in Jerusalem, to the supreme tribunal of the Empire."[53]

We have a gleam of light today about the meat market of I Corinthians 10:25. The Christians in Corinth were concerned about purchasing meat sold in the "shambles" (Greek *makellon*) because it had first been offered to idols. An inscription found in the course of the American excavations was identified as belonging to the meat market, and it may have come from a large commercial building on the northern side of the Agora.[54] An alternative site is on the west of the Agora[55] where a row of shops once stood, each with a deep shaft that led to the underground tunnel that brought water into the Agora. These shafts must have provided cooling for perishable items. An inscription here in Greek corresponds to Latin *Lucius lanius*, that is, Lucius the butcher. The presence of several ruined temples in the area, among them the temple of Apollo on an elevated site just to the north of the market area, provides the setting in which the flesh of sacrificed beasts might have been taken to a nearby shop for sale.

Corinth was also a place of games and theater. Every second year the town was the center for athletic contests known as the Isthmian Games in honor of the god Poseidon. The remains of both theaters and an amphitheater give point to Paul's illustrations in I Corinthians 9:23-27 where reference is made to athletes training to win a fading wreath.

Reference to the important pavement inscription left by a certain Erastus on a pavement to the northwest of the Agora will be made in a later paragraph.[56]

Paul tarried in Corinth "yet a good while" (v. 18) and then passed on to Ephesus, taking with him Priscilla and Aquila. His visit to Ephesus on this occasion was brief, for he was pressing on to Jerusalem to keep the feast (v. 21). He was to return for an extended ministry on his third missionary journey in A.D. 53.

PAUL'S THIRD MISSIONARY JOURNEY AND HIS LAST YEARS

After his return to Jersualem from his second journey (18:21f.), Paul had hurried on to Antioch. The Greek text in verses 22 and 23 gives an impression of haste with its succession of participles. Paul set out by land again and traversed the "Galatic region" (literal Greek), that is, the Galatic Lycaonia and "Phrygia" (probably the whole area including both the Galatic and the Asian). As there was no bar to the way (cf. 16:6), he pressed on into Asia and, having visited his old friends of southern Galatia, he was now ready to conquer new fields. He came to Ephesus where his friends Priscilla and Aquila had instructed a well-

53. W. M. Ramsay, *St. Paul the Traveller and the Roman Citizen*, p. 260.

54. W. F. Albright, *Recent Discoveries in Bible Lands*, p. 119; O. Broneer, *op. cit.*, pp. 79, 89f.

55. W. A. McDonald, "Archaeology and St. Paul's Journeys in Greek Lands," *BA*, Vol. V, No. 3 (1942), pp. 43f.

56. See p. 405.

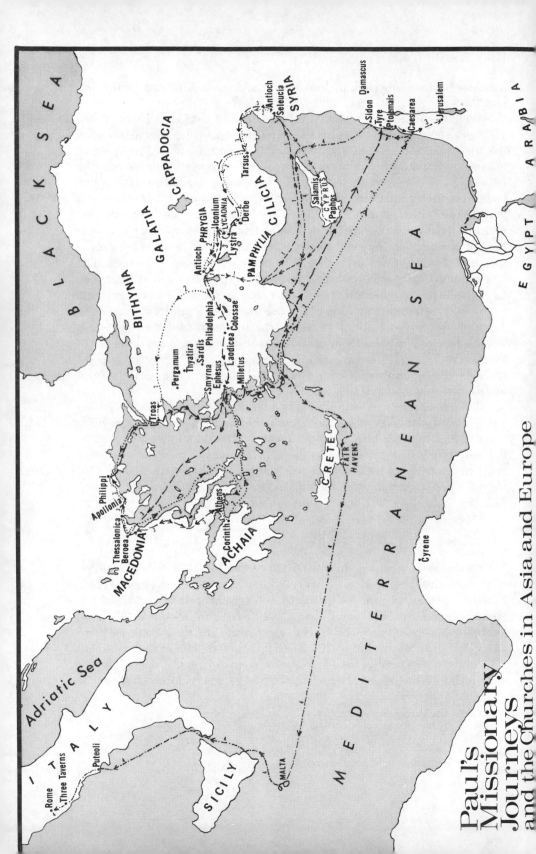

Paul's Missionary Journeys and the Churches in Asia and Europe

informed Jew, named Apollos, about Jesus the Messiah. This man returned to Corinth from whence he had come and taught in the synagogue, "shewing by the scriptures that Jesus was Christ" (18:28).

Paul, as usual, ministered in the synagogue in Ephesus, but after three months he had to move to the school of Tyrannus. It was quite usual in Ephesus for discussions to take place in a school and not in the marketplace as in Athens.[57] Paul's ministry continued for two years, during which time he healed many who were ill, in the name of Jesus. Jewish exorcists then tried to cure those possessed by demons by using the same name. It is a fact that there were Jews who did this kind of thing in those days. There are in existence still several magical papyri in which the sacred name of God, variously pronounced as *Iao*, *Iae*, *Iaoue*, and so on, was used, along with other expressions, in magic spells.[58] Ephesus in particular was renowned for its devotion to magic. The word "deeds" (19:18) is used in a technical sense and seems to refer to such magic spells.

Another word, here translated "curious arts," also had a technical meaning. These magical formulae were destroyed when the practitioners were converted (v. 19). Examples of such documents can still be seen in the British Museum or the Louvre.[59]

Paul's heart was set on visiting Rome. His plan was to pay a quick visit to Macedonia, then Jerusalem, and after that, Rome. He sent Timothy and Erastus ahead of him into Macedonia (19:22) as a first step in the working out of what were to be his final plans. The mention of Erastus here has led to a discussion as to whether this might be the Erastus who was the city treasurer of Corinth, referred to in Romans 16:23 as Erastus the "chamberlain" (Greek *oikonomos*). We are not certain that it is the same person, but there was certainly an Erastus of some importance in Corinth. Paul, who was almost certainly in Corinth when he wrote his letter to the Romans,[60] refers to the "chamberlain" of the city as a man he knew there. There is another reference to Erastus in II Timothy 4:20, where we learn that Erastus abode in Corinth. This is no doubt the same man that we meet in Paul's letter to the Romans. In the course of excavations in Corinth in 1929 Professor T. L. Shear found a pavement bearing the inscription ERASTVS PRO: AED: S: P: STRAVIT, which in translation reads "Erastus, procurator and aedile, laid this pavement at his own expense." An article was later written in the *Journal of Hellenic Studies* by A. W. Woodward, who remarked, "The evidence indicates that this pavement existed in the first century A.D. and it is most probable that the donor is identical with Erastus the friend of Paul who is mentioned in the Epistle to the Romans."[61] The inscription was found in the little square at the north end of the street leading past the theater.

---

57. See above, pp. 396–399.
58. A. Deissmann, *Bible Studies* (Eng. trans., Edinburgh, 1909), pp. 322ff.
59. Adolf Deissmann gives a number of excellent examples in his remarkable book, *Light from the Ancient East*, pp. 254ff., 302ff., 453ff.
60. A. M. Hunter, *Introducing the New Testament* (London, 1955), p. 69, etc.
61. F. F. Bruce, *Are the New Testament Documents Reliable?*, p. 92.

The letters are rather deeply hollowed out and were once filled with bronze held in place by lead.[62]

The question may be asked whether the Greek word *oikonomos* could represent the Latin *aedile*. We discover that these officials, whether Greek or Roman, included in their functions the charge of the financial affairs of the city, and thus the identification seems very probable. Most scholars today are agreed that there is no good reason why the man who prepared the pavement inscription should not be the same as Erastus the chamberlain.

Before Paul could join his friends, a serious riot broke out. It was apparently provoked because the gospel Paul preached was presenting a serious threat to the cult of Diana (Greek, Artemis). In the account in Acts 19:23-41 there is considerable local color, and archaeological research has shown that in these details Luke has given a faithful picture.

Ephesus was the center of the Artemis cult in the East. The goddess Artemis (called Diana by the Romans) was, in a special sense, "Diana of the Ephesians" (v. 28). Her temple was one of the seven wonders of the world. It was considered so sacred and inviolable that not only the Ephesians, but also foreign individuals, kings, and peoples deposited money there for safekeeping. So the temple was a sort of bank. In addition, great gifts were made to the goddess, which added to the wealth of her temple. One inscription tells of the gift of a certain Vibius Salutaris of twenty-nine statues of silver and gold, to be carried in a public procession to the temple. In the light of all this we begin to appreciate the concern of "Demetrius, a silversmith, which made silver shrines for Diana" (v. 24), when the preaching of Paul began to produce a stream of converts to Christ. Demetrius "called together the workmen of like occupation" and pointed out that Paul had "persuaded and turned away much people, saying that they be no gods, which are made with hands" (vv. 24-26). No doubt at every center of sight-seeing to which pilgrims came in the month of Artemison (March-April) to pay their homage to Artemis, a brisk trade was done in souvenirs and objects of devotion. No silver shrines have been found in excavations, although small pottery ones have, along with a great variety of votive gifts.

Artemis, according to tradition, fell down from heaven, and her image was enshrined in her temple. Possibly the origin of the belief was that a meteorite, resembling a many-breasted female, once fell in the region. Despite its former glory, the temple was lost for many centuries but it was found at the end of the last century to the northeast of the city in the low ground at the base of the hill of Ayassoluk, on which later a Christian church was built. Today a plan can be drawn, showing a platform 418 feet long and 239 feet wide, from which a flight of ten steps led up to a pavement, and three more steps led up to the temple

62. W. A. McDonald, "Archaeology and St. Paul's Journeys in Greek Lands, Part III, Corinth," BA (Sept., 1942), p. 46; E. M. Blaiklock, *op. cit.*, pp. 62-67.

The Artemision (temple of Artemis [Diana]) in Ephesus was one of the seven wonders of the ancient world. The immense structure was supported by one hundred columns, some of them sculptured. Pictured here is the marble drum of one of the eight pillars that supported the pediment. (British Museum)

platform.[63] The temple itself was about 343 feet long and 164 feet wide, and contained one hundred columns just over six feet in diameter. Some of these were sculptured. The sanctuary was seventy feet wide and the altar twenty feet square. The statue is thought to have been behind the altar. Fragments found in the excavation prove that brilliant color, as well as gold, was used in the temple decoration.

It was this temple and all that it stood for that was in danger of being "despised" (v. 27), so the excited crowd cried out, "Great Artemis of the Ephesians!" Ramsay points out that this was "a common formula of devotion and prayer as is attested by several inscriptions."[64]

In the uproar, the crowd seized two of Paul's companions and "rushed with one accord into the theater" (v. 29). This is the structure to be seen today by the tourist on the western slope of Mount Pion. It was 495 feet in diameter and would hold about 24,500 people in its heyday. It was connected to the harbor of Ephesus by a fine marble paved street, the so-called Arkadiane, which was thirty-six feet wide, 1735 feet long, and lined with a colonnade on each side, behind which were shops and stores.

The town clerk (Greek grammateus) was alarmed at the riot, fearing the consequences of an inquiry; for he, as the executive officer, was responsible to the Roman provincial administration. He urged the people not to be alarmed for the honor of the great goddess, for everyone knew of her fame and her heavenly origin. Indeed, she had so honored the city as to give it a special title, "Warden of the Temple of Artemis" (Greek neokoros, literally "temple sweeper"). The Authorized Version misses the point by translating, "the city of the Ephesians is a worshipper of the great goddess Diana, and of the image which fell down from Jupiter" (v. 35). This very title, neokoros, once used of very menial temple services, came to be used as a title of honor, and is attested in many inscriptions.[65] It was in fact used very widely of individuals in Egypt and Asia Minor, and sometimes for a people as a whole group. Josephus speaks of Israel as "temple keeper of God," for example.[66] For our purpose it is important to know that the term was in fact used of Ephesus.

One final point comes out of our study of this chapter. It is the reference to "Asiarchs" in verse 31, or as the Authorized Version has it, the "chiefs of Asia." These Asiarchs, or high priests of Asia, were the heads of the provincial cult of "Rome and Emperor." Augustus permitted Ephesus, among others, to dedicate a sacred area to Rome and the Caesar. The Asiarchs are mentioned often in inscriptions and seem to have been chosen from families of position and means

63. M. M. Parvis, "Archaeology and St. Paul's Journeys in Greek Lands, Part IV, Ephesus," BA (Sept., 1945), pp. 67ff.
64. W. M. Ramsay, St. Paul the Traveller and the Roman Citizen, p. 279.
65. M. M. Parvis, op. cit., p. 80.
66. Josephus, Wars V.ix.4.

In the great theater (center) at Ephesus silversmiths who profited by the worship of Artemis led the townspeople in a riot against Paul's preaching. The Arkadiane (right), named for the Emperor Arcadius (A.D. 375–408), runs west from the theater to the harbor ca. three-fourths of a kilometer away; the street's colonnades once stood in front of ships and other buildings. (Ewing Galloway)

to care for the rites of the imperial cult, observed by the league of cities in the Roman province of Asia.

The office was held for one year, but the title was used after the individual retired from office. There could thus be several Asiarchs at once in Ephesus who represented rather public honor than narrow religious fanaticism. Their tolerance of Paul (v. 31) was thus quite in keeping with their general attitude in such cases.[67]

Shortly after, Paul left for Macedonia. Very quickly he visited Greece again, returned to Macedonia, and then set sail for home. He was able to see the Ephesian elders en route (Acts 20:17–38), but proceeded on his way and landed at Caesarea. Nothing could dissuade him from going to Jerusalem, but as it happened, it led to his imprisonment, his detention in Caesarea under the procurators Felix and Festus, and his final journey to Rome.

Three archaeological notes will complete our account. We have already referred to the Temple inscription implied in Acts 21:28,[68] and to the "castle"

67. M. M. Parvis, *op. cit.*, p. 80.
68. See above, p. 331.

or "fortress" in Acts 21:34 being Antonia.[69] The final item concerns the exact title of the "chief man" of Malta where Paul was shipwrecked (Acts 28:7). This title appears on two Maltese inscriptions, one in Greek and one in Latin.[70] The "first man," or *protos*, in this case was Publius. Luke's title is the correct designation of the Roman governor of Malta.

Our discussion has been a lengthy one, but it will have served to show the tremendous value of archaeological research for our understanding of such a book as Acts. Luke is shown to be a most careful recorder of information, whether it be matters of geography and political boundaries, local customs, titles of local officers, local religious practices, details of local topography, or the disposition of buildings in Greek or Roman, Asian or European towns. Most of our information has come from archaeological research, which has only just begun its enormous task.

69. See above, pp. 298, 350, 352, 360.
70. F. F. Bruce, *The Book of Acts* (Grand Rapids, 1954), p. 523.

22

ARCHAEOLOGY, JOHN'S GOSPEL, AND THE BOOK OF REVELATION

AMONG the difficult problems of New Testament study are those of the date and authorship of the books. The writings that appear under the name of John in the New Testament have been the subject of a great deal of discussion, both as to date of writing and as to authorship. Perhaps it is true to say that the world of scholars has not yet entirely made up its mind about these questions. It is not our intention here to raise the issue but only to show how the discoveries of archaeologists have thrown light on two of these books, the Gospel of John and the book of Revelation. Archaeological discovery has brought to bear on the problems connected with these books some solid material evidence. This is refreshing because much of the thinking of the past has been based largely on internal evidence and has lacked the control provided by external points of reference.

ARCHAEOLOGY AND THE GOSPEL OF JOHN

At the end of the nineteenth century and in the earlier part of the present century radical scholars placed this Gospel in the second century A.D. and insisted that it showed Gnostic influences. One Gnostic sect in particular, the Mandeans, was said to have influenced the writer of this Gospel greatly. The dualistic thought of these people was said to be clearly evident in the Gospel, and for this reason it was placed late in the second century.

More conservative scholars were not slow to point out that the external evidence was at the least fragmentary and the internal evidence lacked external

411

controls. Then came the discoveries of the past half-century, and the subsequent mature consideration of their significance. These have seriously affected the discussion.

In some ways the most interesting of all of these discoveries is a small papyrus scrap of John's Gospel found in Egypt and dated no later than A.D. 150.[1] This showed that the Gospel had already been circulated in a provincial area of Egypt, and hence its date of composition must have been earlier in the century at the very least.

Reference has already been made to the topographical references in John's Gospel which have led W. F. Albright to conclude that the author was well acquainted with features of Palestine that were obliterated after the Roman campaign of A.D. 70.[2] We have also noted that there are practically no Jewish remains in Palestine that can be dated to the last quarter of the first century A.D.[3] The Jews were driven out after A.D. 70, and the tombs we have are all before this date. Practically all traces of synagogues have gone, and synagogue remains left today are all from late in the second century. Christians were gathered up in this ruthless destruction by the Romans so that there was an almost complete break in Christian tradition as well. In this connection W. F. Albright has written:

> Any reminiscences of the life of Jesus or of conditions in Palestine in His time must have been carried into the Diaspora by Christian refugees, either voluntarily or otherwise. This means that if there are correct data in the Gospels or Acts of the Apostles which can be validated archaeologically or topographically, they must have been carried from Palestine in oral form by Christians who left that land before or during the first Jewish revolt.[4]

What are some of these first-century items listed by Albright? We have in fact referred to most of them. Thus he pointed out that the name Rabbi (my master) and the equivalent Greek term *didaskalos* (literally "teacher") were both used in a number of places in John's Gospel. But whereas it was once argued that the use of these terms pointed to a late date for John, who used the words far more than the Synoptics, it is now evident that both words were in common use in the days of Christ. The data point rather to an early than to a late date for John.[5]

The names on the ossuaries show that the range of names in John is quite

1. Discussed in detail on p. 435.
2. See above, p. 378; and cf. W. F. Albright, *The Archaeology of Palestine* (London, 1954), pp. 247f.; also W. F. Albright, "Recent Discoveries in Palestine and the Gospel of St. John" in *The Background of the New Testament and Its Eschatology* (Cambridge, 1956), pp. 153ff.
3. See above, p. 369.
4. W. F. Albright in *The Background of the New Testament and Its Eschatology*, p. 156.
5. *Ibid.*, pp. 157f. Some recent discussion would place the Gospel of John before A.D. 70. See J. A. T. Robinson, *Redating the New Testament* (Philadelphia, 1976), pp. 254-311.

he Sea of Galilee, a place often mentioned in the New Testament. The sea is calm, as ı this picture, when the customary west wind blows, but a wind shift to the east can re-ult in sudden and severe storms (see Mark 5:35-41). (Trans World Airlines)

Limestone ossuary, used for secondary burials in Roman Palestine. The chest is painted red and decorated with geometric figures. (Royal Ontario Museum, Toronto)

consistent with the names in common use in Palestine in the first century. Thus the name Laz'ar, an abbreviated form for Eleazar, is common on the ossuaries, as are female names like Maryam (Mary), Marta (Martha), Elisheba (Elisabeth), and Shalom (Salome). All of these names are in good first-century tradition.[6]

We have already discussed the topographical reference to the "Pavement" (Greek *Lithostrotos*; Aramaic *Gabbatha*).[7] And even if there remains some doubt about the exact identity of the site, the reference has the ring of authenticity to it.

Albright also drew attention to a topographical note in John 3:23, where we learn that John the Baptist was baptizing at "Aenon near Salim, because there was much water there."[8] This description suits the area close to Shechem and Nablus where there is still a village of Salim and, close by, the village of 'Ainun. These two lie near the headwaters of the Wadi Far'ah, with many springs in the

    6. W. F. Albright, *The Background of the New Testament and Its Eschatology*, pp. 157f. J. Finegan, *The Archaeology of the New Testament* (Princeton, 1969), pp. 216–219, 237–246. A list of names familiar from the New Testament is given on p. 246.
    7. See above, p. 360; and cf. W. F. Albright, *The Background of the New Testament and Its Eschatology*, pp. 158f.
    8. *Ibid.*, p. 159.

vicinity. Later Christian tradition which identified Salim with Salumias in the Jordan valley was wrong. If John were really baptizing near the Jordan, there would be no need to comment on the fact that there was much water there. Recent study of these names points to the accuracy of the topographical information in John's Gospel at this point and provides a note of authenticity.

Another of Albright's suggestions needs some modification. He argued that Sychar in John 4 is to be identified with old Shechem (or Sychem) which, according to information available in 1956, was not destroyed till the time of the Jewish revolt and was therefore still in existence in Jesus' day.[9] But, according to the latest excavations, Shechem ceased to exist about 100 B.C., so that Albright's point is not valid at present unless, of course, further excavation at old Shechem reveals an area of the town that was occupied during the first part of the first century A.D.[10]

Evidence of the possible early date of John's Gospel has come recently from two most unusual sources: first, from the discovery of some early Gnostic documents from Egypt and, secondly, from the manuscripts found in caves near the Dead Sea. The argument regularly advanced by critical scholars was, as we have seen, that John's Gospel was heavily overlaid with dualistic thought. Now and then a writer would protest.[11] Thus E. R. Goodenough held that the thought of John's Gospel expressed in the prologue presents a view of the Logos doctrine that was more primitive in its philosophy than was the doctrine of Philo (about 20 B.C. to A.D. 50). He accordingly suggested that both Philo and John drew on earlier material. C. H. Dodd also sought to deny the direct influence of the Gnostics. Now, due to archaeological discovery, we are able to approach the problem from two angles. First, we have opportunity to study in some detail and at first hand a set of Gnostic documents from Egypt and, secondly, we are able to study the type of thinking of one of the religious communities in Palestine at, and before, the time of Christ, and this community was not in any way a Gnostic community.

The Gnostic material from Egypt comes from Chenoboskion in Upper Egypt and includes nearly forty lost treatises.[12] The date, judged from a study of the style of writing (paleography), is the late third or early fourth century. Up to recent times our knowledge of the Gnostics had come secondhand, largely from the Church Fathers. Whereas we had only three original codices and seven different writings a few years ago, we now have thirteen codices and forty-four different writings. Of all the Gnostic works mentioned by the Fathers, only a few are now missing. It becomes clear that the picture the Fathers drew was a true

---

9. *Ibid.*, p. 160.
10. See discussion on p. 378.
11. W. F. Albright, *The Background of the New Testament and Its Eschatology*, p. 161.
12. V. R. Gold, "The Gnostic Library of Chenoboskion," BA (Dec., 1952), pp. 70ff. The whole question of alleged pre-Christian Gnosticism has been taken up by E. Yamauchi, *Pre-Christian Gnosticism* (Grand Rapids, 1973).

one. Indeed, on the evidence of the new material, the early Gnostics were even worse heretics than the Fathers indicated. The supposed form of mild Gnosticism that is said to have influenced John was simply non-existent in the second century when the Gospel of John was believed to have been written and when John supposedly came under their influence. By that date the Gnostics were already outrageously heretical. Whence then came the simple dualism so clearly expressed in John's Gospel? It did not come from the Gnostics, for they had a strongly developed and quite non-Jewish dualism. In any case, their whole approach was quite out of keeping with the sublime teaching of John's Gospel.

A study of the Qumran materials reveals that the Messianic sect that produced these documents had a theological system that was characterized by a far-reaching dualism. Perhaps these people were originally influenced by the Persians, but if they were, the system had been greatly modified. If the Persian thinkers spoke of two opposed principles at work in the world, good and evil, both independent of one another, the Qumran sectaries thought rather of two opposing spirits, both created by God at the beginning of time. The dualism is therefore monotheistic and strongly ethical. Indeed we have here an ethical dualism not unlike what we find in the New Testament, and very strongly expressed in both John and Paul. Both John and the Essene sect of Qumran speak of truth and perversity (or lying), light and darkness, and so on.

Concerning the dualism of the Qumran sect, W. F. Albright has written:

> . . . their theology was characterized by a simple dualism, derived from Iranian sources, but thoroughly Judaized in the process of adaptation. There is a Spirit of Truth and a Spirit of Falsehood, both created by God; it is man's duty to choose between them. The Spirit of Truth is substantially the Christian Holy Spirit, but lacks all specifically Christian overtones. This simple dualism, contrasting good and evil, truth and falsehood, light and darkness, appears in the Gospel of John; there is nothing Gnostic about it, and those many N. T. scholars who date the Gospel after the rise of Gnosticism are now proved wrong. The Gospel of John is saturated with phraseology and conceptual imagery reminding us of the Dead Sea Scrolls.[13]

In the light of this study it is clear that John's Gospel is far closer to the ethical dualism of the Qumran sect than it is to the material dualism of the Gnostics. Even so, it is by no means exactly parallel. This much is clear, however, that there is no compelling reason why John's Gospel should not be dated in the first century A.D., for the Qumran documents can be dated from the period approximately 100 B.C. to A.D. 70.

To sum up, then, there is a good deal of interest for us in the archaeological

13. W. F. Albright, *Recent Discoveries in Bible Lands* (New York, 1955), p. 131. A thorough discussion of the parallels and differences between John's Gospel and Qumran is available in J. H. Charlesworth (ed.), *John and Qumran* (London, 1972). Nine essays by significant scholars give good coverage of the issues.

The remains of a fourth-century Christian church at Shavei Zion, Israel. Note the mosaic flooring on different levels. (Israel Office of Information)

Mosaic flooring of the north aisle of the Shavei Zion church. The cross motif has been adapted for use at the head of the chapters in Part III of this book. A partly damaged inscription in another mosaic, in the third level of the church, has reference to Luke 2:2. (Israel Office of Information)

discoveries which bear on John's Gospel. The items we have mentioned all tend to support an early date as well as the authenticity of the book. It would seem, therefore, that we have reached a point in the study of John's Gospel where archaeological evidence practically compels us to agree to a first-century date for its original composition. There is nothing which requires a second-century date and much that suits the first century.

ARCHAEOLOGY AND THE BOOK OF REVELATION

Some years ago Sir William Ramsay wrote a book called *The Letters to the Seven Churches of Asia.*[14] He took up the seven churches mentioned in Revelation 2 and 3, and sought to describe their origin and their relationship to one another. He was able to gather important archaeological material about them as well. It was his idea that the seven churches represented seven postal centers studded along a circular route, each on the center of a Christian circuit.[15]

Archaeology can provide a description of the towns as they stood at the close of the first century A.D. This may contribute something to our understanding of the peculiar problems that faced each of the churches. It cannot, of course, give us any information about the inner faith of the members of these churches.

Details of the town of *Ephesus* have already been given.[16] As we have seen, the town was a center for the worship of Artemis, the great Diana. Emperor worship, too, was practiced here, as well as all kinds of magical arts. Later it became the home of various Gnostic sects. Paul founded the Christian Church here and came into conflict with vested interests (Acts 19). The Church received some commendation in the book of Revelation.

Smyrna was originally founded as a Greek colony more than a thousand years before Christ. It lay on a deep gulf, thirty-five miles north of Ephesus, at the end of a great road. It had a good outlet to the sea a few miles away, and was actually a maritime city that became a close associate of Rome. The people of Smyrna were proud of this fact and regarded themselves as the "first of Asia," a title carried on their coins. Ancient writers often refer to the "crown of Smyrna," which seems to have been a reference to the garland of flowers worn by the worshippers of the goddess Cybele. The foundress of the city in mythology was the Amazon Smyrna,[17] who is depicted on coins and elsewhere armed with

14. (London, 1904). Cf. the more recent book by Wm. Barclay, *Letters to the Seven Churches* (London, 1957).

15. W. M. Ramsay, *The Letters to the Seven Churches of Asia,* p. 191.

16. See above, pp. 403–409.

17. The Amazons were a mythical race of warlike females. Some interesting details about Smyrna are available in E. M. Blaiklock, *Cities of the New Testament* (London, 1965), pp. 98–102.

The Ephesus temple of the Roman emperor Hadrian (A.D. 76–138), built southeast of the theater, helped to make the city one of the most beautiful in the East. (Rosenthal Art Slides)

the double-headed axe of the Amazons and wearing the short tunic and high boots of the huntress and warrior. A high crown rests on her head.[18]

Perhaps the reference to the "crown of life" (Rev. 2:10) had special significance for these people who had heard from childhood about the crown of Smyrna. The true Smyrna would wear a crown suited to the servant of the living God. Ramsay sees in the reference to "faithful" (v. 10) a reminder of the faithfulness that the worldly city had shown to Rome. This constituted a call to the Christians to show a similar faithfulness to Christ. No excavations of any extent have been made at Smyrna up to the present, but visitors can still make out the plan of the ancient stadium and a few other ruins. The modern city unfortunately covers most of the old site and we are almost entirely dependent on literary material.

Pergamum, capital of the province, was sixteen miles inland and fifty miles north of Smyrna. It was a center for several religious cults. Asklepios, the god of healing, was greatly honored here. His symbol, the serpent, is found often on coins. Pergamum was also a center for emperor worship, and there had been a temple here for that purpose since the days of Augustus in 29 B.C. Traditional

18. W. M. Ramsay, *op. cit.,* pp. 266f.

Ruins of the Asclepium (temple of Asclepius, the Greek god of healing) on the south-west outskirts of Pergamum in Asia Minor. Adjoining a broad courtyard flanked by colonnades (center) were a theater (foreground), library, temple of Zeus Asclepius, and the treatment center. (B. K. Condit)

Greek gods like Zeus, Athene the goddess of poetry and learning, and Dionysius the god of wine were likewise worshipped, and these, together with Asklepios, were worshipped in times of national disaster.[19] The city had a certain pride in its religious significance. It was the first, and for a time the only, provincial town to have a temple dedicated to the imperial cult. By the end of the second century it had three, the original one created by Augustus, a second built in the days of Trajan (A.D. 98–117), and a third in the days of Severus (A.D. 193–211). The Augustan temple is represented on coins.

Probably the reference to "Satan's seat" in Revelation 2:13 is to emperor worship. Christians were in danger of showing tolerance to these cults and of compromising their stand for Christ, so as to follow "the doctrine of Balaam" and "the doctrine of the Nicolaitanes" (vv. 14f.). On the other hand, if a Christian resisted the pressure of the society in which he lived, he ran the risk of presecution. Already there had been at least one martyr when Revelation was written (v. 13).

19. *Ibid.*, p. 284.

Excavations have been carried out in Pergamum since 1878, and these have revealed much of the glory of the city, notably its acropolis.[20] One of the important discoveries was the remains of the gigantic altar of Zeus, which was adorned with marvelous sculptures portraying the battle of Zeus against the primeval giants. This altar was restored and reconstructed for display in the Berlin Museum.[21] Another large temple dedicated to the worship of Trajan and Hadrian has been exposed. There is much more yet to be discovered about the story of Pergamum.

Thyatira was a small town between Pergamum and Sardis but lay inland on a main road. It was likewise the center of several cults, among them being those of Apollo and Sibyl, the female diviner. Apollo, the sun god, was the tutelary or guardian deity here, and his worship was coupled with that of the emperors.

The town was founded by Seleucus I about 300 B.C. as a garrison city even though it had no natural defense advantages. It lay on a plain and was an important trading center whose greater period of prosperity was only just beginning at the time Revelation was written. Numerous inscriptions from Thyatira mention all sorts of trades in the city and speak of workers in wool, linen, and garments, dyers, leather workers, tanners, potters, bakers, and bronze smiths.[22] We are reminded of Lydia, the woman of Thyatira, a seller of purple (Acts 16:14).

The letter to Thyatira comes from "the Son of God, who hath his eyes like unto a flame of fire, and his feet are like fine brass" (v. 18). The celestial Christ is thus contrasted with Apollo, the son of Zeus, and the emperor, his incarnation. The church at Thyatira is castigated because she lacked fortitude to resist the insidiousness of these cults. Actually the false teaching of Montanism[23] flourished here after about A.D. 150.

Sardis lay thirty-five miles to the south of Thyatira in the center of numerous trade routes. It was a big city and was formerly the capital of the rich kingdom of Lydia. The original Sardis was an almost impregnable fortress perched on a hill, but later the town spread to the plain below and the old city became an acropolis. Cyrus, the Persian conqueror, took the city from Croesus in 546 B.C., but later it was recaptured by the Seleucid king Antiochus the Great. The patron goddess of the city was the native Cybele, who was identified with Artemis. The ruins of her temple are still standing. Several of the broken columns and two full columns still stand on an area 327 feet long and 163 feet

---

20. C. M. Cobern, *The New Archaeological Discoveries* (New York, 1918), pp. 563f. See E. M. Blaiklock, *op. cit.*, pp. 103–106, for further information on Pergamum.

21. More recently it has been removed to Russia.

22. W. M. Ramsay, *op. cit.*, p. 325; E. M. Blaiklock, *op. cit.*, pp. 107–111.

23. This teaching commenced with Montanus, who was regarded as the incarnation of the Spirit of God. It placed great emphasis on the gifts of the Spirit and held to strict discipline in the Church.

across, and on the sacred way leading to the temple the visitor can see some of the flanking lions.

In A.D. 17 Sardis suffered greatly from an earthquake, but the town was rebuilt with help from Emperor Hadrian, who appears on coins extending his bounty to a kneeling figure. In the writers of that age the town had a bad name for luxury and loose living, and the letter of Revelation 3:1–6 urges the church to watch lest the Lord come in judgment. In later days there was a Christian church there. Excavations by an American expedition in Sardis began in 1910 and revealed the temple of Cybele-Artemis.[24] It was evident that this temple had been taken over by Christians, for the sign of the cross was engraved into the stone in many places, indicating the new use to which the building had been put. One of the most famous bishops here was Melito, who died about A.D. 190. A mortgage deed dating to 300 B.C., found in the ruins of the building, proved that it had originally been dedicated to Artemis. The area was rich in inscriptions, the most famous of which was probably a bilingual text in Lydian and Aramaic, dating from the tenth year of the Persian king Artaxerxes.

Further extensive excavations have taken place at Sardis each year since 1958, so that today we have a vast amount of information about this ancient city.[25] During the course of these years progress in research and excavation has been made while a good deal of conservation and restoration work has gone on. A modern road, the Salihli Highway, separates the ancient town into two parts although these were formerly one. The ruins cover the Roman and Byzantine periods as well as earlier periods, for a deep sounding in one area showed that the site was occupied in the Late Bronze Age. There are good remains of the Lydian, Persian, and Hellenistic periods as well as remains of the later Islamic period. A fine synagogue of the early third century (ca. A.D. 230–250) with numerous sculptured pieces and a menorah (seven-branched lamp) was brought to light in 1963. A large quantity of pottery, coinage, and bronze pieces, numerous inscriptions in Lydian, Latin, and Greek, many types of architecture, masonry, and statuary, fine mosaics, and a host of other items from all archaeological periods make Sardis one of the most rewarding excavations ever carried out in Anatolia.

Among the most impressive of the remains is the Synagogue, which has been partly restored. While much of the remains dates from the third century, it is clear that the construction of the basic form of the building goes back to the period not long after the earthquake of A.D. 17.

Another interesting building is the Artemis temple. The earlier excavations have been extended. Further details have become available about the inner altar and its orientation. It was approached from the east, and the goddess and her priests faced westward toward graves that were protected by Artemis, according

24. C. M. Cobern, op. cit., pp. 565ff.
25. Preliminary reports of the nineteen campaigns held up to 1976 may be found in various issues of BASOR since 1959. These reports will continue.

to Lydian inscriptions. At the southeast corner of the Artemis temple a small Christian church was discovered. Repairs and restoration work have been carried out here. The church seems to have been used in the fourth century A.D. It is now clear that the remains at Sardis are so extensive that future excavation will be involved in an investigation of areas around the central site where traces of further settlement as well as important tomb areas have been identified.[26]

Philadelphia was twenty-eight miles to the southeast of Sardis. It was the center of a wine industry and its chief deity was Dionysius. Its position was strategic for defense and for entry into the heart of Phrygia, so that it was a "doorway." It was to be an "open door" (v. 8) now in a new mission, as formerly it had been the center from which Hellenistic culture had spread. Little has been done in the way of excavation, hence our knowledge rests on literary references, a few inscriptions, and some coins.

Finally *Laodicea*, situated on a spur of hills some forty-three miles southeast of Philadelphia, was a very wealthy center, trading garments and cloth made from the glossy black wool of the local sheep. Today the ruins of this ancient town lie over many acres, but no thorough examination of the site has been undertaken. There was more to be seen a hundred years ago, but since then the local inhabitants have removed a great deal of the remains of ancient buildings in order to build other towns nearby; and, alas, this has been going on ever since the eleventh century.

The letter in Revelation 3:14–22 draws a contrast between the wealth of the city as represented by its woolen cloth, its medical work, and perhaps the eye salve made there on the one hand, and the depth of its spiritual poverty on the other. Sir William Ramsay saw in these verses references to the actual source of Laodicea's wealth.[27] Until serious excavation is done, however, we must remain in ignorance about the full significance of the references to the city.

A great deal still needs to be done in the excavation of these cities. Indeed, only Ephesus, Pergamum, and Sardis have been excavated at all, although some surface surveys have been carried out in all these towns. Yet these places were vital centers of Christian worship in the first century A.D., and the book of Revelation, being a document of early Church history, will yield its primary meaning much more clearly when the archaeologist has unraveled the underlying thought and culture of the society represented in this book.[28]

26. C. H. Grunewalt, "The Sardis Campaign of 1976," BASOR, No. 229 (Feb., 1978), pp. 57–73.

27. W. M. Ramsay, *op. cit.*, pp. 416–419. See also E. M. Blaiklock, *op. cit.*, pp. 124–128.

28. E. M. Blaiklock, *Out of the Earth* (Grand Rapids, 1957), p. 54, and W. M. Ramsay, *op. cit.*, give useful material of this kind.

23

THE NEW TESTAMENT AND THE PAPYRI

ONE of the greatest chapters in the annals of New Testament archaeology is the remarkable story of the discovery and interpretation of the papyri of the centuries surrounding the life of our Lord.[1] As early as the end of the sixteenth century a few scattered samples of papyri were brought to Europe. In 1752 some more were found in Herculaneum, the ruins of which lay beneath the ash thrown out by Mount Vesuvius in A.D. 79. By the close of the eighteenth century some papyri were coming to Europe from Egypt. Though tragic stories are told of peasants burning papyri in order to enjoy the odor of the smoke, it was during the nineteenth century that increasing numbers of these precious documents began to find their way into Europe and their significance became clear even to the peasants of Egypt. The great Fayum depression some fifty or sixty miles southwest of Cairo became a veritable quarry of papyri. In 1877 great masses of these valuable documents were found at the ancient site of Crocodopolis in the Fayum and were sent to Vienna. Then in 1889–1890 Sir Flinders Petrie began scientific excavation at the site of Gurob and found many papyri wrapped around mummies. These he carefully recovered and passed on to other scholars. His work was supplemented by the discoveries of B. P. Grenfell, A. S. Hunt, and D. G. Hogarth, who carried out a systematic search for papyri in Egypt and over several years had remarkable success, notably at Oxyrhynchus. One of the first pieces to come to light bore the familiar noun for "mote" known from Matthew 7:3–5. When eventually the piece was cleaned, it turned out to be a collection of sayings of Jesus, dating probably from the third century A.D.

---

1. J. Finegan, *Light from the Ancient Past* (Princeton, 1946), pp. 321f., gives a good summary.

424

It can readily be seen that such material is likely to provide evidence of a most intimate kind for the life of the people in Egypt and elsewhere, for a piece of papyrus then was as important as a sheet of writing paper now. Letters, receipts, official documents, licenses of all kinds, permits, summonses, title deeds, in fact, written documents of every kind, whether personal or official, feature among the papyri. The documents themselves also provide valuable information about the language of the common people of the time, and this discovery is of tremendous significance for the study of New Testament language.

THE NATURE AND USE OF PAPYRUS

Papyrus is really a swamp plant which grows in great profusion in Egypt. Quite early, perhaps as early as 2500 B.C.,[2] the stem of the papyrus plant was cut into long thin strips which were laid out on a flat surface and soaked in water. A second layer was then placed crosswise on top of the first and the two layers were pressed together to form a single sheet. This was dried in the sun, scraped with a shell or a bone to remove roughness, and then used for writing. The size of the sheets varied according to the need. An average size would be nine to eleven inches long and six to nine inches wide. Sheets could be joined together so as to form a long roll, one such roll being 140 feet in length. The side on which the fiber ran horizontally, and which was normally used for writing, is known as *recto*. The back of the sheet, with the fibers running vertically and not normally used for writing because of its roughness, is called *verso*. Perhaps we see here some explanation of such references in the Bible as Revelation 5:1 where we read of writing "within and on the backside" (cf. Ezek. 2:10).

The oldest piece of papyrus in existence today dates from the fifth Egyptian dynasty (about 2500 to 2350 B.C.). From then on papyrus continued in regular use till long after the time of Christ. From Egypt the use of papyrus spread to other lands, and there was a regular trade between Egypt and Phoenicia and Greece at an early period. One story from about 1100 B.C. tells of a certain Wen-amon who went from Egypt to Byblos in Phoenicia.[3] Among many interesting facts in this story we find a reference to the trade in papyrus. An account of the process of making papyrus comes from the Roman writer Pliny who lived in the first century A.D.[4]

For ordinary purposes small sheets of papyrus were used, the long roll being used for literary purposes. Some of the longer books in the New Testament provide a good illustration. Thus Luke's Gospel would require a roll just over thirty feet long. Perhaps one such roll was as much as could be handled conve-

---

2. *Ibid.*, p. 307. See also F. Kenyon, *Our Bible and the Ancient Manuscripts* (London, 1958), p. 38.

3. J. B. Pritchard, *ANET*, pp. 25-29.

4. Pliny, *Natural History* xiii.11f.

*Letter of Mnesiergus of Athens to his household, the oldest e
tant Greek letter. It was written on a leaden tablet and folded
that the contents were inside (right) and the address outsi
(left). (Antikenmuseum, Staatliche Museen, Berlin)*

niently by the reader, and therefore Luke divided his story into two rolls. Paul
would have written his letters on papyrus rolls. In fact, in one passage in
Timothy he asked his friend to bring with him "the books, but especially the
parchments" (II Tim. 4:13). These "books" were very likely rolls of papyrus.

It sometimes happened that when a piece of papyrus was needed in a hurry,
or when nothing else was available, an old piece would be reused. The original
writing was erased as far as possible and the papyrus given a second application of
writing. Such a rewritten piece of papyrus is known as a *palimpsest.*

Writing was done with a reed pen, and ink made either from lampblack,
gum, and water, or from nut galls, green vitriol, and water. There are references
to pens and ink in the New Testament (II Cor. 3:3; II John 12; III John 13).

In the first century A.D. papyrus was the normal writing material, though
other media were also used. We can think of the New Testament books as being
written on papyrus. It is of some interest to note that the Greek word *biblos*
means "the pith of the papyrus stalk." From this came the word *biblion* for the
papyrus roll. Hence the early Christians referred to the sacred books used among
them as *ta biblia* (plural of *biblion*), "the books." In Latin this became *biblia* and
hence our English word, Bible.

Recent research has made it fairly clear that it was the Christians who
popularized the leaf-book (codex), and abandoned the rolls for church use. It
was necessary for the early Christians both to be able to make rapid reference to
texts in order to justify their interpretation of the Old Testament and to see what

Jesus, Paul, and others had said,[5] and to have a number of different writings conveniently accessible at one time. The page-type of "book" was of more use. A study of the existing manuscripts of the third and fourth centuries A.D. shows that for the third century A.D. nearly eighty-four percent of the Christian papyri are of the codex type, whereas for non-Christian writings which still used the roll form just over six percent are in codex form. By the next century Christian books show a ninety-seven percent preference for the codex, while the non-Christian show sixty-five percent. The Christians on this evidence had the lead in the use of the codex or leaf book.

Passing reference should be made to the very valuable documents known as *ostraca*.[6] These were pieces of broken pottery on which letters, receipts, notes,

5. C. C. McCown, "The Earliest Christian Books," *BA* (May, 1943).
6. A. Deissmann, *Light from the Ancient East* (Eng. trans. London, 1927), pp. 50ff.

A Vulgate palimpsest of the fifth century A.D., found in a northern Italy monastery. A copyist had erased the uncial Vulgate text (larger letters) and had reused the parchment for a sixth-century work of Isidore. The carefully written Vulgate text has proved an important link between Jerome's original (now lost) and Codex Amiatinus, hitherto the oldest extant text. This picture shows Judges 5:5–18. (Herzog August Library, Wolfenbüttel, West Germany; photo by A. Dold)

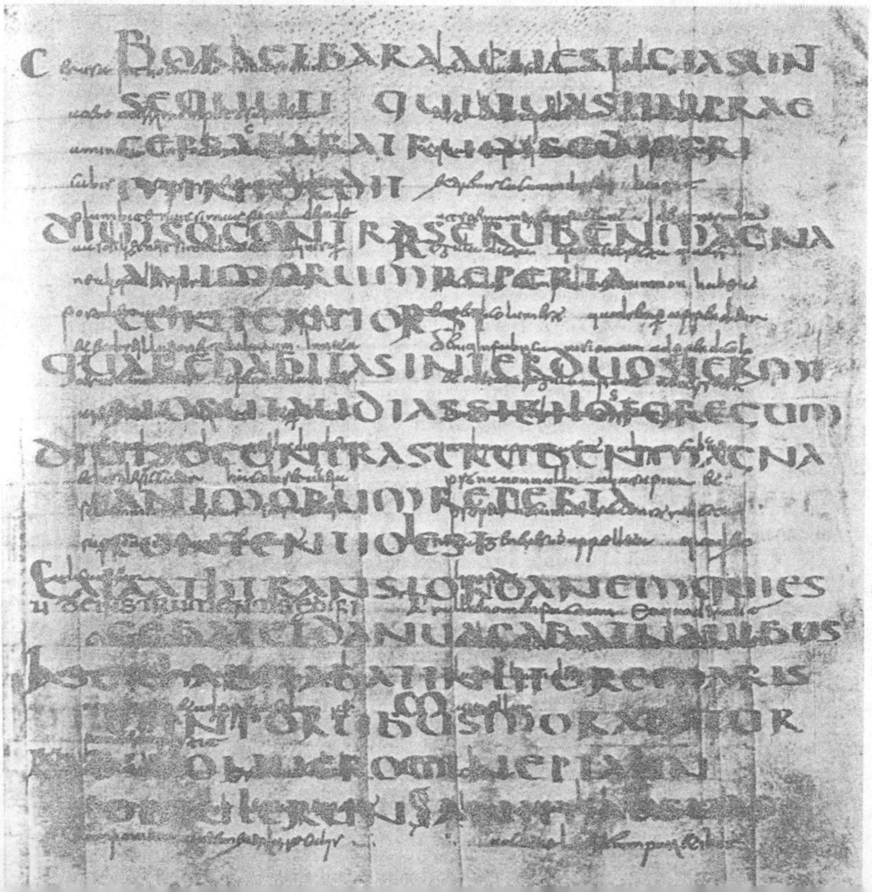

and the like were written in ink. Early excavators threw these away so that they are often found in rubbish heaps, but they are now carefully collected and allowed to make their contribution to the study of the language used in the New Testament. The scantiness of our treatment must not be considered a measure of the very great importance of these precious documents.

THE LANGUAGE OF THE PAPYRI

The language of the papyri was Greek for the most part, but it has been clear for many centuries that it was not the Greek of the great classical writers. It was rather like the Greek of the New Testament, which had been something of a puzzle to the scholars, who regarded it as a sort of Judaic or Hebraic Greek. Some scholars actually suspected that there was a special dialect of Greek lying behind the New Testament, and there are some interesting anticipations of the modern view in the writings of such scholars as Professor Lightfoot and Dean Farrar.[7]

The discovery of the papyri added greatly to our knowledge of a type of Greek which hitherto seemed so strange. New Testament scholars had actually compiled lists of words which they assigned to a so-called biblical or ecclesiastical Greek. But whereas this list once consisted of some five hundred words, it could be very greatly reduced in the light of this new information. The papyri, along with inscriptions and ostraca, had revealed a vocabulary that seemed to be quite well known in the first century A.D. What was the meaning of this discovery? This task was taken up by a German pastor in Marburg, who later became the famous Professor Adolf Deissmann and held the chair of New Testament exegesis in Berlin. He was suddenly struck by the likeness of the language of the papyri to that of the New Testament, and he realized that the key to many of the problems of the language of the New Testament lay here.[8] It seemed to him that the papyri gave the vernacular Greek of considerable parts of the East, Greek as it was spoken and written by the ordinary men and women of the day. It was the common (or *koine*) Greek, and this was the language to be found in the New Testament.

The idea was taken up by other scholars such as J. H. Moulton, and although in their first zeal these early workers arrived at some conclusions that were later modified, their researches gave the correct general interpretation of the language of the New Testament. The subsequent study of many thousands of documents has placed scholars in a position where they know the grammar of Koine Greek, and new lexicons have been written to include this latest vocabulary material. One of the most famous of these is *The Vocabulary of the Greek New Testament*, illustrated from the papyri and other non-literary sources, by J. H. Moulton and George Milligan. It is now accepted that the New Testament

7. G. Milligan, *Here and There Among the Papyri* (London, 1923), pp. 59–62.
8. A. Deissmann, *op. cit.*, outlines the story.

language was under heavy debt to the lingua franca of the day, itself a descendant of Attic Greek of the fifth century B.C. in which the classical Greek literature was written. It had, however, gained from admixture with other kinds of Greek. Even if the problem is a little more complex than we have indicated, it remains true that with the discovery of the papyri the first known examples of a kind of Greek hitherto known only in the Bible came to light. In the absence of such material it is no wonder that the scholars thought that the New Testament was written in the special language of the Greek-speaking Jews and early Christians. Only when the archaeologists produced from the dry sands of Egypt documents that had lain for centuries wrapped around mummies, stuffed into odd corners of collapsed buildings, or cast out into rubbish heaps, did the picture become clear. It was then the task of the linguist to interpret and to translate these documents.

THE LETTERS OF THE FIRST CENTURY A.D.

A great variety of private letters from the days when the New Testament was being written is now available for study. Deissmann has presented a selection of these coming from the centuries ranging from the time of Alexander the Great to Mohammed. He began with the oldest Greek letter then in existence and included letters of Egyptian Christians in the years just before the Moslem invasion of Egypt.[9] This collection makes the nature of the letter form in antiquity very clear.

Letters were written on separate papyrus rolls which, when completed, would be rolled up, fastened with a string, sealed, and addressed on the outside. The postal system of the day was reserved for official messages, and ordinary individuals depended on friends to carry their "mail." Paul's letters were delivered in this way. They were never designed to read as literary treatises but were addressed to personal friends or to groups of Christians and dealt with some of the practical problems that arose in a church or in the life of an individual. Sir William Ramsay stated some years ago that "in the individual case they discover the universal principle, and state it in such a way as to reach the heart of every man similarly situated, and yet they state this, not in the way of formal exposition, but in the way of direct personal converse, written in place of spoken."[10]

The personal note struck by Paul is closely in agreement with the general procedure of other letter writers of his day. It is usual to have opening and closing salutations, and a wide range of regular niceties of expression. Samples of these letters are readily available for the student,[11] but we shall choose two to illustrate.

9. *Ibid.*, pp. 146ff.
10. W. M. Ramsay, *Letters to the Seven Churches* (London, 1908), p. 25.
11. A. Deissmann, *op. cit.*; J. Finegan, *op. cit.*; G. Milligan, *op. cit.*

A good example of a letter of commendation comes from Oxyrhynchus and has been dated A.D. 16. A certain Theon recommended the bearer of the letter, Hermophilus, to his brother Heraclides in the following words:

> Theon to Heraclides his brother, many greetings and wishes for good health. Hermophilus the bearer of this letter is friend . . . and asked me to write to you. Hermophilus declares that he has business at Kerkemounis. Please therefore further him in this matter, as is just. For the rest take care of yourself that you may remain in good health. Goodbye. The third year of Tiberius Caesar Augustus.[12]

The address was written on the verso (back).

We notice that in this letter the writer's name is first, then the name of the person to whom the letter is addressed, and a greeting. At the end of the letter is a parting greeting and a wish. These features are to be found quite regularly in Paul's letters. Indeed Paul also spoke of "letters of commendation" (II Cor. 3:1).

Some of these non-Christian epistles contained, in addition to the usual introductory material, a "prayer" and "thanksgiving" very much like what we find in Paul's letters. Thus in the second century A.D. a young man named Apion, serving with his regiment in Italy, wrote to his father, telling of his stormy trip and giving some details of his present life:

> Apion, to Epimachus his father and lord, many greetings. Before all things I pray you are in health and that you prosper and fare well continually together with my sister and her daughter and my brother. I thank the Lord Serapis that, when I was in peril in the sea, he saved me immediately. When I came to Miseni, I received as journey-money from the Caesar three pieces of gold. And it is well with me. I beseech you therefore, my lord father, to write me a little letter, firstly of your health, secondly of that of my brother and sister, thirdly that I may look upon your handwriting with reverence, because you have taught me well and I therefore hope to advance rapidly, if the gods will. Salute Capito much, and my brother and sister Serenilla and my friends. I am sending you by Eucetemon a little picture of me. Moreover my name is Antonis Maximus. Fare you well I pray.[13]

In the margin alongside the letter the following words are found:

> There salute you Serenus the son of Agathus Daemon, and . . . Turbo the son of Gallonius. . . .

There are similarities of expression and technique between this letter and those of Paul, Peter, and John. Thus the phrase "I pray that you are in health" compares with III John, verse 2. The acknowledgment of the help of the gods is much like the expression of Paul's gratitude to God which we often find in the

---

12. G. Milligan, *op. cit.*, pp. 33f.
13. J. Finegan, *op. cit.*, pp. 327f.

introduction to his letters (Rom. 1:8; I Cor. 1:4; Phil. 1:3; Col. 1:3; I Thess. 1:2; II Thess. 1:3, etc.). The phrase "Salute Capito" is to be compared with such a greeting as that in I Corinthians 16:19, and the salutations from friends can be compared with salutations at the end of several of Paul's letters. Altogether, in the construction of the sentences, in the general absence of connecting particles, and in the whole mold of the letter with its greeting, prayer of thanksgiving, general contents, salutations, and closing valediction, we have much to

A typical first-century-A.D. letter, written in a large, semi-cursive hand. The sender, Procleius, requests Pecusis to have his friend Sotas bring along some drugs to Alexandria. The letter is written on a piece of papyrus ca. nineteen by ten centimeters. (British Museum)

remind us of Paul and of the others who wrote the letters in the New Testament. Our biblical letters are typical of the correspondence of the day.

THE COMMON DOCUMENTS OF EVERYDAY LIFE

There is a great variety of these, and they give detailed information about all aspects of life, family relationships, education, taxation, religion, slavery, petitions of one kind or another, sickness and death, food and dress, and so on. The great value for us is that they give us the typical vocabulary of the common people as well as parallel information to what we find in the New Testament.

Reference has already been made to the official documents summoning people to their home town for the census in the days of Augustus and later.[14] These were found in Egyptian rubbish heaps. We have also mentioned the magical papyri and the incantation texts which have been recovered in great numbers.[15] Many of the letters give interesting details about the relationships inside the family. One letter instructs a wife to "expose" a child about to be born if it is a girl.[16] Another letter from a wife expresses concern for her husband in a time of danger.[17] Other letters from children to parents tell us a great deal about family relationships. Letters referring to bereavements manifest, as we might have expected, deep feelings. Sometimes they are poignantly beautiful. But the Christian cannot help being impressed by their general air of despair in marked contrast with the Christian hope.

At times we have a glimpse into the education of the day, as, for example, in the case of a mother who wrote to a son whose teacher had left him:

> I took care to send and ask about your health and learn what you are reading; he said that it was the sixth book [of Homer] and testified at length regarding your pedagogue. So, my son, I urge both you and your pedagogue to take care that you go to a suitable teacher.[18]

This shows that it was the task of the pedagogue to take the boy to school and to act as his guardian until he reached maturity. We here meet the word Paul used in Galatians 3:24, where he says that the law was a pedagogue (schoolmaster) to bring us to Christ.

Slavery was part of the social structure of those days, and the papyri tell us much about this institution. The pedagogue, for example, was often a slave, but generally a greatly honored one. Even if the slave system was evil in many ways, we have many instances of deep concern for the welfare of the slaves. The

---

14. See above, pp. 381–388.
15. See above, p. 405.
16. G. Milligan, *op. cit.*, p. 93. Unwanted children were left unattended in the open fields or by the roadside to perish; that is, they were "exposed."
17. *Ibid.*, p. 91.
18. *Ibid.*, p. 97.

manumission (setting free) of slaves was used in Christian writings as a picture of freeing men from the bondage of sin to become Christ's bondslaves. Deissmann has an interesting section on such documents and points out many parallels in phraseology between the common and the Pauline usage of this vocabulary.[19]

Some of the expressions that refer to slavery are found in the New Testament, and we may study the everyday usage of such words as "slave," "redemption," and "ransom" in these documents. In this connection the papyri help us sometimes to translate difficult passages in the New Testament. In Romans 8:23, for example, there is a Greek word *aparche,* translated in the Authorized Version as "firstfruits." In classical Greek it was used for the first fruits or the first offerings made to the gods. One papyrus, however, renders it "legacy duty," and another uses it for the "entrance fee" paid by Alexandrian men who became citizens. Sometimes it is used for a "gift" to a god.[20] One special use is where it refers to the "birth certificate" of a free person. This latter meaning has been suggested as the correct one for Romans 8:23. The point is that children of God have the *birth certificate* of the Spirit, which makes them free men even if they still await formal release from the bondage of the flesh.[21]

Other papyri give information about social life. Here, for example, is an invitation to a man to be present at some ceremonial occasion:

> Antonius, son of Ptolemaeus, invites you to dine with him at the table of the Lord Serapis in the house of Claudius Serapion on the 16th at 9 o'clock.[22]

The word for "invite," "request," or "beseech" is regularly used in the New Testament (e.g., Luke 11:37; I Thess. 4:1), and the word "lord" (Greek *kurios*) is regularly used as a divine title. For Paul there is but one Lord, Jesus Christ, despite the claims of other "deities" to be lord. Again, in the phrase "in the house of Claudius," the word "house" does not occur in the text, but must be supplied. This usage is also found in the New Testament, for example, in Luke 2:49 (RV), where the words of Jesus are reported, "Wist ye not that I must be in my Father's house?"[23]

SOME EXAMPLES OF NEW TESTAMENT VOCABULARY FOUND IN THE PAPYRI AND THE OSTRACA

The papyri and the ostraca (broken pieces of pottery on which something is written, a receipt, a brief letter, a note, etc.) enable us to study firsthand the

19. A. Deissmann, *op. cit.,* pp. 320f.
20. J. H. Moulton and G. Milligan, *Vocabulary of the Greek New Testament* (London, 1957), p. 54.
21. G. Milligan, *op. cit.,* pp. 99f.
22. *Ibid.,* pp. 101f.
23. The reasons for this translation are given in the standard commentaries, e.g., A. Plummer, *Gospel According to St. Luke,* ICC (Edinburgh, 1913), pp. 77f.

everyday use to which numerous words in the New Testament were put. Even where classical Greek used certain words, we discover that Koine Greek sometimes had a different shade of meaning and a breadth of common usage which would not have been suspected. In many cases the popular usage is taken over into the New Testament as a metaphor to describe some spiritual experience. We shall take a few examples to show the value of this new material for our understanding of the meaning and usage of such words.

The word "earnest" (Greek *arrabon*) in the New Testament occurs in II Corinthians 1:22; 5:5 and Ephesians 1:14 and seems to indicate an advance payment in expectation of the full payment at a later date. The papyri use the word in precisely this sense. One example comes from Egypt where a woman who sold a cow received an *arrabon* of one thousand drachma in advance. Another document refers to some dancing girls who received money as an *arrabon* on their promised salary.[24] This particular word is in fact used by some classical writers, but it is a direct borrowing from Semitic languages.

The verb rendered "have" in Matthew 6:16 (Greek *apecho*), in the phrase concerning the hypocrites, "they have their reward," is a regular technical word in the papyri for the granting of a receipt. It is also found on many ostraca which were commonly used for the issuing of receipts. This word is found in the classics, although there it has other meanings too. Deissmann, commenting on its use in Matthew, says that "it is as though they [the hypocrites] had already given a receipt, and they have absolutely no further claim to reward. This added touch of quiet irony makes the text more lifelike and pointed."[25] In other words, when the hypocrites had won the applause of men by disfiguring their faces, their right to receive a reward had been realized, and it was as though the receipt had been issued. Here the matter ended.

There is another use of the word in Philippians 4:18, where Paul, expressing gratitude to the church at Philippi for their help, said, "I have [Greek *apecho*] all, and abound," that is, "I give you a receipt in full." Again, in Philemon 15, Paul, writing to Philemon concerning the slave Onesimus who had departed, suggested that this had been but for a time so that "thou shouldest *receive* him [as one for whom he had signed a receipt] for ever."

The word for "seal" in Romans 15:28 (Greek *sphragizo*) was regularly used in commerce, according to the papyri. Paul had remarked that the Gentiles, having shared in the spiritual blessings of the poor saints in Jerusalem, should now share with them the things needed to sustain their bodies. He promised to "secure [or seal] this fruit" for the saints in Jerusalem, and after that to go on to Spain. What does the phrase mean? The verb *sphragizo* occurs in a specialized commercial sense in the papyri, where it is used for sealing up bags of wheat and

24. J. H. Moulton and G. Milligan, *op. cit.*, p. 79.
25. A. Deissmann, *op. cit.*, pp. 110f.

barley.[26] The sealing was the proof that everything was in order for delivery. So Paul, like an honest merchant, would see to it that the gift entrusted to his care would be properly secured for those to whom it was consigned. In classical Greek the word also meant "to seal," though its connotation was wider.

The phrase "in a disorderly manner" (Greek *ataktos*), found in II Thessalonians 3:11, is known in the papyri, from which we discover an interesting usage. One contract from A.D. 66 deals with the apprenticeship of a boy to a master. The boy is to be supported with food and clothing by his father, and the master is to give the boy a monthly allowance. If there are days when the boy "fails to attend work" or "plays truant," the father has to arrange for an equivalent number of days at the conclusion of the contract.[27] The adverb used in II Thessalonians is from the same room as that used here for "play truant" or "fail to attend" and denotes culpable idleness. In Thessalonica there were those who were *ataktos*, "working not at all," that is, they were idlers. Paul deplored this and indicated that even if these people thought that the Lord was coming, the best way to prepare was to be busy at a profitable occupation when He came. Those who played truant were behaving "in a disorderly manner" (Greek *ataktos*).[28]

These examples show the kind of information that is now available from the papyri and the ostraca. And the exciting thing is that the task has only just begun.

THE EARLIEST NEW TESTAMENT DOCUMENTS

The question is often asked whether we have copies of the New Testament books reaching back to the first century A.D. We must admit that we have no such material. The earliest extant manuscript falls just inside the period covered by this book. In 1935, C. H. Roberts noticed in the John Rylands Library in Manchester a scrap of John's Gospel which had been acquired in 1920 by Dr. B. P. Grenfell, but was unnoticed till Roberts examined it.[29] It was a small piece of papyrus, only 3½ × 2½ inches, containing fragments of John 18:31 to 33 and 37 and 38. The style of writing enabled it to be assigned to the first half of the second century. As we have seen,[30] the fact that it was not only written in Egypt but that it had been used in a provincial town in Egypt at this early date points to the fact that John's Gospel, far from being a late second-century production as some had maintained, was in fact far earlier, and more likely to have been

26. G. Milligan, *op. cit.*, pp. 72ff.
27. *Ibid.*, pp. 74f.
28. L. L. Morris, *The Epistles of Paul to the Thessalonians* (Grand Rapids, 1958), p. 100.
29. C. H. Roberts, *An Unpublished Fragment of the Fourth Gospel* (Manchester, 1935).
30. See above, p. 413.

This papyrus fragment of John 18 dates from the early second century A.D. and is the oldest extant manuscript of the New Testament. (John Rylands Library, Manchester, England)

written in the first century, or at least very early in the second. Up to the present this is our earliest piece of the New Testament.

There are other second-century papyri, however, including one at Manchester containing Titus 1:11–15 and 2:4–8, and another at Oxford containing fragments of Matthew 26.[31] Another very early manuscript from Egypt is the Bodmer papyrus,[32] known as Papyrus Bodmer II. It is dated to about A.D. 220 and preserves the Greek text of John 1:1–14:26 almost complete, along with fragments from the rest of John, 14:29–30 and 21:8–9.

But the great manuscripts of the New Testament come from the third and the following centuries and lie outside the scope of this book. It is by no means unlikely that yet other manuscripts of the New Testament dating from the second century will be discovered, for archaeological work is going on all the time.

31. See Nestle's *Greek New Testament*, British and Foreign Bible Society, for a convenient list.

32. F. V. Filson, "A New Papyrus of the Gospel of John," *BA*, Vol. XX, pp. 54–63.

The Chester Beatty Papyrus (p⁴⁶) is the earliest known manuscript of Paul's letters (ca. A.D. 200). This page of the manuscript contains Ephesians 6:20–24 and Galatians 1:1–7. (University of Michigan Library)

GENERAL CONCLUSION

There is something exciting about supplementing the biblical records with information from nonbiblical historians and from the thrilling discoveries of modern archaeology. It is very evident that the biblical records have their roots firmly in general world history. Archaeological discovery supplements, explains, and at times corroborates the biblical story. The happy combination of the biblical records, the nonbiblical histories, and the discoveries of the archaeologists has produced such splendid results to date that we are full of optimism about the future. There is work for many centuries yet to be done. Many sites have yet to be excavated thoroughly and many others remain whose excavation has not yet commenced. If the achievements of the excavator up to the present have yielded such important results, what may not the future hold for us?

APPENDIXES

KINGS OF JUDAH		PROPHETS	KINGS OF ISRAEL	

```
          KINGS OF JUDAH              PROPHETS              KINGS OF ISRAEL

          Rehoboam   922-915                               Jeroboam I    922-901
          Abijah     915-913                               Nadab         901-900
          Asa        913-873                               Baasha        900-877
  9th                                                      Elah          877-876
                                                           Zimri         876
  C                                          E             Omri          876-869
  E                                          L
  N       Jehoshaphat 873-849                I      E      Ahab          869-850
  T       Joram       849-842                J      L      Ahaziah       850-849
  U       Ahaziah     842                    A      I      Joram         849-842
  R       Athaliah    842-837                H      S
  Y       Joash       837-800                       H      Jehu          842-815
                                                    A
  B.C.                                                      Jehoahaz      815-801
                                                            Joash         801-786

  8th     Amaziah     800-783          A                    Jeroboam II   786-746
                                       M
  C       Uzziah      783-742 )   I    O    H
  E                           )         S   O
  N                           )   S     S   S               Zechariah     746-745
  T                           )             E
  U                           )   A         A               Shallum       745
  R                           )
  Y       Jotham      742-735 )   I    )    E               Menahem       745-738
                              )        )
  B.C.                        )   A    )    A               Pekahiah      738-737
          Ahaz       735-715  )        )
                              )   H    )                    Pekah         737-732
                              )        )  M
                              )        )                    Hoshea        732-724
                              )        )  I
                              )        )
                              )        ;  C                 ISRAEL FALLS TO
          Hezekiah   715-687  )        )                    ASSYRIA    722/721
                              )        )  A
                              )        )
  7th                         )        )  H
          Manasseh   687-642  )        )

  C       Amon       642-640
  E       Josiah     640-609
  N
  T                           )
  U                           )   J
  R                           )              NAHUM
  Y                           )   E          ZEPHANIAH
                              )
  B.C.                        )   R
                              )
                              )   E
                              )
          Jehoahaz   609      )
          Jehoiakim  609-598  )   M
                              )
          Jehoiakin  598      )   I          HABAKKUK
  6th     Zedekiah   598-587  )
                              )   A
  C       JUDAH FALLS         )
  E       TO BABYLONIA        )   H
  N
  T
  U
  R
  Y

  B.C.
```

441

	BABYLONIAN, PERSIAN AND GREEK KINGS		THE JEWS
600	**BABYLONIAN KINGS** Nebuchadnezzar 605-562 Amel Marduk 562-560 Neriglissar 560-556 Nabonidus 556-539		586 Fall of Jerusalem
550	**PERSIAN KINGS** Cyrus 539-530 Cambyses 530-522 Darius 522-486		538 Edict of Cyrus 520 Haggai and Zechariah 516 Temple completed
500	Xerxes 486-465 Artaxerxes I 465-424		Esther 458 Ezra Malachi
450	Xerxes II 424-423 Darius II 423-404		445 Nehemiah 432 Nehemiah recalled 407 Elephantine Letter
400	Artaxerxes II 404-358		
	Artaxerxes III 358-338 Arses 338-336 Darius III 336-331		
350	**GREEK KINGS** Ptolemies	Seleucids	
	Ptolemy I 323-283		332 Jews fall under Greeks 320 Ptolemies take control
300	Ptolemy II 283-246 Ptolemy III 246-221	Early Seleucid Kings	Ptolemies in Palestine
250	Ptolemy IV 221-203 Ptolemy V 203-181	Antiochus III 223-187	
200			198 Seleucids take Palestine
		Seleucus IV 187-175 Antiochus IV 175-163	167 Pollution of Temple 166-160 Judas
	Later Ptolemaic Kings	Antiochus V 163-162 Demetrius I 162-150	164 Temple cleansed 160-142 Jonathan 152 Jonathan high priest
150		Balas 150-145 Antiochus VI 145-142 Demetrius II 145-139	142-134 Simon
		Antiochus VII 139-129	134-104 John Hyrcanus 104-103 Aristobulus I
100		Seleucids continue with internal troubles till Roman conquest in 63 B.C.	103-76 Alexander Jannaeus
			76-67 Alexandra 67-63 Aristobulus II 63 Pompey takes Jerusalem 63-40 Hyrcanus II
50			
0			40-37 Antigonus Mattathias 37- 4 Herod

442

LIST OF EMPERORS

EMPEROR	DATE	NEW TESTAMENT REFERENCE
Augustus	B.C. 30-A.D. 14	Luke 2:1
Tiberius	A.D. 14-37	Luke 3:1
Caligula	A.D. 37-41	
Claudius	A.D. 41-54	Acts 11:28, 18:2
Nero	A.D. 54-68	Acts 25:10-12, 27:24
		II Tim. 4:16, 17
Galba	A.D. 68-69	
Otho	A.D. 69 (3 months)	
Vitellus	A.D. 69 (1 month)	
Vespasian	A.D. 69-79	
Titus	A.D. 79-81	
Domitian	A.D. 81-96	
Nerva	A.D. 96-98	
Trajan	A.D. 98-117	
Hadrian	A.D. 117-138	

LIST OF PROCURATORS

PROCURATOR	DATE	NEW TESTAMENT REFERENCE
Coponius	A.D. 6-10	
M. Ambivius	A.D. 10-13	
Annius Rufus	A.D. 13-15	
Valerius Gratus	A.D. 15-26	
Pontius Pilate	A.D. 26-36	Matt. 27, Mark 15:1-5,
		John 18:28-38
Marcellus	A.D. 36-38	
Maryllus	A.D. 38-44	
Cuspius Fadus	A.D. 44- ?	
Alexander	A.D. ?-48	
Cumanus	A.D. 48-52	
Felix	A.D. 52-59(?)	Acts 23, 24
Porcius Festus	A.D. 59(?)-62	Acts 25, 26
Albinus	A.D. 62-64	
Gessius Florus		
(Siege of Jerusalem)	A.D. 64-66	

THE FAMILY OF HEROD THE GREAT

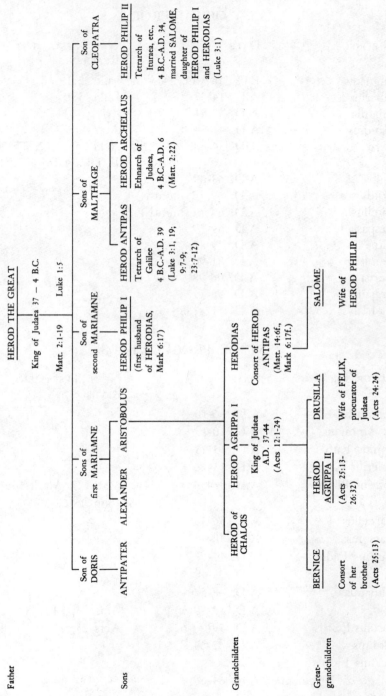

Father

HEROD THE GREAT
King of Judaea 37 – 4 B.C.
Matt. 2:1-19   Luke 1:5

Sons

Son of DORIS

ANTIPATER

Sons of first MARIAMNE

ALEXANDER   ARISTOBOLUS

Son of second MARIAMNE

HEROD PHILIP I
(first husband of HERODIAS,
Mark 6:17)

Sons of MALTHAGE

HEROD ANTIPAS
Tetrarch of Galilee
4 B.C.-A.D. 39
(Luke 3:1, 19;
9:7-9;
23:7-12)

HEROD ARCHELAUS
Ethnarch of Judaea,
4 B.C.-A.D. 6
(Matt. 2:22)

Son of CLEOPATRA

HEROD PHILIP II
Tetrarch of Ituraea, etc.,
4 B.C.-A.D. 34,
married SALOME,
daughter of
HEROD PHILIP I
and HERODIAS
(Luke 3:1)

Grandchildren

HEROD of CHALCIS

HEROD AGRIPPA I
King of Judaea
A.D. 37-44
(Acts 12:1-24)

HERODIAS
Consort of HEROD ANTIPAS
(Matt. 14:6f.,
Mark 6:17f.)

Great-grandchildren

BERNICE
Consort of her brother
(Acts 25:13)

HEROD AGRIPPA II
(Acts 25:13-26:32)

DRUSILLA
Wife of FELIX,
procurator of Judaea
(Acts 24:24)

SALOME
Wife of HEROD PHILIP II

444

10

Birth of Jesus Christ, 6 B.C.?

0

10

20

Ministry of John the Baptist

30

Death of Christ. Birth of the Church
Martydom of Stephen
Conversion of Saul of Tarsus, A.D.35

40 Church in Antioch
James beheaded. Peter in prison

Paul's famine visit to Jerusalem
First missionary journey begun, A.D. 47

50 Second missionary journey, A.D. 50-51   I and II Thess., Gal.?
                                               I Cor. (Gal.? Phil.?)
                                             II Cor., Rom.

End of third missionary journey and arrest,
A.D. 56. End of Caesarea imprisonment,
A.D. 58. To Rome, A.D. 59

60

End of first Rome imprisonment, A.D. 61   (Phil.?), Eph., Col., Philem.
Further journeys   I Tim., Mark, Titus, II Tim., Heb.
End of second Rome imprisonment and
death, A.D. 64
Jewish revolt, A.D. 66

70   Fall of Jerusalem
       Fall of Masada, A.D. 73   Matt.? Luke-Acts?

80   Josephus, *History of Jewish War*

90   Josephus, *Jewish Antiquities*

                                               Rev., II and III John?
                                             John, I John

100

BIBLIOGRAPHY

The Bibliography that has been collected in the following pages is at best a selection of useful books now available for study. The complete list is, of course, very extensive. For the most part the present suggestions include only books in English, although a few in French and German have been included where they are thought to have special value. Articles from journals have not in general been included here, although in the case of specially significant ones they have been listed in the appropriate chapter. The footnotes in the body of the present book will direct the reader's attention to many more valuable articles in scholarly archaeological journals.

GENERAL BIBLIOGRAPHY

BIBLICAL GEOGRAPHY AND TOPOGRAPHY
Aharoni, Y., *The Land of the Bible*, 1966 (Burns & Oates, London)
Aharoni, Y., and M. Avi-Yonah, *The Macmillan Bible Atlas*, 1968 (Macmillan, London)
Baly, D., *The Geography of the Bible*, 1957 (Harper, New York)
du Buit, M., *Géographie de la Terre Sainte*, 1958 (Les Éditions du Cerf, Paris)
Grollenberg, L. H., *Atlas of the Bible*, E. T. 1956 (Nelson, New York)
———, *Shorter Atlas of the Bible*, 1959 (Nelson, New York)
Kitchen, J. H., *Holy Fields*, 1956 (Eerdmans, Grand Rapids)
Kraeling, E. G. (ed.), *Rand McNally Historical Atlas of the Holy Land*, 1959 (Rand McNally, Chicago)
Rowley, H. H., *The Teach Yourself Bible Atlas*, 1960 (English Universities Press, London)
Smith, G. A., *The Historical Geography of the Holy Land*, 25th ed., 1931 (Hodder & Stoughton, London)
Van der Meer, F., and C. Mohrman, *Atlas of the Early Christian World*, E. T. 1958 (Nelson, New York)

Wright, G. E., and F. V. Filson, *The Westminster Historical Atlas to the Bible*, rev. ed. 1958 (Westminster, Philadelphia)

OLD TESTAMENT HISTORY
Albright, W. F., *The Biblical Period*, 1950 (Blackwell, Oxford)
———, *From the Stone Age to Christianity*, 2nd ed., 1957 (Johns Hopkins University Press, Baltimore)
Bright, J., *A History of Israel*, 1961 (Abingdon, New York)
Gordon, C. H., *The World of the Old Testament*, 1960 (Phoenix House, London)
Harrison, R. K., *A History of Old Testament Times*, 1957 (Zondervan, Grand Rapids)
Hayes, J. H., and J. M. Miller, *Israelite and Judaean History*, 1977 (SCM, London)
Herrmann, S., *A History of Israel in Old Testament Times*, 1975 (SCM, London)
Kitchen, K. A., *The Bible in its World*, 1977 (Paternoster Press, Exeter)
Noth, M., *The History of Israel*, E. T., 2nd ed., 1960 (Harper, New York)
Orlinsky, H., *Ancient Israel*, 1960, 2nd ed. (Cornell University Press, New York)
de Vaux, R., *Histoire ancienne d'Israel des Origines à l'installation en Canaan*, 1971 (J. Gabalda, Paris)
Wiseman, D. J. (ed.), *Peoples of Old Testament Times*, 1973 (Oxford, London)

TRANSLATIONS OF ANCIENT RECORDS
Beyerlin, W. (ed.), *Near Eastern Religious Texts relating to the Old Testament*, 1978 (SCM, London)
Breasted, J. H., *Ancient Records of Egypt*, I–IV, 1906–7 (Chicago University Press, Chicago)
Budge, E. A., and L. W. King, *The Annals of the Kings of Assyria*, Vol. I, 1902 (British Museum, London)
Grayson, A. K., *Assyrian Royal Inscriptions I–II*, 1972, 1976 (Harrassowitz, Wiesbaden)
Luckenbill, D. D., *Historical Records of Assyria*, 1926–1927 (Chicago University Press, Chicago)
Pritchard, J. B., *Ancient Near Eastern Texts*, 1955 (Princeton University Press, Princeton)
———, *The Ancient Near East*, 1958 (Princeton University Press, Princeton)
Thomas, D. W., *Documents from Old Testament Times*, 1958 (Nelson, New York)

BIBLE DICTIONARIES AND ENCYCLOPEDIAS
Black's Bible Dictionary, 1954 (A. & C. Black, London)
The Illustrated Bible Dictionary, Parts I–III, 1980 (Inter-Varsity, London)
The International Standard Bible Encyclopedia, Vol. I, 1979. Other volumes to follow (Eerdmans, Grand Rapids)
The Interpreter's Dictionary of the Bible, 4 vols., 1962 (Abingdon, Nashville)
McKenzie, S. L., *Dictionary of the Bible*, 1966 (Geoffrey Chapman, London)
The New Bible Dictionary, 1962 (Inter-Varsity Press, London)
The Zondervan Picture Encyclopedia, M. C. Tenney (ed.), 1975 (Zondervan, Grand Rapids)

Chapter I: BIBLICAL ARCHAEOLOGY TODAY

Albright, W. F., *Archaeology and the Religion of Israel*, rev. ed. (Johns Hopkins University Press, Baltimore)
———, *The Archaeology of Palestine*, rev. ed., 1956 (Pelican, London)
———, *The Bible After Twenty Years of Archaeology (1932–1952)*, 1954 (Funk and Wagnalls, New York)
Avi-Yonah, M., *Encyclopedia of Archaeological Excavations in the Holy Land*, Vols. I–IV, 1975, 1976, 1977, 1978 (Massada Press, Jerusalem)

Burrows, M., *What Mean These Stones?*, 1941 (American Schools of Oriental Research, Baltimore)

Chiera, E., *They Wrote on Clay*, 1956 (Chicago University Press, Chicago)

Finegan, J., *The Archaeology of the New Testament*, 1969 (Princeton University Press, Princeton)

———, *Light from the Ancient Past*, 2nd ed., 1959 (Princeton University Press, Princeton)

Franken, H. J., and C. A. Franken-Battershill, *A Primer of Old Testament Archaeology*, 1963 (E. J. Brill, Leiden)

Free, J. P., *Archaeology and Bible History*, 1950 (Scripture Press, Wheaton, Ill.)

Kenyon, K. M., *Archaeology in the Holy Land*, 1960 (Ernest Benn, London)

———, *Beginning in Archaeology*, 1952 (Phoenix House, London)

———, *The Bible and Recent Archaeology*, 1978 (John Knox Press, Atlanta)

Lapp, P. W., *The Tale of the Tell*, 1975 (Pittsburgh Theological Monograph Series, No. 5)

Lloyd, S., *Mounds of the Near East*, 1963 (Edinburgh University Press)

Owen, G. F., *Archaeology and the Bible*, 1960 (Revell, Westwood)

Parrot, A., *Discovering Buried Worlds*, E. T. 1955 (SCM, London)

Paul, S. M., and W. C. Dever, *Biblical Archaeology*, 1973 (Keter Publishing House, Jerusalem)

Pritchard, J. B., *Archaeology and the Old Testament*, 1959 (Princeton University Press, Princeton)

Unger, M. F., *Archaeology and the Old Testament*, 1954 (Zondervan, Grand Rapids)

Williams, W. G., *Archaeology in Biblical Research*, 1965 (Abingdon, New York)

Wiseman, D. J., *Illustrations in Biblical Archaeology*, 1958 (Eerdmans, Grand Rapids)

Woolley, C. L., *Digging Up the Past*, 1937 (Pelican, London)

Wright, G. E., *Biblical Archaeology*, 1957 (Westminster, Philadelphia)

———, *An Introduction to Biblical Archaeology*, 1960 (Westminster, Philadelphia)

Wright, G. E., and D. N. Freedman (eds.), *The Biblical Archaeologist Reader*, 1961 (Doubleday, Garden City)

Chapter II: ABRAHAM THE MIGRANT

Glueck, N., *Rivers in the Desert*, 1959 (Weidenfeld, London)

Gordon, C. H., "Bible Customs and the Nuzi Tablets," in *BA*, Feb., 1960

Gurney, O. R., *The Hittites*, 1955 (Pelican, London)

Heidel, A., *The Babylonian Genesis*, 2nd ed., 1951 (Chicago University Press, Chicago)

———, *The Gilgamesh Epic and Old Testament Parallels*, 2nd ed., 1949 (Chicago University Press, Chicago)

Lambert, W. G., and A. R. Millard, *Atrahasis, The Babylonian Story of the Flood*, 1969 (Oxford)

Matthews, V. H., *Pastoral Nomadism in the Mari Kingdom (ca. 1830–1760 B.C.)*, 1978 (Americal Schools of Oriental Research, Cambridge)

Parrot, A., *The Flood and Noah's Ark*, E. T. 1955 (SCM, London)

———, *The Tower of Babel*, E. T. 1955 (SCM, London)

Pfeiffer, C. F., *The Patriarchal Age*, 1961 (Baker, Grand Rapids)

Rowley, H. H., "Recent Discovery and the Patriarchal Age," *BJRL*, Sept., 1949

Thompson, T. L., *The Historicity of the Patriarchal Narratives*, 1974 (Walter de Gruyter, New York)

van Seters, J., *Abraham in History and Tradition*, 1975 (Yale University Press, New Haven)

de Vaux, R., "Les patriarches Hébreux et les découvertes modernes," *RB*, 1946, 1948, 1949

Woolley, C. L., *Excavations at Ur*, 1954 (Barnes & Noble, New York)
————, *Ur of the Chaldees*, 1940 (Pelican, London)

Chapter III: IN THE LAND OF THE PHARAOHS

Alt, A., *Die Herkunft der Hyksos in neuer Sicht*, 1954 (published in *Kleine Schriften* by
    C. H. Beck'sche, Munich)
Cottrell, L., *Life Under the Pharaohs*, 1956 (Evans, London)
————, *The Lost Pharaohs*, 1955 (Evans, London)
Engberg, R. M., *The Hyksos Reconsidered*, 1939 (Chicago University Press, Chicago)
van Seters, J., *The Hyksos, a New Investigation*, 1966 (Yale University Press, New
    Haven)
Vergote, J., *Joseph en Egypte—Génèse 37–50 à la lumière des études égyptologique récentes*,
    1959 (Publications Universitaires, Louvain)
Wilson, J. A., *The Burden of Egypt*, 1951 (Chicago University Press, Chicago)
Yahuda, A. S., *The Accuracy of the Bible*, 1934 (Heinemann, London)
————, *The Language of the Pentateuch in Its Relation to Egyptian*, 1933 (Oxford Univer-
    sity Press, London).

Chapter IV: FROM EGYPT TO CANAAN

De Wit, C., *The Date and Route of the Exodus*, 1960 (Tyndale Press, London)
Garstang, J. and J. B. E., *The Story of Jericho*, 1940 (Marshall, Morgan & Scott, London)
Glueck, N., *The Other Side of Jordan*, 1940 (American Schools of Oriental Research,
    New Haven)
————, *The River Jordan*, 1946 (Westminster, Philadelphia)
Kenyon, K., *Digging Up Jericho*, 1957 (Ernest Benn, London)
Kitchen, K. A., *The Egyptian Nineteenth Dynasty*, 1980 (Aris & Phillips, Warminster)
Mendenhall, G. E., *Law and Covenant in Israel and the Ancient Near East*, 1955 (The
    Biblical Colloquium, Pittsburgh)
Montet, P., *L'Egypte et la Bible*, 1959 (Delachaux et Niestlé, Neuchâtel)
————, *Le drame d'Avaris*, 1941 (Paris)
Pfeiffer, C. F., *Ras Shamra and the Bible*, 1962 (Baker, Grand Rapids)
Rowley, H. H., *From Joseph to Joshua*, 1950 (Oxford University Press, London)
Van Zyl, A. M., *The Moabites*, 1960 (E. J. Brill, Leiden)

Chapter V: SETTLING INTO THE LAND

Albright, W. F., "The Rôle of the Canaanites in the History of Civilisation," 1960 (in
    The Bible and the Ancient Near East, G. E. Wright [ed.], Routledge & Kegan Paul,
    London)
Bulliet, R. W., *The Camel and the Wheel*, 1975 (Harvard University Press, Cambridge,
    Mass.)
Driver, G. R., *Canaanite Myths and Legends*, 1956 (T. & T. Clark, Edinburgh)
Garstang, J., *Joshua-Judges*, 1931 (Constable, London)
Gottwald, N. K., *The Tribes of Yahweh*, 1979 (SCM, London)
Gray, J., *The Legacy of Canaan*, 2nd rev. ed., *VT Supp. V*, 1965
Jacob, E., *Ras Shamra et l'Ancien Testament*, 1960 (Delachaux et Niestlé, Neuchâtel)
Kenyon, K., *Digging Up Jericho*, 1957 (Ernest Benn, London)
Macalister, R. A. C., *The Philistines, Their History and Civilisation*, 1913 (Oxford Univer-
    sity Press, London)

Ringgren, H., *Religions of the Ancient Near East*, 1973 (S.P.C.K., London)
Weippert, M., *The Settlement of the Israelite Tribes in Palestine*, 1971 (SCM, Studies in Biblical Theology, Second Series, 21)

Chapter VI: ONE NATION—ONE KING

Glueck, N., *The River Jordan*, 1946 (Westminster, Philadelphia)
Kenyon, K. M., *Jerusalem: Excavating 3000 Years of History*, 1967 (Thames and Hudson, London)
Parrot, A., *The Temple of Jerusalem*, E. T. 1957 (SCM, London)
Phillips, W., *Qataban and Sheba*, 1955 (Harcourt Brace, World, New York)
Simons, J., *Jerusalem in the Old Testament*, 1952 (Brill, Leiden)
Unger, M. F., *Israel and the Arameans of Damascus*, 1957 (James Clark, London)
Vincent, L. H. and A. M. Steve, *Jérusalem de l'Ancien Testament*, 1954, 1956 (Librairie Le Coffre, Paris)
Yadin, Y., "New Light on Solomon's Megiddo," *BA*, 1960

Chapter VII: THE KINGS OF ISRAEL

Caiger, S. L., *Bible and Spade*, 1936 (Oxford University Press, London)
Conteneau, G., *Everyday Life in Babylon and Assyria*, 1954 (Arnold, London)
Crowfoot, J. W., and others, *Early Ivories from Samaria*, 1938 (Palestine Exploration Fund, London)
———, *The Buildings of Samaria*, 1942 (Palestine Exploration Fund, London)
Dupont-Sommer, A., *Les Araméens*, 1949 (A. Maisonneuve, Paris)
Encyclopedia of Archaeological Excavations in the Holy Land, Vols. I–IV, 1975, 1976, 1977, 1978 (Massada Press, Jerusalem), for details about specific towns
Luckenbill, D. D., *Historical Records of Assyria*, Vols. I, II, 1926, 1927 (Chicago University Press, Chicago)
Olmstead, A. T., *History of Assyria*, 1923 (Scribner's, New York)
Parrot, A., *Nineveh in the Old Testament*, E. T. 1955 (SCM, London)
———, *Samaria*, E. T. 1955 (S.C.M., London)
Thiele, R., *The Mysterious Numbers of the Hebrew Kings*, 1958 (Chicago University Press, Chicago)
Thomas, D. W. *Archaeology and Old Testament Study*, 1967 (Oxford Press, London)
———, *The Prophet in the Lachish Ostraca*, 1946 (Tyndale Press, London)
Torczyner, H., *The Lachish Letters*, 1938 (in *Lachish I*, H. Torczyner [ed.], London)
Unger, M. F., *Israel and the Arameans of Damascus*, 1959 (James Clark, London)
Wiseman, D. J., *Chronicles of the Chaldaean Kings*, 1956 (British Museum, London)

Chapter VIII: THE KINGS OF JUDAH

Caiger, S. L., *Bible and Spade*, 1936 (Oxford University Press, London)
Encyclopedia of Archaeological Excavations in the Holy Land, Vols. I–IV
Kenyon, K. M., *Jerusalem: Excavating 3000 Years of History*, 1967 (Thames and Hudson, London)
Kitchen, K. A., *The Third Intermediate Period in Egypt*, 1972 (Aris & Phillips, Warminster)
Mazar, B., "The Campaign of Pharaoh Shishak to Palestine," 1957, *VT Supp. IV*, pp. 57–66
Parrot, A., *Nineveh and the Old Testament*, E. T. 1955 (SCM, London)
Thiele, E. R., *The Mysterious Numbers of the Hebrew Kings*, 1958 (Chicago University Press, Chicago)

Chapter IX: CITIES OF JUDAH AND ISRAEL IN THE DAYS OF THE KINGS

Aharoni, Y., "Arad: Its Inscriptions and Temple," 1968, *BA*, Vol. 31, pp. 2–32

Amiran, R., *Ancient Pottery of the Holy Land*, 1969 (Massada Press, Jerusalem)

Biran, A., "Tell Dan—Five Years Later," 1980, *BA*, Vol. 43, pp. 168–182

Crowfoot, J. W., and G. M. Crowfoot, *Early Ivories from Samaria*, 1938 (Palestine Exploration Fund, London)

Crowfoot, J. W., K. M. Kenyon, and E. L. Sukenik, *The Buildings at Samaria*, 1942 (Palestine Exploration Fund, London)

Encyclopedia of Archaeological Excavations in the Holy Land, Vols. I–IV, 1975, 1976, 1977, 1978 (Massada Press, Jerusalem)

Kenyon, K. M., *Jerusalem: Excavating 3000 Years of History*, 1967 (Thames and Hudson, London)

Lamon, R., *The Megiddo Water System*, 1935 (Chicago)

Pritchard, J. B., *The Water System at Gibeon*, 1961 (University of Pennsylvania)

———, *Winery, Defenses and Soundings at Gibeon*, 1964 (University Museum, University of Pennsylvania)

Reifenberg, A., *Ancient Hebrew Seals*, 1948 (The East and West Library, London)

Shiloh, Y., "Elements in the Development of Town Planning in the Israelite City," *IEJ*, Vol. 28, 1978, Nos. 1–2, pp. 36–51

———, "The Four-room House, Its Situation and Function in the Israelite City," *IEJ*, Vol. 20, 1970, pp. 180–190

Wright, G. E., *Shechem, The Biography of a Biblical City*, 1965 (G. Duckworth, London)

Yadin, Y. (ed.), *Jerusalem Revealed*, 1975 (The Israel Exploration Society, Jerusalem)

Chapter X: DAYS OF EXILE

Albright, W. F., "An Ostracon from Calah and the North-Israelite Diaspora," *BASOR*, No. 149, 1958, pp. 33–56

Conteneau, G., *Everyday Life in Babylon and Assyria*, 1954 (Arnold, London)

Dougherty, R. P., *Nabonidus and Belshazzar*, 1929 (Yale University Press, New Haven)

Howie, C. C., *The Date and Composition of Ezekiel*, 1950 (*Journal of Biblical Literature* Monograph Series IV)

Janssen, E., *Juda in der Exilzeit*, 1956 (Vandenhoeck und Ruprecht, Göttingen)

Koldewey, R., *The Excavations at Babylon*, 1914 (Macmillan, London)

Lane, W. H., *Babylonian Problems*, 1923 (John Murray, London)

Neusner, J., *A History of the Jews in Babylonia*, Vols. I and II, 1965, 1966 (E. J. Brill, Leiden)

Parrot, A., *Nineveh and Babylon*, 1961 (Thames & Hudson, London)

Wiseman, D. J., *Chronicles of the Chaldaean Kings*, 1956 (British Museum, London)

Chapter XI: THE RETURN OF THE JEWS FROM EXILE

Kenyon, K. M., *Jerusalem: Excavating 3000 Years of History*, 1967 (Thames and Hudson, London)

Olmstead, A. T., *The History of the Persian Empire*, 1948 (Chicago University Press, Chicago)

de Vaux, R., *Les décrets de Cyrus et de Darius sur la reconstruction du Temple*, 1937 (*Revue Biblique*, Paris)

Whitcomb, J. C., *Darius the Mede*, 1959 (Eerdmans, Grand Rapids)

Chapter XII: THE PERSIAN PERIOD IN PALESTINE FROM 500 B.C. TO 330 B.C.

Aharoni, Y., "Investigations at Lachish, 1973–1977," 1978, *Tel Aviv*, Vol. 5, pp. 41f. "The Residence"

Banks, F. A., *Coins of Bible Days*, 1955 (New York)

Encyclopedia of Archaeological Excavations in the Holy Land, Vols. I–IV, 1975, 1976, 1977, 1978 (Massada Press, Jerusalem)

Ghirshman, R., *Iran*, 1954 (Penguin, London)

Olmstead, A. T., *The History of the Persian Empire*, 1948 (Chicago University Press, Chicago)

Simons, J., *Jerusalem in the Old Testament*, 1952 (Brill, Leiden)

Wright, J. Stafford, *The Building of the Second Temple*, 1958 (Tyndale Press, London)

———, *The Date of Ezra's Coming to Jerusalem*, 2nd ed., 1958 (Tyndale Press, London)

Chapter XIII: THE JEWS OUTSIDE PALESTINE IN THE FIFTH CENTURY B.C.

Cowley, A., *Aramaic Papyri of the Fifth Century B.C.*, 1923 (Oxford University Press, London)

Cross, F. M., "The Discovery of the Samaria Papyri," 1963, *BA*, Vol. XXVI, pp. 110–121

Driver, G. R., *Aramaic Documents of the Fifth Century B.C.*, 1957 (Oxford University Press, London)

Dupont-Sommer, A., *Les Araméens*, 1949 (Maisonneuve, Paris)

Kraeling, E. G., *The Brooklyn Aramaic Papyri*, 1953 (Yale University Press, New Haven)

Chapter XIV: THE COMING OF THE GREEKS

Bevan, E. R., *Jerusalem Under the High Priests*, 1904 (Arnold, London)

Farmer, W. R., *Maccabees, Zealots and Josephus*, 1956 (Columbia University Press, New York)

Lapp, P. W., *Palestinian Ceramic Chronology 200 B.C.–A.D. 70*, 1961 (American Schools of Oriental Research, New Haven)

Lapp, P. W. and N. L., *Discoveries in the Wadi Ed-Daliyeh*, 1974 (American Schools of Oriental Research, Cambridge). Note ch. 5

Pfeiffer, C. F., *Between the Testaments*, 1959 (Baker, Grand Rapids)

Russell, D. S., *Between the Testaments*, 1960 (John Knox, Richmond)

Chapter XV: THE RELIGIOUS COMMUNITY OF QUMRAN

Allegro, J. M., *The Dead Sea Scrolls*, 1957 (Pelican, London)

Black, M., *The Scrolls and Christian Origins*, 1961 (Nelson, London)

Bruce, F. F., *Second Thoughts on the Dead Sea Scrolls*, 1956 (Eerdmans, Grand Rapids)

Burrows, M., *The Dead Sea Scrolls of St. Mark's Monastery*, Vol. I, 1950 (American Schools of Oriental Research, New Haven)

———, *The Dead Sea Scrolls*, 1956 (Secker & Warburg, London)

———, *More Light on the Dead Sea Scrolls*, 1958 (Secker & Warburg, London)

Charlesworth, J. H. (ed.), *John and Qumran*, 1972 (Geoffrey Chapman, London)

Cross, F. M., *The Ancient Library of Qumran and Modern Biblical Studies*, 1958 (Duckworth, London)

Driver, G. R., *The Judaean Scrolls*, 1965 (Blackwell, Oxford)
Dupont-Sommer, A., *The Essene Writings from Qumran*, 1961, trans. G. Vermes (Blackwell, Oxford)
Fritsch, C. T., *The Qumran Community*, 1956 (Macmillan, New York)
Gaster, T. H., *The Scriptures of the Dead Sea Sect*, 1956 (Doubleday, New York)
Greystone, G., *The Dead Sea Scrolls and the Christian Faith*, 1956 (Moody Press, Chicago)
Milik, J. T., *Ten Years of Discovery in the Wilderness of Judaea*, 1959 (SCM, London)
Murphy-O'Connor, J. (ed.), *Paul and Qumran*, 1968 (Geoffrey Chapman, London)
Stendahl, K. (ed.), *The Scrolls and the New Testament*, 1958 (SCM, London)
Sutcliffe, E. F., *The Monks of Qumran*, 1960 (Burns & Oates, London)
Van der Ploeg, J., *The Excavations at Qumran*, 1958 (Longmans, London)
de Vaux, R., *Archaeology and the Dead Sea Scrolls*, 1961 (Oxford University Press, London)
Yadin, Y., *The Message of the Scrolls*, 1957 (London)

Chapter XVI: THE DAYS OF HEROD THE GREAT

Avigad, N., *Archaeological Discoveries in the Jewish Quarter*, 1976 (The Israel Exploration Society, Jerusalem)
Encyclopedia of Archaeological Excavations in the Holy Land, Vols. II and III, 1976, 1977 (Massada Press, Jerusalem)
Jones, A. H. M., *The Herods of Judaea*, 1938 (Oxford University Press, London)
Mazar, B., "Excavations Near Temple Mount Reveal Splendours of Herodian Jerusalem," *BAR*, Vol. VI, No. 4, 1980, pp. 44–59
Netzer, E., "The Winter Palaces of the Judaean Kings at Jericho at the End of the Second Temple Period," *BASOR*, No. 228, 1977, pp. 1–27
Perowne, S., *The Life and Times of Herod the Great*, 1956 (Hodder & Stoughton, London)
Wilkinson, F. J., "Ancient Jerusalem, its Water Supply and Population," *PEQ*, 1974, pp. 33–51
Yadin, Y. (ed.), *Jerusalem Revealed. Archaeology in the Holy City*, 1975 (Israel Exploration Society, Jerusalem)

Chapter XVII: HISTORY OF NEW TESTAMENT TIMES

Barrett, C. K., *The New Testament Background: Selected Documents*, 1957 (S.P.C.K., London)
Blaiklock, E. M., *Rome in the New Testament*, 1959 (IVF, London)
———, *The Christian in Pagan Society*, 1956 (IVF, London)
Bruce, F. F., *New Testament History*, 1969 (Nelson, London)
Bouquet, A. C., *Everyday Life in New Testament Times*, 1953 (Batsford, London)
Jones, A. H. M., *The Herods of Judaea*, 1938 (Oxford University Press, London)
Josephus, F., *Antiquities of the Jews* (Loeb Classical Library, trans. H. St.-J. Thackeray and R. Marcus)
———, *The Jewish Wars* (Pelican, London, trans. G. A. Williamson)
Judge, E. A., *The Social Pattern of the Christian Groups in the First Century*, 1958 (Tyndale Press, London)
Perowne, S., *The Later Herods, the Political Background of the New Testament*, 1958 (Hodder & Stoughton, London)
Reicke, B., *The New Testament Era, The World of the Bible from 500 B.C. to A.D. 100*, 1969 (A. & C. Black, London)
Ridderbos, H. N., *When the Time Had Fully Come*, 1957 (Eerdmans, Grand Rapids)

Chapter XVIII: ARCHAEOLOGY AND THE ROMAN OCCUPATION OF
PALESTINE

Albright, W. F., *The Archaeology of Palestine*, 1960 (Pelican, London), pp. 146–176,
238–249
Avigad, N., *Archaeological Discoveries in the Jewish Quarter*, 1976 (The Israel Exploration
Society, Jerusalem)
Banks, F. A., *Coins of Bible Days*, 1955 (Macmillan, New York)
Blaiklock, E. M., *Out of the Earth*, rev. ed., 1961 (Eerdmans, Grand Rapids)
Bouquet, A. C., *Everyday Life in New Testament Times*, 1953 (Batsford, London)
Bruce, F. F., *The New Testament Documents: Are They Reliable?* 5th ed., 1960 (Eerdmans,
Grand Rapids)
Cobern, C. M., *The New Archaeological Discoveries and Their Bearing on the New Testa-
ment*, 1922 (Funk & Wagnalls, London)
Dalman, G. H., *Sacred Sites and Ways*, 1935 (S.P.C.K., London)
Guttman, S., "Gamla: The Massada of the North," *BAR*, Vol. V, No. 1, 1979, pp.
12–27
Parrot, A., *Golgotha and the Church of the Holy Sepulchre*, E. T. 1957 (SCM, London)
Pritchard, J. B., *The Excavation at Herodian Jericho, 1951*, 1958 (AASOR, XXXII–
XXXIII for 1952–54) (American Schools of Oriental Research, New Haven)
Unger, M. F., *Archaeology and the New Testament*, 1962 (Zondervan, Grand Rapids)
Yadin, Y., *Masada, Herod's Fortress and the Zealots' Last Stand*, 1966 (Weidenfeld and
Nicholson, London)

Chapter XIX: THE JERUSALEM THAT JESUS KNEW

Avigad, N., *Archaeological Discoveries in the Jewish Quarter*, 1976 (The Israel Exploration
Society, Jerusalem)
Dalman, G. H., *Sacred Sites and Ways*, 1935 (S.P.C.K., London)
Encyclopedia of Archaeological Excavations in the Holy Land, Vols. I–IV, 1975, 1976, 1977,
1978 (Massada Press, Jerusalem)
Finegan, J., *The Archaeology of the New Testament*, 1969 (Princeton University Press,
Princeton)
Jeremias, J., *Jerusalem in the Time of Jesus*, 1969 (SCM, London)
———, *The Rediscovery of Bethesda*, 1966 (New Testament Archaeology Monograph
No. 1, Louisville)
Levertoff, B. A., *Jerusalem in the Time of Christ* (S.P.C.K., London)
Parrot, A., *Golgotha and the Church of the Holy Sepulchre*, E. T. 1957 (SCM, London)
———, *Land of Christ*, 1968 (Fortress Press, Philadelphia)
———, *The Temple of Jerusalem*, E. T. 1957 (SCM, London)
Yadin, Y. (ed.), *Jerusalem Revealed. Archaeology in the Holy City 1968–1974*, 1975 (Israel
Exploration Society, Jerusalem)

Chapter XX: FIRST-CENTURY TOWNS IN PALESTINE AND SYRIA

Caiger, S. L., *Archaeology and the New Testament*, 1948 (Cassell, London)
Cobern, C. M., *The New Archaeological Discoveries and Their Bearing Upon the New
Testament*, 9th ed., 1929 (Funk & Wagnalls, New York)
Finegan, J., *The Archaeology of the New Testament*, 1969 (Princeton University Press,
Princeton)
Fritsch, C. T. (ed.), *The Joint Expedition to Caesarea Maritima*, Vol. I, 1975 (American
Schools of Oriental Research)

Hamilton, R. W., *A Guide to Bethlehem*, 1939 (Jerusalem)
Humphrey, J. H., "A Summary of the 1974 Excavations in the Caesarea Hippodrome," *BASOR*, No. 218, 1975
Netzer, E., "The Winter Palaces of the Judean Kings at Jericho at the End of the Second Temple Period," *BASOR*, No. 228, 1977
Sukenik, E. L., *Ancient Synagogues in Palestine and Greece*, 1934 (London)
Yadin, Y., *Masada, Herod's Fortress and the Zealots' Last Stand*, 1966 (Weidenfeld and Nicholson, London)

Chapter XXI: LUKE THE HISTORIAN

Blaiklock, E. M., *Cities of the New Testament*, 1965 (Pickering and Inglis, London)
Bruce, F. F., *The Book of Acts*, 1952 (Eerdmans, Grand Rapids)
———, *The New Testament Documents: Are They Reliable?* 5th Ed., 1960 (Eerdmans, Grand Rapids)
Finegan, J., *The Archaeology of the New Testament*, 1969 (Princeton University Press, Princeton)
Marshall, I. H., *The Gospel of Luke, A Commentary on the Greek Text*, 1978 (The Paternoster Press, Exeter)
Metzger, H., *St. Paul's Journeys in the Greek Orient*, 1956 (SCM, London)
Ramsay, W. M., *The Bearing of Recent Discovery on the Trustworthiness of the New Testament*, 1914 (Hodder & Stoughton, London)
———, *The Cities of St. Paul*, reprint 1960 (Baker, Grand Rapids)
———, *St. Paul the Traveller and the Roman Citizen*, reprint 1960 (Baker, Grand Rapids)
———, *Was Christ Born in Bethlehem?*, 1898 (Hodder & Stoughton, London)
Reicke, B., *The New Testament Era*, 1969 (A. & C. Black, London)
Robertson, A. T., *Luke the Historian in the Light of Research*, 1920 (T. & T. Clark, Edinburgh)
Schürer, E., *History of the Jewish People in the Age of Jesus Christ*, new edition, G. Vermes, F. G. B. Miller, and M. Black (eds.), 3 vols., 1973f.

Chapter XXII: ARCHAEOLOGY, JOHN'S GOSPEL, AND THE BOOK OF REVELATION

Albright, W. F., "Recent Discoveries in Palestine and the Gospel of St. John," in *The Background of the New Testament and Its Eschatology*, 1956 (Cambridge University Press, Cambridge)
Barclay, W., *Letters to the Seven Churches*, 1957 (Westminster, Philadelphia)
Cadoux, C. J., *Ancient Smyrna*, 1938 (Blackwell, Oxford)
Charlesworth, J. H. (ed.), *John and Qumran*, 1972 (Geoffrey Chapman, London)
Gold, V. R., "The Gnostic Literature of Chenoboskion," *BA*, Dec., 1952
Hemer, C. J., "Unto the Angels of the Churches," 1975—a series of four articles in *Buried History*, a quarterly journal of biblical archaeology, Vol. XI (The Australian Institute of Archaeology, Melbourne)
Morris, L. L., *The Dead Sea Scrolls and St. John's Gospel*, 1960 (Westminster Chapel Bookroom, London)
Ramsay, W. M., *Letters to the Seven Churches*, 1908 (Hodder & Stoughton, London)
Roberts, C. H., *An Unpublished Fragment of the Fourth Gospel*, 1935 (Manchester)

Chapter XXIII: THE NEW TESTAMENT AND THE PAPYRI

Deissmann, G. A., *Light from the Ancient East*, 3rd ed., 1927 (Hodder & Stoughton, London)

———, *The New Testament in the Light of Modern Research*, 1929 (Hodder & Stoughton, London)

Finegan, J., *Light from the Ancient Past*, 2nd ed., 1959 (Princeton University Press, Princeton)

Greenlee, J. H., *Introduction to New Testament Textual Criticism*, 1964 (Eerdmans, Grand Rapids)

Kenyon, F., *Our Bible and the Ancient Manuscripts*, 1958 (Harper, New York)

Milligan, G., *Here and There Among the Papyri*, 1923 (Hodder & Stoughton, London)

———, *The New Testament Documents, Their Origin and Early History*, 1913 (Macmillan, New York)

Moulton, J. H., and G. Milligan, *The Vocabulary of the Greek New Testament* (Eerdmans, Grand Rapids)

INDEX OF SUBJECTS

INDEX OF PERSONS

462

INDEX OF PLACES

INDEX OF AUTHORS

INDEX OF BIBLICAL REFERENCES